GET A
CAMERA...

GET SOME
STOCK...

GO SHOOT A
DOC...

**Continuum International Publishing Group**
80 Maiden Lane, New York NY 10038
The Tower Building, 11 York Road, London, SE1 7NX

ISBN: PB: 978-1-4411-8367-5

Layout and design by Andrew Zinnes.

# THE DOCUMENTARY FILMMAKERS HANDBOOK

## 2ND EDITION

### BY
### GENEVIEVE JOLLIFFE AND
### ANDREW ZINNES

continuum

# ACKNOWLEDGEMENTS

We would like to thank all the contributors in this book for sharing with us their experience and expertise. And to all the filmmakers in our Case Study section who have been very open and honest about the ups and downs of making their documentaries.

To Chris and Jo Jolliffe, Lynn and Stan Morris and Allen and Ilse Zinnes for their continued support in our choices to pursue the ridiculous careers of publishing and filmmaking.

To Casey Mae who makes every day worthwhile by giving us both a smile.

To Chris Jones for his technical wizardry, advice and friendship.

To David Barker our editor for his unending patience and encouragement.

And to the documentary filmmakers of the world, thanks for fighting the good fight!

## LEGAL DISCLAIMER

# THE DOCUMENTARY FILMMAKERS HANDBOOK INTRODUCTION TO 2ND EDITION

It's hard to believe nearly six years have passed since the first edition of this book. But what a six years it has been! In 2006, shooting HD was considered a luxury, no one had ever heard of Facebook or Twitter and streaming was something you did by a small river. Alternative distribution was the exception instead of the rule. Crowd funding was in its infancy. Things have truly changed dramatically for the documentary filmmaker – for the better! No longer is one tied to old models of distribution. No longer does one have to wait months for their film to be released. No longer does one have to worry if they will see any royalties from selling their film. Technology has made it possible for the documentary filmmaker to have more control over their work, more opportunities to monetize it and the ability to have it seen across the world instantaneously.

Given all of this, we've had to adapt with the times as well. While we still have our classic Q & A format with industry experts and working filmmakers (by the way – don't expect formal, grammatically correct interviews – they are conversational and colloquial and always have been since 1995), we've slanted our questioning towards dealing with social media, digital technology and new distribution models. And since filmmaking has gotten leaner and meaner with smaller HD cameras, DSLRs, compact flash audio recorders and editing systems on laptops, we've trimmed down too with a streamlined format that's more "user friendly" to the mobile APP wielding filmmaker.

So it is with great pleasure that we introduce the *The Documentary Filmmakers Handbook, 2nd edition*. We hope it will enlighten, educate and inspire a whole new generation of filmmakers – who will blog and tweet their hearts out about it!

Genevieve Jolliffe and Andrew Zinnes

3:26am, November 14, 2011

# CONTENTS

## INTRODUCTION

## CHAPTER ONE - GETTING STARTED

## CHAPTER TWO - LEGAL

## CHAPTER THREE - ORGANIZATIONS

## CHAPTER FOUR - FUNDING

## CHAPTER FIVE - BROADCASTERS

## CHAPTER SIX - PRODUCTION COMPANIES

## CHAPTER SEVEN - GLOBAL PERSPECTIVE

## CHAPTER TEN - SALES AND DISTRIBUTION

## CHAPTER ELEVEN - DOCUMENTARY MASTERS

## CHAPTER TWELVE - CASE STUDIES

## JOIN THE WEBSITES

www.guerillafilm.com
www.filmmakerjunction.com

The web component of this book is where you can go to:

- Watch videos of the filmmakers interviewed in this book.
- Listen to podcasts of filmmakers and experts.
- Download contracts and forms for use in your projects.
- Find links to cool filmmaking sites to help you make better films.

We plan for both sites to be so much more as they evolve with you, the filmmakers. So stop on by and get involved. Also check out our blogs at **www.guerillagal.com** and **www.chrisjonesblog.com.** Join our Facebook group **Guerilla Film Maker.**

# WORDS OF WISDOM FROM OUR FRIENDS

*"Documentary - its a journey that can change you forever - what makes the journey possible is the collaboration you have with other directors, camera people, editors, sound people and the subjects of your film."*

BARBARA KOPPLE, Director

*"One third of your work comes from your own emotion; one third comes from your energy; and one third comes from pure work!"*

LUC JACQUET,
Director, March of the Penguins

*"Stay within yourself and embrace the unknowing."*

STACY PERALTA
Director, Dogtown & Z-Boys, Riding Giants

*"Be tenacious, persistant and just keep with it."*

ROSS KAUFFMAN,
Director, Born Into Brothels

*"Find a subject that you are passionate about because it can take many years to make a film and you want to be able to stick to it."*

Jessica Sanders
Director, After Innocence

*"Surround yourself with as good a team as you can. You don't have to have everything figured out - the documentary process is one of a discovery as you go along. Collaboration is the key."*

MARILYN AGRELO,
Director Mad Hot Ballroom

*"To make real insightful documentaries you have to give your life, family, bank balance, sanity and day to day existence as an ordinary human being."*

SEAN MCALLISTER,
Director, The Liberace of Baghdad

*"Don't compromise your own personal integrity and your own personal ethic when you're making a film."*

CATHY HENKEL,
Director, The Man Who Stole My Mother's Face

*"To make a film you need an army and in order to be a good filmmaker you have to work with all the members of that army. "*
STEVE SABOL,
NFL Films

*"Documentary is a new wave of social activism. No longer do you have to speak about the atrocities that exist in the community. You can tell these stories visually and that hits people more. That's a lot of power."*
KEITH BEAUCHAMP,
Director, "The Untold Story of Emmitt Louis Till"

*"The best films I've seem weren't necessarily made by professional filmmakers, but were films where people really got involved."*
ANAND PATWARDHAN,
Director, "War and Peace"

*"My tip to any filmmaker is never give up. That's the key to your success."*
ELLEN PERRY,
Director, "The Fall of Fujimori"

*"To make a great film, you need life experience, so travel and engage in life. Working in a coal mine is better than learning the Avid at age 18. Life experience is huge in becoming a great filmmaker."*

NINA SEAVY
The Documentary Center

*"Pick up a camera and go out and shoot it. It's accessible and affordable. Just make sure you have a good story. Story is king."*

KERRY DAVID,
Producer, "My Date with Drew"

*"Don't be afraid to take a point of view. It's an illusion to think that you can know how to shape a story if you don't commit to your point of view."*

ROSE ROSENBLATT,
Co-director, "The Education of Shelby Knox"

*"This is your film. Trust your gut. Make your voice heard. Even after you sell the film, never be afraid to speak out on decisions that are being made - you know your film better than anyone.*

SHEENA JOYCE,
Prodcer, "Rock School"

# CHAPTER ONE
# GETTING STARTED

## THE DOCUMENTARY FILMMAKERS HANDBOOK

FINDING YOUR
SUBJECT

MARK HARRIS
PROFESSOR/
DOC FILMMAKER

**Q – What should a documentary filmmaker bear in mind when choosing their subject matter?**

*Mark* – It should be something that you feel strongly about. It should be meaningful to you, a subject worth spending the time on that it takes to make a film. And that can vary from maybe a year if you get financing right away, to 4-5 years if it takes a long time to raise the money. The older I get, the more I question if I really care deeply about the subject before I start a documentary. I have been very fortunate that most of the films I've done have had a long life. One of the first films I did was about Caesar Chavez and the grape strike. I knew that something important was happening in Delano and I was right because 40 years later the film still has a life. It proved that my instincts were good and that I should trust them.

**Q – Once their subject is chosen, how should filmmakers start on the path?**

*Mark* – A lot of preliminary research. You need to know who are going to be the main characters. I think casting a documentary is one of the most crucial decisions you make as a director. Whom are you going to be focusing on? Through whose eyes is this story unfolding? Casting is as essential for documentary filmmaking as it is for narrative filmmaking. In fact many of the most successful recent documentaries are character driven. Even documentaries about social issues, like *Waiting For Superman*, have strong central characters at their core. After casting, the next thing you need to figure out is what is the question you are examining. Godard said something I often quote to my students: *"a good film is a matter of questions properly asked."* What is the question you are exploring? What's your point of view on your subject? That can change as you go through the film, but I always have some attitude toward my subjects when I start.

---

 mharris@cinema.usc.edu          www.usc.edu

18

*Q – Do documentaries tend to have any rules to them regarding form?*

*Mark* – I think documentary films have more in common with fiction films than differences. I write fiction, novels and screenplays. I teach screenwriting. I think there are certain basic narrative rules. When I start out, I don't think so much in three acts, but I do think about a beginning, middle and end. How is this going to unfold? How do I keep the audience involved? The biggest aesthetic issue of documentary is always structure.

*Q – How planned can documentaries be?*

*Mark* – It depends on the kind of film. Recently, I have been doing mostly historical documentaries. The events are over and you can very much plan what's going to happen. History is not going to change. What's important is your interpretation of history. For these and my observational films, I end up doing a detailed treatment beforehand. It helps me organize my thoughts and they are often based on a lot of research. But there's always a tension between what you think is going to happen and what actually happens. So I sketch out a structure as to how I think the film is going to unfold, but I'm not tied to that. I did a film on Peace Corps groups in South America in the late 1960's. I did a month of research in Colombia trying to figure out which one I was going to focus on. I came back and wrote a 12-15 page treatment based on what I'd seen there. I went back and started shooting and had to throw the treatment away. When I was preparing to cut the film, I looked at the treatment and while the scenes were not the same, the structure was. Treatments help me know what dramatic elements I need for the film.

*Q – Is it important to have a specific style in your documentary?*

*Mark* – I think content dictates form or style. A verité film is different from a historical film where you are using a lot of stock footage. I've shot interviews that are against the same kind of textured or black background and I've shot interviews on location in people's homes. It depends on the nature of the film.

**MARK'S FILMS**

*Living in Emergency: Stories of Doctors Without Borders*, 2009
Producer

*The Defector*, 2009
Writer, Producer

*Darfur Now*, 2007
Producer

*Where Do The Children Play*, 2007
Producer

*Into the Arms of Strangers, Stories of Kindertransport*, 2000
Winner Academy Award ™ for Doc Feature

*The Long Way Home*, 1997
Winner Academy Award™ for Doc Feature

*Redwoods*, 1967
Wiiner Academy Award™ for Doc Short

*Q – How do make your subjects feel comfortable during interviews?*

**Mark** – I spend a lot of time with them beforehand. I always try to establish a relationship with them. That might mean going out to breakfast with them beforehand or a pre-interview phone call. I always spend at least an hour beforehand somehow. I think it's essential that you don't go in cold.

*Q – How much time do you block off for an interview?*

**Mark** – At least a couple of hours. For my historical documentaries, if I can do two interviews a day, that's about right. A good interview in a documentary can be very revealing. When people are talking intimately about their lives, I want to see their faces and expression. I try to only use them on camera when they are talking emotionally.

*Q – Are there any tips on getting good interviews?*

**Mark** – Besides spending time with them, I think it has to do with how you respond to them. I really listen to the music as much as the words. I'm always trying to listen to the underlying emotions of my subjects. And my interventions are not so much questions of facts as they are questions of emotion. Instead of asking, *"what happened next?"* I might say "That must have made you really feel sad," or something comparable. I suppose my model is more of a therapeutic one. I have been doing a lot of films on the Holocaust where people are talking about extremely traumatic events. When you're in that situation,

## CHARACTERS

**Heroes**
They need to be relatable and sympathetic even if they are an anti-hero. If they have a special talent, that helps.

They need to have flaws – both internal and external. Internal – low self esteem eminating from child abuse. External – won't get close to anyone.

They must resolve both internal and external issues by the end of the story in order to show character growth.

**Villains**
The same as the hero, but opposite.

The best villains are sympathetic. You can understand why they do what they do, you just wouldn't go about doing it that way.

it's important that the subject know that you aren't going to flinch from their pain. That you're going to sit there and tolerate the pain that they went through. If it makes you at all anxious or uncomfortable, they aren't going to tell you about their lives.

*Q – How do you feel about the adage of having the interviewee repeat the question as part of their answer?*

*Mark* – It helps sometimes. I try to train people beforehand to do that. Sometimes they remember and sometimes they forget. I hate to break the flow, so I listen carefully and think if I can pick this up later. If I can't, then I interrupt. But usually you can pick it up. I sometimes give people a hand signal to remember, but when we're talking about emotional things, I don't like to stop the flow.

*Q – What are the common mistakes that you see documentary filmmakers make?*

*Mark* – One thing is that they haven't thought clearly through what the audience needs to know to understand this film. They're so immersed in it, they make assumptions that the audience knows what they know. People are afraid of narration. It's sometimes the easiest way to get from point A to point B and to provide the exposition that you need. People are fans of observational film and they don't think you need to set things up.

*Q – What advice would you give a new documentary filmmaker?*

*Mark* – You have to really love the process of filmmaking. I've been making documentaries for over 40 years. It's not only my vocation; it's my way of experiencing the world. It's a way for me to discover things about myself. Every film that I've made, successful or not, it has been a great learning process for me. And I love the process.

**THE DOCUMENTARY DOCTOR**

**FERNANDA ROSSI**

*Q – How do you define doctoring?*

*Fernanda* – As an interactive decision-making process. I used to believe my job was to spot problems, not any more. I don't believe the film broken and needs to be fixed. That approach is disempowering to the filmmaker, and it would be quite arrogant of me to think I have the answer. On the contrary, I assume that the film or fundraising trailer is what it needs to be at this very moment for the filmmaker to learn something and move on. All documentaries have the potential to be better if the filmmaker is willing to dive in. Not every film will be great, but every one can be transformed. Doctoring helps the filmmaker see the dynamic of their story, what's going on and why, and then I present them with tools that will help the them find solutions consistent with his or her vision.

This process is in direct opposition to just presenting solutions unilaterally. Out of fear, insecurity and other things, we get a committee of people around us who make decisions for us, rather than getting people to educate us on how to make better decisions by and for ourselves. Ultimately my job is to adapt to the story and creative needs of the filmmaker I'm working with.

*Q – What's the difference between opinions, feedback and doctoring?*

*Fernanda* – Opinions are what people say about a film from an emotional place. It's an emotional reaction that's immediately rationalized or justified. Someone may like something or not and they tell you why. I don't think opinions are bad, I think they're just misused. When someone says that they don't like a certain part of the film, I don't think people should change it. They should ask themselves, What are the characteristics of

---

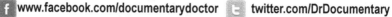

info@documentarydoctor.com   www.documentarydoctor.com

www.facebook.com/documentarydoctor   twitter.com/DrDocumentary

22

this person? Is this my target audience?

Then there's a consultant's feedback. Feedback is useful. It's a step above opinions because they're not only telling you how people feel but rather what they think is or isn't working. They can be sometimes more precise and technical in their approach. I think it's still misleading because it's still putting the center of attention on the other person, the de facto consultant. But it's useful because sometimes you get lost and it's good to have an outsider saying, *"This is the problem"*. Unfortunately, as soon as we put the authority on someone else, we lose ourselves.

There is also the feedback of those who have gone through the same before you, namely other filmmakers. But they've already attached a sense of success to a specific methodology. If I call a famous filmmaker for feedback, he or she has already a way of doing things that has worked for him/her. So to this filmmaker there are one, two, three ways of doing things that have proven infallible for her. Personally, I've seen all kinds of people succeed with their own method or strategy. In this business you have to be willing to try, be wrong and try again. The minute you are working by formulas – especially other people's formulas – you lose your personal vision and voice.

My suggestion is that we have to remain quiet and listen to answers from the inside. I help people to find their voice rather than tell them what I would do. My answers – and any outsider's answers - will be limited compared to the research that a filmmaker has done for his or her own film.

**Q – Since most documentaries rarely have a script, isn't it easy for people to get lost?**

*Fernanda* – Yes. Every film is uncharted territory and it gives us that sense of utter despair when we're half way into making it. Opinions are easier to dismiss if we disagree with them, but feedback is much harder to turn down. Because if you're really lost, any lifesaver is thrown, you'll grab. That's why I think feedback is so dangerous, it gives you that false feeling that you have resolved something. For real definite solutions you have to dig deep. Sometimes a filmmaker will hire anybody in a moment of creative anxiety, not just consultants but editors, producers, without checking credentials or just believing what a website says. They're looking to appease that dread that maybe there is no film among all that footage. That sudden knee jerk reaction can give the filmmaker some temporary piece of mind but it backfires long term. Once I had a filmmaker call me to ask me what to do about an editor

## 3 ACT STRUCTURE

**Act 1:**
Set up the world.

Set up the tone.

Introduce main characters including your villain.

Inciting incident: some kind of external event gets the action rolling.

Act 1 break: the lead character makes a conscious decision to go on a journey or exploration.

**Act 2, Part 1:**
The lead character works on their goal.

Lots of obstacles, which create tension and drama.

A moment (Syd Field calls this a "pinch") where the lead character is tested for the first time.

---

that wasn't really delivering, I asked her how she chose this editor. She said, *"Oh this editor was the first one to answer my email."* Filmmakers spend more time choosing an iPod than the time willing to spend on checking who we are going to get involved with months on end. It's not that filmmakers don't know, it's that at a moment of creative or story anguish, we'd do anything, even hiring a pivotal person based on how fast they answer an email!

**Q – When do people usually approach you?**

**Fernanda** – Twenty percent call me as soon as they have an idea. They want to see if it's viable and what it would take to make it happen. Most people come when they have shot some footage and they want to make a fundraising trailer or plan for the rest of the project – brainstorm on where they story could go and prepare for that. They also might want help knowing how to fundraise.

Another twenty percent call me when they're about halfway through their shooting. They've shot 70 hours and they still don't know where they're standing with the story. And then the remaining 50% is divided into two groups. Those people who are about to start post-production and want to maximize their budget by not getting lost in the cutting room where they're paying $2,000/week. And those who've been in the cutting room for several weeks and they still don't have anything to show. Or they might have a rough cut but it's not what they wanted.

Also, some people call me after all festivals have rejected them. They've received the same consistent feedback. Unfortunately many times they don't know what to do with such feedback because they're either dealing with a great deal of anger regarding those rejections or are unable to figure out how to transform that feedback into a tangible plan of action. I'm happy to say that in those cases once they've got over the frustration of having to go back to the cutting room, a few structure tweaks landed them into several festivals and even got them a theatrical release. So I join at several stages. The nature of what I do changes depending on the phase the film is on, but the methodology is the same.

**Q – What is your process once you are hired?**

*Fernanda* – People contact me via e-mail and then I send them a questionnaire, which helps me evaluate if and how I can be part of their team. Then we talk on the phone, discuss the main problems with the film and I explain how I work. If that's what they are looking for, we set a date for a phone consult if it's a trailer or short documentary or even written material like a proposal. If it's a rough cut, we meet in person and it can take one to two days of work. The sessions start with some exercises and depending on the stage they're at, we either do a scene breakdown or story development or whatever needs to happen. At the end of day, we do a plan of action. After that, people go execute the plan they decided upon and then we have a follow up over the phone. Most people are done after that. The work is very thorough and I give my all in those sessions, people like to come back not because I held anything back but because they like the exchange, it's inspiring and the only time they can let their guard down.

**Q – How can you tell if somebody can be helped? And if they can't be helped, what do you do?**

*Fernanda* – Both the questionnaire and the phone conversation tells me if I can work with a person. I take for granted that all films can be improved no matter the state of it if the person is ready.

There're two types of people who aren't ready for a consultation: people that want to consult to get approval and those who want to prove to me they know better. In the first case, they don't seem to have any problems with the film. They just want me to watch it and get my blessing. Well, my opinion on a film doesn't really matter. I only work with filmmakers who need to take their stories to the next level, whatever that may be.

In the second case, they usually say something like,

## 3 ACT STRUCTURE

*A midpoint where a discovery is made that raises the stakes for the second half.*

**Act 2, Part 2:**

*A moment in the second half where the hero begins to fall and the villain gains strength. Pinch #2.*

*Act 2 break: an "all is lost" moment for the hero. They seem like they will not achieve their goal.*

**Act 3:**
*The hero picks themselves up off the floor and continues towards resolution.*

*All characters resolve their arcs.*

*Confrontation with villain.*

*They win or lose.*

*"I'm a very experienced filmmaker and I'm having some issues. I don't know whether you can help me."* And I say, *"You're right. I don't know if I can help you."* These people are transferring their fears or anger to others. They're looking for someone to fight with and I don't need to be the punching bag. Most of the time they're just frustrated. Or they've had some tough things said to them. They're defensive. If I see I can work around those emotions, I might go ahead.

Most people, however, really need an outsider who understands story structure and can guide without interfering, like a shrink, they don't live your life or tell you how to live it, they give you tools to have a better life. Any filmmaker through enough trial and error can eventually figure their story out. The key question is at what expense of time, money and creative energy. Working with a qualified person in this capacity can shorten the time, save some money and get you to the finish line without hating your film!

### Q – How much do you charge?

**Fernanda** – I try to stay within reason. It's a flat fee, there are no surprises, no bait and switch, no gimmicks, no *"if you buy in the next five minutes you also get..."* I'm primary an independent scholar, not a salesperson, so the fee is secondary to the main issue which is the work. The issue to take into account is what the filmmaker will get out of this experience. The average filmmaker I work with saves in the range of the five figures because they cut down the production and their post production time significantly. Unfortunately, this is only evident after they are done, but it also means I get a lot of repeat clients. I also become friends and friendly with many of the people I work with, I value the relationship and the person above everything else.

### Q – Do you travel to your clients?

**Fernanda** – Many sessions happen over the phone. For the in-person ones, I'm based in New York but I take 20 trips a year between lectures at conferences and markets and my own signature workshops. I live on a plane practically and New York is my home just because that's where I do my laundry! Many filmmakers come to New York and get other things done while in town. I give them a discount to help with travel expenses and in many cases make recommendations for accommodations. Others meet me in between wherever I'm lecturing. Occasionally, I'm flown over, but generally only big production companies do that.

### Q – When a filmmaker gets an idea, should they stop to do research or jump in and begin shooting?

**Fernanda** – I think it depends a lot on the deadline of the topic. And the funny thing is all filmmakers think their film has an immediate deadline. There are some things like the Kumbamela in India, which happens every 12 years, so you better get on the plane now. Then there are the imaginary deadlines. The problem with making imaginary deadlines real is that the grant makers and everybody around them know better. In my book, I

## TRAILER MECHANICS

Length: 1-5 minues for online and initial meetings, 10-20 minutes for grants.

Use full scenes, this is not a movie trailer.

Start with an engaging character or attention grabbing visuals.

Tell the story and leave your audience wanting more.

Think of it as a short trying to prove three things:
- A story
- You're the one to tell it.
- You're the person with the access.

spend a lot of time talking about making the film in your head. And the more you make the film in your head the more things will flow. There's something funny about us humans, we resist change and the unknown. So if you chart the territory, you will go much faster – we fool ourselves into believing is not that unknown after all. I have a few exercises in my book on how to work with that. I don't believe in scripting a doc, but I do believe in seeing yourself making the doc. That is, foreseeing the possibilities and expanding the scenarios and storylines.

Research is a tricky thing, too. It can become a writer's block. You always believe that you have to research one more thing. So the key issue here is balance – listen to yourself. Have I truly researched enough? Or am I getting blocked and research is a safe place? That situation can be avoided by envisioning yourself in the process. I do that when people get scared to release the film. It is the fear of exit 5 – one of the five points where people can drop the film. They're delaying locking picture because they know that the next step is going to be a challenge for them.

**Q – What should filmmakers think about before they begin their film?**

**Fernanda** – Why they want to make it and what they expect to achieve. All throughout the making of the film, filmmakers fear that there's no story or the story isn't good. People want to be certain that they are investing their time, money and enthusiasm into something that will be successful. Success means different things for each person. Awards, money, etc., there are many variables that determine such success and we have control over only one of them – the product. We have no control over the other variables:

other films in the market, the need of the market at that moment, the reviews that you will get. So if we can only control one variable of many, how can we predict success? So it's good to have a good story as a starting point, but you make the films because we want to comment on the world or because we want to bring something to the commonwealth, not because of success.

**Q – How important is a fundraising trailer to a documentary film?**

*Fernanda* – Now that everyone has access to a camera and a desktop editing system, people assume that you can afford to make a trailer. So I 'd say, *"Absolutely"*. There's hardly a production or post-production grant, which doesn't require a work-in-progress, sample tape or fundraising trailer. Development grants will give you money to make such demo. But as soon as you get past the development stage, every grant asks for something audiovisual to support the paperwork. And private investors - it drops out of their mouth, *" Do you have something?"* People are more keen on watching even the sloppiest of teasers than read one page. And even if they like to read, images make a stronger impression because after all we're fundraising to make a film not writing a novel.

**Q – How long should a fundraising trailer be?**

*Fernanda* – It all depends on the venue and circumstances where it'll be shown. Short trailers, 1-5 minutes are good for online and first meetings. Longer trailers, up to 20 minutes, are more customary for grants. People tend to make a fundraising trailer as a cross between a movie preview and a music video; that's a very bad idea. A fundraising trailer, work-in progress or sample work should be a short without an ending. If it has an ending, then grant panelists and investors will say that if it works as a short, why should they fund a feature length piece? With these fundraising demos you want to prove three things. There's a story, you're the one to tell the story and that you have access to that story. For that you need full scenes not a flashy montage.

**Q – What are the most common problems that you see in documentaries?**

*"Most people need an outsider who understands story structure and can guide without interfering. Like a shrink, they don't tell you how to live. They give you tools to have a better life."*

*Fernanda* – I think filmmakers confuse good topics with good stories. Some topics make great photograph books or magazine articles, but because they're filmmakers, they feel they have to make films out of every topic they like. In the editing room, one common problem is trying to cut the film in the order that it's going to be shown. That puts a lot of pressure on both the editor and the director. Another problem is not being able to sustain the story. The middle of a film is a challenge, especially in documentaries where you don't have a conflict driven structure. It's a huge mistake to apply a conflict driven structure to a non-conflict driven film. When they apply the wrong model to their film, they think that their film is wrong. But it's the model that has been misused.

**Q – What advice would you give a new filmmaker?**

*Fernanda* – If you look for clarity inside first, then the answers will come from outside.

*Q – How far back do your archives go?*

*Clara* – The NBC News Archives go back to 1948 with NBC's first network nightly news program, Camel News Caravan with John Cameron Swayze. We also have some footage from the first half of the 20th century, including the Universal Newsreels from 1920-1960.

*Q – What collections do the NBC Universal Archives include?*

*Clara* – In February 2011, we launched a new website, www.nbcuniversalarchives.com, that presents, for the first time, the archives of several NBC Universal brands on one e-commerce platform. The collections available for licensing are NBC News (including MSNBC), NBC Sports, NBC Radio, NBC Artworks (graphics), Universal Studios stock footage, Telemundo (Spanish language network), the Weather Channel, etc.

*Q – How does one go about ordering footage from you?*

*Clara* – Professionals can research, select and license our footage online or offline. You can view and buy clips online at and for full service offline, or for any questions, you can email us at or call us at.

*Q – If one knows that something aired on NBC, but can't remember when or can't find it in the database, do you have in-house researchers who can help?*

*Clara* – We have experienced researchers who can not only help you find something specific but also suggest other stories or rare footage related to your topic.

---

 footage@nbc.com          www.nbcuniversalarchives.com

*Q – How does one screen the footage before ordering?*

*Clara –* You have several options to screen and select footage. First, a portion of our collection is viewable and downloadable online at www.nbcuniversalarchives.com. Second, you can order a viewing copy from our staff who will compile a screener for you. Finally, you can visit our offices in New York at 30 Rockefeller Plaza to screen film and tape material. This option is particularly helpful when your project requires deep research, extensive screening or a large volume of film material that is costly to transfer.

*Q – On what format do you provide the footage?*

*Clara –* We can provide footage on any format. Some of the most frequently requested formats currently are Quicktime and DVD for screeners and Quicktime, Beta SP, Digibeta and HDcam SR for masters.

*Q – How fast is the turnaround time once an order is placed?*

*Clara –* We are continuously reducing our turnaround time to meet clients' increasingly short deadlines. Nowadays our clients can download some of our content directly from our website. For offline service, we can deliver within a few hours in some cases (e.g. digital delivery) to several days (e.g. film transfer). Turnaround time depends on several factors namely the amount of footage ordered, the complexity of the research and underlying rights and the original format of the footage.

*Q – Do you require a producer to credit NBC anywhere in the film if they use your footage?*

*Clara –* We request an end credit, "NBC Universal Archives."

*Q – Is it possible to order footage with either the NBC logo on it or voice over?*

*Clara –* We usually license footage without any NBC branding or talent. However, in some cases, our clients request clips that include on-air NBC reporters or logo. These requests are reviewed on a case-by-case basis and we ask for a description of your production including how the clip(s) will be used as well as a script or treatment if these are available.

*Q – How much does a license cost?*

*Clara –* License fees are based on three main criteria: the use or media - theatrical, public television, all television, DVD, online, etc; the territory, e.g. US only, worldwide, etc.; and the term - 5 years, 10 years, in perpetuity, etc. Therefore the more extensive the rights are - for example, all media, worldwide, in perpetuity - the higher the license fee will be. Our e-commerce is based on a per clip licensing model whereas our offline sales are based on the traditional per-second license fee. We offer volume discounts when a

# ARCHIVAL HOUSES

*For a more comprehensive list of international archives go to the National Public Library's website under Public Moving Images @ www.loc.gov/film/arch.html*

**ABC News VideoSource - NYC**
*www.abcnewsvsource.com*

**BBC Motion Picture**
*www.bbcmotiongallery.com*

**Getty Images**
*www.gettyimages.com*

**Pond5**
*www.pond5.com*

**Archives Canada - Ottawa**
*www.archivescanada.ca*

**National Geographic Digital Motion - Washington, DC**
*www.digitalmotion.com*

**WPA Film Library - Illinois and International**
*www.wpa.org*

**The New Zealand Film Archive - Wellington**
*www.filmarchive.org.nz*

**ITN Archive House , London**
*www.itnarchive.com*

client's project requires a large amount of footage so we strongly encourage producers to come to us early in the production process to discuss how we can work together within their budget parameters.

*Q – Any tips for filmmakers when approaching you?*

*Clara –* Archival and news footage can add a lot to a documentary both on the content and the creative levels. Licensing footage can also be cost effective if done properly. Therefore we would highly recommend to filmmakers to reach out to us early in the production process so that we can explore together how they can best use our archives, discuss content suggestions and plan according to their budget and schedule. Communicating with our team is key as we know our archives and can guide you in the footage licensing process.

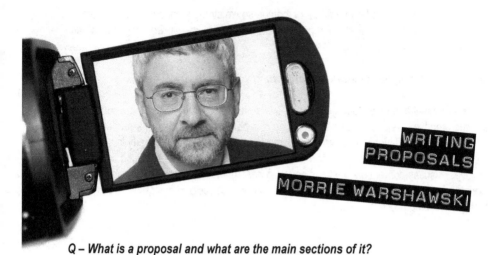

*Q – What is a proposal and what are the main sections of it?*

*Morrie* – The best way to answer that question is a proposal is whatever the funder wants! Every funder will want something different. Barring that, there's a general template for what would be in a proposal. It would include a description of the project, a description or a statement proving that there's a need for the project, which is very important. Then there's always something about the intended audience for whom you're making the piece. The treatment is often the most important part of the proposal and for some reason filmmakers have trouble writing treatments. Maybe it's because filmmakers are visual people. But then again, the treatment is totally visual in nature. It doesn't say anything about why I'm doing it or what I intend to prove out of this. In words you describe what people will visually see on the screen. Next in the proposal you need something about your timeline and production plans. You need information about the personnel and a detailed budget. Another important part of the proposal is distribution and outreach plans. Filmmakers screw up this part of the proposal a lot.

*Q – What should filmmakers think about with regard to distribution and outreach?*

*Morrie* – They need to think about who the audience is and as many ways as possible to get the project out to those audiences. Funders are looking for very rich, interesting and varied distribution ideas and plans. And they're also looking more and more for community outreach plans as well. In fact, in my work I've eliminated the word "audience" and try to get my clients to think only of "community." This is the huge sea change that the Internet and social networking has made. Many funders are demanding that you have a website; expecting a website so people can see what you're doing. They are assuming that you will be using the power of the Internet to add value to your project.

---

 morriewar@sbcglobal.net　　 www.warshawski.com

*Q – What in your opinion makes a proposal stand out from others?*

*Morrie* – The word I like to use is "compelling." Funders are looking for a proposal that grabs them, that says this project has to be made and these people are the ones who have to make it. The writing has to be good and compelling. Another word I say to filmmakers is "story." The proposal has to tell a good story - that's what people are looking for.

*Q – Do you give any advice on how to create a good story?*

*Morrie* – I tell filmmakers to personalize it. I always look at the level of language and if it's too abstract and theoretical, it is not going to work for a full proposal. You must balance the macro with the micro. You can say, *"Here is why I am making it. To save the planet."* But then you should say, *"And in order to do that I am going to show the story of Juan Valdez in Venice Beach."* Then you're going to tell me a story that really grabs me. Use active verbs and tell them about some very visceral things that they'll see. You want to be very specific and visual. The treatment seals the deal.

*Q – How many pages is a typical treatment?*

*Morrie* – I like a two page, single-spaced treatment for a piece that might be as long as two hours. Some funders allow you more room than that and few would allow you less. But, again, the right answer is whatever the funder will allow or prefers.

*Q – Is it good to include any awards that you've won, letters of support or video footage?*

*Morrie* – Yes, all of that. I'll always tell filmmakers to get letters of support for a film. Kudos letters, I call them. You always want one or two from a distributor. Those are like gold. And you always want a couple from a potential user of the film - whoever is going to see it or buy it. And if you're going to do a project on a special subject, you want to get an expert in the field to write you a letter of support. So if you're doing a piece on water, then you want a water expert, an author or academic, to write you a letter saying that this is a great project and this person knows what they're doing. All of this stuff is to help shore up your credibility. The funders want to know that you're going to get it done. Footage is a separate topic. Fernanda Rossi has written a whole book on the subject called *Trailer Mechanics*. Bottom line, you need to have something to show people as soon as possible. And that footage must be compelling - there's that word again. Now funders are expecting to be able to see a clip on your website, and/or on sites like YouTube or Vimeo.

*Q – What about the budget?*

*Morrie* – Yes, you need to include one. That's often a weak spot for filmmakers because the filmmaker will configure it such a way that it might lose the grant for them. The budget might not be understandable, it might not be detailed enough, it might have squirrelly figures in it that aren't explained. I think it's important every time you see a figure in your budget that people might question, you write a note about it. Most filmmakers don't do that. They just assume you'll know about it. Some filmmakers that come out of the commercial world include things like "contingency." That's usually a mistake in the nonprofit world because most funders don't understand it. Most budgets fail for me because they don't include distribution, marketing or PR. If I see a budget that doesn't have a figure for production stills, I get angry. Festival fees, screeners, press kits should be included as well.

**Q – Do most funders understand these budgets?**

**Morrie** – The ones that fund media do, but most don't. And that's why you have to write notes for them. And don't forget that if they don't understand it they're smart enough to give it to someone who does.

**Q – If you're going to shoot film or video, do you have to explain why?**

**Morrie** – Only if it is important for some reason. Most funders won't care.

**Q – How has proposal or treatment writing changed over the last few years given funders needs and digital technology?**

**Morrie** – The basic writing has not changed, while everything else around it has changed dramatically. For the new 3rd edition of my book *Shaking The Money Tree: The Art Of Getting Grants And Donations For Film And Video Projects*, I went out looking for recent successful proposals that I could put in the appendix as exemplars. I fully expected just to find the same kind of well-written proposals I'd seen in the past. What surprised me was that the level of sophistication in the newest proposals was much higher than in the past. For one thing, they just looked a whole lot better! People were incorporating more visuals and the layouts were nicer. Most funders are accepting - and many are requiring that the proposal be submitted electronically, so I'm seeing more PDF file proposals. Instead of submitting a work sample, people are providing a url link to where the clip can be seen online.

"It's a mistake to think that you can just send a proposal in without making any contact at all and stand to have a great chance of getting the money."

**Q – Is it important to know people in the organizations, foundations or entity that you are soliciting?**

**Morrie** – Yes. And that is why it's a slow, long process. You have to be strategic about it and about whether or not you want that kind of money. It takes years to establish those relationships. So

## CASTING YOUR CHARACTERS

*They must be open and honest.*

*They should not always give you one word answers.*

*They must be flawed.*

*They must look good as well as speak well on camera.*

*They must be comfortable with the camera and crew being around.*

*They should be introspective.*

*Hopefully they have stills and home videos of their lives that they are willing to share.*

*If the person you want doesn't fit the above criteria, then find someone else.*

if you're an emerging filmmaker and you haven't applied anywhere or you don't know anyone, you have to start down that long path of making connections. In my experience, many proposals hinge on some kind of personal contact. It's a mistake to think that you can just send a proposal in without making any contact at all and stand to have a great chance of getting the money.

### Q – Do you find that most people in these entities are amenable to that contact?

*Morrie* – No! Why should they be? That's the whole trick! If they were amenable that would be easy. But let me differentiate between public funders and private funders. Any government funder like the National Endowment for the Humanities has to talk to you. They can't refuse your phone call by law. They're a public servant. Somebody has to talk to you and give you the information that you need. So there's no reason in the world for any filmmaker not to take advantage of that. Now with private funders, that's not true. They don't have to talk to you and some won't talk to you. Most set up structures to make it difficult for you to talk to them because they don't want to be inundated with conversations with filmmakers. One of the ways that they shield themselves is in their guidelines. They'll say *"don't call - send a letter of inquiry before submitting a formal proposal."* I'm somewhat controversial on this, but I tell people never to send the letter unless there's no way around it. Try to talk to them. It's also important to make the right contact. You have to do a lot of research and know your stuff or you're dead. One of the important things is to really know what the funder is about before you call. If you call up and ask questions that are already in their guidelines or ask things that have nothing to do with them, you're dead.

## WHAT GOES IN A PROPOSAL

A statement stating why the project is important. Personalize it!

A descripton of the intended audience.

A treatment outlining the narrative of the film. Keep it to two pages.

A description of what kind of access you have to the subject matter.

A real cost budget. Make sure to include a fee for yourself.

A timeline of production and post.

Production Team bios. Include your advisory board as well.

Distribution plans inlcuding social outreach and alternative distribution.

Kudos letters from orgranizations that support your film.

A work sample. If you don't have one, then use one of your crew members'.

**Q – Should you start at a junior level and work up or start at the top and work down?**

**Morrie** – Get as high in the chain as possible. Get to the decision maker if you can. For many of the private funders, you're going to have to go to a program officer even though the board of trustees will be making the decisions.

**Q – If you have written a proposal, can you send it blindly to anybody?**

**Morrie** – NO! That is a big mistake! That is a major error. I call it the shotgun method. If you send one general proposal and send it out to everyone, you're dead. You won't even hear back. You have to tailor each proposal to each funder individually. And that is why I like to have one big file of everything the filmmaker needs and then you jerry rig it and change it and massage it every time.

**Q – What is the most important thing to make clear in your proposal?**

**Morrie** – A need for the project to be made. You must prove that the world needs this program. And that can be done by doing basic research that most filmmakers don't do - like being able to name similar projects and why yours is different. Talk to experts, distributors, Google it. I was just working for a year on a project with a filmmaker and I asked him if he knew if anyone else has done anything like it. He said he didn't know and we did a little research. I get a call from him a week later and he says that someone just made this film! He had to switch gears dramatically and it was a devastating blow. What is weird is that this is not unusual.

*Q – Do the funders understand the power of the documentary medium or media in general as far as promotion of their cause or message?*

*Morrie* – No. There's a small handful that do and they like to fund media projects. Most funders don't. They are scared of it. Confused by it. They think it's too expensive. That means that when filmmakers are getting support from a foundation, it is despite the fact that they are making a film not because they are making a film. And what lures them into feeling they have to do it, is that you're covering a subject that they really believe in or are interested in such a powerful manner that they have to support it. So, many a funder that says "we don't fund media" has supported a media project because the filmmaker gave them a proposal that was so close to their mission. So I should say they're aware of the power of the medium, they are just not convinced that they need to be involved or can afford to be involved.

*Q – Has social media come into play at all?*

*Morrie* – As they say, OMG. Social media is a major part of the landscape and will continue to grow in importance. I cannot imagine any filmmaker doing fundraising now without some social media presence. That's both a wonderful and horrible thing. On the upside, there are now so many more avenues for asking for money, for growing your community, and for marketing your work. On the downside, it means that there are even more things that you have to do. Social media is not "instead of" but rather "in addition to" and that's a big issue for filmmakers who do not have enough time, energy, or resources to begin with.

*Q – Are you getting a sense that these days there is more or less money available for funding documentary projects?*

*Morrie* – It depends if you are looking at the whole pie or slivers of the pie. I think the whole pie is bigger. I think portions of the pie are smaller. Government support is definitely down over the last ten years. No question. Private foundation support, however, has grown. That is only because the private foundation sector has exploded. There are more foundations now than ever and they have more money than ever. Individual money is still around and there's a lot of it. It's just a matter of tapping into it. The recent Recession has had a major effect on fundraising. There's still money out there, it's just taking longer to do the fundraising for each project.

*Q – Most filmmakers don't think about their careers beyond the here and now.*

*Morrie* – And they should because it is absolutely essential. If a filmmaker wants to consult with me, I send them a stack of materials to fill out. And at the top of the stack is their personal mission statement as a filmmaker. 99% of them don't have one and ask

## THE TREATMENT

The treatment is a written expression of your visuals.

The treatment should convey the mood of the project.

You don't want to put anything business-like in the treatment. If you have access to a person or place, imply it in the story.

The treatment shouldn't be any longer than 2-3 pages.

Always go for story over character when writing your treatment.

When starting, write down all the things that you like about your subject via free-writing.

Your treatment doesn't have to be precisely what you use to lock picture. Production is fluid and most funders know that.

me why they need that. What I've learned is that if you cannot clarify a couple of big issues like mission, you are never going to be good at fundraising and make it through the process of looking for money. You have to show the funder that you have a backbone - that you're a person with a purpose. The competition is so stiff for money that the funder can pick and choose whomever they want to give money to. So you need differentiators and the first one is *"are you a person with a sense of purpose?"* - because if you aren't I don't want to be with you. The second thing is that once you decide on the mission you can focus on the style of the fundraising you want to undertake. There are lots of ways to raise money. So in the non-commercial side of things, you can go to individuals with personal asks or conduct direct mail campaigns. Or you can write grants to public agencies or foundations. Or you could go get corporate money or support from small businesses. But the smart filmmaker will say to him or herself, *"What kind of career do I want to have in filmmaking?"* And, what is the right path for looking for money in the path I want to take? Once you have a bead on that you can be strategic every time you take on a project. What you are actually doing is thinking two or three projects ahead and you're beginning to build a base of both contacts and learning that you can work off of. Otherwise you will waste a lot of time. An example of this is if I'm working with a filmmaker and the second thing I ask about is vision of career path. If they say that they *"...eventually want to be making narrative feature films, but the project I am working on now is a documentary"* - I say that if that is true, you don't want to spend a lot of time learning how to write grants because what you will be doing later on is raising money from individuals. That's going to be your path. So let's start going down that path and learn those skills.

*Q – So for documentarians who want to do social issue projects, you would teach them how to write grants?*

**Morrie** – That's right. And actually for people doing projects on social issue work, they have the largest panoply of ways to get money. Almost all the avenues are open and appropriate including occasionally corporate money. So we'll teach you how to do the research and talk to the funders and teach you how to write grants. In addition, I'm telling all my nonprofit clients to set up structures - usually an LLC - so that they can also accept investments. There is a whole range of people out there who are just more comfortable making an investment instead of a donation, even if they know that the chances for ever seeing a dime back on their investment is zero.

*Q – What are the biggest mistakes that documentary filmmakers make in their proposals?*

**Morrie** – Lack of research. The second thing is lack of self-awareness. Sometimes they lowball their budgets. The thinking is that if I come in low enough they may be more likely to fund me, so I will cut this and that and make it look doable. That is a mistake because they will send the budget to someone like me and I will call back and say they can't do it for this. The other thing is what if you get the money? Now you have to do it for that price and you lied. You're in trouble.

*Q – What advice would you give a filmmaker?*

**Morrie** – Writing proposals is the tip of the iceberg. And that writing a grant is the lesser art and grant hustling is the greater art. They key to a good proposal is really understanding the project well and being able to articulate it. If you don't have good writing skills, you can always hire a good writer or write a rough draft and have them look at it. On the low end, you are looking at $20-$50/hour and $100-$150/hour on the high end. The other thing is that you want to balance passion with reason. You need both of those in a proposal. And do your research. Think from the mind of the funder. Ask yourself what they want and then you're more likely to be successful.

**PITCHING**

**ELIZABETH RADSHAW**
**HOT DOCS PITCHING FORUM**

*Q – What is the Hot Docs Forum?*

**Elizabeth** – It's a two-day pitching festival that happens during the Hot Docs industry event. We do it alongside conferences, panel and workshops for industry professionals. The Forum is separately accredited from the Hot Docs Festival and we show around thirty projects - most that have been pre-selected and one that has been picked out of a hat. In the Forum, you have seven minutes to present your project, perhaps even show a clip and then there are seven minutes of guided feedback by our selected moderators. And this is all observed by about four hundred of your industry peers, such as sales agents, producers and broadcasters.

*Q – Who are the moderators?*

**Elizabeth** – Traditionally, the moderators were only broadcasters, which worked well when the documentary broadcast climate was strong, but we've seen fewer and fewer places for one off docs. Many of those funders have shut down and the commissioning budgets for those kinds of films have shrunk. What we are really trying to do is bring different kinds of individuals in addition to the broadcasters and we have identified several main areas there. They are broadcasters, foundations and funds, crowd funding and brands and agencies. So, we've opened up the Forum to include series projects and interactive projects as well as one offs. So around the table we have invited other market partners such as distributors, foundations, film funds like Ford Foundation or The Sundance Institute. And whereas before you had to have a broadcaster on board in order to get into the Forum, now you can have any market partner. Even crowd funding from Kickstarter counts as a trigger.

*Q – What are the most important things to get across when you pitch?*

---

 forumrkt@hotdocs.ca       www.hotdocs.ca

*Elizabeth* – Well, first, before you even start pitching other people, there are a lot of questions you need to answer. The biggest question is: why? Why here? Why now? Why you? Why are you the right person to make this film? And why should your audience care? When you have good responses to those answers, then you are in a good position to build your pitch and tell your story. You don't have to verbatim bring those answers out, but the exercise that you take in answering those questions is going to come out in your story and your pitch. The next important thing to realize is who is the audience. Who is the film for? But also to whom are you pitching? Are you pitching for money? Are you pitching for support? Are you pitching to a foundation? Are you pitching to a brand or agency to support a greater campaign for the film? And then what are you actually asking for from them? Being clear is critical here. What does that pitchee have at stake? What is a broadcaster's budget like? What is their audience share like? Has it gone down? Maybe you are pitching to the wrong person. And then the big question is: why should they care? Why should the audience care? Why should the broadcaster care that you are making this film? That is critical. It will be the root of an emotional and visceral response to the project. When you nail that question, people get it.

**Q – Are there any tips in how you pitch to the four kinds of funders?**

*Elizabeth* – There are no tips, per se. But it's the obligation of the filmmaker to have done the research on these organizations before you pitch to them at the meeting. Check out their websites and talk to people who have received funds from them. Get in touch with the filmmakers and find out what it was like to pitch to and work with them. And when you are at the meeting, ask the questions that will get you the information that you need. Maybe something wasn't clear on their website. You cannot treat them all the same because they all have different objectives. Foundations and NGOs have constituents that they are trying to get a message to. Broadcasters have an audience that they are trying to retain at their channel. Agencies and funds have consumers that they want to reach. You have a community that you want to reach and source around your film via crowd funding. You have a direct link through social media to reach out to them. They are all people. But once you understand what their goals and objectives are, then you can be effective. Also remember that you are interviewing them just as much. It has to be an equal partnership.

**Q – Some filmmakers never think about how they pitch - the performance so to speak.**

*Elizabeth* – I totally agree. People forget that it is a performance. Here's the thing: documentarians are epic storytellers. They do it better than anyone else. They are able to identify in reality incredible stories and bring them across. It's

*"You have to recognize that if you aren't the person who is a natural salesman and you aren't comfortable schmoozing a cocktail party, then you need to find a partner who is."*

tricky when you know that you're a person who can't give a performance. When you know that you can't give them a hook and feed them a little magic so that they ask you more. I think there is a lot in practice - in feeling comfortable with your content - that you are able to get it across in your sleep. If you can pitch your Mom and her knitting buddies and they get it, then you've nailed it. But you also have to recognize that if you aren't the person who is a natural salesman and you aren't comfortable schmoozing at a cocktail party, then you need to find a partner who is. It's a hard thing to recognize because you basically have to give away control. But in terms of performance, you have to be able to drop a little magic. It's what every child asks for when they want their parent to tell them a story.

### Q – Does it help to bring in visual aids or some of your subjects?

**Elizabeth** – At the Forum, 99% of the projects show trailers. It's just what people do. If they haven't shot yet, then they will do a slideshow with stills and have a musical score underneath it to create emotional. I think when you are in a one on one meeting, you need to come prepared with visuals. But I've also seen pitches without a trailer, without a piece of paper and they just nailed it.

### Q – After the pitch, what are some of the common questions that come back from the pitchees?

**Elizabeth** – My favorite one is: *are you going to make a broadcast length version?* I'm not trying to discourage feature length docs, but you need to know to whom you are pitching. If you are pitching a broadcaster with no feature length doc slot on his channel and you are making a feature length doc, then they don't need to know that until later when they are interested. The other typical questions are: *why does it cost so much?* If they have a snapshot of your budget and they see that your R&D is huge. Or maybe your production budget is massively inflated because you have to travel around the world four or five times. You have to explain that in your pitch. Maybe you have a massive cross media app that you need to build. Or you have a huge campaign around it. After that it depends on the project itself.

*Q – If someone likes your pitch, what typically happens?*

*Elizabeth* – At the Forum, we do two things. First, all the pitches are transcribed and emailed to you. So about an hour after you pitch, you should have all the notes of what everybody said at the pitch. It's good to have because you might not be paying complete attention because it's nerve wracking. Then we get people to fill out Let's Talk Later cards. So after every fourth pitch, we collect those from the financiers and email it to the filmmakers, introduce each other and give them a place to chat upstairs or in another place at the Forum where they can meet. Ideally, their inbox gets flooded with information and we make it instantaneous so the meetings can happen quickly. In general, you will get a one on one meeting with a financier and they will ask you those key questions. Hopefully, they will have had time to read deeper in your treatment or watch the trailer a few more times. And hopefully they will have some hard questions about what you hope to achieve. Then they will talk about where it fits on their channel and after that they will talk about budgets and deliverables. Many times the broadcasters have to go back and discuss the information with their controllers. Very few can green-light at the meeting. But they can express interest. And the same goes for fund and foundations. One thing those people can do is help you out to make your application even more desirable.

*Q – What are the common mistakes you see filmmakers make when pitching?*

*Elizabeth* – At the Forum, because it is a timed event, they sometimes try to answer a question that is very long winded. So I would tell them to not answer the question and say, *"I look forward to meeting with you in person and answering that question."* In general, in a one-on-one meeting, its offering too much information at the wrong time. Sometimes you don't have to be as detailed as you think you have to be because you are in the forest and you cannot see the trees. So instead of reaching out to the person you are pitching and guiding them around the forest, just give them a little tour. It's hard to drop someone in from the sky. Have a little bit of perspective and remember they haven't been sweating, crying, living and breathing with the idea as long as you have.

*Q – What advice would you give a new filmmaker?*

*Elizabeth* – Diversification. You want what you love to do to be your bread and butter, but also understanding that good storytelling is good storytelling and being to diversify within the genre, within the deliverables that you create within the form, is ideal. Also be nimble, responsive, entrepreneurial and innovative. While specialization is key - I just want to direct - that's great, but knowing that you can make a doc and then a really great commercial and then some innovative media cross platform project, that's imperative too.

**Q – How different is pitching a broadcaster versus a foundation or individual investor?**

*Carole* – In general, you need to create a basic pitch that can be altered depending on whom you're pitching. For example, an investor wants to know if they're going to get a return on their investment – go bottom line. A foundation wants to know if your film fits their guidelines. And a broadcaster wants to know if your film fits their audience. Your pitch must address their needs, not yours.

**Q – What tips would you give for pitching?**

*Carole* –The pitch must be a visual description of the film. Stay on the story and don't confuse the issue with technical information because most of those people don't know what a HD camera is. They fund stories so don't give them the history. Remember that people give money to people as stated in the art of film funding: alternative financing concepts. Pitch yourself, who you are and why you are making the film. Tell them a heart-felt story and touch their hearts. We communicate through the heart chakra, so speak from your heart to their heart. You will get 60% of your money from people so pitching people is your greatest asset.

**Q – What do you think is the most important element of your pitch?**

*Carole* – After listening to thousands I think it's a "sticky story." Not just a story, but one I can easily remember. When you pitch someone it's an opportunity to spread the word about your film to all their friends, right? Yes, but only if they can remember it. *Made to Stick* by Chip and Dan Heath says that *"too often you are cursed with too much*

general@fromtheheartproductions.com

www.fromtheheartproductions.com  www.facebook.com/fromtheheartgrants

*knowledge."* Bringing that wealth of info into a simple sticky story is the key to the perfect pitch. I highly recommend this book for all filmmakers. A "sticky story" is one where you take all the knowledge you have on your film and transform it into a simple story, one that is easy to remember. The first rule is to keep it simple, find the core of the idea. You may have paragraphs of info; keep taking things away till you can't take anything else out or you lose the essence.

So step one, find the core. Think of journalists who create lead copy for articles and you get the story in a few words, they prioritize. So can you. This simple story needs something unexpected; this is to be sure you get their attention. You might ask a question that the film needs to answer. It can be a surprise like a shocking fact or a point of interest they will remember or a massive change in direction for the film. You need something concrete, like specific people doing specific things or give them some facts. Concrete ideas are easy for people to remember and they create a foundation.

Credible information makes people believe your story. This can be a place for truthful core details and please make them as vivid as possible. We need to see your film from the pitch. Emotion is next. I say, *"Touch my heart and I reach for my pocket book."* We communicate through the heart chakra, so touch me with your story. You can do this through one of your characters, let me feel them.

When you pitch me your "sticky story," I want to walk away with your film in my mind forever. Then I can tell my friends that I invested/donated to your film and brag about it. Remember, you have carried this film for several years and your audience is just hearing about it. That's why brevity and a sticky story are needed to transmit your knowledge to someone who knows nothing about it. This is an excellent way to create your pitch.

### Q – How long should a pitch be?

**Carole** – Under three minutes. I like a two-minute pitch. It should engage people. I should be able to see your film as you are talking. You want me to start asking questions that will let you to tell me more about your film. So have an introduction pitch and then have other information ready to give me. Sometimes the person doesn't ask the question that you want them to ask. So I tell my filmmakers to do what the politicians do – tell them what you want them to hear.

### Q – How important is your log line?

**Carole** – It's paramount to you and to your financing. There is an old Hollywood story of a writer who passed an envelope with a hand written log line saying, *"Romeo & Juliet on dope."* That film was made from that bold move and it is known as *Panic in Needle Park*. This one line description of your film keeps you on track during production and editing. If it doesn't fit your log line, don't include it. Irony is a key to log lines, we all love irony and that log line is what fills up the seats at your screenings and buys your DVDs.

**Q – Should support material be brought into a pitch?**

*Carole* – It all depends on if they are allowed and where you're pitching. The most important part of the pitch is that it's part of you. It must come from your heart and not your head. You need an urgency to close people, if you don't have one, create one. For example: I need to raise $10,000 by 5-11 to enter my film in Sundance. Remember pitch yourself your passion and why you are making this film and tell him your sticky story. Then he can tell his wife/mother/brother about why he donated to your film. Never ask for the full budget, cut it up into $10,000 or $20,000 chunks and work on one chunk at a time. Don't be afraid to offer something for larger donatons. Be creative. Cook dinner for them and show your trailer for $350.00. Whatever your talents are, use them to make money for your film. Clothing, jewelry and art are all things people like to take home with them after making a donation for your outstanding pitch.

**Q – How important is your physical presentation?**

*Carole* – Very important. You must look like the Rock of Gibraltar. You will never fail. You have the patience of job and you are full of ideas and never have any doubts about raising the money or finishing the film. You must project this. We are all looking at you carefully to see if there is a chink in your armor. Can you take it the pressure of working two to five years to make a film. Show us with your posture, your smile, your total faith in yourself and your film that you will finish this film and that we will love every minute of it.

**Q – How important is a funding trailer?**

*Carole* – It's the second most important funding tool you have. This trailer has to grab me in 30 seconds or my mind is thinking other things. Don't hit me with tons of copy at the beginning. Give me the essence of the story. Start with an engaging character or attention grabbing visuals. Remember, we watch hundreds of them when we are judging grants. Tell me the story and leave me wanting more with your fund raising trailer.

"Touch my heart and I'll reach for my pocketbook!"

**Q – How long should a proposal be?**

*Carole* – It should be as long as your funder requests. I tell my filmmaker that when they get the idea for a project they're passionate about, they should write down all their ideas and thoughts they have about it. It may take two weeks, but put all your emotions and feelings in writing. Give it a week and then go back to it. In those thoughts you will find the proposal. Go through and find the words or sentences or paragraphs that fully describe your thoughts because you have to knock me off my feet with a dynamite proposal. If this is for the LA Film Grant, you might be one of a hundred applications. And I read one after another, so if you have something good, it will wake me up. If you're having trouble with the story, then your film is underdeveloped and don't worry, it will emerge through this writing/talking method. To me the overview is the most important. That's where I can read the full story in three paragraphs. Make it good and I will read every word of your proposal. Grab me at the beginning of the proposal like you do with the trailer, then reel me in!

*Q – So story should always win out over character?*

**Carole** – Absolutely. In America, we like character driven docs, so your characters are most important. But put the info into a story for me - one I can remember and repeat. Introduce me to your character through the story. We fund stories and we like engaging characters.

*Q – So your proposal should really talk emotionally about how your subject matter fits their mission statement.*

**Carole** – Yes. Let's go back. Once you have written all those pages on your idea – cut it down to about ten pages and now you have your template for your vision. Then edit it down to meet each funders required length. They'll also have certain requirements. Like the Roy W. Dean Grant wants films that are unique and make a contribution to society. I like it when people write in their proposal, *"This film is unique because..."* Or, *"This film makes a contribution to society because..."* That way I know they have read my guidelines and know what OUR needs are. We like that. You have to think like they think. For investors of documentary films, it's important to get your story down to two pages and give them some visuals of the people and locations you plan to shoot. I love pictures in my proposals. It's branding. I won't forget it.

*Q – What should filmmakers know about budgets for proposals?*

**Carole** – I like to see general budgets of under $500,000. It doesn't have to be super-detailed, but I want to know that you know that you can do it for what you think you can do it. However, many grants are based on the budget so never under budget. Get on the phone and talk to all your vendors and get prices for your personal film. For docs, make a budget even though you know you will never use it. Make it as close to what you think you will use then add your 10% contingency. Use that number and throw away the budget. You should come close to that number in the end. You must have a goal for funding and you need to make it a game to stay under budget.

*"The most important part of the pitch is that it's part of you. It must come from your heart and not your head."*

1. Do research on the people you're pitching so you don't tell them something that has no chance of being funded. If it's a broadcaster, watch their channel. If it's an organization, read their mandates!

2. Rehearse your pitch and try it out on friends.

3. Have more than one version of your pitch. A really short one to get people's attention and a 2-3 minute one to really engage them.

4. Try to only pitch people one or two projects at a time. Most broadcasters and funders hate the "shotgun" approach.

5. Stay on the story. Don't tell them about the technical aspects or the style until the end.

6. Have energy and passion! Being upbeat and positive can swing someone sitting on the fence.

7. Eye contact is important. It engages the people to whom you are speaking.

**Q – How important is it to show access in the proposal?**

**Carole** – Very important. You have to show that you have the rights to the story so we know that your film can be made without any problems. If it is with a person, we want to know that you have an agreement with that person or their family. If you have letters you should include them.

**Q – Is it a good idea to contact people who have received grants or funds from particular funders?**

**Carole** – I don't think that works well. Usually they won't share their work. Look online for proposals from award winning films. I get them from the winners of my grants and put them online. Also, you should look at current winners so you are more up to date with what funders want.

**Q – If you fail to get a grant, is it a good idea to go back to that funder and reapply with changes?**

**Carole** – Yes. I know a filmmaker who went to ITVS three times and failed. Each time she received guidance on how to make it better and by the fourth time, they accepted her. Every person who enters my grants, I promise to give them a 15-minute interview where I go over their proposal and give them guidance on getting funding. I get to know them and can feel into the passion. Of course, I want them to come back, especially when I see that they are committed to making that film. The film A Girl And A Gun won my NYC grant after applying three times. I am honored to work with Cathryne Czubek. She made the film better each year and was very excited to win. Tenacity is the backbone of the filmmaker.

**Q – Where's a good place to look for individual investors and what's a good way to ask for money or services?**

*Carole* – When you ask for money, you get advice. When you ask for advice, you quite often get money. Remember that people don't give money to films; they give money to filmmakers. They're going to fund you. It's you they're interested in. You could go to an established production company with your project and ask that you work on the film with them as a co-producer. Or if you want to do it on your own, then you have to ask yourself who would be interested in this film. Look for people with vested interests, people are interested in the same issue as the film.

### Q – What advice should you ask for?

*Carole* – Let's say you have a film and you have a list of people who've invested in that type of film. You can get that list easily through the 990 forms from non-profit organizations. That form tells you where the company received their money and who they gave it to. So say you want to do a story on an opera singer. You can easily find donors to the Metropolitan Opera and others. But to walk in and ask them for money is a long shot. Instead, put a lovely proposal together and send it to them with a cover letter stating that you need their advice. *"I know that you're a patron of the arts and I need help in many ways. Would you be interested in mentoring me?"* Now the best way to get to them is to make friends with their secretary. That's the person who can fund your film. If they take it into their boss and say, *"I think you should really look at this. It's a great concept and the filmmaker needs your help."* They trust their assistants and will listen to them. Once you have good advisors and they see what you're doing, they're more apt to give you money. Invite them to all your meetings – production, scouting, whatever you're doing. And whenever you create paperwork for your proposal run it by them so they see everything you put together.

### Q – Is it likely that you can raise money from product placement?

8. *Look professional. You don't have to wear your best suit, but you shouldn't look penniless either.*

9. *If appropriate, bring visual samples. Video and photographs help executives get a clear understanding of the project. And they can tell if your subject works well on camera.*

10. *Never leave anything behind. They may misrepresent your idea to their bosses and screw up your chances. Get a second meeting and do it yourself.*

11. *No matter how the pitch goes, ask questions, chat and form allegiances. This is where you start building your business connections and network.*

12. *Follow up the meeting with a phone call or email a few days to a week later to find out if you are moving forward or not.*

## FUNDRAISING PARTIES

*If you don't have access to or have been turned down by larger funders – all is not lost. You can still attract cash by going right to private investors by holding fundraising parties, giving your pitch and asking for contributions on the spot.*

*Have a trailer and other visual aids to get investors excited.*

*Have one of your subjects there to make the film seem more personal. It's like having Julia Roberts there!*

*Connect with organizations who are interested in your subject matter who might have a place to screen your film and can advertise through their membership.*

*Make their donations tax deductible by having 501 (c) 3 status through a fiscal sponsor.*

*Food, drink and music all make for a festive atmosphere. Try to tie these to your subject matter or theme.*

*Pitch, but don't oversell. And answer everyone's questions!*

**Carole** – I wouldn't say for first timers that they'd get money. But I'd say product itself is a good idea. Someone I know who works in product placement was able to get a computer for a documentary filmmaker because the computer was used in the film. Also realize the audience of the product needs to be the audience of your film. If you are going after Coca-Cola then you should have a clean, family oriented film. The trick is to look online for the product you want and find who manages that company. Product placement companies are between the corporation and the filmmaker. They are the ones who decide if your film fits their image. So find who has your products and send them an outline of the film to get approved.

*When you ask for money, you get advice. When you ask for advice, you quite often get money.*

### Q – What are in-kind donations?

**Carole** – That's when you get goods and services for free or at a discount. A good way to do that is to go to the vendor with a one-page proposal and ask them for whatever you need.

### Q – What are the grants that you offer?

**Carole** – We have the New York Film Grant that closes every April 30th that offers goods and services from places in the New York area. You can apply for this grant if you live anywhere in the US, but you get more out of it if you live in and around New York. In LA, I have two grants that close June 30th and August 30th. They're set so that if you don't get into the finals in June you can reapply for the August round. They're donations from people in the industry and they give you goods and services either free or at discounts. Plus you get contacts at these top companies and once you get in there, you can work all sorts of deals. It's up to you to pitch the donors and get ongoing good prices after you use the grant allowance.

*Q – What are the common mistakes that you see documentary filmmakers make?*

*Carole* – Clearly defined films get funded. That's my motto. When people start telling me a murky story that I cannot follow, I have to work with them to clear it up. When you can see your film, then you can bring it from that level into the physical universe. We need to clearly see what you film looks like and feel your characters, that's how you manifest your film.

*Q – What advice would you give a new documentary filmmaker?*

*Carole* – Passion powers your film. Commitment to your film is crucial. You must have faith and believe in your film. Test it out first. Get a Facebook page and put it out there see if you can get a following. If not, find another film. You must know your audience before you start to make the film.

ETHICS AND
BALANCE

KEES BAKKER

**Q – When in the life of a documentary do ethics apply?**

**Kees** – Always. When we consider ethics as a practical philosophy – and the conception, writing, producing, shooting, editing, showing and viewing (etc.) of a documentary are actions, then in all of these stages ethics are an issue. Up till now, ethics in documentary has mainly been discussed when talking about the relation between the filmmaker and his subjects. But the audiovisual representation itself (the truth-claim, questions of objectivity/subjectivity, rhetorical strategies), the distribution, the programming and showing of a film (the selection by cinemas, festivals, broadcasters, etc.) are actions that – thus – imply ethical values. In the same vein, the act of watching a film implies an ethical stance. The spectator isn't that innocent anymore. With the proliferation of audiovisual messages – especially in the so-called Western world – the average spectator knows quite well how to value the images and sound and how to position himself in relation to those audiovisual messages. The spectator's interpretation of documentaries is not free from moral and ideological values, and in my eyes it's to some extent his responsibility to be conscious of the fact that as well the representation he's watching as his own interpretation of it are guided by the world views of respectively the filmmaker and the spectator.

**Q – Do documentary filmmakers have a responsibility to their subjects? And what is "informed consent" and would that cover a filmmaker from being sued?**

**Kees** – Documentary filmmakers should be aware that the representation of subjects in a documentary film could have an important impact on the daily life of these subjects. This can be a positive or a negative impact, or hardly any impact at all. The filmmaker has a moral obligation to inform his subjects of how they'll be depicted in the film, and how this might affect when the film is shown. When the subjects agree to be filmed, after

---

 info@keesbakker.eu           www.keesbakker.eu

being informed of how and with what possible consequences, this agreement is called 'informed consent'. In theory, this is quite simple, but in practice it's not always that easy. Not necessarily because the subject doesn't want to, but because it depends very much on the moment and situation during the shooting. Informed consent depends on the honesty of the filmmaker, but we have to be aware that the filmmaker can't foresee all possible interpretations and effects of his film on the private life of the subjects. And with the current inflation of lawsuits, a filmmaker is never covered from being sued.

**Q – What are the ethics involved when paying someone to be in your documentary?**

**Kees** – Yes. This puts the notion of 'informed consent' under pressure because it's a kind of bribery; the appearance in the film has become a paid contract. It can be useful in some situations of investigative journalism, but at the same time this could put the credibility of the subject and the reliability of his account under pressure: *"If you tell me what I want to hear I pay you, if you don't tell me what I want to hear you get nothing."* Here the filmmaker has to find an ethical balance and decide for himself how far to go in order not to discredit his own film.

**Q – Does a documentarist have to pay his actors?**

**Kees** – In general, I don't think so, but it may depend on the (narrative) structure the filmmaker is looking for. And in general documentaries aren't that good investments; they rarely make profit. But there are exceptions, like *Etre et Avoir*, which became a huge box-office success. It led one of the subjects, George Lopez to sue the producers and the director Nicolas Philibert, probably because he wanted to have a part of the pie. He accused the director and the producers of counterfeit (claiming to be co-author of the film because fragments of his courses were depicted in the film) and of infringement of his "image rights". All claims were nonsuit: there was informed consent. Lopez couldn't be considered co-author since he didn't participate in the creative process of the filmmaking itself; the film was not reproducing elements of his courses for which he could claim copyrights; the judge considered that Lopez and the kids had only been filmed in their "natural habitat."

**Q – What is 'The Television Without Frontiers Directive" of the European Union and how does this apply to documentaries in Europe?**

**Kees** – It regulates the free movement of television broadcasting services in the European Union. It concerns the production and distribution of European works, television advertising, protection of minors etc. What's interesting in relation to documentary is that the Directive stipulates a quota that broadcasters have to spend on independent productions. More interesting is how this Directive relates to national legislations, in which there are often quotas for specific programs, e.g. sports, factual programming, entertainment, fiction, advertising, etc. Reality TV, for example, has been labeled as 'factual programming', instead of "entertainment", in order to meet those quotas with financially lucrative programs instead of with 'boring' documentaries. What in spirit may be a quota to support independent (documentary) production, has become a means for certain broadcasters to put more "infotainment" in their programming schedules in order to attract more advertisers. A former chief of France's biggest TV channel TF1 put it once nicely: *"What we are selling to Coca-cola is the available time of human brains,"* meaning that the programs in between the commercials are destined to prepare the television spectator for those commercials. Maybe this is good sales ethics, but for the independent producers of television content it is very questionable.

**Q – In the USA, TV news has gone from news = truth, to news = opinions, entertainment and competition for ratings. Is there a danger of broadcasters imposing this new form of journalism onto documentaries?**

**Kees** – The problem is that broadcasters are the big financers of documentaries. They're in their right when they commission a film to impose some demands. This dependence on television channels makes the documentary very vulnerable. There's less and less space for 'stubborn' documentary filmmakers who think of themselves as artists and whose documentaries present a distinct way of looking at the world. Audiovisual journalism doesn't have the same force, nor the same mission, to stimulate the spectator to reflect on events or opinions. Its main mission is to inform. In the last decade this domination of the journalist attitude within the broadcasting world has led to a kind of uniformization of the documentary. It has become synonymous with audiovisual journalism; an enormous impoverishment of the documentary, in which creativity, subjectivity and aesthetics were the strong points. Personally, I don't mind that much that news for some channels has become a vehicle for opinions and entertainment, as long as it's presented as such and as long as there are other channels to counterbalance. It becomes more problematic when such 'newscasts' become the only source of information of a spectator. I know there are many people that only stick to a single news source, and then it becomes worrying.

**Q – Is it a good idea to have opinionated documentaries out there? How can one ensure balance in the documentary field so it's never one sided?**

**Kees** – Why should there be a balance? I think it's more honest to be one sided than to pretend to know what the world is like. When Joris Ivens had made *The Spanish Earth*, one of the critiques was that it was one sided. He hadn't filmed from the fascist point of view. His reply was that it would've needed a second film made by someone else. How can you be objective about the other side when you condemn the other side's worldview? Actually, I don't think there are unopiniated documentaries. And those who pretend to be unopiniated should be handled with extreme distrust. The balance one should look for is more in the openness, sincerity and coherence of the arguments and opinions.

**Q – Is there a ruling body that can reside over news programs?**

**Kees** – There is, fortunately, not a world wide ruling body, but most countries have some kind of controlling body. Their task is often interesting, but very, very sensitive. Apart from the statistical controlling mechanisms related to quotas, like advertising or the time newscasts spend on political parties in election time, these controlling bodies sometimes lean towards a censorship that is based on an ideology that may not correspond with public opinion, and neither with the law. In the latter case it becomes very problematic. A controlling body should be well defined regarding its missions, and not appropriate a power (of censorship) that goes beyond law.

*Q – Is there a journalist code of ethics that has to be adhered to?*

*Kees* – Journalist codes of ethics differ from country to country. That's why the Council of Europe established a resolution on the ethics of journalism to get some unity in it. It's not an obligation to adhere to it, but more a guideline for journalists. In that sense it differs from the European Convention of Human Rights, which has the status of an international treaty to which signatory states adhere to; it has the status of law. It also includes articles on the right to freedom of expression, the right to information and sometimes there can be a tension between these different rights, especially when it comes to public figures. There are journalists that have less respect for the private life of their subjects, but in general my impression is that most journalists respect the major ethical codes related to their profession. When they don't, the subjects may have a case before a tribunal. There's no official code of ethics for documentarists, but apart from common law they often implicitly adhere to journalist codes of ethics.

*Q – What are the true dangers to documentary filmmakers when they explore something sensitive and should documentary filmmakers hold back if their society's morals are different from others?*

*Kees* – Well, the true danger is to be killed by an intolerant bastard. Theo van Gogh, the filmmaker, was killed because of his stance against Muslim fundamentalism in his writings and in his film *Submission*. Van Gogh was someone who wouldn't hold back, and sometimes he crossed the borders of decency. Unfortunately, we live in a world where some people think they have the right to play judge, jury and executioner, without following the legal – national or international – procedures. Some people think you can impose respect by using violence. If we let our lives be determined by these kinds of people, we give in to fear and moral weakness. It's not up to me, nor to the authorities, to decide for others how they should position themselves. If a documentary filmmaker works in a society with different moral standards, he should take them into account, but this does not mean that he may not denounce what he thinks necessary to denounce. But by denouncing people, systems

"There's no official code of ethics for documentarists, but apart from common law they often implicitly adhere to journalist code of ethics."

## JON ELSE ON ETHICS

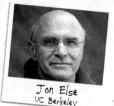

Jon Else
UC Berkeley

*Q – What are the ethics in pushing your subject to answering questions?*

*Jon – We have all the power, and to pretend otherwise is silly. All the great documentarians are forthright that they made constructions, even in cinema vérité. All we and the audience have is conscience. That sounds high minded, but we all got into this in order to get as close to the truth as we can. Yes, we can debate all day about 'truth,' but in blunt practical terms for those who get up every morning and make documentaries, the difference between truth and untruth is pretty clear. In interviews, that means letting people tell their version of the facts. And when we cut the interview, trying to represent in a broad sense what that person's opinion is. You don't put words in people's mouths and you don't tell them what to say. I've adopted a couple of techniques where I think that it's important that the audience hear the interviewer's voice to be reminded that someone is conducting the interview. It becomes tricky when you are interviewing someone you hate or think is evil. And there is a great temptation to use a different ethical standard for those we detect as the moral other. You have to use the same standards on your enemies as your friends.*

*Q – What do you think about one-sided sensationalist political documentaries?*

*Jon – There's nothing wrong with sensationalism. There's nothing wrong with propaganda as long as the audience knows that's what it is. An interesting example is Super Size Me, which is a very partisan film and in some ways sensational, but it's loaded with vetted, factual material, and the director is very up front about his sentiments. The danger comes when documentaries purport to be vetted, objective and factual and in fact aren't. We need advocacy based on evidence.*

or religions, you make enemies. Some enemies are not that bad: they use their freedom of expression to hit back. Other enemies, often by lack of arguments, have restort to violence. What's important to know is that the use of our freedom of expression is nevertheless limited (e.g. slander and incitement to discrimination, hatred or violence are in most national laws not allowed), and definitely guided by ethical considerations.

In the case of the Danish cartoons, initially they were intended to denounce the use of religion to justify terrorism. That may, and did offend people, but in my eyes that was not the primary motivation of these cartoons. But once the riots started, the motivation for republishing these cartoons became different: the attitude of *"we want to show you that we stick to our freedom of expression"* became more a freedom to offend; republishing the cartoons for the sake of it. From an ethical point of view I find that motivation much more problematic than the initial denunciation. But in both cases, the proper way to protest is by legal procedures. The riots that occurred in protesting against the cartoons laid bare an enormous hypocrisy with many people. For decades they have burned flags, portraits, crucifixes, and the like, so apparently there are people that appropriate rights they want to deny to others. In peaceful protest, I suggest to drop millions of copies of George Orwell's *Animal Farm*.

*Q – Should docu-dramas be taken as seriously as documentaries? Can a documentary filmmaker recreate a scene, even rehearse their subject?*

*Kees* – Unless they're parodies, docu-dramas should be taken as seriously as documentaries or fiction films. A filmmaker is free to choose the form in which he wants to put his story. Fiction films should be taken seriously too, because they often can teach us serious things about our own real world. It's not the use of an actor that changes the value of the story; neither does the use of an actor imply that the story isn't about the real world. In the first decades of documentary film it was common practice to use actors and to stage scenes. This wasn't to mislead the spectator, nor to make a fiction film, but to better convey the story.

*Ford Transit* by Hany Abu-Assad was labeled 'docu-drama' because of the limited knowledge of documentary by the broadcasting organization that commissioned the film. Not because the film is a docu-drama, but for the simple fact that the director used an actor to tell his story and to give his view on the effect of Israeli occupation on the daily life of Palestinian people. If we continue to follow that logic, we have to rewrite documentary film history. Everything before was fake or fiction. Unfortunately, television imposes more and more its standards of storytelling onto documentary, leading to a narrowing down of the concept of documentary, based on the idea that documentaries should tell the truth and telling the truth cannot be done by using fictional elements other than 'faithful' re-enactments in docu-dramas. I find such an attitude very shortsighted, first because it's based on a positivism that thinks there exists only one truth and secondly because it leads to an enormous impoverishment of the film language. Third, there is sometimes more truth in fiction films than in news programs. Fourth, we should stop thinking of documentary as being the opposite of fiction film – it is not. And five, we should not put documentary at the same level as audiovisual journalism. So yes, when it's up to me, documentary filmmakers may recreate and rehearse scenes if it supports the story they want to tell.

*Q – Are there any rules that should never be broken in documentary filmmaking?*

**Kees** – No other than defined by law. All other rules are conventional (actually, law is conventional too, of course), and I don't mind when films, be they documentaries or fiction films, play with the conventions of the genre. It's often a way to make the spectator aware of the arbitrariness of rules, the artificiality of the film language and leads to a better understanding of that language and how it represents reality. Furthermore, transgressing bounderies - even those defined by law - can sometimes provoke important and desired changes in an existing situation. The choice of a filmmaker to do so is normally, or should be, the result of an ethical dilemma, discussing the pros and cons of such a transgression.

*Q – What are the ethics of an interviewee nudging their subjects in interviews to go somewhere that might be too sensitive, painful – all for exposing the cause? What about ethics in using music in documentaries which will manipulate the audience?*

**Kees** – If it's for mere sensationalism it's very disputable. If it's for exposing the cause, it may be defendable. Whether it concerns harsh interviews or imposing new meanings by adding music or editing the interview, it would be very important to have the subject's consent after he or she has seen the final result of the film and has been explained the possible consequences of showing the film to wide audiences. But when the interviews concern public figures and their public functions there's much more freedom for the documentary filmmaker to manipulate without having an informed consent, than with private citizens in the privacy of their lives. Manipulations are sometimes very effective to denounce manipulations. Of course, the spectator may dismiss a film because of this kind of manipulations, but that is probably something the filmmaker is aware of from the start. We can think of the films of Michael Moore, but also most of the engaged or militant documentaries. Sometimes the form of the film may present an "objective" stance, but, as I said before, the spectator of today may well be capable to see through it. Again, in my opinion, we should not impose journalist codes of ethics onto documentary filmmaking. Regarding documentary we should accept a subjective discourse and the creative and/ or aesthetic way in which it is presented, including a more or less manipulative use of music, editing, lighting or whatever cinematographic technique the filmmaker wants to use to convey his message.

*Q – What common ethical mistakes do documentary filmmakers make?*

**Kees** – It's difficult to talk about 'mistakes' when it comes to ethics. You might not subscribe to the same ethics as someone else. We may not agree, but that does not mean it's a mistake. In general, I think the deontology of documentary filmmakers is quite reasonable. The thing that disturbs me most, but this is my personal stance, is the attitude or pretension of objectivity that many documentarists have, which in my eyes is more misleading than an explicit subjectivity.

*Q – What advice would you give a documentary filmmaker?*

*Kees* – Be sincere. Believe in yourself and in what you want to tell and show.

# CHAPTER TWO
# LEGAL

## THE DOCUMENTARY
## FILMMAKERS HANDBOOK

**Q – When should a documentary filmmaker approach a lawyer?**

*Michael* – At the conception stage. When you wait, it just drives the bills up. Find someone that you like and then stick with that person.

**Q – What should people consider when hiring a lawyer?**

*Michael* – The first thing a filmmaker ought to do is educate themselves about the issues they are likely to run into. If they are working on a movie with a lot of clearance issues, they should get a book like *Clearance And Copyright* to get up to speed, so that when they go talk to a lawyer, they have the language and vocabulary to understand what the conversation is about. Also you'll not be asking fundamental questions at $400 an hour that you could have gotten out of a $25 book. I'm shocked at how many filmmakers think a one-on-one consultation with a lawyer is the best way to learn about the fundamentals of clearance and copyright. Finally, and maybe most importantly, when a filmmaker is informed, they'll be able to separate the baloney from the real thing as far as choosing a lawyer is concerned.

**Q – What is Fair Use and to what extent does it go?**

*Michael* – Fair Use is a concept that exists in some form in all copyright laws all around the world. It recognizes the fundamental truth that every creation is built upon something that goes before it. Fair Use is expressly stated in the United States where we deal with copyright as a property – as an asset.

The U.S. law sets out four issues which always have to be addressed by the court when deciding a fair use case. If you take from other people's work without permission you have to meet certain tests. One is that you have to do something different with it. For

---

 www.michaelcdonaldson.com   www.donaldsoncallif.com

instance, you're doing a film on the rating system for the MPAA and you need to show certain scenes that cause movies to get certain ratings. You need to show those scenes to tell your story. So you have a right to go into those films and cut out those scenes and put them into your documentary. This kind of use is totally transformative. You have taken these passages from narrative films and changed them into an intellectual examination of a ratings system.

Two is how much did you take compared to the length of what you took it from. If you took three lines from my *Clearance and Copyright* book, it would be Fair Use no matter what you did with it. There are a lot of lines in that book. But if you took three lines from a haiku poem, there wouldn't be anything left. It's the percentage of the underlying work that you take.

The courts also consider whether what you took was the "heart" of the work or a less important piece. Four, a concept that confuses a lot of people is whether your use replaces the market for the underlying work. For instance, if you take something that was shot for a news clip and use it on another news program you are replacing the market for it. Even if it's very fast-breaking news that is very important and raises public awareness, taking from one news story to use in another news story is not Fair Use. There are a couple of very clear cases on that around the taping of the Reginald Denny beating in 1992 during the Los Angeles riots following the Rodney King verdict. Another example is the 19-hour Elvis Presley documentary where they took almost all of his appearance on *The Steve Allen Show* and put it in the documentary. Using that much of a television appearance really used the footage more for the entertainment value of the underlying work than the informative value. It stole the market for the underlying work. If you are making a documentary, you can determine fair use by asking three questions: Is the material you are using a good illustration of the point you are making in you film? Do you only use as much as you need to illustrate the point? Is the connection between your use and the point you are making clear to the average viewer? If you can honestly give a strong "yes" in answer to each of these questions, your use is a fair use.

*Q – What are the ramifications of answering your three questions with a "no"?*

*Michael* – If your use of someone else's copyrighted work fails to meet the fair use test, you infringe their copyright. And their case is usually pretty strong because it's obvious that what you used came from their work. In fact, you admit that at the opening of the fair use argument.

*Q – So if the footage that you take satisfies the fair use test, then you do not have to pay to clear them?*

*Michael* – If you have a legitimate Fair Use situation, there's no requirement to pay anyone. If there were no Fair Use in the copyright law, no one would be able to write a very interesting critique. You often could not make a documentary or if you did make it, it would not be very interesting because you could not afford the amount of material to cinematically illustrate your presentation.

*Miss Representation* is a documentary about how the media misrepresents women. The filmmaker had to use clips from television and film in order to illustrate the points that the talking were making in their interviews. *These Amazing Shadows* is a documentary about the National Film Registry: who makes the selections, how the films are selected, and the types of films that are selected. Showing the films that are being discussed is essential to demonstrating the points that are being made by the documentary.

### Q – Does Fair Use cover music?

**Michael** – As you can see above, music is covered. But music is very difficult because the typical song is so much shorter than a film. By the time you have taken what you need to illustrate your point, you have often taken a pretty big piece. Secondly, it's very hard to say that music is transformative as far as a film is concerned. There have only been a few cases where music survived the Fair Use test. Recently, a filmmaker came into our office wanting to use fifteen seconds of John Lennon singing his song *Imagine*. We worked with the filmmaker to help them correctly set out in the film exactly why they were using the song. We were able to obtain insurance. Yoko Ono sued. She lost. Big time. The judge said we were right in our opinion that in this film that talked about the lyrics that were used, such a use was a fair use. We are now able to obtain insurance for a lot of music, this was not true 10 years ago.

### Q – What should you be aware of when using photographs in a documentary?

**Michael** – When you use a photo you are often showing 100% of it. Not good. And typically you are not transforming it – you are using it for exactly the purpose it was intended. So photos are tough. There was a case a few years ago in a New York court where they found a poster of a quilt that was up for a couple minutes in a dramatic TV show to be copyright infringement. But the court went on to say that if the poster was in a documentary about the museum or a documentary about the woman who made the quilt, it might have been Fair Use. So the court left the door open. In fact, a picture in the background of an interview should be Fair Use. A photo used to identify someone being discussed should be all right for two or three seconds. But there are no cases yet that say exactly this same thing. So know that you are traveling in waters that are less well charted when you use photographs in your documentary pursuant to Fair Use.

You will not cast anything in "false light." All your statements about someone or something must be true.

### Q – How was Morgan Spurlock able to use the McDonald's logo and advertising throughout *Super Size Me* and not pay a fortune?

**Michael** – Trademarks and logos from copyrighted material. Trademarks are the opposite of copyright. In

## COPYRIGHT

The owner creates it and owns it 100%.

You need to get permission to use the property in most cases.

Lasts for 75 years and can be renewed.

When copyright isn't renewed, work falls into the Public Domain and can be used without clearing it.

## TRADEMARK

Exists through use.

Tells people the source of what they are buying.

You can show a trademark without getting permission as long as you don't alter its appearance.

copyright, the owner creates it and owns it 100%. They can put it in their drawer and say nobody can use it. A trademark only exists through use. Trademarks are to tell people the source of whatever it is that they are buying. People make soap and put the word "Ivory" on it – that's a trademark and it is only good for that line of products. Look at the Universal logo. You see that and you know they are selling movies. But you could have a Universal Hair Salon, because that is a very different product and the public will not be confused. So a filmmaker can show any logo in a movie without clearing it as long as they show it accurately and it's being used the way it was intended to be used.

**Q – Are there any privacy issues that documentary filmmakers should be aware of and can you probe public figures further than private figures?**

**Michael** – The answer to both of those questions is "yes". You want to think of privacy like a balloon. Private people have a very big bubble that you cannot get into. Public people who go out and try to get press have a very small bubble. If you run for President of the United States, it's like there is no bubble at all. And if you are President of the United States, your sex life becomes everybody's business. But if you are a very private person, the same information would be a real invasion of privacy. Privacy is about the expectation of a reasonable person. You can also invade someone's privacy by physically entering a private space such as a bathroom, a bedroom, or – according to one case – an ambulance taking someone to the hospital. More than any other area of the law, privacy is wildly different from country to country.

### Q – How about defamation?

**Michael** – Like privacy, the right not to be defamed is a personal right that everyone has. Defamation is when you say something that is not true in a factual manner and that harms somebody. Documentary filmmakers need to know that when someone they interview defames someone else and that remark is included in the film, the filmmaker becomes liable as a republisher of the defamatory remark. When you hear something that is presented as a fact and could harm a person's reputation, be a good journalist and check it out. Be sure you have at least one other independent source for the information.

### Q – What is False Light?

**Michael** - False light is the kissing cousin to defamation. It comes about when you misrepresent someone. A good example was when Clint Eastwood was out having dinner with a woman and a reporter said he was having an affair with her. It wasn't true. The reporter said it didn't hurt him because it enhanced Clint's image as a leading man. But Clint sued and won. False light. Of all the personal rights that documentary filmmakers must be most careful, it is this one. You must be accurate in what you say, even if your inaccurate statement does not harm the person.

### Q – What is De minimus Copyright Doctrine?

**Michael** – If you go into a courtroom and sue over 5 lines out of over 5000, the judge will not even go through the analysis. It's de minimus. That means that it's too small to bother the courts with.

### Q – When do documentary filmmakers need to have signed releases and whom do they need them from?

**Michael** – You want to get them from the person that you're interviewing unless the person is a minor. Then you need to get it from their parent or guardian. Most insurance companies and broadcasters want to see those releases.

### Q – If you get someone on camera giving you their permission to film them, does that hold up?

## EXCEPTIONS TO LIMITED LIABILITY

Owners of a corporation or LLC can be held personally liable if...

1. They personally and directly injure someone.
2. They personally guarantee a bank loan or a business debt on which the corporation defaults.
3. They fail to deposti taxes withheld from employee's wages.
4. They are neglingent in hiring or supervising their employees.
5. They do somethign fraudulant or illegal,that causes harm to the company or someone else.
6. They treat the corporation as an extension of their personal affairs, rather than a separate legal entity.

**Michael** – Absolutely. However, insurance companies and broadcasters like to see it on paper, even though the on-camera release is often better for court.

**Q – If you're shooting an interview and there are people walking around in the background, do you need to get all of their releases?**

**Michael** – In the example you just gave, the answer would be "no". However, broadcasters and insurance companies will often require you to get them. They don't want to bother with the litigation.

**Q – Does E&O Insurance cover you if you break the Fair Use rules?**

**Michael** – This is the big change since your first edition. Every insurance company who issues E&O insurance policies for filmmakers now offers coverage for items used pursuant to Fair Use. Our office negotiated the first such "Fair Use rider" just after your book came out with Media Professional. Chubb quickly followed and then every company fell into line. This changed the whole landscape of Fair Use. The insurance companies each have lists of approved law firms across the country.

**Q – If you have gotten someone's permission to use their likeness and then they change their mind, do they have any legal recourse?**

**Michael** – They have a right to change their mind, but that doesn't cancel their

## MAKING A CONTRACT

*Always consult a lawyer to help you sort out the legalese that is needed to make a contract ironclad. Verbal agreements can often be disputed.*

*1. If someone wants to break a contract, they can and only expensive legal action can stop them. They may be betting you can't afford it.*

*2. Get as much money up front as possible. If you can get it on the signing of the contract, even better. Anything can happen down the line – your investor or distributor might die, go bankrupt, get bored etc.*

*3. ALWAYS have a contract for everything, even if it's between friends and family. Many friendships have disintegrated because there was no partnership agreement in place defining the boundaries of each party.*

*4. When entering a deal with a goods or services supplier, get a written quote. People change jobs, get fired or die so have evidence.*

*5. Follow your instincts – if something is too good to be true, it probably is.*

*6. ALWAYS sign a contract before work begins.*

*7. Read and understand all the text of the agreement, including the infamous fine print. Beware of loop holes for in one section you may be given a right, but later on in the contract its taken away or nullified.*

*8. If in doubt, always consult your lawyer.*

*9. When you do consult your lawyer, make sure that both you and they absolutely understand how you will be charged (i.e. by the hour, a percentage of the movie). Make sure that each time you call with a simple question, you're not going to be charged for a full consultation fee.*

*10. If push comes to shove (by that we mean you're in DIRE STRAIGHTS), sign a bad contract, take the money and get the movie made. It's better than no movie at all.*

permission. Too bad. The release covers it.

*Q – What is the most common mistake that documentary filmmakers make?*

*Michael* – They don't educate themselves on these kinds of issues until they're deep into it. They know all about the subject matter they're investigating. They know how to operate the camera and how to do the lighting and the sound. They can stretch a dollar until you can hear it squeal all across the country. And they just don't educate themselves on these clearance and copyright issues. That gets them into trouble.

*Q – What advice would you give a documentary filmmaker?*

*Michael* – Don't think you have to ask anyone's permission to go out and make a film. Pick up your camera and start shooting. If there is a story you want to tell, go for it. There is always a way to get your project finished.

*Q – Should a filmmaker form a company prior to starting their film?*

*Stephen –* Yes! I always suggest that a filmmaker do that for a couple of reasons. Mostly because the filmmaker is going to be taking someone else's money to make their film – either a network or an investor. It's important for the filmmaker to shield themselves from personal liability either with respect to the money or to the content of the film.

*Q – What company should a filmmaker form?*

*Stephen -* They have a choice of two structures: One, a corporation; the other, a limited liability company or LLC. They both have very similar if not identical benefits in terms of acting as a protection against personal liability. You want to structure them so that the money coming into them isn't taxed until it comes out into the hands of the owner of the company – the member. Both of these entities are treated by the law as separate people. So the government will normally tax money when it's received by the company and then again when it's aid out to the shareholder. But with Subchapter S-Corporation, it provides that the government doesn't get two bites. LLCs are treated the same way. There are additional costs involved, at least in New York in setting up an LLC, that don't apply to a corporation, which can be meaningful or a small entrepreneur or filmmaker. It runs into the four figures in the process of setting up LLCs.

*Q – Is it possible for someone to get a 501 (c) 3 designation?*

*Stephen –* It's very difficult to do it by yourself, because what's involved for qualifying, not only involves setting up the entity, which isn't that complicated, but it's a different kind of entity that the normal for profit corporation or LLC. Beyond that, once you have set it up, there's a fairly elaborate IRS process that you have to go through in order to qualify. It's more advantageous to use a company that is already set up as a 501 (c) 3, and come in under their banner, especially for a one off project. Those companies can receive grants on your behalf because they have non-profit tax status and then they will charge an administrative fee which varies. Shop around and find the best one.

*Q – Should filmmakers create deal memos for their crew?*

*Stephen* – Yes. People are better off if there's a simple piece of paper that lays out what they think they've agreed to.

*Q – What is cross-collateralization?*

*Stephen* – It's when a distributor puts up costs for more than one film, and does not pay out any revenue until all of the expenses from all of the films have been recouped. So if one film is selling like gangbusters and the other is a dog, you are not going to get money on the successful film until all of the costs on both films are earned out. Normally one would resist cross-collateralized accounting. You want each film to stand or fall on it's own.

*Q – How much should a filmmaker set aside for legal expenses?*

*Stephen* – Figure that the line item for leal will run between 1.5-2% of the budget I have seen slightly over if it's a very complicated budget and it can get up to 2.5%.

*Q – What common mistakes do you see documentary filmmakers make?*

*Stephen* – Documentary filmmakers out of frustration take short cuts to clearing stuff. It's understandable, not because its complicated, but it certainly qualifies as a pain in the ass. It's difficult to find who owns what rights and it may be expensive. It's like Spring cleaning – nobody wants to do it. They take their chances and don't clear things and hope that nobody will come along. That you see a lot.

*Q – What advice would you give a new filmmaker?*

*Stephen* – Try as much as you can to tell stories that you're really interested in. That sounds kind of obvious, but what makes documentary film wonderful when it's wonderful, is that documentary filmmakers tell stories that they care about. They're really invested in it and want to tell their version of what they think is true. You want to try not to make a film just because it's there to be made. It's too hard and nobody is going to get rich making a documentary film. So tell the stories that you're passionate about telling.

**Q – How can The Rights Workshop help documentary filmmakers?**

*Brooke* – We provide music supervision, music licensing and clearance. We clear film clips, art, and photography – image and likeness, and also provide composer contracts and negotiation. But the core business is creative music supervision and clearance.

**Q – What type of music rights are there that a filmmaker should be concerned about?**

*Brooke* – There are three ways of providing music to your film. One way is to hire a composer using a work-for-hire agreement. The second way is to seek music from a music production library which you usually find in post-production houses. The third way is using commercial music. That's in the order of how expensive it is to acquire that music.

Commercial music tends to be the most expensive and the reason why is that there are two permissions needed to be granted. One is from the songwriter for the song from the publisher and the second is from the performer through the record label. To get permission from the writer, you have to go to a publisher to ask permission and a quote is generally given. The performer permission, which is called the master right, usually comes from the record label. You have to request it, get permission and receive a quote for it. That's why commercial music is the most difficult and that's why most people use our service. We have good relationships with record labels and publishers that help you secure the right, or tell you very quickly if you can not get permission to use songs.

**Q – Of the three examples, which one would you say is the most common to a documentary film and what problems could arise if you don't clear something?**

*Brooke* – Probably clearing commercial music, but then again, a lot of documentarians save money, and headaches, by hiring a composer. The problem that documentary

---

 info@rightsworkshop.com      www.rightsworkshop.com

filmmakers have more than other filmmakers is that when you're recording on the spot, your microphone is open and you can inadvertently record commercial music. You're still going to have to clear that music if you decide to use the clip in your film. So if you're walking down the street taping your subject and there's a Bruce Springsteen song going on in the background and you pick up that song, you're going to have to pay for it. The only time you're not going to have to pay for it is when your lawyer claims that it may fall under the Fair Use waiver. But other than that, you're going to have to clear the music and that's when documentary filmmakers really get into trouble.

If you don't clear a piece of music you can receive a "Cease and Desist" letter, which means you need to stop using that piece of music in your film and you must take it out. The cost involved is usually a penalty that arises out of using the music and can range from $1500 to $7k to $24k. That fee is based on how many times that film has been exhibited and the medium in which it's being used. Then there's additional costs of actually taking out that piece of music – you have to go back into the edit suite and substitute it in with something. Also if you base your whole film, like the guy who did the Nirvana documentary, on a band and you don't have clearance or permission from the estate or the composer then the whole film is going to be all for naught.

### Q – What are your thoughts on Fair Use?

*Brooke* – I don't rely on it. Fair Use for music is an entirely subjective decision. And that decision to claim something might be Fair Use needs to be looked at on a very individual basis. So you can't say, *"I only used four notes from something. I don't need to clear it."* That's simply not true. I've had to clear four notes of Herb Albert before because it's undeniably Herb Albert. It has nothing to do with how many notes you're using. It has to do with the purpose and character of the use, the nature of the copyrighted work, the amount used and the effect on the use of the song in the market place. As a music supervisor, my job is to administer the position of the lawyer who's overseeing the film. If the lawyer says it's not Fair Use, that's when I come in and have to clear the piece. But if we both agree the use could fall under fair use, then we generally claim such.

### Q – When you clear something, are you usually clearing it in perpetuity or is it for a certain amount of time? And does it matter whether it's for theatrical, DVD or streaming?

*Brooke* – It totally depends on what the medium is, which could be television, cable, art house theatrical, theatrical, DVD, home video, internet only (streaming, digital download), conference only, in flight, military bases, etc. There are so many different mediums out there it's incredible, so when I do clear music for a documentary filmmaker, unless the film has been picked up by a distributor already, we do a film festival license with an option for other mediums. Or we do

*Read the Case Study of 45365 to see why music is so important to your doc.*

***Synchronization
Rights:*** *the right to use
music in conjunction
with a film where the
music is synchronized
against the picture.
These rights are
obtained from the
songwriter or composer
via the publisher.*

***Master Rights:***
*the right to use an
existing sound recording
of the music in a film or
television project. These
rights are from by the
performer and are given
by the record label.*

***Mechanical Rights:***
*the right to record
and release a specific
composition at an
agreed-upon fee per
unit manufactured
and sold. Right to
use a song owned by
someone else on a
recording.*

an option for all rights in perpetuity, as sometimes it's more cost effective. It depends on who the client is, how big their pockets are and where they think their film is going. If their film is going to PBS, then they don't have to clear the music as the Corporation for Public Broadcasting agreement covers the licenses. But when you have a show air on PBS, generally PBS wants to repackage those shows for DVD. So when you air them on PBS then the only rights you have to get are home video rights for DVD and digital download. Or maybe it might be for "free" television outside the US. If that's the case we clear a) the DVD/DD/streaming rights, and b) Free television outside the US. In those cases home video rights aren't that expensive. They can range from a few hundred dollars up to a thousand dollars per license. Outside the US, public TV tends to be a lot more expensive but it just depends on where the client is going to be exhibiting their films. So price is entirely dependent on exhibition.

***Q – Say you made the mistake of putting in music that you just couldn't clear and now you have to replace it, in your experience have you found that doing this can hamper the sale of the film?***

***Brooke*** – I've never been on the sales side so I'd have no idea if it's actually hampered a sale. However, I've been in the situation where a film was sold with a song in it but we did have to take it out. In that case, the filmmakers got the composer to do a song that sounded just like it or we did everything possible to find a song by that artist that we could clear. Some broadcasters will provide money to clear music rights if they feel it is important to the film.

***Q – If filming, your subject starts singing a song – what rights would you have to clear?***

***Brooke*** – Only publishing rights or what's called the synchronization rights because the master rights are owned by the person performing it - your friend on camera or the footage owner. You get a release to film the singer, which covers their image and likeness as well as hopefully the clearance of the composition if they wrote the song.

**Q – How much is it to clear Happy Birthday?**

*Brooke – Happy Birthday* must always be cleared but again it depends on the media. For a film festival it could probably be $350 for one year. For television in the US, it's probably about $1,500 for five years. Outside the US, probably the same. But it also depends on the budget of the film. If you're talking about a major Hollywood motion picture, then you're probably talking about $2,500 or $5,000. But you don't have to generally clear the performance of it, you only have to clear the publishing if it is being sung in a documentary. Don't worry, they don't ream you on this song.

**Q – If a filmmaker is making a documentary with lots of music, would you advise the filmmaker to approach a company and make a deal with them early on for clearing the rights?**

*Brooke* – Yes. Clear the music before you finish the film because you have to know if you can use select songs. There are very few films that become moneymakers right off the bat, so I think the licensors, if they're smart and they know that it's being distributed by someone big, they might ask for a step deal where they get paid once and then again if your film does well at the box office. It's imperative to talk to publishers or record labels about a catalog of songs before even shooting if your subject is dependent on those songs.

**Q – What are some of the things a music supervisor can do for a filmmaker in suggesting music?**

*Brooke* – A good music supervisor will be able to make good suggestions that will be helpful to support the emotion of the film. First of all, the supervisor should get along with the filmmaker as this is a creative process and there needs to be mutual respect for one another. A good music supervisor will be able to help provide the director with the right sorts of music for their budget. So no music supervisor is going to suggest a Ben Harper song when he doesn't license his music in film and TV. If you get somebody like that then you're doomed. Why would they get you excited about something if you can't use it? Be careful - if you use your best friend because they have a cool record collection the reality is that person might not understand the licensing process, how to acquire the rights and the nuances involved on getting a musician involved on a project. I was talking to a filmmaker today who was hesitant on bringing a music supervisor on board, but the director is getting in such a crunch that they can't actually see straight due to editing. So if you can't get a piece of music that you like, what you can do is go to a music supervisor and within 24 hours they should be able to turn around

*Yes, you have to clear the song "Happy Birthday." You have to get the publishing rights if someone starts singing it in your doc.*

and give you some other options of other songs that you can use at a decent price. Another great thing about a music supervisor is they can get you deals on a great song before an artist has a hit - therefore it's cheaper.

**Q – Do you help find composers?**

**Brooke** – Yes, we can suggest composers.

**Q – Is it common for documentary films to have music supervisors?**

**Brooke** – It depends on the size and level of their documentary. I've worked on *Ballets Russes* as a music supervisor and we cleared 90% of the music, I worked on *The Devil and Daniel Johnson* and it was my relationship with the publisher that enabled them to get a deal with the publisher in 24 hours at a super price. I'm working on a film now that is about bullying and offering creative suggestions that parallel the budget is the key to working with a good supervisor.

**Q – When should a documentary filmmaker approach you?**

**Brooke** – Sooner than later. Most people go to a supervisor in post-production and that's OK. If you can go earlier, that's even better. This also pertains to rights clearances. If you're doing a documentary on a particular musician or artist then you're going to want to involve a supervisor even sooner because you'll want to make sure you're going to get that music. We worked on a documentary film about a guitar collector and he has to have *The Immigrant Song* by Jimmy Paige and Robert Plant. He has three people in a recording studio recording the song and we just got the "no." If he'd started a month ago, he could've gotten another song. He can use it in the soundtrack, but he can't use it in the film. Things are rejected for two reasons – money and contextual reasons like religion, violence or sex.

**Q – Do you negotiate a soundtrack and are they popular for documentaries?**

"It's important to talk to publishers or record labels about a catalog of songs before even shooting if your subject is dependent on those songs."

**Brooke** – Some are, and it depends on the film. Yes we do soundtracks. It's a little different when dealing with a documentary, but it can be done. It's generally conceived with a record label in mind. The music gets cleared afterwards but what's challenging when you're doing a soundtrack is that the soundtrack should be released at the same time as the film. Record labels need at least 6-8 months before the film's release to put a soundtrack out so you need to have that time in order to clear it.

**Q – Who pays for the soundtrack?**

**Brooke** – The record label. They'll give an advance

MUSIC RIGHTS TIPS

**MUSIC RIGHTS TIPS**

Hire a composer to create all your music. It's a work-for-hire so you own the copyright.

Negotiate a fee before your film gets out into the world. If your film gets into Sundance, licensors will jack up the price.

Get licenses in perpetuity (lasts forever) and in all windows of distribution. This way you will never have to go back and renegotiate.

The right to use a song is usually turned down for two reasons: money and film content. Not enough cash or too much religion, violence or sex can scuttle a deal.

Many unsigned bands and artists will give you a song for fee in exchange for exposure.

Don't wait until the last minute to clear music. This way you have time to find replacements.

for the royalty-bearing artists on the soundtrack and to the producer/director. Those percentages range from 3% - 5% for the producer.

*Q – What kind of a fee should a filmmaker allow for music supervision?*

**Brooke** – For all music in the budget, I always say you should allow 10% of your overall film budget towards music. That includes music supervisor, music composer and all licensed music.

*Q – When you're done clearing everything, is there any paperwork that you have to give to the filmmaker and distributor?*

**Brooke** – Oh my God, my whole desk is paperwork! Everything I do is via fax and email and everything has to printed up and documented. Nowadays, distributors want double signed contracts and it's becoming harder and harder for me to get that from the companies. All they want is their money and they don't give counter signed contracts. The filmmakers get a draft memo that's a sign off with the quotes on it, as they need that for their E&O. We also provide music cue sheets for certain clients who request them. Usually that's the editor's job but we've done them! They're incredibly important!

*Q – Would you recommend using public domain songs?*

**Brooke** – Yes. People can use public domain songs that are free and clear. The only pitfall is to make sure that it's public domain. If it isn't, then you have to clear it. You

## PUBLIC DOMAIN

*If the copyright has expired, it falls into the public domain. You can use that work in your film without getting permission. Here's some PD tips.*

*1. Any work that was published, but never copyrighted is in the public domain.*

*2. Any work that cannot be copyrighted, such as government publications, are in the public domain. Government publications must have credited references to the agency that created them.*

*3. As a rule of thumb, any work published prior to 1922 probably is public domain. But the copyright may have been renewed and you must go by the most recent date. For music you must go by the date of the recording you wish to use, not the composition's original date. Even if there isn't a date, check anyway as new laws state that a modern work does not have to have a date present to still be copyrighted.*

*4. Works created outside of your country should be checked with a copyright lawyer. Something that is public domain in the US might not be in another country.*

*5. Contact the Library of Congress Copyright Office, www.loc.gov/copyright/ or go to www.publicdomain.com to find out if a work is in the public domain.*

might have to pay for the research to confirm that the song you are using is in the Public Domain. You can go to publicdomain.com to check out what's in public domain.

*Q – What are the common mistakes that you see documentary filmmakers make?*

*Brooke* – The biggest mistake I see is when an client or filmmaker comes to us too late. They've started to do music clearances themselves, and ultimately get higher rates than us. They come in to us to clear up their mess. That is hard!! On the flip side I've also seen some filmmakers come in with licenses in place where I've said, *"Oh my God! You've actually contracted for this amount, I can't believe it!"* Because they don't realize that when you go out and request a license, that person comes back with an answer and a figure but that's still negotiable. It's not something that you actually have to take as the end all price. So the biggest mistake is had they worked with someone like us it would have, a) alleviated the licensing maze and frustration and b) gotten a much better price. People hire us and pay us sometimes to get things for free!

*Q – What advice would you give a new documentary filmmaker?*

*Brooke* – Be aware and knowledgeable of new medias and the ways in which your film is going to be ultimately distributed.

# SAMPLE PERSONAL RELEASE FORM

Date: As of [INSERT DATE]_____, 20XX

Project: [INSERT PROJECT DESCRIPTION] _____ presently entitled
"[INSERT PROJECT TITLE]_____".

In consideration of the possible inclusion of the Materials (as hereinafter defined) in the Project and for other good and valuable consideration, the receipt and sufficiency of which are hereby acknowledged, I, the undersigned, hereby irrevocably grant and assign to YOUR COMPANY NAME their agents, successors, assignees and licensees (collectively, "Company"), and Company will own, all rights, title and interest of any kind or nature (including without limitation the copyright as a work made for hire or otherwise) in and to the Materials (as defined below) and the Project, exclusively and irrevocably, without restriction, throughout the universe in perpetuity, to be used and disposed of without limitation as Company will in its sole discretion determine, in any and all media now or hereafter known or devised including without limitation theatrical, television, videogram, radio, print, internet, and any and all advertising, marketing, promotion and publicity of any kind or nature in connection therewith, without any liability to me, and no compensation will be payable to me at any time in connection therewith.

"Materials" will be defined as my voice, name, photograph, performance, appearance, likeness, biographical information, and/or any material based upon or derived therefrom, as photographed, filmed, recorded and otherwise captured and/or identified visually, on audio and/or audiovisually, by Company or otherwise, in any manner or media whatsoever, including without limitation in on film, video and/or audio tape, still photography, and/or any and all other formats now or hereafter known or devised, disseminated, transmitted, distributed, reproduced, exhibited, digitized, broadcast, displayed, compressed, edited, dubbed, added to, subtracted from, modified, combined with other material and/or otherwise used and/or exploited, all as Company will determine in its sole discretion. I hereby waive all rights of "droit moral" or similar rights, and I will have no consultation or approval rights in connection with the use of the Materials.

I represent and warrant that I have the full right and authority to enter into and perform this Agreement and to grant the rights granted herein, that I am over 18 years of age (or if under 18, my parent or legal guardian will sign below to signify consent on my behalf to the terms and conditions of this Agreement), that the rights I have granted hereunder will not violate, conflict with or infringe upon any rights of, or any commitment, agreement or understanding I have or will have to or with, any person or entity, and that the consent of no other party is required for Company to exercise its rights hereunder. I will not have, institute or support any claims, actions or demands against Company arising out of the Project, the Materials or Company's exercise of any rights hereunder, and I hereby release, indemnify, hold harmless, and discharge Company, its successors, licensees and assigns, and any representatives thereof, from and against any and all claims, actions, demands, damages, losses, costs, expenses and/or liabilities of any kind or nature (including without limitation attorneys' fees and expenses) arising out of or in connection with or incurred by reason of the use of the Materials and/or the Project and/or the inaccuracy, breach or alleged breach of any representation, warranty or undertaking I have made herein. I understand that Company is proceeding with the production and exploitation of the Materials and the Project in reliance upon and induced by my signing this Agreement.

Company will not be obligated to produce, release or use the Materials or the Project or to continue such production or release or use if commenced. My sole and exclusive remedy for any breach, termination or cancellation of this Agreement or any term hereof will be an action at law for damages, and I agree that I will not have and I hereby irrevocably waive any and all right to enjoin or restrain the production, distribution or other exploitation of the Materials, the Project and/or any elements thereof or rights therein and/or otherwise to seek or obtain equitable or injunctive relief. The grant of rights, representations, warranties and indemnities hereunder will survive the expiration or other termination of this Agreement. This Agreement (i) will be governed by the laws of YOUR STATE OR COUNTRY applicable to agreements made and entirely performed therein, (ii) may be licensed or assigned by Company, in whole or in part, to any persons or entities whatsoever, and upon such assignment Company will be released from its obligations hereunder, (iii) may not be assigned by me, in whole or in part, (iv) will inure to the benefit of and be binding upon the parties' respective successors, licensees and permitted assigns, and (v) reflects the complete understanding between the parties and supersedes all prior discussion and understandings, oral or otherwise, between the parties and cannot be modified except in a writing signed by both parties.

Signature:_____

Print Name:_____

Address:_____

Telephone:_____

# CHAPTER THREE
# ORGANIZATIONS

## THE DOCUMENTARY
## FILMMAKERS HANDBOOK

### Q – How can IFP help documentary filmmakers?

*Milton* – Support for documentaries exists primarily in three programs: The Project Forum of Independent Film Week (formerly called the IFP Market), IFP's Independent Filmmaker Labs, and our fiscal sponsorship program. The Project Forum section of Independent Film Week devoted to docs is "Spotlight on Documentaries" and is a meetings-centric forum that includes 60 new documentaries-in-progress, with the mission being to connect these projects with potential financing, broadcast, and distribution partners. The Independent Filmmaker Labs are for new docs from first-time feature directors. It's very selective, and 10 projects at the rough-cut stage are chosen for year-long support and mentorship on finishing, marketing and distributing those projects. Fiscal sponsorship, available through numerous non-profits, is a way that those selected projects can use the umbrella of IFP's non-profit status to raise funding from foundations and individuals, who receive charitable tax deductions for those contributions. We sponsor both documentary and narrative works working in any film or video format or platform, but about 60-70% of our sponsored projects are documentary.

### Q – How do you choose those films?

*Milton* – I head up a team that's comprised of other programming staff at IFP. We have some additional outside screeners in the early stage of evaluation who have experience of looking at documentary work, but the final selection is made by a small team of about three people. The primary basis for selection is that this is a documentary that we feel will have interest from the range of industry who attend this event - funders, sales agents, production companies, US and international broadcasters, theatrical and non-theatrical distributors, and festival programmers. There has been a very high level of documentary production over the past few years, so in a selective program like this, it's not a matter of just separating the good from the bad, the professionally made from the amateur, or anything like that. These days it's not about which docs are "worthy of

mtabbot@ifp.org    www.ifp.org    twitter.com/ifpfilm

http://independentfilmmakerproject.blogspot.com

a spot" because there are way more that are worthy than we have slots. Although the top 10 or 15 are easy and are chosen on uniqueness and outstanding quality alone with no regard to where they'll end up in the world, the rest is more a balancing act because we're selecting for an "audience" of a very specific group of industry attendees, few of which gravitate to the same kind of work. So we can't have too many of any one kind of doc - not too many POV-style or HBO-style - not too many on arts & culture or too many environmental, war docs, kids competition docs, etc. Beyond the subject matter, after a point this comes down to slight differences between projects in the overall impact of the written material submitted and the sample material from the doc that we are able to see. We also try to strike a balance in the overall selection between projects at the different stages of pre-production, production and early post-production, and late post-production. Generally projects that are further along are going to get more traction than those still early in production, unless the filmmaker is a "name." And of course subjectivity unavoidably plays a part. But essentially, by selecting a project to present here, IFP is putting its imprimatur on it.

**Q – Do you have any documentaries that are in the script stage?**

**Milton** – No. A documentary must have begun production to some degree and have sample edited material to submit In addition to the written application.

**Q – What do you want to see in that edited sample?**

**Milton** – We can see anything from a few scenes or a trailer to a rough cut or fine cut, but it is the primary element on which selection is made. The documentary section is very competitive, so the submitted sample should be the very best presentation of the project that can be produced by the deadline. While a good teaser trailer might be effective for catching a buyer's initial interest, it alone is not enough for us to consider at the application and selection stage. A trailer of four minutes or less must be supplemented by at least an additional 10 minutes of material that gives us a sense of the material and how the film actually works – not just the high points in a trailer.

**Q – Does it help to have any financing in place?**

**Milton** – A project must have some financing in place, even if it's only the filmmaker's personal funds invested to date. Of course, additional financing shows a level of interest by other entities in the documentary and gives confidence to others who might want to get involved.

**Q – Apart from getting potential meetings with companies, what other benefits to filmmakers exist at Independent Film Week?**

**Milton** – Part of our goal is creating a space where the filmmakers, the creative community, and industry can meet, mix, and interact. We tell filmmakers that a lot of what they're doing here is meeting their peers from around the country who are people

## IFP NY MEMBERSHIP

*$35 fee/community level - NYC members w/ access to online content and filmmaker tools.*

*$100 fee - gets you full benefits, free or discounted access to many local programs.*

## OTHER IFP LOCATIONS

*IFP Minnesota: www.ifpmn.org*

*IFP Chicago: www.ifpchicago.org*

*IFP Phoenix: www.ifpphx.org*

*IFP Seattle: www.ifpseattle.org*

*Check websites for membership fees and programs.*

## INDEPENDENT FILMMAKER LAB

*Application fee: $50.*

*For first time filmmakers.*

*Ten projects chosen every year.*

*Each project is assigned an experienced working doc filmmaker as a mentor.*

*Three key members of filmmaking team are invited to attend thee immersive lab weeks during the year.*

*When chosen, you're included in the Project Forum during Independent Film Week.*

## PROJECT FORUM INDEP. FILM WEEK

*2nd or 3rd week of September, following the Toronto Film Festival.*

*Networking week inlcuding social events, filmmaker Conference, 35 panels, conversations and case studies.*

that they will be working with in the future. It's a professional networking week that also includes social events and a week-long Filmmaker Conference comprised of about 35 panels, conversations, and case studies.

*Q – How many distributors come to the market?*

*Milton* – There are usually 350-400 different companies from festivals to production companies. However, in the documentary world it's smaller subset of that - probably around 100 companies represented.

*Q – When is the deadline for the application?*

*Milton* – Both the early and final deadlines are in May at the beginning and end of the month. They change every year by a few days so check our website.

*Q – Is there a fee for the Project Forum/Independent Film Week?*

*Milton* – There's an application fee of around $60. If a project is selected, there are no additional fees to participate.

*Q – What changes in submissions or success at IFW have you seen in recent years.*

*Milton* – There has been an increase in numbers and quality of submissions due generally to technological advances in the cameras and editing systems that are more accessible and affordable to filmmakers. Many documentarians can get further with less upfront funding. There is the same or less funding at the back end, however, so competition for those dollars is intense. Despite increasing digital platform outlets, many are accessible only through aggregators. But broadcast and these digital platforms - and the filmmaker's own ability to hold onto certain rights - are the primary ways for a documentarian to both monetize their work and have it seen. These are areas we try to educate filmmakers about in our conferences and particularly in our labs.

*Q – What is the Independent Filmmaker Lab for documentaries, and how does it work?*

*Milton* – This program was created to identify promising features from first time filmmakers (there's a narrative lab strand also) whose success we could help ensure by providing creative feedback at the final post-production stage, and continued mentorship in the areas of marketing , outreach, audience definition, and distribution. The labs are supervised by senior IFP staff, along with Lab Leaders who are working producers. Additional workshop leaders in specific disciplines are also brought in to lead lab sessions, and each project is also assigned an experienced working documentary filmmaker for continued mentorship as the film is completed. Because so much of the lab is tailored to the specific projects selected, only 10 are chosen each year, and three key

## 501 (C) 3

501 (c) 3 is the US Tax Code for non-profit organizations. Many funders can only give to places that have this designation. If you have this status any contributions to your film become tax deductible for the donors. The easiest way to take advantage of this is to join a non-profit organization that will act as your fiscal sponsor. Foundations and donors will donate to the organization with the funds earmarked for your project. The organization then takes a fee to cover their overhead – usually around 5%.

The other option is to get non-profit status for your own company. It's very possible to do and you won't give up that 5%, which is a big deal if you have a large budget. But the red tape and strict accounting you have to adhere to can be a real pain and means you need a good tax lawyer and accountant (which you should have anyway!)

members of each filmmaking team are invited to attend the three immersive lab weeks which are held over the course of the year. The Labs provide community, mentorship, and project-specific strategies to help filmmakers reach their artistic goals, support the film's launch, and maximize exposure in the global marketplace. The Labs focus in the first spring session on creative feedback and the finishing process (editing feedback, working with a composer, post sound, post production budgeting, deliverables, archival, music rights and Fair Use, festival strategy, etc) followed by audience engagement and marketing and web strategies in the fall, and ending in December with distribution plans and options just as these projects finish and have begun festival submissions. The labs have expanded from one week to three because of the increasing demand on independent filmmakers to be involved in the marketing, outreach, and distribution of their films - including the need to understand the world of digital rights management.

All projects in the documentary lab are automatically included in the Project Forum of Independent Film Week, and take meetings there with the industry, in addition to their own Doc Lab sessions held during that week.

### Q – What is the submission process for the lab, and what is the deadline?

*Milton* – A written application, and the submission of a rough assembly or rough or fine cut. We must see most of the documentary to be able to see how it is working as a whole. A trailer or short sample is not adequate. Apart from a $50 application fee, the labs are free to the participants. The deadline is usually in March of each year. The evaluation and selection process is identical to that of Independent Film Week.

*Q – Do you give grants to filmmakers?*

*Milton* – Currently the only documentary grants we give are to projects already in either the Project Forum or the Independent Filmmaker Labs, and those grants depend on outside sponsorship from year to year.

*Q – What single piece of advice would you give new filmmakers?*

*Milton* – Know the landscape - educate yourself on documentaries that have come before you and those that are being programmed on various platforms and in festivals now - from the traditional to the most esoteric. Know where you fit in that continuum. Also learn as much as possible about what outlets or partners would be most interested in the documentaries you are making - because any one film won't be of interest to everyone - and the industry respects knowledgeable filmmakers who know what they (the industry) do.

**Q – What kind of programs does Women Make Movies have?**

*Debbie* – We have a distribution program where we're the largest distributor of films by and about women in the world and we also have a Production Assistance program that helps about 200 filmmakers raise money for their projects. We don't actually raise the money, but we help them in seeking funds from corporations, individuals, government and other non-profit funding sources. Films from both programs have won awards at Sundance or been nominated or won Academy Awards, including this years' *Pariah* by Dee Rees which won at Sundance and *From Sun Up*, which was nominated for an Academy Award for Best Short Subject Documentary.

**Q – Why the emphasis on women?**

*Debbie* – Just look at the Academy Awards and you will know why. Or look at just about any festival in the world and what you will find is rarely more than 25% representation of women. Women still have a lot tougher time. Their budgets are lower both in production and marketing. Women just don't have the same opportunities men do especially when they're making films about women's subjects.

**Q – Why do you think that is?**

*Debbie* – I think it's because the industry is still so male dominated on every single level. And this is true whether it's distributors or production executives, producers, film festival directors, the people on the jury or the film critics. You are often times pitching to men. I really believe that men and women experience film in a different way. They're interested in different things and men aren't as interested in women's subjects. And vice versa is the

---

 dzimmerman@wmm.com     www.womenmakemovies.com

 www.twitter/womenmakemovies.com

 www.facebook.com/womenmakemovies

same too. What we want to see is equality. We want to see an equal number of women in power. And an equal number of women filmmakers.

**Q – Does the playing field get level if a woman has a completed film?**

**Debbie** – Absolutely not. We have actually been doing a study in looking at funding patterns over the last five years at government and foundation sources and it's absolutely appalling. With some funders, less than 20% of funding goes to women. And again those percentages go way, way down when you're talking about women making films about women's subjects.

**Q – How does your Production Assistance program work?**

**Debbie** – We have a deadline three times a year and any woman can apply to our program. Our application is on our website and they have to be the director of the film. They don't have to be the producer – we want to support men producers who are producing films by women directors! The films in the Production Assistance program do not have to be about women – they can be about anything. They can be features, documentaries, or shorts. Some of the films that came out of the program include *The Oath* by Laura Poitras, *Boys Don't Cry*, *Nerakoon (The Betrayal)* by Ellen Kuras.

A key part of the program is fiscal sponsorship, which allows filmmakers to apply for grants from foundations and government agencies that can't give money to individuals and provide tax benefits to individuals and corporations that want to make donations. There are tax benefits for the filmmakers. As long as the funds are spent on non-salary items, the filmmaker doesn't have to declare the funding as income.

Filmmakers can submit a proposal and sample during any time of production as long as they are looking to raise at least $50,000. The criteria that we use include the quality of the proposed film, whether we think you can really finish the film and whether we think you can raise the money. Once you're accepted into the program we'll consult with you on your proposal as well as your sample and help you get the best materials together so you can present that project to a variety of funders. We will let you know when deadlines are coming up. We have a great diversity of resources on our website – sample proposals and budgets, etc.

We have a series of workshops in New York twice a year that focus on the business side of the business and this year we will start doing online workshops as well. The workshops are on fundraising and distribution and we bring in panelists experienced in all phases of production and marketing

*"I encourage filmmakers to go to film festivals whether or not they have a film in a festival. They're a great way to learn about the industry and make contacts."*

93

*Q – What is the overhead percentage you take on the fiscal sponsorship?*

**Debbie** – 5%. Though we are considering increasing it! It's the lowest percentage that almost any film organization takes.

*Q – Does the filmmaker get some sort of Women Make Movies stamp when they're in your Production Assistance program or does that only happen when you distribute the film?*

**Debbie** – I think it happens in both programs. Being able to say that this project is sponsored by Women Make Movies gives you an entrée. People maybe take you a little more seriously. Foundations know there is a non-profit organization with 30 years experience behind you and that will make sure that the funds received will be used in the way the funds were proposed to them.

*Q – How does your distribution program work?*

**Debbie** – We are a small boutique distributor with an alternative approach to distribution. We create very customized distribution strategies for all the films we acquire and only acquire about 20 each year. We work closely with our filmmakers on community outreach programs. We distribute to all markets including theatrical. We don't do that with every film, as a theatrical release is not always appropriate. Because we focus on documentaries, it's harder to get them into the theater. A lot of the films that we do aren't even feature length. For those films we try to use the broadcast or community

**WOMEN MAKE MOVIES PRODUCTON ASSISTANCE PROGRAM**

Only women can apply.

The films do not have to be about women.

Program provides fiscal sponsorship for 5% fee.

Funding is not declared income (as long as the funds are spent on non-salary items.)

Must be looking to raise at least $50,000.

Submit proposal and sample during any time of production.

Financing consultation help available.

Access to fundraising and distribution workshops.

Deadline is 3 times a year.

Will help you present your project to a variety of funders.

engagement campaigns as a way of getting the film to the general public. In the past five years we've had many films on PBS through *Independent Lens* and *POV*, as well as the Sundance Channel, HBO and other broadcast outlets. After theatrical and broadcast, the film goes into educational distribution where it goes to universities as well as museums, schools, film societies, community groups, and all kinds of other educational and cultural centers. In addition we have six films out on iTunes and are in the process of setting up an online digital delivery platform.

*Q – Do you take any kind of commission from the sales of these films?*

*Debbie* – Our distribution contracts are the same as any other distributor, but the money we earn has to go back into the organization in order for us to retain our non-profit status. The staff doesn't get a share of the profits. And as a non-profit, we can receive grants. One such grant we received was from the National Endowment of the Arts in order to increase our broadcast sales domestically and to research the international market. Being non-profit also enables us to be able to take on films that are risky because they don't have a commercial market.

*Q – What else gets you excited by a film?*

*Debbie* – Quality. We want great films. We're also looking for films that challenge audiences in one of two ways. Either it brings information that you're not getting from the mainstream media or the form challenges us to think about film in a different way. When those two things happen together it's a great film. We are looking for feminist films – whatever ones' personal notion is of feminism.

*Q – Where are the places you go to look for your films?*

## ONLINE DOC COMMUNITIES

**Doculink**
www.doculink.org

**The D Word**
www.thed-word.com

**Documentary Films**
www.documentaryfilms.net
www.docos.com

**International Documentary Association**
www.documentary.org

**Documentary Archive**
www.documentaryarchive.com

**Docs In Progress**
www.docsinprogress.org

**Documentary Organization of Canada**
www.docorg.ca

**Fractured Atlas**
www.fracturedatlas.org

**Third World Newsreel**
www.twn.org

**The Documentary Filmmakers Group**
www.thedfg.org

**Debbie** – Every year I go to Sundance, Toronto and Cannes. We sometimes go to Berlin and Rotterdam. We also go to the Amsterdam International Documentary Festival in November and Hot Docs in Toronto. I usually have to turn down a lot of invitations because there are so many. We also work with a lot of women's film festivals around the world that are just starting up. In the last few years, we worked with the Mexico City Women's Festival, an Israeli Women's Film Festival, Filmor, a women's film festival in Istanbul and a number of others.

*Q – Are there any tips on distribution and marketing that you think are important?*

**Debbie** – I encourage filmmakers to learn as much as possible about distribution and marketing before they finish their films. I encourage them to go to film festivals whether or not they have a film in the festival. Festivals are great ways to learn about the industry and make connections. One thing that I tell people all the time in my distribution workshops is there are three things you can get out of distribution: fame, fortune and a good conscience. You aren't always going to get all of them. Sometimes you're making a film to be a calling card in order to build your career. In that case, you want to create a really great festival strategy for your film. If you're making a film for a particular audience you need to be thinking about that while you're in production and you need to come out of production with a really great list of organizations that are going to be interested in the films afterwards. And then create a marketing strategy that will get it out to those groups or individuals.

*Q – What are the common mistakes that you see documentary filmmakers make?*

*Debbie* – Not thinking about distribution or marketing. Also, people come up with the same ideas. There are so many subjects that haven't been covered. Use your imagination. And when you get an idea do your research to find out what other films have been made on the subject. You can learn so much from watching those films about what you should and shouldn't put in your film. Look at the end of a film and see who funded it – that's a great place to start in terms of funding your film. Another thing I have to say is be nice. Filmmakers are Type A personalities. They have to work so hard to get their films made and once they're made, they need to shift gears a bit. It's very important to be the kind of person someone wants to go into business with. That's part of our decision-making. When you sign a distribution contract, you're signing a contract that is for five to seven years. I always say that festival programmers have it easy. When they show a film, it's like going out on a date -- and you can go out on one date with almost anybody. But when we acquire a film, it's like you are getting married. It's important not to be so pushy that you alienate the people that you are trying to appeal to. And that is true for filmmakers that accost broadcasters, funders or distributors in bathrooms, or that stick DVDs in your hand. Or people that send us something and call and call and call. I'm not saying don't follow up, but be conscious of treating people how you want to be treated.

### Q – What advice would you give a new documentary filmmaker?

*Debbie* – It's important to understand that you are not going to succeed overnight; it takes a lot of hard work. Also, when filmmakers, especially first time filmmakers, say they don't have enough money to make a trailer, I look at them like they are crazy! You have to invest that. You can barter yourself – you work for free so someone else will do your sound or whatever you need done for free – get that trailer finished. Or raise money through crowd sourcing. Also, you might not want to make a feature documentary first time out of the gate. Short films have even more opportunities on the festival circuit – major film festivals show shorts, doc fests show shorts and there are even specialty short film festivals. Short films make great calling cards to help you raise money for your next film and give you a great introduction to the industry and vice-versa.

**THE EAST BAY MEDIA CENTER**

**MEL VAPOUR**

*Q – What production services do you offer documentary filmmakers?*

*Mel* – Project consultation and equipment rentals such as cameras, microphones, lighting and editing systems. While most doc producers today prefer to edit and post themselves, we do have editors that people can use.

*Q – Do you have a fiscal sponsorship program?*

*Mel* – Yes. I would suggest that producers go to our website and look under "Fiscal Agent." We require an agreement between producers and The East Bay Media Center and it's very accessible and easy to initiate.

*Q – What other programs do you have for filmmakers?*

*Mel* - We produce the Berkeley Video and Film Festival. The BVFF has grown to include international producers and some of the best docs being made by indie producers today. We screen at the Landmark Shattuck Cinemas Multiplex in Downtown Berkeley. In addition, we provide production workshops, the Documentary Workshop and have added an incredibly successful and dynamic Screenwriters Workshop.

*Q – Why are community based media centers important to the arts?*

*Mel* – The arts must reflect the complexities and nuances of the communities where the arts are produced and generated. Community based media centers provide access, expertise and insights into the very fabric of the issues facing all communities. There is an ever pressing need to provide members of these communities with technology and access that can be a viable component to solving local issues.

*Q – What are the common mistakes you see filmmakers make?*

---

 **www.eastbaymediacenter.com**    **maketv@aol.com**

*Mel* – Organizing a project from initiation to completion is the most glaring. The East Bay Media Center usually starts from the back end and works forward in consulting filmmakers. There is an enormous amount of detail and minutia in producing films, and filmmakers are generally passionate about their work, while leaving many of the mundane nuts and bolts details aside.

*Q – What advice would you give a new filmmaker?*

*Mel* – Be optimistic. Be focused on your end goal and put your passion into the technical and aesthetic craft of filmmaking first and foremost. Make liaisons with individuals and groups that can assist in the technical production of your film. Take advantage and utilize the web as a vital source of knowledge. Find like minds in the fields of business and the promotional aspects of your film, once it's completed. Go on - make your film!

# CHAPTER FOUR
# FUNDING

## THE DOCUMENTARY
## FILMMAKERS HANDBOOK

**ITVS**

**CLAIRE AGUILAR**

*Q – What is ITVS?*

*Claire –* ITVS is a funder, presenter and promoter of independent programs by independent producers for public TV.

*Q – What kind of funding is available?*

*Claire –* There's the bread and butter funding that people know us for, which is for completion funding for single programs that is via our Open Call program. We try to differentiate the funding because it's not a grant. Grants have generally no strings attached, but this is really a production license agreement. So in exchange for the financial support, we contract with the producer a license for public TV.

*Q – Do you get a piece of PBS's license fee?*

*Claire –* No. Basically let's say the project needs $150,000 for completion support. We'd give the producer that amount in exchange for licensing the program for exclusive public TV. It's usually for three or four years. On the other hand, we're able to give that kind of support to a lot of projects. But we also have other initiatives for R&D.

*Q – Do you ever get involved in licensing for theatrical or DVD?*

*Claire –* We just want TV, but we have to approve theatrical to make sure that the TV premiere is the first and it doesn't get tied up with waiting for theatrical. That has worked out for films like *Goodbye Solo,* which we financed and was a drama, but it had a number of theatrical runs. We don't take any home video or DVD rights.

*Q – What kind of film would you fund?*

---

 itvs@itvs.org

 www.facebook.com/itvsfans

 www.itvs.org

 www.facebook.com/itvsfans

*Claire* – The mission of ITVS is to fund films from independents that are compelling, that tell stories that haven't been told before, that are innovative in either form or content and that push the civic discourse. That means that it's going to spawn debate. So they're usually social issue films and mostly documentaries. We're open to all genres including experimental films and documentaries and animation. We're really interested in drama, but the budgets tend to be very high for us. And with our international shows we're looking for a view on global issues for American audiences that they haven't seen either. One of the first programs we did for that was a story about Arab women living in Israel who started a pickle factory. It's an interesting film because it's about Arab women who are disenfranchised because they're women and they're widows and they're trying to improve their lives by starting a business.

*Q – What would you never fund?*

*Claire* – We don't fund any lifestyle kind of television. We don't do "how-to's", nature or entertainment. That said there are a lot of entertaining films that may not seem like they're in the ITVS mandate, but they are. It depends on the show and how you look at it. There's a film that we funded called *King Corn* where these two guys plant an acre of corn in Kansas and they track the corn to where it goes. It goes everywhere from animal feed to high fructose corn syrup for Coca-Cola. It's done in a fun sort of reality show way, but those issues we're interested in.

*Q – With the international films, are you doing a similar deal with them as you would the domestic films coming to you for support?*

*Claire* – They're more co-productions than acquisitions. There's a similar license, but since it's international the window is a little longer. On the other hand, we don't control theatrical, home video or other TV markets. We are only interested in American TV and that contains public TV, cable and the free broadcasters.

*Q – How does a filmmaker approach you for funding and what is the process?*

*Claire* – There's an application process. Go to our website and go to the "for producers" section in the funding section, look at the guidelines and see if you are eligible. You have to be over 18 and a US citizen or resident. Unless you're international. Then it's the opposite. You have to have a prominent role in the film and have completed a previous film where you are the director or producer. It can be a student film – just so long as you have something under your belt. For Open Call, you have to be in production and have a sample of the program. So a trailer or selects are required. If you qualify for all of that, you send in an application and we have two rounds a year. The deadlines are in February and August and it's a competitive peer panel review process. The other initiatives are for development for diverse producers. One is for a station partnership. The average contracts that we give are $150,000. So the applications go through different rounds of review and it would be read internally and externally. There are three tiers of review and if it goes to the final tier – the final panel review, which is pretty good, there will be 30 projects in that pool and 10 will be funded. If you're chosen, the contract negotiations begin. The whole process takes about six months. We also do some outreach, but most people have heard of us. And there are some filmmakers that we do seek out if we have worked with them in the past or we hear they have a good project. We do answer some questions about how to apply, but we cannot pre-evaluate proposals.

**Q – And if it's a filmmaker that you're seeking out?**

**Claire –** An example is a filmmaker named Stanley Nelson who we've worked with before on a film called *A Place Of Their Own* about his family. He is a middle class black man whose family vacationed in Martha's Vineyard. He came and pitched a program he wanted to work on about black sexuality in Hollywood as it has created controversy every since *Guess Who's Coming To Dinner* to *Shaft*. We said we would put in some R&D for that so he could come up with a reel and then we'd look at it and decide if we want to put in production funding in the future.

**Q – What makes for a good proposal in the eyes of ITVS?**

**Claire –** People have to have to put in a three-page treatment. There's another element, which is a half page synopsis of what the project is about. But with the treatment you hopefully say what the film is about, but how it's going to be told, what is it going to look like, what are the different elements in it. We really want to know if you can visualize the project in words. We look at other things like samples, too, but the treatment is really key.

LINCS (Linking Independents and Co-Producing Stations) provides matching funds up to $100,000 to partnerships between public television stations and independent producers.

LINCS funds single non-fiction public television programs and demonstration projects that include both broadcast and transmedia elements on any subject and from any viewpoint.

LINCS proposals are accepted on an ongoing basis. Producers must be U.S. citizens or legal residents.

The people who review are internal staff and external people that we engage. They are people just like the applicants, really - independent filmmakers, TV people, educators, outreach people and writers. They have seven criteria that they evaluate the projects on. Is it compelling? Is the treatment clear? Does it speak to an underserved audience - ethnic minorities, the elderly, etc? Does the project have the access that it requires? Why do they want to make the film? Is it going to be something for public TV? If it's more a theatrical film then this is the place to talk about that. Everyone wants to make feature docs and that makes sense, but they are a bit of an oil and water situation with TV. It's hard to schedule 90-minute documentaries. Is the production team strong and is the budget reasonable? Are they first time filmmaker or do they have people on their team that are really good? Is the amount that they are requesting reasonable? And while the treatment is important, we do look at the other materials. If the treatment is beautiful, but the video is really bad or vice versa, we look at them together. We have an essay on our website called *How to Write a Better Treatment* that talks about these issues. How to put into words any visualization and style. And what not to do, such as dropping names.

**Q – Do you want to see a classic three-act structure?**

**Claire –** People have said that about us, but I don't think that is the case. On the other hand, when a program definitely has a three-act structure then we have to look at the story that way. And so many documentaries are being structured that way in terms of narrative filmmaking and character based. So if it has that form, then we look to see if it is working. It's really the filmmaker who states that.

1. Carole Dean said it best, "When you ask for money, you get advice and when you ask for advice you get money."

2. Do research to know what broadcasters and organizations are the best fit for your project.

3. Do research to find out if there are any competitive projects that have come out recently or are about to come out. People don't like funding the same thing.

4. Fundraising parties are a good way to talk directly to the people who would be most interested in supporting your film.

5. Get 501 (c) 3 status so someone's donation can become tax deductible.

6. Co-productions are a good way to get chunks of money from different countries. You can take advantage of certain tax breaks, government incentives and soft money this way.

7. Cash isn't the only thing to ask for. In-kind donations help, too, so find a way to get a free editing system or camera.

8. If you fail to get a grant in one cycle, try again. Many filmmakers get funded on the third, fourth or even fifth try!

**Q – What is a way someone can get a character-based doc through?**

*Claire* – Having video on them is really helpful. Sometimes people haven't had a chance to put together any production materials on the main character, but they pull together things like news footage or reportage or something so we know whom they are talking about and if they're going to work on TV.

**Q – In your opinion what makes a good documentary program?**

*Claire* – The level of storytelling. Something that's really engaging and talks about things that we would never know before. If you go to a film festival and you read the blurb of a film, you wonder to yourself why you would want to see a 15-year-old girl in the penal system who has bursts of violence. Then you see the film, *Aimee's Crossing*, and you are riveted by the character and the skill of the filmmaker.

**Q – If someone was a first time filmmaker and had a good idea, how would they convince you?**

*Claire* – There are different ways. Some people pair up with a more experienced person such as an executive producer or a co-producer. That's usually the way to get into ITVS. There's a great film called *Farmingville*, which was on POV and was produced by two people. One was Catherine Tambini who had done a number of documentaries before and her partner was Carlos Sandoval who was an attorney and an activist. He partnered with her and she was the main applicant. It was his first film and he did a great job. They were funded the first time they came to Open Call because the material was so strong. For an emerging filmmaker, he wasn't emerging in terms of his life. But even if someone has expertise or great access, we hold tight to this rule because so many people

that apply just don't have that experience and they need to partner.

**Q – Do you do short films?**

*Claire –* We acquire them through *Independent Lens* for American TV rights. We don't go into production funding for shorts unless they are 30-minute pieces that we could put on PBS. People send in shorts through Independent Lens and we look at them and then package them into an hour programs. Or if we need them as interstitials to round out the hour, then we look at them. Shorts are so great, there just isn't a lot of room for them. We're going to have an online shorts contest this year and we'll put them on our website.

**Q – What is Independent Lens?**

*Claire –* It's a multi-week series of independent programming – everything from documentary to drama to experimental to animation. It was conceived as a way to get independent voices on the air in primetime, works with *POV*, which airs in the same time slot but the rest of the weeks of the year – during the summer. Some of the shows are ITVS funded films and others are acquisitions. Sometimes they follow the PBS calendar themes like February they might have black films on and in June they might do gay and lesbian themes.

**Q – When the projects come in do you designate slots right up front or when they are done?**

*Claire –* We try to do it up front, but sometimes it's not possible. We may see something that we want on *Independent Lens*, but we have to make sure that PBS is on board with that. Some of our shows already have commitments to other PBS shows like *American Masters*, but we try to control the distribution of all our funded shows. And we work with the producers to find the best place for it.

**Q – What is ITVS community and ITVS community classrooms?**

*Claire –* It's an outreach program that is the umbrella of all the engagement and outreach programs that we do. That ranges from something called the ITVS Cinema Series where we go to different places and screen ITVS programs to people who are involved with the film and the issues of the film. ITVS Classrooms is where we put out study guides to work with educators to get out the word on certain issues. And not only classrooms, it can be care-givers and people in the health fields. We have a department here that does this and they work with the filmmakers to do the activities.

**Q – What is LINCS?**

*Claire –* It is a funding initiative where a filmmaker partners with a public TV station and what ITVS will do is match up to $100,000 of the money that the station puts up. So you would go to WGBH and say I have this program, can you put in $100,000 of post and promotion? Then I could go to ITVS and get $100,000 cash for the project. It's great. It has generated at lot of interesting programs. A recent LINCS example is *We Still Live Here - As Nutanyunean* by Anne Makepeace. It was done in partnership with PBS station WGBY out of Springfield, Massachusetts. The film is about the Wampanoag nation of southeastern Massachusetts, which ensured the survival of the first English settlers in America, and lived to regret it. *We Still Live Here - Âs Nutayuneân* tells the story of the return of the Wampanoag language, the first time a language with no native speakers has been revived in this country. Spurred on by an indomitable linguist named Jessie Little Doe, the Wampanoag are bringing their language and their culture back.

### Q – Are you seeing any trends in documentary filmmaking?

*Claire* – We are still seeing hundreds of projects about international and global subjects from independent filmmakers - the world is certainly getting smaller. The subjects range from economic globalization, migration, democratic uprisings and revolutions, women's rights and empowerment, environment, art and culture, etc. And one of the trends are the many films that ask us what the effect of Islam is on the world, on the US and on difference communities - although this might be attributed to a repercussion after 9/11, it is also an attempt to understand one of the most widespread and misunderstood religions of the world.

### Q – Is PBS constrained by the same censoring regulations as the rest of American TV?

*Claire* – They are now ever since the Janet Jackson incident at the Super Bowl - the wardrobe malfunction. So the FCC really cracked down on what you can show on commercial TV, not cable, but commercial TV, which PBS is part of. Then PBS went and issued a policy statement of what you can and can't show. You can't really get away with anything now. You can't even say "God" on PBS without it insinuating some kind of curse. You can't say "ass" even though Jon Stewart says it every night.

*Q – What are the common mistakes that documentary filmmakers make?*

*Claire* – They don't read the guidelines or follow the directions. And I can understand in your enthusiasm not doing that, but it is better if you do. Like when we ask for a three-page treatment, don't turn in six pages because you have a lot of material. The other thing is to really think about the material for television. That means an hour show.

*Q – What advice would you give a documentary filmmaker?*

*Claire* – It's sort of obvious, but don't give up. Be resolute to what you have to do. And that is the same thing for us. We have to reject 95% of the proposals, but that doesn't mean that the project doesn't have value or that you cannot come back again. That's the spirit of making a film and that is ours as well. Don't take no for an answer.

**Q – What is the California Documentary Project?**

*John* – It's a competitive grant program from the California Council of the Humanities (CCH) that supports documentary film, radio and new media projects about California subjects and issues. We look for projects that are of relevance to both California and national audiences and that are deeply informed by the humanities. The Council has made 104 grants through CDP since 2003.

**Q – When you say the humanities, what do you mean?**

*John* – We look at the humanities in two ways. We look at it both as humanities content that is evident in the piece itself and as a methodology, meaning that the project has a rigorous intellectual foundation and an approach based on humanities research and scholarship. In other words, we want to know what the story is as well as how the filmmaker is going to explore it. These projects should also take a critical, analytical and open approach to the subject matter. We want to know how you'll research the subject and which advisors will help you along the way.

**Q – What wouldn't you fund?**

*John* – We don't fund outright advocacy. So we won't fund projects that are a politically one-sided and lack critical and analytical perspective. We won't fund projects that are overly celebratory or promotional. And we don't fund post-production exclusively. Our grants are intended to come in while a project is still in production.

**Q – For your Production and Research, you need to be matched one to one by**

---

info@calhum.org     www.calhum.org

www.facebook.com/pages/California-Council-for-the-Humanities

http://twitter.com/Cal_Humanities

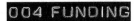

non-federal sources. Does that mean you have to have private money in place before you apply?

*John* – Well, no. The match can be made through in-kind or cash sources. Those funds do not have to be in place at the time of application, though they need to have been contributed and verified when the project is submitted for final report. So in the review we look closely at the proposal's fundraising strategy to assess whether there's a good chance of securing the funds necessary for completion or not.

### Q – What are the available grants?

*John* – The Research and Development Grant is awarded at the very early stages of a project to support the development of humanities content and the overall approach to the subject matter. You can use R&D funds to produce trailers, but we like to see a majority of the funds go toward working with humanities advisors and developing the humanities content or approach. The Production Grant awards up to $50,000 and, as the name implies, supports projects in production, the rationale being that this is when humanities advisors can play the most significant role. If you're already in post and there haven't been any humanities advisors in place all along, it's really too late for them to do anything but review rough cuts. The Production Grant has become increasingly competitive and the number of proposals received has tripled in the past three years. Then we have the Public Engagement Grant, which is intended to capitalize on the potential of these projects to reach and engage audiences above and beyond broadcast. We're excited because we haven't been able to support our projects in areas like this in the past.

### Q – Would that include film festivals?

*John* – Potentially. But it's more about reaching beyond the obvious audience and getting people to understand the issues. At present the guidelines are fairly open. We want to support well-defined specific activities, but this could mean screening and discussions, developing educational curricula, translation and subtitling, targeted distribution, reversioning of content for new audiences, or even an associated transmedia project.

### Q – How would someone apply for one of these grants?

*John* – For the Production and R & D grant, there's an annual deadline in the fall. Once the guidelines are posted on the CCH website read them thoroughly. If there are any questions after reading them, then feel free to contact me. You then submit a proposal, budget and work samples by the posted deadline. You can also sign up for the Council's eNews to receive notification once the guidelines are posted.

> "What doesn't tend to work so well are one to two minute, splashy fundraising pieces that don't really give a good sense of what the final project will actually be like."

**Q – What do you like to see in a proposal?**

*John* – Because we tend to be an early funder, we place more emphasis on the written proposal than some others. First and foremost, we want people to follow the structure of the guidelines and be succinct. I also advise people to take what they think is common knowledge and question it because the people who are reviewing your proposal may not be as informed on the subject as those that are making the project. Yes, reviewers will have media experience, but some may also be humanities scholars and you need to satisfy both audiences. We also look for proposal narratives to address both the micro and the macro story. So for example if you are doing a biography, we don't just want to know the biographical details of the person's life, we want to know what the relevance of that information would be to society at large. None of these subjects exist in a vacuum and as much as you can establish the larger context for them, the more competitive you'll be. And then we are looking for great stories. The humanities component is important, but we also want these projects to be engaging, compelling and accessible.

**Q – So you are not so much interested in what cameras are being used and other technical aspects.**

*John* – Exactly. We ask for a treatment, but we don't need people to go into that level of specificity. It's important to state that we absolutely encourage adventurous film, radio and new media techniques and styles, but the nuts and bolts of how you do this is not necessary for the proposal.

**Q – What do you want to see in the budget?**

*John* – By definition, these grants are for somewhat experienced media makers and we assume they have some knowledge on how to create a budget. However the budget and the timeline are very revealing. You can have a fantastic proposal narrative, but if we see that there's only a tiny amount of money in the budget for post without any explanation then you know there's some experience lacking. It differs between film, radio and new media but generally we see total budgets for film projects ranging from around $150,000 on the low end to well over $1 million. Most film projects come in at the $300,000-$500,000 range, and radio is much less. We look for as complete and accurate a budget as possible so having realistic amounts for post production and rights and clearances are important. Reviewers don't want to see any sign that the project isn't going to be completed or not completed at a high enough technical quality.

**Q – What are you looking for in the work samples? How could a first time filmmaker get involved in your grants?**

*John* – For the Production grant, applicants have to submit a work-in-progress and a previously completed production. Generally a ten minute work-in-progress is about the right length. And the ones that tend to do best give a sense of the story and style and have something very compelling right at the outset, rather than a trailer that takes a long time to build. That said, we see works-in-progress at all different stages from rough assemblies of interview excerpts to very finely crafted fundraising pieces. What doesn't tend to work so well are one to two minute, splashy, fundraising pieces that don't really give a good sense of what the final project will actually be like.

**Q – Do you need a fiscal sponsor to get the grant?**

*John* – Yes. CCH doesn't make grants to individuals. You have to work through a non-profit.

**Q – Do you recommend applicants having humanities advisors?**

*John* – We require that projects actively involve humanities advisors to provide context, depth, and perspective. These can be university professors, independent scholars or they can be culture bearers, meaning their life experience gives them a perspective that will inform the project in ways others can't. The more engaged with the project your advisors are, the more competitive your proposal will be. There's no requirement that these advisors need to actually be in the piece, but they should be used as a resource. Most filmmakers that I've spoken to afterward have said that they benefited from the experience of

*"The more engaged with the project your advisors are, the more competitive your proposal will be."*

## ACTIVIST MEDIA ORGANIZATIONS

**Outreach Extensions**
Develops and implements solution-baed media outreach campaigns that extend the impact of documentaries beyond TV and their local communities. Works with dozens of non-profit organizations like United Way and the American Diabetes Association.
**www.outreachextensions.com**

**Working Films**
Their motto says it all: "Linking non-fiction film with cutting edge activism." Their film campaigns change "toxic environments, influence equitable public policies, making communities more inclusive, and inspiring principled individual actions." They have resources for filmmakers as well like social media outreach seminars and guides.
**www.workingfilms.org**

**Active Voice**
Helps filmmakers spark social change by putting a human face on the issues of our times. Mostly focus on immigration, criminal justice, health care and sustainability.
**www.activevoice.net**

working with advisors.

**Q – Do you need to be a California resident to apply for the grant?**

*John* – No. For us, it's about the subject matter.

**Q – If you fail to get funded, can you reapply? And if so, how many times?**

*John* – There's no limit on how many times you can reapply. However I'd encourage an applicant who wants to reapply to contact us and find out why they were declined. If they're still interested, then they can make those improvements and apply again. What I don't encourage though is either trying to force your project into fitting our requirements or applying as if it was the lottery. It's a lot of work to prepare an application and it's a lot of work for us to review them.

**Q – Can you have more than one film per cycle?**

*John* – No. You can only submit one proposal per grant round. The Public Engagement grant is a little different because it's intended to support previously funded CDP projects.

**Q – What are the common mistakes you see filmmakers make?**

*John* – Not reading the guidelines thoroughly is big. The other big one is not understanding the humanities requirements. Grant reviewers often ask, *"Is this film a humanities based inquiry?"* If it's pure entertainment, advocacy, or celebratory, and doesn't use the humanities to provide context, depth and perspective, then it wouldn't pass. We also see a lot of historical documentaries and it's a pretty common mistake for these proposals not to make a clear and direct case for contemporary relevance.

*Q – What advice would you give a documentary filmmaker?*

*John* – To learn as much as possible from those that are more experienced than you.

**Q – What is the NEA and how does it differ from the NEH?**

*Alyce –* The NEA is The National Endowment for the Arts. The NEH is the National Endowment for the Humanities. The NEH covers things like literature and history whereas our portfolio covers areas such as visual arts, dance, music and the media arts – although we do consider literature an art form and provide grants in that area, too.

**Q – How would documentary filmmaking fit into the NEA?**

*Alyce –* Two fold. Through our Arts and Media section, this has been traditionally known as Radio and Television. We revised the guidelines to be more inclusive of all the platforms which one has access to. This initiative has been designed to capture the arts on every media platform – television and radio, but also mobile, game platforms and web-based media. The projects funded under these guidelines will be about the arts and media as art. We're even funding dramatic narrative under Arts in Media. Then we have Art Works, which includes film and media art festivals, service organizations such as the Independent Feature Project or Women Make Movies, community based media centers, but media creation as well.

**Q – What are the monetary levels of the grants?**

*Alyce–* The smallest is $10,000 and it generally goes up to $200,000.

**Q – How would a filmmaker apply for a grant?**

*Alyce –* Through our website. We don't fund individuals, but we do fund organizations. So a filmmaker would have to be affiliated with a 501(c)(3) such as IFP, Women Make

---

webmgr@endow.arts.gov          www.nea.gove

www.facebook.com/NationalEndowmentfortheArts

http://twitter.com/NEAarts

Movies or the Filmmakers Collaborative. We aren't able to fund an individual artist through a fiscal sponsor; therefore, the relationship with the nonprofit organization must extend beyond using them as a pass-through. The organization has to be registered through www.grants.gov and their proposal would come in through there as well. The 501(c)(3) has to have a DUNS number. Applying can be a bit cumbersome so we really encourage filmmakers to get everything in order and not wait until the last minute.

*Q – What else would you require in an application and what gets your attention?*

*Alyce –* We require a narrative description of the project and a budget that outlines the expenses that will be accumulated during the course of the grant. We require a listing of key personnel including the track record a filmmaker has of making documentaries; who have they tried to reach? what successes have they had? We also ask our applicants what their strategy is for attracting an audience. Do they have an outreach, engagement, or marketing plan? Do they have a social media strategy? Do they have distribution in place at the time of their application? In the past, how have their projects been distributed? Ultimately, how are people going to know that this project exists and will they be so compelled by the promotion to give their time?

*Q – Do you require filmmakers to show you either samples of previous work or of work in progress?*

*Alyce –* Yes, both.

*Q – Is an NEA grant typically first money in or one that comes in down the line?*

*Alyce –* It can be either. We convene peer review panels and it really depends on how the panel feels about the work. Needless to say, first money in for a first time filmmaker is probably not going to happen. First money in for a seasoned filmmaker is more likely.

*Q – What could a first time filmmaker do to increase their chances?*

*Alyce –* Have a brilliant trailer.

*Q – Would it help if they teamed up with a more established producer?*

*Alyce –* Not always. It has to be clear as to what that established producer is really going to be contributing; we don't want it to just be a name on the proposal. Are they really going to have any involvement and if so, what?

*Q – Who populates the panels?*

DUNS Number
Data Universal Numbering System

Need it to apply for a federal grant. Indentifies your business.

Call Dunn & Bradstreet to get it. 1-866-705-5711. It's free!

## APPLYING FOR AN NEA GRANT

*You can get between $10,000 and $200,000. Check www.nea.gov for deadlines.*

*1. Register with www.grants. gov.*

*2. Go to www.nea.gov and download application from The Arts in Media section under Grants.*

*3. Fill out Application for Federal Domestic Assistance.*

*4. Fill out the Project/ Performance Site Location(s) Form.*

*5. Fill out the NEA Organization & Project Profile Form.*

*6. Complete and attach required items to the Attachments Form (work sample, project narrative, budget, etc.)*

*7. Submit application electronically through www. grants.gov.*

**Alyce** – It depends on the nature of the panel. If we have a panel coming up that looks at film festivals then it will be comprised of people who have been affiliated with the running of film festivals in one way or another. We always have a lay person on the panel who is not directly involved with the field. They are there to represent the general American public. We generally choose these people from those that inquire about being in that position.

*Q – Do you have to be an American citizen or organization to receive the funding? And does the film have to be about an American topic?*

**Alyce** – Yes on citizenship. No on the content having to be American.

*Q – Does the project have to end up on PBS?*

**Alyce** – No, and I think that is one of the misconceptions. Projects need to reach a broad audience and television remains an important vehicle, but it doesn't have to be public television; if you had an offer from HBO or a basic cable network, that would be fine. However, you can put something on TV or up on the web and it's available to the whole nation or in the case of the Internet, the world, but unless it's strategically promoted, it doesn't mean it's going to reach an audience. What are you going to do to ensure it does?

*Q – If someone wanted to have a theatrical release of their film, are you okay with that?*

**Alyce** – Absolutely.

*Q – Does the NEA require you credit them?*

**Alyce** – Yes. We ask that they credit the Endowment and we do ask for a final report that states how the funds were used and whether or not the grant was effective.

*Q – If one fails to get a grant, can they resubmit for the same project?*

*Alyce* – Yes, there's no limit to how many times people can submit one project but you can't reapply in the same year. There have been cases where projects look very promising but it's just too early in the process and the panelists didn't feel that it was appropriate to invest. The panel will say that they are favorable and encourage them to reapply.

### Q – Can someone call the NEA before starting the process to see if their project is appropriate?

*Alyce* – Absolutely, but we really have just about all of the answers to most questions on our website. Our guidelines are posted there along with a series of FAQs, but we are always here to help if need be.

### Q – What are the common mistakes that you see filmmakers make?

*Alyce* – I would say not clearly and succinctly articulating the story that we will experience through their film. Very often they will put the rationale of why this film should be made – why this film is important. But at the end of the day our questions are: what are we going to see? What story are you going to tell and how are you going to tell it?

### Q – What advice would you give a new filmmaker?

*Alyce* – Raising money is hard and if you're looking to foundations and government funders for that money, you need to clearly state the how and why of your film in terms of engaging your audience. An example of that would be engagement campaigns that have been developed by organizations such as Outreach Extensions, Working Films, or Active Voice. Develop partnerships with organizations interested in your film's themes that then serve as part of your distribution plan. This is what's of interest to funders especially those that come on earlier rather than later. Make sure you read a funder's website and see what their missions are. Your film needs to speak to that.

## APPLYING FOR AN NEA GRANT

8. Mail materials to NEA for staff review.
Media Arts Office/The Arts in Media
Room 729
NEA
1100 Pennsylvania Avenue, NW
Washington, DC 20506-0001

9. Eligible proposals sent off to panelists for review. Panels meet for 1 to 5 days to discuss projects.

10. Panel sends recommended proposals to National Council where they are reviwed in open session.

11. Council recommends proposals to Chairman who makes final decision on granting and amount of grant.

12. Notificiation

*Q – What is IndieGoGo?*

*Danae* – It's the largest open funding platform in the world. It helps raise money from more people, faster. We launched in 2008 at Sundance and since then we're now in over two hundred countries, run over 26,000 campaigns and distributed millions of dollars. We allow anybody to use our platform whether they be entrepreneurs, publicists, technology developers, app developers, food trucks owners or restaurants. Creative people can use it as well, so musicians, writers, filmmakers, photographers are welcome. In addition, we are open to anybody who wants to raise money for a cause or charity. We have a lot of activists, community gardens, cancer research teams and individuals raising for their own personal endeavors. For example, we have a couple raising money for IVF. We have a young volleyball team in Utah raising money to go to the Junior National championships in Georgia. There's a man named Pastor Marion who for years has been saving lives from execution in the Congo. When his kidneys started failing, a CNN reporter who's been covering his work for years launched an IndieGoGo campaign to raise money for a kidney transplant. In the end, they raised $50,000 and he was able to fly to South Africa and have the surgery.

*Q – How did IndieGoGo come about?*

*Danae* – After college, I worked on Wall Street in finance in a media group. I'd meet a lot of filmmakers and producers at nighttime events. One time, I met a 70-year-old producer who Fedexed me his proejct thinking that I could finance his movie. It broke my heart to think that a man with a lifetime of experience was begging me, a young girl aged twenty-two with no experience, for money. It seemed that Hollywood was well financed, but not the independent world. I went back to business school so I could start a fund to help independent creative endeavors. There, I met my co-founders who also had experience

 www.indiegogo.com      http://www.indiegogo.com/blog

 www.facebook.com/IndieGoGo      http://twitter.com/IndieGoGo

with fundraising. Eric Schell had founded a theater company in Chicago and my other co-founder, Slava Rubin, created a fund to raise money for cancer research. So we all came together and very quickly realized the way to make it the most impactful business was to make it global, be democratic in our approach and allow anybody from around the world to raise money. That meant using the internet. We had enormous visions and still do. You have to have that kind of mentality if you want to build anything real. That's why we called ourselves IndieGoGo. We're all about the independent spirit happening.

*Q – How can IndieGoGo help documentary filmmakers?*

*Danae* – It's a vital tool for doc filmmakers for it helps get their projects off the ground. If you can show that you can execute something with a small amount of money, such as a fundraising trailer, it validates your overall project. That's very important to investors. In fact, there are five major benefits to crowd sourcing. First is money, obviously and the more you can get the better. Second, is market validation. When people donate to you it's like they're voting for your project with dollars. Other investors see this and realize they have less risk by putting in money when others have. This also helps ease distributors' nerves becuase they see there's a market for your project.

Third is marketing and awareness building. The one mistake filmmakers make is that they take years to make an amazing film, putting in tons of sweat equity, and only when they're done do they tell people about it. They expect people to show up out of nowhere. That's not the world we live in anymore. They should tell people about it from day one. They should use production as a new form of promotion. They should share snippets, dailies, progress updates and stories. People today are active consumers. We want to be part of things, we want to participate, give feedback, give our reactions, thoughts and comments on a product. So if you can create awareness of your project early on and give the public a way to interface with it, you will draw larger crowds when you're ready to release your film to the world.

Fourth is participation, which is allowing people to engage with you. On IndieGoGo, we allow people to leave comments, ask questions and keep a dialogue going about a project. The campaign owners can do video updates such as stating they got a great new interview and how it's going to help the perspective of the film. It allows filmmakers to have dialogue throughout production or post-production of the film in a way that allows your audience to participate - maybe give ideas. We had one filmmaker, Roberta Grossman, who had a couple of campaigns on IndieGoGo to raise $13,000 for a documentary about a famous Jewish song that everyone dances to. It was a very heartwarming project. She started her campaign, got a ton of feedback and people reached out to her. It flew around the internet and it ended up in the inbox of the granddaughter of the man in Israel who wrote the song. She reached out to her saying that they had seen her campaign on IndieGoGo and she wanted to be a part of it.

The fifth thing is the idea of curbing serendipity. Morrie Warshawski talks about this a lot. When you share information with the world, positive things can come back to

## 5 BENEFITS OF CROWDSOURCING

1. Money.

2. Market Validation. When investors see others have invested in you, it provides less risk. Also helps distributors realize there's a market for your film.

3. Marketing and Awareness. Telling people about your project from day one. Use production as promotion. Share snippets, dailies, program updates and stories from the field as a way to engage and involve your audience.

4. Participation. Allowing people to engage, ask questions and start a dialogue with you while you are making the film.

5. Serendipity. You never know who is out there that can help.

help you. With Twitter, Facebook and other social media, it's easy to share and you never know who's listening. The reason someone decides to do a documentary film is because they're passionate about the subject. And they feel that other people would be passionate about it too. At this point, that's an assumption. But what happens is when they do a campaign, they start raising money from people they know, then they start raising from people they don't know via friends of friends or Facebook. Then it goes from an assumption to being real. People are out there, are interested in the project and start sending in money. That's the icing on the cake for a documentary filmmaker.

*Q – What would you say is the advantage of crowd funding?*

*Danae* – Years ago there were lots of obstacles to anyone who wanted to break into filmmaking and very few ways around them. These days, the obstacles are still there, but crowdfunding allows someone who doesn't have a trust fund, credit cards or an in to main funding opportunities, a way of getting their project started and completed. It's an exciting time for creative people. There's no excuse for a documentary filmmaker to not make their film these days. Marketing is free and the equipment is cheap.

*Q – Why do you think people will give money to someone they don't know?*

*Danae* - There are a lot of different reasons. One is people want to support in what they believe. Two, they want some kind of perk that might be offered for investing. Three, they want to be part of something bigger than themselves, but can't due to their busy lives. They can satisfy those urges by living vicariously through the campaign. And four, there's a certain element who just look for cool stuff to support. The most successful campaigns get validation from the donations of people that they know. Then we provide a ton of tools and tips of how to go out to the communities that would care about your project and engage with them for fundraising.

*Q – How would a doc filmmaker go about running a successful campaign?*

*Danae* – There are three key elements. The first is a great pitch that's personal and authentic. Don't be somebody else. You aren't going after an investor with his or her own objective. This is your fan base. These are people who care about your project, so just be yourself. That means telling them why you're passionate about making this film and why it's important that it gets out to the world. Often times filmmakers just pitch the project, but in the social funding world, people fund people. So make a video pitch with you in it stating what I just mentioned. You should also come up with some unique and exclusive perks that are personalized or customized. For example, you could give away signed tee shirts or offer a chance to watch an editing session. There's also financial perks such as they will get the DVD before anyone else does or for half price. Then there's exclusivity perks, which might be that you only give out a limited number of a certain object and then it's unavailable. Then you need to engage participation from your funders. So when you're running your campaign, put out progress reports as well as updates on whatever your film is about. A great example is *100 Yen*, a film about the Japanese arcade experience. They had a tee shirt campaign and in the middle of it, they asked their funders to vote on the tee shirt style. With *Sound It Out* a UK doc by Jeanie Finlay, they were very authentic. They showed the story and themselves. The second key element is being proactive. Doing updates and reaching out to influencers makes a big difference. The *100 Yen* guys were great at this. They reached out a quirky, niche video arcade blog online. They went right to their core audience and raised $12,000 in a couple weeks. The readers of that blog saw the campaign and thought, *"Sweet, I want in."* The third element is having an audience that care. If you're making a film about paper clips, you have to make sure that there are people in the world that care about paper clips.

*Q – Some filmmakers want to do everything themselves. Does it help to have help?*

*Danae* – Totally. We've noticed that and films that have four to six members raise 72% more than just one person. People who do more than eleven updates do 137% more.

*Q – When you do a campaign, is it better to do it in small chunks?*

*Danae* – We encourage people to start small, especially if they're new to crowd funding. Run a $1,000 campaign to get comfortable with it. It teaches people what it takes to be out there and authentic.

*"With Twitter, Facebook and other social media, it's easy to share and you never know who's listening."*

Be specific with your use of funds and be transparent. So say that your film is going to cost $50,000, but you are raising $1,000 because you have to shoot a trailer in order to take the next step. You have to put in the energy and time to make it work, but if you remember that the whole reason for making the film was to impact people and share a story, then why not start at the beginning?

### Q – Any suggestions for documentary filmmakers to increase traffic to their site?

**Danae** – Everything that I just talked about. Be proactive. Do updates. Reach out to influencers like bloggers and organizations with newsletters. We have a campaign called E-maker for inventors in the UK. One group created some 3D printers and over a week they raised over $107,000. They made it onto a blog called Gizmoto, which went to their core audience. When you reach out to influencers, don't just ask them to cover your campaign. Go to the ones who can be helpful. Maybe they are someone who you'd want to interview for your project. Also the people you interview could tell their friends via Facebook or something. The way it usually works is you put out an email to your friends and family. Then you go on Facebook and get the Twitter stuff going. Then you reach out to the influencers and hopefully they will drive traffic your way. Then it's about to maintaining your updates and giving reasons for people to re-share.

### Q – How is IndieGoGo different from Kickstarter?

**Danae** – We don't curate so we allow anyone to post. We don't believe it's our decision on who should be successful or not. We are international, so anyone in the world can create a campaign as long as you have a bank account. We don't just support creative projects. Entrepreneurs, causes and charities can be with us, too. What's interesting is that since our launch in 2008 we now have over two hundred competitors and we are still the only ones that are broad. The other difference is that you keep the money you raise and we provide you an incentive so you pay a lower fee if you reach your goals. We integrate with Paypal and allow you to use credit cards while they force you to use Amazon Checkout, which a lot of people have a hard time using. It's not very common.

### Q – How much can you realistically raise?

"There's no excuse for a documentary filmmaker to not make their film these days. Marketing is free and equipment is cheap."

**Danae** – It all depends on who you are and how big your audience is. If you're Kevin Smith, you're going to raise a lot of money because you connect with a huge amount of active fans. If you're a first time filmmaker out of film school, you're not likely to raise a million dollars. Emily Hagen made a film called *My Sucky Teen Romance*. She's a high school filmmaker and she raised $9,000 to help get the film underway. Then she got the buzz going and did another campaign and raised $6,000 for post. She raised that a lot faster because she was connected to Harry Knowles of Ain't

## RUNNING A SUCCESSFUL CAMPAIGN

1. Great Pitch. Personal and Authentic. Be passionate and explain why your project is important. This helps get the word out.

2. Make a video pitch.

3. Offer unique and exclusive perks that are personalized and customized to entice people to donate.

4. Engage your funders and let them participate. Put out project reports and updates frequently. Have proactive blogs. Allow the funders to choose certain things about the campaign such as what t-shirts will say or what kinds of clips go up next.

It Cool News. He blogged about it and his fans came through.

*Q – What are partner pages?*

*Danae* – Certain organizations have pages on IndieGoGo so they can tout their own campaigns. One of them is the Sheffield Doc Fest. When you go to their page, you will see all these docs that are related to the festival. It's extra marketing. And another difference between Kickstarter and ourselves is that some of our partners are non-profits like Fractured Atlas and the San Francisco Film Society. They allow for donations to be tax deductible without paying double fees. Normally they would pay us a fee of 4% and then 6%-7% to the non-profit on whatever they raise. We came up with a flat 6% for both so the filmmaker can keep more of the cash.

*Q – What is the GoGo Factor?*

*Danae* – It's an algorithim that measures how active a campaign is. We want to reward people who work hard. So if you're working hard to promote, share and update your funders and your community is working hard commenting, sharing and funding you, then you get a high GoGo factor. At that point, we'll promote you to the press and feature you. We're very democratic. Everyone has an equal chance for success. It's all based on how hard you work.

*Q – What common mistakes do you see filmmakers make?*

# FUNDING ORGANIZATIONS

**A.J. Muste Institute**
www.ajmuste.org

**Arthur Vining Davis Foundation**
www.avdf.org

**Creative Capital**
www.creative-capital.org

**Dance Film Association**
www.dancefilms.org

**Ford Foundation**
www.fordfound.org

**Frameline Film & Video Comp. Fund**
www.frameline.org

**Guggenhiem Fellowship**
www.gf.org

**The Jerome Foundation**
www.jeromefdn.org

**Latino Public Broadcasting**
www.puffinfoundation.org

**The LEF Foundation**
www.lef-foundation.org

**MacArthur Foundation**
www.macfound.org

**Nathan Cummings Found.**
www.nathancummings.org

**Nat'l Black Programming Consortium**
www.nbpc-online.com

**National Fund for Jewish Documentary**
www.jewishculture.org

**Native Public Television**
www.nativetelecom.org

**The North Star Fund**
www.northstarfund.org

**Open Meadows Foundation**
www.openmeadows.org

**Pacific Pioneer Fund**
www.pacificpioneerfund.com

**The Playboy Foundation**
www.playboyenterprises.com

**Puffin Foundation**
www.lpbp.org

**Rockefeller Foundation**
www.rockfefellerfoundation.org

**Roy W. Dean Film and Writing Grants**
www.fromtheheartproductions.com

**The Sister Fund**
www.sisterfund.org

**The Unitarian Universalist Fund.**
www.uua.org

**For more info on grants go to: www.foundationcenter.org**

**Danae** – They have the belief that *"if they build it, they will come."* Nothing in the world works that way. Even if you have an amazing pitch and video, if all you do is put it up and walk away then when you come back two months later, you won't be successful. You have to put yourself out there. You will have a much higher success rate if you speak for yourself as well. That's the importance of making it personal and putting yourself in the video to show who you are. And then the last mistake is not being themselves. You aren't pitching Hollywood studios. You don't have to be somebody else. If people don't believe you because you are trying to pull some song and dance, then you won't be successful.

**Q – What advice would you give a new filmmaker?**

**Danae** – Action speaks louder than words. Just do and the momentum will build. Then more people will want to jump in because people like to be part of action. So if you are having a hard time raising $5,000, then try and raise $1,000. Then go off and do something real with that $1,000 and then come back and say, *"This is what I did."* Do that enough, then people will know you can execute and will want to be a part of your project.

# CHAPTER FIVE
# BROADCASTERS

## THE DOCUMENTARY
## FILMMAKERS HANDBOOK

### Q – What is your job?

*Nancy* – My title is Senior Vice-President, Documentary Programming and I, along with others in our department, develop new ideas for HBO to produce as documentaries. We also acquire documentaries and give completion funding for works-in-progress. For a certain number of the shows that HBO is producing or commissioning, I'm the supervising producer. I'm responsible for overseeing all the day-to-day operations and editorial direction of those productions.

### Q – What kind of documentary films does HBO look for?

*Nancy* – Our main focus are documentaries that deal with contemporary social issues in the United States, but we do also have a number of international films each year. The hallmark is films with a present-tense storyline and a verité style, but there certainly are also exceptions to that. They tend to be strong, character-driven films, and are mainly feature length.

### Q – What kind of film proposal would get you excited?

*Nancy* – In terms of a written idea, without any footage to back it up, it would have to be very persuasive. And by that I mean it shouldn't seem familiar, it shouldn't feel like you've seen it before, it shouldn't seem like something that would be appropriate for another channel because of its genre or subject matter. For our purposes, it should be a story that's really character-based or access-based, that's following a present tense, unfolding story, not something that has happened primarily in the past. So, if the action is yet to come, how do you write a proposal about that? It mostly depends on the characters. Why are they compelling? What's going on with their lives? What's going to happen to them - something that we are going to follow? And there should be a sense of why and how the specific story line relates to a bigger social issue that's relevant and important.

---

 **www.hbo.com**

*Q – Would you like to see some footage or a rough assembly before getting involved with a film?*

**Nancy** – Yes. We will consider and we have developed things from written proposals, but it helps to have at least a few minutes of footage. If it's a character-driven piece, then a few minutes with the main character is helpful. If it's access-driven, then a few minutes of the institution or whatever it is.

*Q – Do you work with first time filmmakers and if so how can one improve their odds of attracting HBO as a distributor?*

**Nancy** – Yes, we do work with first time filmmakers. For a first time filmmaker it's helpful to supply some footage with your proposal. And then, on top of that, one should be open to the possibility of working with another qualified person - an established producer perhaps. We've often made those marriages, and many of them have been very successful collaborations.

*Q – Does HBO prefer one off documentaries or series?*

**Nancy** – Our hallmark is the one off documentary, usually feature length. So that's what we're primarily looking for. We also do some shorts, 30 – 40 minutes in length.

*Q – Do you generate any of your programming ideas in-house or do they come from outside producers?*

**Nancy** – It's about half and half.

*Q – What kind of budgets do you like to work within?*

**Nancy** – There is a huge range. If it's something we're commissioning, then whatever it takes to do it properly. Most of our projects take over a year to produce. We can follow a story over many years, if necessary, which is a luxury. And since our films' stories often come together in the edit room, we make sure there is ample editing time budgeted.

*Q – Does HBO have on site editing facilities that filmmakers can use?*

**Nancy** – Yes, but we only do a few shows in-house each year.

*Q – When you acquire a film, what kind of deliverables do they need to bring you?*

**Nancy** – They're extensive and are outlined in the contract that you sign. I wouldn't want to begin to describe it myself! We have a great post-production department here that handles all that.

*Q – Do you allow your films to have a theatrical release prior to airing on HBO?*

*Nancy* – It depends. It's really on a case-by-case basis. Most of our documentaries premiere on HBO prior to a theatrical release, excluding festival exposure and special screenings. But we're sometimes open to the possibility of a different arrangement. There are some documentaries that we come to at a later stage, after the theatrical release is already underway, that we then acquire. It just depends on the film and how it fits into our overall picture.

**Q – How would a filmmaker approach you with a project for your regular and Late Night programming?**

*Nancy* – Our Late Night programming is long running and extremely popular. Pitches can be made the same way as regular documentaries, but we do most of the shows in-house, so there is a very limited number of ideas we're taking from the outside.

**Q – What's your process for evaluating material and deciding what gets acquired?**

*Nancy* – For cold, unsolicited submissions that come in, one person will look at it and write coverage initially. If it's favorable, it'll get passed on to me or one of the other supervising producers. If we like it, we'll pass it along to Sheila Nevins. But along the way, we all share things with each other. *"What do you think of this?"* It's not always black and white. But, because we don't have a huge number of slots, we are looking for something that really jumps out. Sometimes you'll see a rough cut that has potential – a germ of an idea worth exploring. We would then work with the filmmaker to do that.

**Q – How hands on is HBO either in the production or editing stages of your films?**

*Nancy* – An idea is developed and we all have to feel good about it going in, but during the whole shooting process we're not too involved. It's a very intimate process between the filmmaking team and the subjects. Where we do get very involved is in the editing phase. We spend a lot of time at that point and are very hands on. No matter how good a film is, we're seeing it at a stage when it can still be better. There's not necessarily a clear roadmap, so to get the best film you have to pull it and push it in different ways. We often have all day screenings with filmmakers to go through the film frame by frame. So it isn't like we're just e-mailing notes. It's more collaborative. A lot of the time you don't know what's wrong, you just know something is. So we sit together and try to figure it out by trying different things.

**Q – What do you see as the future of documentary filmmaking?**

*Nancy* – I think the future is very bright for non-fiction. It only seems to be getting more exciting and more broadly defined. There's a bigger and bigger audience acceptance of non-fiction. From a programmer's perspective, the whole accessibility of technology in terms of making a documentary is both a blessing and a burden. There's a lot more out there to wade through in order to find something good. But there's also a lot more good

## CO-PRODUCTIONS

Many broadcasters can't give you your whole budget so you have to get it from different sources.

Allows broadcasters to defray the risk, so if you can get one interested, you may be able to get others.

Start making relationships with foreign and domestic broadcasters even when making lower budget films. It will pay off later!

Co-productions can be complicated so get a good lawyer.

Your subject needs to appeal to every broadcaster so an American baseball doc won't do well in Europe.

material. The reality is that, unlike a scripted narrative film, you can get your documentary film off the ground relatively cheaply and on your own. So that's exciting. I think all these things go through cycles and we're in an upswing right now. But I don't think we're going to slide back too much.

**Q – What common mistakes do you see filmmakers make?**

**Nancy** – In terms of pitching, the classic one that happens all the time, is that people don't have a sense of what your channel is and what types of documentaries you do – even when the information is readily available. In addition to that, people should have a sense of the general documentary landscape around them. If you're doing a verité film, you have to provide as much information as you can to explain why you think your characters are worth following.

**Q – What advice would you give a filmmaker?**

**Nancy** – To have a healthy sense of self-criticism. Sometimes people get enthralled by the worthiness of their subject. They become lax in the telling of their story. Be creative. Have high standards. Think in advance about legal issues. Get advice from peers from the documentary community. Learn from other people's work and get them to help you with yours.

**Q – What are some terms that describe what is an A & E show?**

**Steve –** Big characters, high stakes, unique access and closed ended episodes with resolutions. When you look across the board, we have big characters in Gene Simmons, the cast of *Storage Wars, Billy the Exterminator, Dog the Bounty Hunter,* the detectives on *The First 48* and the list goes on. A great character can come from anywhere and we're always looking to add more to our roster.

**Q – What about the other terms?**

**Steve –** High stakes. On a scale of one to ten, what's the worst thing that can happen to you? You die, right? On *Intervention*, all the addicts are tracking towards death. If you've ever seen *The First 48*, every episode starts with a dead body in the alley. Unique access. Take *Dog the Bounty Hunter* for example, he and his team are breaking down doors to grab people who don't want to go to jail. The way the cameras gets that coverage certainly qualifies as unique access. Furthermore, seeing Gene Simmons on stage spitting fire and gargling blood in front of 25,000 KISS fans, and then seeing that same guy at home with his wife and kids, that's unique access. Close-ended episodes with resolutions are what we like. With our business model, it's important the viewer can surf in and out of a series and not be completely lost due to a continuing storyline that they need to catch up on.

**Q – How can you tell if a project is right for documentary or reality TV?**

**Steve –** That's one of the things I try to teach documentary filmmakers all the time. The two things to ask are: is there a long running series out of this concept? Or is this merely a one-off 90-minute documentary? The golden ticket for a filmmaker trying to break into the lucrative industry of non-fiction programming is to develop a documentary that can be produced over and over again. It's no coincidence that some of the most successful programs on cable television possess these attributes. For example, *Deadliest Catch,*

 www.aetv.com

*Beyond Scared Straight, 30 Days* and *Ice Road Truckers* are just a few from this ever growing list. When researching topics, ask yourself; *"Can the material fit within the four elements of the filter terms mentioned earlier?"* History Channel did a one off special called *Ice Road Truckers* that had great ratings and was able to explore that world and define and craft what the show should be. A&E's highest rated premiere was *Beyond Scared Straight*, based off Academy Award-winning Director Arnold Shapiro's 1979 documentary *Scared Straight!* The documentary followed a group of juvenile delinquents who spent a very up-close and personal three hours at Rahway State Prison with the goal of deterring them from a life of crime. Our series is the same format of the film, just condensed and put into a nice package of a 60-minute TV show.

**Q – Is there a percentage of your programming that is geared toward reality as well as documentaries?**

**Steve** – It's all defined as non-fiction. We don't produce anything that doesn't have the potential for being a series. For a network to successfully broadcast documentaries, it would need to curate a doc-series in the similar way ESPN did with their *30/30* series. As a documentary filmmaker, wouldn't you like to have some marketing behind your project? Wouldn't you like to have radio and magazine promotion? It's not cost effective to do one-offs. Think about it in terms of big budget films. They spend $5-$10 million in P&A. That money is not only for getting the audience there the first couple weekends, it's for ingraining the knowledge of that product to the consumer for ancillary benefits such as DVD distribution and pay-per-view purchases. They don't market something too heavily after that first round and the same thing goes for us. We don't have the budget to constantly market to one-time screenings.

**Q – So where do Jesus Camp and The September Issue fit into that model?**

**Steve** – *Jesus Camp* and *The September Issue* were strictly for theatrical release and distribution. A & E makes fantastic topical and thought provoking documentaries, with the main focus being theatrical release. Our development team embraces the documentary community and understands that with limited funding available everywhere it can sometimes feel like hitting the lottery is easier than getting their documentary made. This is why I encourage doc filmmakers to look at their ideas as potential series. You're going to put in the same amount of work in developing the idea either way so why not consider doing something bigger than a one-off film?

**Q – How hands-on can a producer expect the network to be when working on a series at A&E?**

**Steve** – It's a collaboration all the way through with a varying degree of involvement. If there's something that's semi-viable, we work with the producer to craft

*"The golden ticket for a filmmaker trying to break into the lucarative industry of non-fiction programming is to develop a documentary that can be produced over and over again."*

# NATIONAL GEOGRAPHIC TELEVISION INTERNATIONAL

*NGTI looks for quality factual programming, within the following sub-genres: natural history, science, history, culture, people & places, ancient civilisations, adventure, environment and society.*

*To discuss your idea, email your request to ideas@natgeotv-int.com and you'll be contacted within 7 working days (except around the time of major markets and festivals when this may be longer).*

*Submissions of ideas with a story treatment, budget, producer bio, sample of producer's work, production schedule/delivery date and a trailer and/or rough cut (if available) can be emailed directly. The contact details can be found online at www.natgeotv-int.com/pages/contact*

*All submissions will be reviewed and the producer responded to within 6 weeks from date of submission. NGTI's head of acquisitons and co-productions will review the submission, looking for fit with the NGTI brand and catalogue and its potentional in the international marketplace.*

**www.natgeotv-int.com**

# TRU-TV

*Tru TV, is an American cable network owned by Turner Broadcasting, a subsidiary of Time Warner. Programming for the channel focuses on 'caught on video' reality programs such as Cops, Operation Repo, Hot Pursuit, Foresnic Files, Most Shocking. Go to their website for submission information.*

**www.trutv.com**

that into an amazing concept. Maybe there's a character missing or some scenes are missing. Once it receives the green light, development executives are very hands on, shaping and molding the pilot to provide it the best opportunity of moving forward to a series.

*Q – Can you speak about some of the promotional things that may need to be created when working with a network?*

**Steve –** I work in the programming and development department and one of my duties is being the brand manager for all my shows. So it's my job to give all of the departments, such as the promo department or the marketing department, as much prep and runway leading up to the launch of the show so that you as the producer have the best marketing. So that may mean getting rushes from the shoot so the promo department can get an idea of how to promote the show at the Upfronts and for internal senior management meetings. The more our ad sales team knows about the show, even if it's very rough lifts from the editing timeline, the more anecdotes they can take and present when they're on the phone with a client and pre-sell the hell out of it. A producer may think that as long as I get the network the finished product seven to ten days before the broadcast that's all that's needed. That's the furthest from the truth.

*Q – With social media is there anything different about how you develop or promote shows?*

**Steve –** In development, it's outside our purview. We do use social media to market and promote our shows as well as build a fan base via interaction with our viewers. We acknowledge the negative and constructive comments that are made and take those into account. But it doesn't entirely define the creative of what the show will be.

*Q – What are the common mistakes that you see filmmakers or producers make?*

**Steve –** Thinking about things like product integration, cross platform or mobile app - all these ancillary revenue streams and other reasons why you think this thing is a goldmine. However, the bottom line is the only thing that turns into a goldmine is a great show. So worry about making a great show and everything else will fall into place.

*Q – What advice would you give a new filmmaker?*

**Steve –** They need to learn and expose themselves to as many facets of the filmmaker food chain as possible. From lighting to shooting to editing to line producing - it's all too common that there's a left-side brain/right-side brain that people gravitate towards. That's OK, but you should always force yourself outside the comfort zone.

Upfronts
Yearly presentation of American and Canadian shows to advertisers. How much ad time is sold can mean whether a show gets picked up or not.

**Q – When you look to program a documentary film, what subject matter excites you?**

*Christian* – We're open to any subject matter to be perfectly honest. What's important to us is the story told. Is it interesting? Is it compelling or dramatic or is it entertaining and funny? I think that because we are part of the Sundance family, what's important to us is the quality of filmmaking. So we look for an interesting story, well told by a skilled filmmaker. Sundance and the Channel have always been about the filmmaker. Not about the filmmaker in the way that IFC focuses on the process, but literally what is the filmmaker's vision and how we can we best bring that to the network.

**Q – Is there any particular style of documentary film or storytelling that you prefer? Say vérité over archival footage dominated films?**

*Christian* – I wouldn't say one is better than the other. If it is between vérité and a heavily narrated film, to be perfectly honest, our taste would lean toward the vérité project. Because it is style that reflects a strength in storytelling and filmmaking. But you can make a great film using lots of archive footage. In those films, you're talking more about the editing. So if you have too much narration, it means, in our opinion, that you probably haven't told the story well enough in your filmmaking.

**Q – Where do you find the films that you program?**

*Christian* – I have an acquisitions director that works for me as well as two program managers. Between the four of us we go to major film festivals and TV markets and documentary markets. We go to Sundance, Berlin, MIP-TV and MIP-COM, which are the two markets in Cannes. We go to Tribeca and the market in Marseilles in June. We go to IDFA in the fall. Toronto. A lot of the smaller or territory-based markets will fly us out. We

---

 **www.sundancechannel.com**   **http://twitter.com/SundanceChannel**

 **www.facebook.com/SundanceChannel**

can't afford to go to everything, but if it's over a weekend and we're invited as guests, we try to hit a lot of the smaller ones. You never know what you are going to find.

**Q – Do you solely do acquisitions or do you create projects in house?**

*Christian* – We generally have been an acquisitions based channel, but recently we have gotten involved in creating one-off documentaries. Now this is all changing and fluid so by the time this book is published or someone reads this, we might be fully financing documentaries. This subject is constantly evolving. But the philosophy now is that we are last in for North American rights and it would never be for more than 20% of the overall budget. Beyond that, we are doing development and production of non-fiction series, but that is out of our original programming department. Those are done through experienced producers and their productions companies.

**Q – With those pre-buys, would you consider a first time filmmaker?**

*Christian* – We don't want to discourage anyone from bringing us a project, and this goes for first time filmmakers with completed films as well. If you really are a new filmmaker, you should seek out an experienced producer or sales agent or in the case of a series, start with production companies because they are going to have the access. On my side, I deal with acquisitions. We try to see everything that is submitted to us, but what we watch first are films that come to us through sales agents with which we have relationships. I trust that a good sales agent will know my network's taste and that they know what we pay for films. When and if we decide to do a deal, it's hard with first time filmmakers because there are a lot of moving parts that have to be explained in terms of delivery, clearances, insurance and masters. I'd rather deal with a sales agent here instead of my staff spending hours or weeks on the phone with the producer making sure the film is deliverable. We buy two hundred films a year and we can't work on explaining delivery to someone.

**Q – What do you think filmmakers should be looking in a sales agent from your perspective?**

*Christian* – Find a sales agent who represents films of a similar size and style to yours. You don't want to go with a sales agent where you are a tiny documentary on a slate of several medium independent features with talent because you aren't going to be their priority. There are a few sales agents that focus exclusively on docs. Try to find them and ask other filmmakers who used them how they did. Did they return your calls? Did they make a lot of sales? With the representations that they made to you, have they tried to live up to them?

*"If you have too much narration it means, in our opinion, that you probably haven't told the story well enough."*

**Q – Do you interface with the Sundance Labs and The Doc Institute?**

*Christian* – We're sort of the end game. They don't want to hear from us right away because usually I think the filmmakers that get that far have an idea of getting a theatrical release or some sort of big festival attention. They don't want to jump to the end of the story and sell it to TV right away. Some people understand that their film is a really great TV documentary; I'm going to try and fund it through various TV networks in Europe and North America. But the Lab people want the freedom to shop it around. That said, we're very supportive. When a film comes out of the Labs or Sundance we try to see all of them and if something fits our programming model then we will do our best to support them and get it on the air. And if someone from the festival or the Labs call us to tell us about a film, we take their world very seriously.

**Q – What kind of things should a filmmaker be thinking about when a deal is struck and a contract comes in?**

*Christian* – Number one, and I hate to be negative and I know that documentaries have gotten a lot of attention in the last few years, but I think you have to look at how many documentaries that did well in festivals got real theatrical releases and made any money. At this stage of the game, documentary filmmakers really need to temper their expectations because there are only a small handful of documentaries that may have any impact theatrically at all. I wish more would, but the market forces don't work that way. And because of that TV in both the US and internationally as well as home video is really where you can make back your money, if you can. You shouldn't go into documentaries to make money. Anyone is lucky if they break even. Having a good sales agent can help you navigate those pitfalls. Another thing is clearances. We aren't going to pay your clearances. Broadcasters don't do that. I run into situations all the time where people are counting on my money to pay their clearances, but I for one, at this network, I can't pay until a film is delivered. So that theory doesn't work. But every network's policy is different. Insurance in something that is expensive and something that people don't want to deal with, but I cannot air a film without it. And networks don't usually provide that for filmmakers – it is part of delivery. Those are the two things that hang up deals the most with us. Format you can always get around. Usually we like to get a NTSC Digibeta or a D5 is great.

*"You shouldn't go into documentaries to make money. Anyone is lucky if they break even."*

**Q – Do you handle a deal differently if you are considered a foreign distributor?**

*Christian* – Not really. The same issues come up that do with domestic films. We buy up to 50%, maybe even 60%, if not more of our documentaries and fiction from foreign. We still need things to be cleared and we still need E&O insurance. We do our best to help foreign producers find E&O insurance. It has always been a big deal for them because it's not something that is required in foreign territories. Also it's difficult to get a NTSC tape from foreign producers – it's usually PAL. But we will figure out a way to get it converted.

*Q – Do you program documentary shorts?*

*Christian* – Yes we do. We buy a lot some years and not so many others. It all depends on how we can use them. Sometimes we do shorts blocks and sometimes interstitials.

*Q – What are the common mistakes that you see?*

*Christian* – The only thing other than insurance and clearances, and this goes to managing expectations, films have come in that we have liked and the filmmaker will put us and other networks off in hopes of a big theatrical or festival release. Then it doesn't come to fruition because it is very rare and then they see interest from TV go away. You need to have a clear eye about what the realistic opportunities for distribution are.

*Q – What advice would you give a new documentary filmmaker?*

*Christian* – If you can, partner with a good producer because the business side and the paperwork can always come back to haunt you.

**Q – What kind of documentaries does Super Channel like to program?**

*Justin* – Super Channel programs feature length documentaries that have ideally done the festival circuit and/or had a theatrical release. We have two documentary slots. The first is called Shock Docs, Tuesdays at 9pm ET on Super Channel 2, and it tends to be documentaries with subject matter of any sub-genre that might be considered shocking in some way and skew more male in demographic. The second slot is called DocuMondays, Mondays at 8pm ET on Super Channel 3, and tends to be documentaries that are more character driven, arts and culture, social-political in nature and skew more female in demographic.

**Q – What kind of docs would Super Channel never program?**

*Justin* – Super Channel, as a subscription pay television service, looks to air documentaries that are more theatrical in nature, or could be about the movie business, therefore we try to avoid documentaries that are more ideally suited for television.

**Q – Where do you find your films? Do you produce any docs or are they all acquisitions?**

*Justin* – We work closely with the Canadian documentary community to pre-license Canadian certified feature films with an eye to a theatrical release before their premiere on Super Channel. We also acquire Canadian and non-Canadian documentaries for our two documentary slots.

**Q – What is a typical license fee/length of license that Super Channel offers?**

*Justin* – The length of a license on Super Channel would be 18 months. Our license

---

 **www.superchannel.ca**　　 **http://twitter.com/SuperChannel**

 **www.facebook.com/SuperChannel**

fees vary depending on whether it's a pre-license with or without Canadian Media Fund involvement or an acquisition.

*Q – How does Canadian content and CAVCO affect the kinds of films you select? Can a non-Canadian be in one of the main positions?*

*Justin* – Super Channel only pre-licenses Canadian Content documentaries. We do also acquire and air Canadian and non-Canadian documentaries in our two documentary slots and throughout the service.

*Q – Are the US and Canada considered one territory these days or are they separate when it comes to distribution rights?*

*Justin* – They are considered separate territories. In fact, Super Channel only takes the English Canadian territory and all other territories are left to the producers and /or distributors for sale. It is imperative though, that a sale within the US does not come into Canada and infringe on our exclusivity within the English Canadian territory.

*Q – Do you have a certain percentage of your programming that must be Canadian?*

*Justin* – Yes, 30% in prime time and 25% out of prime time, must be Canadian Content for each of our 6 channels. As per our license, we must spend 32% of our gross revenue on Canadian content each fiscal year as well as a commitment to a development loan expenditure of $2 million per year; these are interest-free development loans, repayable on start of principal photography.

*Q – How does one submit a proposal for a doc to Super Channel?*

*Justin* – For pre-license, please contact myself with a treatment, ideally a trailer and a finance structure for review. For development, please refer to www.superchannel.ca/ producers/ for further information.

*Q – Do you do co-productions? If so, how should a producer approach you with that?*

*Justin* – Yes we do. As long as the production abides by the Canadian Content rules to qualify as a Canadian production, this is acceptable. We expect producers to pitch us with a finance structure and a production that qualifies within these rules at the time of pitching.

*Q – What kind of deliverables do you require? Do you have to have an HD master?*

*Justin* – Yes, producers have to have an HD master that comes fully closed captioned. Producers must have E&O insurance for the duration of the window plus one year. The qualifying Canadian Content number must be delivered before or during the broadcast license. And all promotional materials must be deliverable before the license period.

**Q – Do you notice a difference in story type, tone or artistic style in Canadian docs than those from other countries? How do the French Canadian films differ?**

**Justin –** I think Canadian filmmakers continue to look to success in the International marketplace and try to stand out on the world stage. Hopefully our films stand out as great films, and aren't asking to be accepted because of where they're from. The benefit French Canada has is an audience who desire films in their language and therefore there's more of an acceptance of homegrown films as part of mainstream culture. In English Canada, we are competing more directly with the US and therefore have a harder time getting a larger audience for our films. Luckily, pay television is the perfect home and a great supporter of Canadian film!

**Q – What are the common mistakes you see documentary filmmakers make?**

**Justin –** Firstly waiting for financing in order to move forward with shooting. Documentaries are often not fully financed while they're in production and often don't get their first source of financing until after they've shot a lot of footage and put a trailer together. So I'd recommend always moving forward while simultaneously applying to any and every funding opportunity available; often shooting in documentary constitutes research whether the footage makes the final cut or not. Secondly, not being aware of every source of funding available to you, whether production and/or development financing; make sure you don't miss an application or opportunity that can help you move forward. Third, not knowing the needs and desires of every broadcaster and/or funding source so you can tailor your pitch to them specifically. Fourth, not making your partners feel invested in your project and be honest. That will create a lot of good will. Lastly, persevere.

*Q – What advice would you give a new documentary filmmaker?*

*Justin* –– See as much as you can, learn as much as you can, be knowledgeable and just do it. Don't be discouraged if your first project has to be DIY, impress the industry with one and they'll want to help you do the next!

# CANADIAN FILM COMMISSIONS

*National Canadian Fed. Tax Credit:* www.pch.gc.ca/cavco

*National Film Board of Canada:* www.nfb.ca

*Telefilm Canada:* www.telefilm.gc.ca

*Powell River Regional Film Commission:* www.prfilm.ca

*Sooke Film Commission:* www.film.bc.ca

*Manitoba Film & Sound:* www.mbfilmmusic.ca

*Newfoundland Film Commission:* www.nlfilm.net

*Northwest Territories:* www.nwtfilm.com

*Nova Scotia Film Commission:* www.film.ns.ca

*South West Shore Film Commission:* www.yarmouth.org/swsfc

*Ontario Media Development Corp.:* www.omdc.on.ca

*Toronto Film and Television Office:* www.toronto.ca/tfto

*Prince Edward Island:* www.gov.pe.ca

*Province of Quebec Film & TV Office:* www.qftc.ca

*Saskatchewan Film Commission:* www.saskfilm.com

*City of Regina:* www.regina.ca

## CANADIAN FILM COMMISSIONS

*Arrowsmith Film Commission:* info@qualicum.bc.ca

*Burnaby Film Office:* www.burnaby.ca/cityhall/

*Comox Valley Film Commission:* www.investcomoxvalley.com

*Cowichan Motion Picture Association:* www.film.cowichan.net

*Greater Victoria Film Commission:* www.filmvictoria.com

*Island North Film Commission:* www.infilm.ca

*Town of Ladysmith:* info@town.ladysmith.bc.ca

*Nanaimo and Mid-Island Film and Video Commission:* www.filmnanaimo.ca

*Okanagan-Similkameen Film Commission:* www.okfilm.bc.ca

*Regional Alberta Film Commission:* www.albertafilm.ca

*Alberta Motion Picture Industries:* www.ampia.ca

*BC Film Commission:* www.bcfilmcommission.com

*Calgary Film Commission:* www.calgaryeconomicdevelopment.com

*Edmonton Film Office:* www.edmonton.com/for-business/edmonton-film-office.ca

*Yukon Film Commission:* www.reelyukon.com

*Alberni Clayoquot Regional Film Commission:* www.islandfilm.bc.ca

**Q – What kind documentary films are you looking to program?**

*Kate* – We program every kind of documentary film in all shapes, sizes and lengths. We do a lot of award winners, film festival selections as well as films that are submitted to us by independent filmmakers. Also, we consider the channel a movie channel, so we're not into reality TV. We're in it to present documentary films to the US audience because there isn't another channel like us out now. And a lot of people don't go out to film festivals to see the films in a theater.

**Q – Do you need a TV premiere to accept a film?**

*Kate* – No. We will do second and third runs. But a US TV premiere would be our first choice.

**Q – Do you ever program themed months?**

*Kate* – We do. It helps with marketing and PR. Some of our more popular themes have been, for example, *Black History Month* in February and *Music Documentary Month* in June. That one's very popular because at the beginning of summer people start going to concerts. You have that outdoor feel. In July, we do an *Across America* map/postcard type theme. So we do films that take place in Connecticut or the Wild West.

**Q – How does one submit a film to you for your review?**

*Kate* – We have a submission page on our website. You just fill it in and send us your film. There is an FAQ on our website, which will really help filmmakers before they submit to us. It will streamline their submissions a lot.

---

www.documentarychannel.com    http://twitter.com/DOC_Channel
www.facebook.com/DocumentaryChannel

**Q – Are there any specific things to watch out for?**

**Kate** – We need to know if they have E&O insurance. If they don't, then they need to get it. You really need to have it. Music clearances are the next deal breaker for us. Many people bring us great films with amazing music in them. And when I screen them I say, *"Wow! That's great that you got that Who song."* And they say, *"Actually I haven't gotten it yet."* That always sets back the deal. I need films that are ready to go. I want to pop a film right on the air. I don't want to wait for a filmmaker to go back and see if the rights are available.

**Q – Are film festivals part of your search?**

**Kate** – Yes. We get a lot of programming from going to film festivals, as well as having long standing relationships with distributors . We also have relationships with universities, which we would like to expand. We also have a special series called Doc U where we do a collection of films from places like the University of Texas – Austin, the New School in New York City or USC. These are done in conjunction with the documentary departments of the schools. So we welcome student films, but sometimes it can be a bit bureaucratic because the university owns the rights, not the filmmaker.

**Q – Do you ever produce documentaries?**

**Kate** – We are mainly acquisitions. We have co-produced a few documentaries from filmmakers who have brought us projects that are almost finished and maybe need some finishing funds. We are planning on producing many, many, many more. But to be frank, the money that it would cost to make one film, $50,000-$100,000 on the lower end, I could buy fifty films for $1,000 each. We are a start up channel so we don't have the luxury of a studio output deal with a huge cushion of inventory. Right now the most important thing is our air and what our viewers are seeing. So they are seeing things like *Born Into Brothels* and *Paper Clips*.

**Q – Can the documentaries be shot on anything?**

**Kate** – Yes. We aren't HD yet, so that restriction doesn't come into play quite as much, but it will. At some point down the line we will probably have to request HD only. But at the moment not as much. You can shoot a doc on your iPhone if you want. In fact, we're working with the Academy of Motion Pictures Arts and Sciences to restore older documentaries from the 1960's and 1970's so they can get back on the air. We are the only channel to have a relationship with them as well as the International Documentary Association.

**Q – When a filmmaker signs with you, what kind of deal can they expect?**

**Kate** – License fees and terms vary and they will be evolving as the channel evolves.

Without naming numbers, I will say that at the present, our license fees are quite low. So as of the printing of your book, we do everything from a free license to $10,000, which is standard. A filmmaker will do a free license usually in exchange for getting it on the air in the US. That way it gets exposure and sold in our online store. Viewers are impulse buyers so every night DVDs get sold. Occasionally, we will foray into slightly higher license fees like $15,000-$25,000 for extreme tent pole titles or films we co-produce. It may seem very low today, but we're going to be here for years to come and so if you start a relationship with us now, greater things will lie ahead. That said, we understand that filmmakers and vendors need to recoup their funds, so I am very patient and don't take offense if they decide to shop their film around to get a larger license fee. If you still haven't sold your title after a year or whatever, you can always come back to us. As for length of the deal term, it's usually two or three years depending on the circumstance. Our tech specs are really just the best master you can provide. Some people give us hard drives. Some people give us HD. We can work with Beta SP, too.

### Q – What can a filmmaker do to help promote the film? And what do you do to promote the film?

**Kate** – We have a head of marketing development and his team contacts the filmmakers to help us promote their film. That's one of the questions I ask all filmmakers when I do a deal with them – will you help us promote your film? And 99% of the time they say yes. We do everything possible to promote the film. We do day and date premieres. We have a ton of press that goes out. You can see all our press clippings and releases on our website. We do film festival sponsorship. We use our Facebook account. And we do a series called DocTalk where we interview filmmakers about their films, intercut it with clips and we air them every Friday night. We love getting email lists from filmmakers and doing big blasts. We want to do all of this together with the filmmaker.

### Q – Do you look for non-English speaking language films?

*Kate* – English speaking is our first choice. It's easier for the American viewing public to watch them rather than have to read subtitles. Not to say that we don't air subtitled films, we do and in fact have co-produced a few.

### Q – What is your store?

*Kate* – It's like Amazon.com, but for documentary films. We have films in the store that might not even be on the channel, but all the ones that are appear there. So when your film airs, there's a little discreet lower third graphic that pops up stating, *"If you'd like to buy this film, go to the Documentary Channel store."* And people buy them. We sell thousands and thousands of DVDs a month. It's a non-exclusive deal, so you can sell them elsewhere if you wish. Sometimes we buy them wholesale from your distributor and take the profit. Sometimes a filmmaker will give us say ten and we see how they do. The deal in this case varies a lot. It could be 50/50 or 60/40 or something else; it just depends on the case.

### Q – So they can still shop their DVD and digital rights?

*Kate* – Yes. It's totally non-exclusive. It's a simple one-page agreement.

### Q – What is Doc World?

*Kate* – It's our community of forums and message boards for filmmakers and fans to share information about all things documentary. And it's always evolving.

### Q – What are the common mistakes that you see filmmakers make?

*Kate* – Blowing too much money and becoming frazzled and desperate. I think that filmmakers need to be realistic goals so they don't get so upset or broke.

### Q – What advice would you give a new documentary filmmaker?

*Kate* – Don't forget the real reason why you wanted to make your film. And think about who do you want to see this film? Hold onto that.

# CHAPTER SIX
# PRODUCTION COMPANIES

## THE DOCUMENTARY
## FILMMAKERS HANDBOOK

**Q – How did NFL Films start?**

***Steve*** – NFL Films started with a wedding present. My father was in the overcoat business and hated it. But his hobby was home movies and as a wedding present he got from my grandmother a 16mm wind up Bell and Howell movie camera. Everything that I did, as his only son, he captured on film. My first pony ride, my first haircut, my first football game. And he filmed every football game that I played in up until I was a senior in high school. When I left to go to college in Colorado, my Dad decided that he would quit his job and try to make a living doing his hobby - making movies. In 1962, he found out that the film rights for the NFL Championship game had been sold to the highest bidder for $1500. In 1962, he doubled the bid. Pete Rozell, when looking at my Dad's application was very happy that someone would think that highly of the National Football League to pay $3000 for the film rights. But he was a little concerned about my Dad's experience when all my Dad had was filming his 14-year-old son. I remember that night I got a phone call from my father. He said, *"I see by your grades that all you have been doing out there for the last four years at Colorado is playing football and going to the movies. So that makes you uniquely qualified to help me."* I quit school and came back and helped him film the first championship game in 1962. Then we won the rights in 1963 and 1964.

In 1965, my Dad had the entrepreneurial vision to tell the NFL, *"Why don't you start your own film company and we'll document all the games. We'll make highlight reels for you and preserve the history of the sport."* Pete Rozell thought it was a good idea and convinced the twelve owners to put up $20,000 and they bought our film company – which was called Blair Motion Pictures – named after my sister.

**Q – So you didn't really have a background in filmmaking?**

---

 **sales.facility@nfl.com**

 **www.nflfilms.com**

 **www.facebook.com/NFLFilms**

 **http://twitter.com/NFLFilms**

**Steve** – No I was an art major. There weren't any film schools in the late '50's and early '60's. I studied Picasso and George Braque. A lot of the classic and cubist painters and a lot of the things that I learned from them I applied to our films. So even though I had no experience making films, I had a feeling about how I wanted it to look. I always looked at the game in dramaturgical terms. To me it wasn't about the score, it was about the struggle. The way the players looked with the grease paint under their eyes. The helmets and the passage of time and the weather. To me football fascinated me because it was a game of bold gestures and grand passions and that's the kind of thing that translates into movies.

*Q – What are some important things to know about interviewing athletes?*

**Steve** – One of things that I've found is that you don't have to be very slick. I think that sometimes interviewers are more concerned about how articulate and knowledgeable they seem and sometimes they intimidate the athlete. I've found it's better to stammer and stumble along and in some ways it makes the athlete more comfortable during the interview. And since almost every interview I do is on film, I'm not really worried about myself. I can always go back and redub my questions which I do a lot of times because I'm not a concise interviewer. I know the subject, but sometimes I tend to ramble in the questions. I don't worry about that because I think when you tend to ramble, it gives the person a chance to collect their thoughts. This is all interviewing on film that can be edited afterwards – this is certainly not the kind of technique that I would advocate if someone were doing a live interview. But to me, the most important thing is to make the person feel relaxed and not worry about how knowledgeable you might sound. Also, since the most important thing is to get the most out of the subject you're interviewing, make sure that you are in a setting where you can get his attention. It's not after a practice or in a locker room. We like to do it in a hotel room or back at the player's house where you get their complete attention.

*Q – When you're shooting a game – how many cameras do you use and what kind of film stock do you use?*

**Steve** – We shoot Super 16mm with the 16x9 ratio – the wide screen. We have a formula where we have three cameras at most of the games. We have a top camera – he's called a tree. He's rooted into position and he's usually on the 40 or 50 yard line. He shoots at 32 frames and covers all the action. Then we have a mole – a ground handheld camera with a 12-240mm zoom, sometimes with an extender to make it go out to 400mm. He shoots anywhere from 48 frames to 200 frames. It's his job to give you that eyeball-to-eyeball ground level look at the game. To me when we started that was one of the philosophies. I wanted to show the game the way I experienced it as a player with the sweat flying, the snot spraying and eyeballs bulging. And that's the camera that gives that classic NFL Films look. Then we have another camera called the Weasel. His job is to shoot everything but the action. He focuses on the bench, the fans, the details, the sun coming over the stadium and the cleat marks in the mud. When I was an art major, I remember Paul Cezanne said that all art is selected detail and that is the job of the

Weasel - to get the little bits of artistic shots that you sprinkle in to make it more than just a highlight film. Very often the Weasel is attached to a soundman. Sometimes we put microphones on the pads of players or on coaches and we will shoot them from across the field on a telephoto lens. But a Weasel is a handheld, 12-120mm lens and he shoots all the little story telling shots and very often sync sound.

### Q – What about slow motion? You use this a lot.

*Steve* – That goes back my art training. I took an approach sort of like the old Cubist painters of the 1930's – Picasso and Braque. What I try to do is take a single image and look at it from multiple perspectives and separate moments in time. So shoot at 32 frames, 48 frames, shoot at 128 frames and get it from across the field and from the end zone. So we would have two or three cameras all shooting the same thing but at different speeds and from different angles. What Picasso did with a bowl of fruit or a woman's face, in essence, we were doing the same thing with a football play. We were fracturing the time and space.

### Q – How much independence do your camera people have? Are they flying on their own?

*Steve* – I started out as a cameraman and I found it very annoying and distracting having someone telling me what to do. If I'm an artist and a cameraman, drop me in the situation and rely on my point of view and my talent. I didn't want somebody back in a truck telling me how to shoot. When I became our DP, I always used the philosophy that Teddy Roosevelt used when he charged San Juan Hill and got all the Rough Riders together and he said, *"Do what you can with what you have, where you are."* And that's what cameramen want. We have a little meeting before the game and each one is left up to their own devices. We've worked together for so long that you know each guy's style. One guy follows the ball in the air, another guy zooms down to the receiver, some guy shoots in the squatting position, other guys standing up and would rather be in the end zone. Donnie Marx who is generally accepted as the greatest sports cinematographer in the world, he is full time for us, but he also does the Olympics, baseball and basketball. Steve Andrich, Hank McElwee, guys that have been working with me for 25-30 years and you know exactly how they shoot and what they're good at and they are on their own. You never know what's going to happen. There are no retakes in this business.

*"To me, words are like medicine. If they are doled out properly they can work wonders, but an overdose can be fatal."*

### Q – How do you come up with your music? Who composes it?

*Steve* – Music is such a big part of our lives. You get married to music, you get buried to music, you go to war to music and you make love to music. Music has always been a part of football. Every kid that's ever been to a football game can think of the thump of that base drum as the teams prepare to come out on the field. I just wanted us to have our own distinctive music. As a kid my favorite music was *Peter and the Wolf* where they used leitmotifs. A bassoon as the grandfather, the menacing French horns as the wolf, the piccolo would be Peter. So we decided to take certain melodies, old campfire melodies, that conveyed a rhythm and a storyline and re-orchestrated them with really big 60-70 piece orchestras and that became the style of NFL music. I've always felt our movies were made, not to make you think but to make you feel and nothing makes you feel more than music. Our original music was written by Sam Spence. Now it's written by Dave Robidoux. He's full time staff.

**Q – What tips would you give for capturing fast moving objects?**

**Steve** – Number one – be in the right position. Have an understanding of where the object is going to move, how fast it is going to go and to be in a position where you don't have to pan as much. Some of our best shots come from the catty corner where you don't have to swish pan and the action comes into you. Make sure that you have an eyepiece with a space around the receptacle, so you can see as much as you can. Our cameras are specially designed racecars, the motor is French, the viewing system is English, the body casing is built in America and they are balanced like sniper rifles for each one of our cameraman. Shooting football is difficult because not only do you have to follow the ball and the action but you can get hit! Guys get whacked on the sidelines.

**Q – Do you have problems with breakage of equipment?**

**Steve** – Not that much. The weather used to be a big problem, but not so much anymore.

**Q – How do you handle your narration? Who writes it?**

**Steve** – Originally football films were written in a very breezy, clever style that was like, *"Milt Plum makes a peach of a pass to become the apple of Coach George Wilson's eye."* Clever, but I wanted to write less script. I felt that the pictures and the music and the sounds of the game would convey the drama of the game. There was a newscaster in Philadelphia by the name of John Facenda who had this great oaken voice – he was the Walter Cronkite of Philadelphia. We hired him to read the scripts because we wanted to write less, not more. To me words are like medicine, if they are doled out properly they can work wonders, but an overdose can be fatal and Facenda could deliver these very terse tight sentences. When you are writing for film you don't need adjectives. My rule is that you could take any script and just take a pencil though almost every adjective and adverb and it would make the script stronger. Good scripts are good verbs, nouns and that's it because everything else you can see. The writing should add something to what the audience is seeing, not repeat or describe what the audience is seeing. All of our producers write their own scripts and that is the type of writing that I look for.

**Q – How hard is it to find good writers?**

*Steve* – The most elusive talent in our business is writing. When we hire someone that's the first thing we look for. If a person cannot write, we don't even consider them. A person that can really write well, we feel we can teach them how to edit and construct a film. When you see something in sports television that's written well, it brings you right up out of your chair.

**Q – How do you find writers for NFL Films?**

*Steve* – I have a file here of 560 applications. We get applications here at a rate of 10 a week. Then we ask for writing samples and we have an intern program. We hire people as interns for 6 months because one thing about making a film, it's an art form, but it's not like a painter who has just a brush and a canvas or a writer that's got an pencil and a piece of paper. To make a film you need an army and in order to be a good filmmaker you have to work with all the members of that army and you have to be able to get along with all the members of that army because filmmaking is such a temperamental, personal, emotional profession and you deal with people who are temperamental and emotional. And unless you can understand that and deal with people like that, you'll never be any good as a filmmaker. We have very few temperamental assholes. We weed them out. That's one thing that should be taught in all film schools is people skills. I've seen a lot people come though that have some talent, but because they are such pricks nobody wants to work with them. On the other hand, I have people with very average talents, but great people skills and everyone rallies around them and wants them to succeed. When you think of our business and how many layers go into just our *Inside the NFL,* which airs on Showtime. You hope it's a good game, and if it's a good game, did the cameraman have a good day? Then is the film processed properly? Then is it edited properly? Then is the script written? Then is the music laid in right? Is the mix done right? Every step of the way you can get screwed and that's why there are so many steps that make the business so difficult and that's why you so see so few good films because there are so many stages that a film has to go through and at each stage you need someone that is personally involved, really committed to doing the best job possible. If you have a mixer that doesn't pay attention or a music cutter that doesn't lay the music in right - that can diminish all the work of everyone that has gone on before.

"The most elusive talent in our business is writing."

**Q – What editing tips can you give about making sports documentaries exciting?**

*Steve* – I think that you have to let the sport be the most important thing in your mind. To me sports has a beauty onto its own. The editing should be like a Fred Astaire-Ginger Rodger musical. The best shot was a head to toe with no cuts because you really got to see the teamwork, the grace and the flow. The minute you start editing, then you

### SHOOTING SPORTS

Watch the sport so you know the rules and can use them to build drama.

Watch how the balls, players and officials move so you can anticipate action.

Slow motion looks great with sporting events - especially those that are physical.

Athletes will give you canned answers. They are trained not to look bad!

Be careful when interviewing athletes before their competition. You don't want to throw them off their game.

If things go right, get into the celebration. If things go wrong, give them space.

Try to get cameras in the action by putting them on a helmet or inside a racecar.

Shoot the crowd! Joe Fan is colorful and by buying a ticket he's given consent.

Get the details of the sport. Adds color and tension. CU of faces are always good.

You must get permission from the team, the venue and perhaps a broadcaster to shoot in the stadium or arena. Do your research!

start adding something artificial. When we have a great play, we like to let it go from the beginning to the end. You can repeat it, but sometimes when you start editing you can over cut things because there is such a plethora of things on TV, that everybody wants to do highlights to make theirs different – cut it quick or speed it up. I hate that. To me, the beauty of what we do is that athletes are the subject, not the filmmaker. And when the filmmaker decides that he is more important or he is going to inflict his point of view on it, you destroy the experience for millions of fans who want to watch Barry Sanders run or Dan Marino throw the ball. That is something that I have noticed creeping into more and more sports documentaries – overediting.

**Q – Do you need to get releases from athletes and fans when you shoot?**

**Steve** – Yes, unless it is from inside the stadium on gameday. Most fans love to be on NFL Films and if anything we have to keep them out of the camera. They are yelling and screaming and it is the opposite for us. It is hard to get some authentic shots when everyone is posturing. The thing we ran into when we started in the 60's and 70's was that the fans were actually spectators. Now fans are part of the spectacle themselves. You go to an NFL game and it looks like a Halloween party every weekend. Everyone comes in costume and they are clamoring to be part of it. They expect to be part of it.

**Q – Can people license footage from NFL Films?**

**Steve** – Yes.

### Q – How do you tell the story of one game?

**Steve** – It is about choices and decision. We try to explain the reasons that one course was taken instead of another. I look at a football game as a big artichoke and you peel back the layers of the game. The strategy, the tactics, the emotions, the spirit, the situations and then we rely heavily on our music and our sound and we look on each game as a story. And what make shows we do like *Game of the Week* or *Inside the NFL* unique is that there is no other network or sport that treats a current game with the detail and the analysis that we do. The game is played on Sunday and we come back Wednesday night complete with a written narration, sound, music – all the elements that go into a documentary film and we do it in 48 hours. Most shows, if you want to see something like that you go to the Classic Channel and see something that was played in 1975. We are the only show that comes back with a comprehensive, detailed account of a current game in a one-hour format. And it isn't regurgitated broadcast tapes; it's in Super 16mm film. It's the game looked at from a totally different perspective.

### Q – How much footage do you shoot and how many editors?

**Steve** – We have about five editors that work on it and we shoot about twenty miles of film. We shoot nine hundred miles of film each year on football. We are Kodak's biggest client. We have three cameras. Each camera shoots about fifteen rolls of films and each roll is four hundred feet. Thirty-five rolls on a *Game of the Week*. Each roll is four hundred feet.

*Q – What production services do you offer at NFL Films?*

*Steve* – We have a complete mixing facility. We have a lab that processes 35mm film as well as 16mm. We have telecine. We have full video post production. We do everything here except make the film. We even have recording studios that can handle a seventy-two piece orchestra. We have two sound stages. It's Hollywood on the Delaware River.

*Q – Can anyone use them?*

*Steve* – Yes. You have to call ahead because we're pretty busy.

*Q – What advice would you give a new documentary filmmaker?*

*Steve* – It's so hard to get started in this business. I would try to get in at any level doing anything you can. Even if you think you want to be a cameraman and there's an opening in sales – go for it. When we started NFL Films it was great combination in that my dad was the great entrepreneurial vision and I was the creative director. We were in a profession that had never been done before. That old saying by Mark Twain, *"All you need is ignorance and confidence and success is sure."* Be persistent, have patience and try to get yourself in a situation where you have an opportunity. You might think you're going to be a good cameraman but might end up being a better editor. You might think you want to be a salesman, but you have a good eye to be a cameraman. You don't want to cubbyhole yourself.

POV
SIMON KILMURRY

### Q – What is POV?

**Simon** – It's a series that has been on PBS for 24 years. We showcase the work of emerging and veteran independent documentary filmmakers from the US and around the world. The series originally started as an acquisitions venue where it would be best described as an anthology series packaged under the POV banner to give documentaries a clear home on public television. Since then it has evolved beyond just broadcast where we are now actively involved in developing engagement campaigns around all of our films. We do about 450 community engagements a year and have produced ancillary materials around all the films so if people want to find out more about the characters or the issues of the film or how they can get involved, there's a whole series of resources that allow them to do that. And we are more deeply involved in the production and support of filmmakers as they are in the process of making their films. We also provide finishing funds and help people find additional funding as well as help people by giving them editorial and technical support.

### Q – What kind of film would POV want to get involved with from a producing and funding angle?

**Simon** – We're trying to be supportive of emerging filmmakers. One of these programs is the Diverse Voices Project where we look to fund people making their first feature length documentary film for public television. The kind of support we can give depends on the project. So for a film like Stephanie Wong-Breal's, *Wo Ai Ni*, which was about a Long Island couple adopting a child from China, we were able to give her substantial money for funding, which I believe was her first money for production. And we were able to give her a lot of editorial support and editorial feedback. We helped her plan the outreach and engagement campaign as well as the festival strategy for the film. By the way, when I say we give editorial support, we don't take editorial control. We have people here, my

---

 **www.pbs.org/pov**         **http://twitter.com/povdocs/**

 **www.facebook.com/povdocs**

colleagues and myself, who have watched thousands of films over the years and we try to bring that experience in order to give some support to emerging makers.

Another example would be the film *My Perestroika* by Robin Hessman. Robin showed us a ten-minute trailer of the film and we decided to take a gamble on it because we liked the material. We probably watched ten or fifteen rounds of that film in various stages of production. We actually wanted to broadcast it in 2010 first, but we decided to hold off so she could do Sundance and other festival work as well as get a theatrical release. I'm glad we did because it did well on the theatrical circuit. So after that we will broadcast it close to the 20th anniversary of the fall of the Soviet Union. It was a bit of serendipitous timing but it was also planned as we all sat down to map out a release strategy.

## Q – What are characteristics of films that POV is looking for?

**Simon** – I think we use films that use cinematic language. We look for films that have an emotional resonance. We look for films that aren't just informational, but have an emotional engagement in character. We look for a bold aesthetic with a clear perspective. We look for strong storylines and for films that surprise and challenge pre-conceived notions. So *Kings of Pastry,* which is not our normal big social issue film, showcases excellence through a couple of characters for whom you really root. And then we have a film like *Sweetgrass*, which is this minimal, vérité, monumental look at the American West. Every shot in that film is so beautifully framed – it's breath taking. And then we look for films that address issues that aren't being spoken about elsewhere or a film takes an unusual angle on that issue. We have films called *Better This World* and *If A Tree Falls*, which both emerge from a post-9/11 security mindset for what defines a terrorist. But the issues aren't front-loaded. The issues come out organically in the filmmaking process.

## Q – What are some of the outreach and educational programs that you offer filmmakers?

**Simon** – With each of our films we sit down with the Outreach and our Engagement and Education team who all work together with the filmmakers to develop public awareness campaigns of which the educational work is one element. So in 2010 we had three films that addressed the concept of adoption, but they were all very different stories. They showed how varied and diverse families are these days. So we decided to raise awareness by doing an online competition called *This Is My Family* where people submitted short films to show what their family looks like. A panel of judges selected one to get a prize and we also had an audience award. So while this was unique to adoption films, it speaks to the kind of engaging ideas we try to create to get us to promote the films and raise awareness of a topic.

## Q – What is the DVD library?

**Simon** – We partner with schools and non-profit organizations to use films that are under license via a lending library. Our community engagement team oversees this. We have

## NETWORKING

1. Form as many contacts as possible through business and social events. People do favors for those they know.

2. Stay informed. Find out the lastest news about projects and the needs of production companies and networks.

3. Set breakfasts, lunches, drinks and dinners with people you want to meet. Pick fun places so you are associated with an upbeat, friendly feeling.

4. Research the person you want to meet and their company and try to fit your strengths to their needs.

5. Have a plan when you talk to people. Know what you want to get out of a meeting or phone call so that the other person does not feel like you're wasting their time.

6. Use connections that you have already to get introductions to new people. A phone call placed on your behalf can make a stranger more open to listening to you.

7. Meet other filmmakers as they may be able to help you, give advice and put you in contact with ther people from new organizations, foundations, production companies, networks or distributors.

8. Do activities out of work with your contacts (some that may even become your friends).

9. Create customer loyalty by using the same rental companies over and over again. They are more likely to cut deals with people that they know personally.

10. Join organizations and documentary online communities in your own country, but also overseas.

11. Be respectful to assistants. They have lousy jobs and low pay, but they are the gatekeepers to their bosses. Further, they may soon be the next person in power that can help you.

over a thousand educators and organizations that have signed up through our community engagement network. We don't tell people which ones to screen, but they're organized by theme and topic and we make suggestions about what might be appropriate for certain organizations. And we give them lesson plans, discussion guides and facilitation materials because some of these films deal with difficult and polarizing issues. There are many ways to engage with these films. You can sit down and watch them on TV, you can watch them online, but sometimes it's best to bring people together to talk about them. That last one is part of our Host Screenings events.

### Q – Who creates the educational materials?

*Simon* – There are consultants and educators that draft those for us. We show them to all of our filmmakers to make sure they are comfortable with how we are positioning things or what focuses we are taking on different topics. Then the materials and clips adhere to different classroom curriculum standards. It's not always possible in the classroom setting to see a 90-minute film or even a one-hour film. So we provide a way for teachers to access the films and the topics when they can and give them some step-by-step lesson plans.

### Q – Does POV Borders still exist?

*Simon* – No. That was a fantastic stand alone online project a few years ago, but what we find with stand alones is that they're great places to experiment, but unless you have a lot of promotional resources, it can be very hard to bring audiences to it. So that's why we are focusing on the main POV site where you will see things like *This Is My Family*. We do have a new project called *Behind The Lines*, which goes back into the POV archive. We have 24 years of interviews with filmmakers, a lot of which has not been available. At the time, we would have used a minute of the footage from the interviews on broadcast, but now we are going back to the source material and cutting longer versions to put online. And then we are going back to the filmmakers to get updates so we can get a sense of how their work has evolved over the years. When you take these as a whole, we can see how the industry and filmmaking has changed. Before this might have been a special online site, but now we want to integrate it into the main site so it's more accessible.

### Q – Do you generally need films to be shot on HD?

*Simon* – Preferably, but not necessarily.

### Q – When you mentioned you offer editorial support, do you also offer editing equipment for filmmakers to use?

*Simon* – When we moved to Brooklyn down by the waterfront, one of the things we wanted to build out is a public space – one where we can do workshops and screenings. And we've also built out some post-production facilities where we're going to make

## MINORITY FILMMAKING WEBSITES

### AFRICAN AMERICAN
www.uafw.org
www.dvrepublic.com
www.blackfilmmakers.net
www.blacktalentnews.com
www.blackfilm.com
www.blackflix.com

### ASIAN
wwwnaatanet.org
www.asianamericanfilm.com
www.theworkshop.org
wwwasiancinevision.org
www.capeusa.com

### LATINO
www.lasculturas.com
www.nalip.com
www.latinfilmnetwork.com
www.blackandlatinofilm.com
www.sho.com

### NATIVE AMERICAN
www.nativenetworks.si.edu
www.nativetelecom.org
www.aifisf.com
www.piccom.org

available a couple of editing suites for POV filmmakers. This way they can possibly save a lot of money on post. So we are looking at doing master classes in the workshop space, panel discussions, rough cut screenings – that kind of activity. We are also considering a filmmaker in residence program where we can bring them in for a year and give them a stipend. This way they can be around people in the industry and be around the community and engagement team and be thinking about all this stuff when making their film.

**Q – A few years ago, you had a distribution deal with Netflix and Docurama that filmmakers could opt for. Does that still exist?**

**Simon** – Not anymore. But we have lots of relationships with distributors – especially theatrical distributors that we can lead filmmakers to when they get to that stage. And we do still have relationships with DVD and other home video distributors. So Zeitgiest, Women Make Movies, Docurama, Icarus, PBS Video – we still deal with them all. The original Docurama deal was OK, but the numbers weren't always that great for the filmmakers. Some filmmakers wanted to do self-distribution or a hybrid so we are trying to be flexible with that.

**Q – How does a filmmaker apply to POV?**

**Simon** – We have an open call every year, which happens in June. And we have specialized open calls around different projects such as our Diverse Voices Project. People should go to our website and sign up for our newsletter or join us on Facebook and they will get that information automatically. We still go to film festivals like Hot Docs, Sheffield, Full Frame, Silver Docs or IDFA to look for films as well. And we are looking for filmmakers still working on films as well. Even if something is out of cycle, we still want to know about it. So people should be in touch with us all year round by dropping us an email or calling us.

We want to hear about what projects are out there.

*Q – What are the common mistakes you see filmmakers make?*

**Simon** – Giving me a DVD that has not been labeled with the name and emails address on the disc itself – that information should always be on the disc. It's also important that people take time to look at our website to get a sense of the kinds of films we do, what topics we have covered so that they are approaching us with appropriate ideas.

*Q – What advice would you give a new filmmaker?*

**Simon** – Don't be afraid to approach commissioning editors about a project. I am on the circuit with the BBC, Danish TV and Finnish TV – all these places from all over the world. The reason people are on that circuit is because they want to hear about projects. They want to talk to filmmakers, but it can be intimidating to go up to and talk to a commisioning editor and ask for five minutes of their time. But that is why we are there so they should take advantage of those moments. Just be comfortable and relaxed and talk to people. We're all human beings.

### Q – What is Independent Lens?

**Lois** – *Independent Lens* is the largest independent documentary showcase on public or commercial television. Broadcast weekly on the PBS prime time schedule from October through June, Independent Lens presents social issue documentaries like *Waste Land*, personal docs like *The Order of Myths, Hip Hop: Beyond Beats and Rhymes, A Place of Our Own*, and *King Corn*, point of view docs, biographies that profile individuals whose lives exemplified social change like *Billy Strayhorn: Lush Life, No Subtitles Necessary, Negroes with Guns*, and *Jean Michel Basquiat*, and films that innovate new styles like *Marwencol* and *Dirt! The Movie*. We feature films with broad audience appeal like *Young@Heart Wordplay*, and *Chicago 10*, award-winning investigative documentaries like *Enron: The Smartest Guys in the Room, Crips and Bloods: Made in America*, and *The Weather Underground*. We love to present films about subjects no one has explored before like *Helvetica, Between The Folds*, and *The Wild Parrots of Telegraph Hill*. We're committed to championing the work of new and emerging filmmakers, and iconoclasts like Frederick Wiseman, Albert Maysles, Kim Longinotto and Jon Else. We describe the series as a "film festival in your living room" - an opportunity for viewers across the country to see award-winning and vital independent documentaries without leaving home.

### Q – What do you require from a filmmaker?

**Lois** – We require the U.S. broadcast television premiere and a 3-year exclusive domestic television license. We also have an exciting new initiative called IndiesLab. If filmmakers elect to work with us, we pay an additional fee to acquire the digital (or New Media) rights. We work with the filmmakers and select digital partners (iTunes, Amazon. com, Hulu, etc.) to create a digital release for their film that rolls out in conjunction with the broadcast premiere.

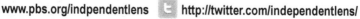

 www.pbs.org/indpendentlens    http://twitter.com/independentlens/

 www.facebook.com/independentlens

*Q – Can you go into more detail about IndiesLab?*

*Lois* – Several years ago ITVS did a survey of independent filmmakers and a very large number of them were not exploiting their digital rights. We felt it was important that independent work supported by public media be a part of the growing digital marketplace. For most films, digital distribution offers an opportunity to reach new audiences, especially younger viewers - one of our core constituents. It can also create revenue for filmmakers. Of course that varies widely among films. It also allows social issue documentaries to be available to future audiences when opportunities arise that create new interest in the film. For example, if an issue suddenly lands in the mainstream news cycle (political uprising, environmental catastrophe, a specific region or country), good digital distribution allows an audience immediate access to a film on that subject. Most public television stations finalize their schedules weeks or months in advance so it is difficult to respond to news stories, but with digital distribution we can make your film available immediately for anyone to buy or stream, and take advantage of the demand and current interest. It creates a second or third life for some documentaries.

*Q – Do your shows have to be an hour long running time?*

*Lois* – No, we broadcast films at various lengths. Each season about one-third or slightly more are feature length documentaries with a total running time (TRT) of 83:25 minutes. A half to two-thirds of our slate is films broadcast at a "TV hour" length with a TRT of 53:25 minutes. We've also broadcast two-hour documentaries including *Bhutto, An Unreasonable Man*, and *The Calling*, and several four and five hour mini-series including *Have You Heard From Johannesburg?*, *The New Americans*, and *Lion in the House*. It depends on the program and the content.

I encourage filmmakers to think about multiple versions for their film while still in production. Most international broadcasters have a running time of 52 minutes so filmmakers need to think about that version to meet most international sales interest. A shorter, "TV hour" length is sometimes also the best length for U.S. television audiences. Television is very competitive, with 700 channels and everyone holding a clicker and having the ability to disengage at any moment. Some films can sustain one length for the theatrical and festival versions but a shorter length is more effective on television. I often ask filmmakers, *"How many 84 or 90-minute documentaries did you watch on television last week?"* That said, many stories that our filmmakers capture cannot be told in an hour and they need more time to unfold. I look at it case by case, and consider each film individually.

*Q – What would characterize an Independent Lens doc from some of the other shows on PBS?*

*Lois* – Most PBS series are committed to a single genre. For example *NOVA* does science, *Nature* does natural history, *Frontline* does current affairs, *American Experience* does American history. We're most similar to *POV*, who by their definition present point of view documentaries. *Independent Lens* is an eclectic series that covers the full spectrum of independent filmmaking - innovative documentaries, shorts, animated work - all united by the creative freedom and vision of a different independent filmmaker each week.

Another hallmark of *Independent Lens* is our deep commitment to diversity, both in the filmmakers we feature and the stories we tell. Recently, a public television programmer said to me, *"Independent Lens is America. You showcase our differences and the strength of that diversity."* That's a great mission to strive to achieve every season.

**Q – What would you say is not an Independent Lens film?**

**Lois** – We try not to duplicate what other PBS series are doing. It's probably easier to say what we are, rather than what we're not. I encourage filmmakers to look at our website to see the range of the more than 230 films we have featured on *Independent Lens* in our first nine series. It provides a very good idea of who we are as a series. Often someone will say, *"I saw such and such a film on Independent Lens and mine is a lot like that."* Generally speaking, we're interested in new ideas and new ways of looking at issues so if we've been there before it's harder to make a case for another film on that same topic.

**Q – Do you look for the films or do people mostly submit to you through your website?**

**Lois** – It's a mix but most of our films are scouted at film festivals and have their *Independent Lens* broadcast after a festival run. Our open submission deadline is the final Friday in September every year. We do the bulk of curating between September and April each year. My summer months are primarily devoted to production work including working with filmmakers who need to trim the film for television; writing and shooting the host introductions; packaging films; and preparing for the launch of the new season each fall.

"Most international broadcasters have a running time of 52 minutes, so filmmakers need to think about that version."

I encourage filmmakers to review our submission guidelines at http://www.pbs.org/independentlens/about/submissions.html and to contact us if they have questions about the submission process.

**Q – Do you need to be an American citizen to get on the series?**

**Lois** – No, absolutely not. Every year we feature a range of international content. We've had a film about how Native Americans are portrayed in Hollywood movies, *Reel Injun* by a Native Canadian filmmaker, a film about democracy in a Chinese grade school, *Please Vote For Me* by a Chinese filmmaker, a film about contemporary South African politics by South African filmmakers, a film about an ex-Mujahid fighter, *Recycle* by a Jordanian filmmaker, and many more. We strongly believe it is important to bring international stories to American viewers. Sometimes the best person to tell that story is a filmmaker from that region or country.

**Q – *What can a filmmaker do to make their film stand out?***

**Lois** – That's a great question because there certainly are more films by more filmmakers than ever before. It obviously helps if your film has been accepted into a major film festival. That doesn't guarantee it's the right fit for us, but it almost certainly guarantees that I will hear about it. In addition to screening their work, many filmmakers attend festivals to network with curators and commissioning editors like me. I've also found films through recommendations from filmmakers I admire, so if you know someone who has been on *Independent Lens* or another PBS series ask him or her to send a note to introduce you and your film. I also read as much as I can about new films. That's how I found *The Desert of Forbidden Art*. I saw a story in an arts journal and the photographs that accompanied the article were so vivid and the story so intriguing that I called the filmmakers and asked them to send me a copy.

I also want to add that we actively seek out first-time and emerging filmmakers. I'm really proud of the number of new filmmakers who had their first television broadcast on *Independent Lens*. Many of them have gone on to make more great films.

**Q – *How long is your license?***

**Lois** – PBS asks for a 3-year license that allows stations to broadcast 4 times.

**Q – *How much is the license fee?***

**Lois** – Our license fee is based partly on market demand. We've paid more for many films, including six figures for some Academy Award nominated and high profile titles.

**Q – *Do you require E&O insurance?***

**Lois** – Yes. Filmmakers are required to have E&O insurance in place for the broadcast. It doesn't have to be in place to submit the film for *Independent Lens* consideration.

**Q – *When we last spoke HD wasn't really prevalent. How has it affected you?***

**Lois** – There's been a big change in that area. When we launched the series in January 2003 we didn't present any films shot on HD. Two years later we had our first full HD show. Now more than 70% of the films are shot partially or completely on HD. It took awhile for independent filmmakers to catch up because of the cost and also because they had already been shooting projects on other formats. Now HD is required by almost

171

all broadcasters so if it isn't delivered on HD we upconvert it. Most filmmakers want their films to look as good as possible so if they have the financial ability they shoot on HD.

**Q – How has social networking changed your series?**

**Lois –** It's huge for us. The good news is that new technology has helped *Independent Lens* do what we do best: storytelling, diversity and engagement. It's why our social media numbers are the second highest of any PBS series. It's why our audience is growing when most series saw a decline in viewership. It's why the *Independent Lens Community Cinema* program has expanded to 106 cities, allowing us to connect viewers with organizations and educators on a local, national and increasingly international level. Social media and new technology provides the apparatus and opportunities to create short-term and long-term engagement and interactivity.

Some of our viewers - especially younger and more diverse viewers - don't watch PBS consistently, but social media allows us to engage with those viewers consistently. In addition to Facebook, Twitter and our very active blogs, we've committed a lot of resources to help our filmmakers design and produce a wide range of transmedia projects. We funded a *Garbage Dreams* game to increase awareness around environmental issues, a 3D virtual mine game for *Deep Down*, and mobile apps for films like *More Than a Month*.

**Q – What is Project 360?**

**Lois –** That's a funding initiative we created three years ago to support transmedia, multi-platform projects that can help promote the broadcast and also stand alone to give the content impact online. We're very committed to helping independent filmmakers see their work as more than "just" a film or television show. It goes back to what I was saying earlier about multiple versions. In addition to the feature length and the TV hour length, filmmakers now need to think about the three-minute short or mobile application, in addition to how they want to promote and market their film while still in production. Project 360 is one way we hope to help independent filmmakers begin their transmedia thinking and planning as early as possible in the life of their project.

**Q – What are the common mistakes you see filmmakers make?**

**Lois –** My two mantras right now are "think transmedia" and "embrace multiple versions." The abundance of content makes it really difficult to break through, but new technologies provide more opportunities than ever for filmmakers to have some control over reaching an audience. That said, sometimes filmmakers get so involved in the "new" opportunities that they lose sight of their first job, which is to make a really compelling film.

The other thing I really appreciate is when I see filmmakers find ways to keep their overhead costs down. This gives them a lot more freedom both in terms of the deals they make when the film is finished and their ability to make more films. If you sink many hundreds of thousands of dollars into a project you might have to sell the film in ways that are not best for the film, or that don't match your goals for the film. Filmmakers who have managed to keep a lower "break even" point are in a great position to negotiate the best distribution deals and control opportunities for their film.

**Q – What advice would you give a new filmmaker?**

**Lois** – You have to be passionate. Then the word "no" just means "not yet." And take up a physical exercise because being an independent filmmaker requires stamina.

# CHAPTER SEVEN
# GLOBAL PERSPECTIVE

## THE DOCUMENTARY
## FILMMAKERS HANDBOOK

EDN

OVE JENSEN

### Q – What is EDN?

**Ove** – European Documentary Network is a member-based organization for professionals working with documentary film and TV. EDN supports, stimulates and creates networks within the documentary sector. We provide documentary consulting and inform about possibilities for funding, financing, development, co-production, distribution and collaboration across borders. This is done via individual consultancy on documentary projects, activities like workshops, seminars and conferences as well as through the two indispensable publications DOX Magazine and The EDN Financing Guide. We have over 1100 members from more than 60 countries and we're open to both newcomers and established filmmakers.

### Q – What is the EDN Media program and how does it relate to documentary filmmakers?

**Ove** – The MEDIA program is run by the European Union, not EDN. MEDIA supports EDN activities like Docs in Thessaloniki, Lisbon Docs and some other of our workshops. The MEDIA program is an important resource for development and funding of documentary projects.

### Q – What is DOX Magazine?

**Ove** – DOX is the leading European magazine focusing on documentary film. DOX gives you insight into the latest developments at the international documentary scene and includes: critique of the latest interesting documentaries, features on new developments in the genre, interviews with leading documentary professionals, reports and updates from important events and personal essays & POV articles. DOX is released four times a year and always comes with a full-length documentary DVD.

### Q – How can EDN help find funding and distribution? What about crowdfunding?

 edn@edn.dk           www.edn.dk

*Ove* – EDN can help filmmakers and producers find funding in several ways. One way is the direct consultation on projects and finished films, which all members can get. Other ways is through the pitching sessions and match making activities we are offering. We offer online pitching sessions, where pitching teams present new projects to a selected group of potential financiers. We also offer advice, information and resources on crowd funding.

**Q – What kind of events does EDN program? Is there anything specifically for documentary filmmakers?**

*Ove* – All EDN activities are aimed at documentary professionals. We organize pitching sessions, development programs, market activities, seminars, workshops and master classes. We've recently developed a number of online formats including online pitching sessions, online master classes and online sessions with financiers. We are also working with new formats for knowledge sharing, trying to collect and produce useful information through special online working groups among our members.

**Q – How has social media affected what you do?**

*Ove* – Social media has made it possible for us to communicate our activities and events more directly to potential participants and also to make EDN wider known. The great thing about our Facebook and Twitter presence is also getting a lot of direct feedback and comments on what we do. This has been very helpful in developing new ideas and initiatives.

**Q – What is the EDN Financing Guide?**

*Ove* – The EDN Financing Guide is an essential tool for documentary filmmakers, producers, distributors and program sellers working on the international market. The guide provides documentary professionals with the information needed to navigate in the evolving landscape of documentary financing, where new approaches to funding and distribution have become increasingly important. The EDN Financing Guide provides detailed information about over 500 documentary strands, 400 documentary departments, over 400 commissioning editors and buyers, over 300 distributors including VOD, over 200 film funds and relevant crowdfunding platforms.

**Q – What kind of help does EDN provide for pitching?**

*Ove* – We offer individual consultation, pitching workshops and at our website we offer resources on how to pitch. This includes examples of good pitching trailers and well written project presentations.

**Q – What are the most important documentary events in Europe these days?**

# HELPFUL EUROPEAN WEBSITES

**Cineuropa**
www.cineuropa.org

**Film File Europe**
en.unifrance.org

**European Film Promotion**
www.efp-online.com

**Holland Film**
www.hollandfilm.nl

**VAR Flemish Audio Visual Fund**
www.vaf.be

**Flanders Image**
www.flandersimage.com

**Film Fund Luxemborg**
www.filmfund.lu

**Greek Film Centre**
www.gfc.gr

**Danish Film Institute**
www.dfi.dk

**Film France**
www.filmfrance.net

**Commission Nationale de Film France**
www.cnc.fr

**Rhone-Alpes Cinema**
www.rhone-alpes.com

**The German Federal Film Board**
www.ffa.de

**FilmFoderburg Hamburg**
www.ffhh.de

**German Film**
www.german-films.de

**Bavarian Film and TV Fund**
www.fff-bayern.de

**Berlin/Brandenberg Film Board**
www.filmboard.de

**North Rhein-Westphalia Film Fund**
www.filmstiftung.de

**Austrian Film Commission**
www.afc.at

**Swiss Film Center**
www.swissfilms.ch

**Irish Film Board**
www.irishfilmboard.ie

**Instituto do Cinema, Portgual (ICAM)**
www.icam.pt

**Film Net, Ireland**
www.filmnet.ie

**Institito de Cine (ICAA) Spain**
www.cultura.mecd.es

**Audio Visual Producers Assoc., Prague**
www.asociaceproducentu.cz

**Estonian Film Foundation**
www.efsa.ee

**Czech Film Center**
www.filmcenter.cz

**Polish Culture**
www.culture.pl

*Ove* – This is very much depending on who you are and what you are working with. For many documentary professionals it is important to be at IDFA and the FORUM in Amsterdam because it is the biggest professional documentary event of the year. For others it might be important to be at Docs in Thessaloniki, because there they can meet the relevant financiers for their particular project in development.

*Q – What are the common mistakes you see filmmakers make?*

*Ove* – Often I see filmmakers underestimating the importance of production value, both when it comes to their films and the presentation of it. If you are asking an audience to spend an hour or 90 minutes seeing your film, you must give them a certain standard. The same goes when you are asking financiers to back your project. How can you expect them to back your idea if you do not present something of high standard? Another issue is making thorough project development. Unfortunately many documentary professionals still present projects not developed to the standards needed for international co-production. So make sure you know your story and how you want to produce it or you will look unprofessional to your potential collaborators.

*Q – What advice would you give a new documentary filmmaker?*

*Ove* – Network! Filmmaking can be a lonely business. A good network will make life as a filmmaker easier, you will make better films and you will have more fun!

**Q – What is BBC Storyville?**

**Jo** – Storyville is a BBC documentary strand that looks for very narrative films with distinct voices from all over the world. We commission 26 films each year for BBC Four and each title is funded in co-production with other broadcasters and finance partners. We will consider films in all stages of production - from funding developments to acquiring finished titles. We support our projects throughout the filmmaking process, from helping to source finance to the cutting room and beyond. We welcome ambitious projects and are happy to accommodate films with theatrical distribution - we don't think of documentaries as belonging solely to TV.

**Q – What are you looking for in a Storyville film and is there a particular style to a Storyville film?**

**Jo –** We look for narrative and ambition and no we don't have any particular style. Our films are enormously diverse. We tend to avoid subject areas that are well covered by other areas of the BBC, like History and Science.

**Q – As a broadcaster, do ratings come into play with what you acquire/program?**

**Jo –** Ratings are not paramount and we encourage original work, but we are looking for films that work for our television audience.

**Q – How do filmmakers pitch their ideas to Storyville and what makes it stand out?**

**Jo –** We like to receive a one page outline with a synopsis of the narrative, a short selection of shot and edited material and brief bios of the filmmaking team. Background information to subjects/places etc. is always useful, but essentially we want to know what story the film is going to tell. A taster tape is essential for pitching an observational film as we need to get an idea of look, tone, characters, pacing, etc. before considering.

---

 www.bbc.co.uk/storyville     www.facebook.com/pages/BBC-Storyville

*Q – Do you have to be British or do you welcome proposals worldwide?*

*Jo* – No, you don't have to be British. We work with filmmakers globally.

*Q – Do you take proposals from new documentary filmmakers?*

*Jo* – Yes, we will consider all projects and quite often work with newcomers.

*Q – Would you advise a new filmmaker to work with an experienced producer or one you've worked with before?*

*Jo* – I think it depends on the nature of the project, the individuals concerned and their particular experience and the complexity of the co-production. For instance, we might advise a relatively new filmmaker who hasn't worked outside of their domestic market before to team up with a producer who is more experienced internationally.

*Q – Do you fully fund productions and/or do you work with certain partners as a co-production?*

*Jo* – All our films are made in co-production with other broadcasters and finance bodies. The deals are bespoke for each film so I would hesitate to generalize as the set of relationships are different each time.

*Q – How long is the process of putting together finance for a film once it's got the greenlight?*

*Jo* – The average is about 9 months. However, sometimes it can be much longer, depending on the project.

*Q – With a co-production, does the filmmaker retain any control over his or her film?*

*Jo* – Again, each deal is different as the rights packages vary from territory to territory. I would always recommend any production with three or more investors to keep a re-versioning contingency in their budget. This means that they can then meet the specific needs of each investor and produce a directors cut of their film should they wish to.

*Q – How does Storyville work with the producers/filmmakers on projects?*

*Jo* – We are available to support a production at any point, but we are particularly hands on during development and in the cutting room. We would not expect to get involved in the day to day decision making, but do expect to screen films at rough cut and fine cut stages, be consulted over any scripts, translations etc. and told of any issues or problems arising with the production. We always have a BBC Exec Producer attached to each

# HELPFUL UK & IRELAND WEBSITES

**Film London**
www.filmlondon.co.uk

**The British Council**
www.britishcouncil.org

**The Prince's Trust**
www.princes-trust.org.uk

**Natl. Endowment for Science, Tech, Arts**
www.nesta.org.uk

**Channel 4 Brit. Doc. Film Foundation**
www.britdoc.org

**The Winston Churchill Mem. Trust**
www.wcmt.org.uk

**Arts Council of England**
www.artscouncil.org.uk

**Scottish Arts Council**
www.scottisharts.org.uk

**Arts Council of Northern Ireland**
www.artscouncil-ni.org

**Northern Ireland Screen**
www.northernirelandscreen.co.uk

**North. Ireland Film and TV Commission**
www.niftc.co.uk

**Arts Council of Wales**
www.artswales.org.uk

**Sgrin Cymru Wales**
www.walesscreencommission.com

**Isle of Man Film Commission**
www.gov.im/ded/iomfilm

**The Scottish Documentary Institute**
www.scottishdocinstitute.com

**Glasgow Film Office**
www.glasgowfilm.com

**Documentary Filmmakers**
www.dfglondon.com

**Documentary Filmmakers Group**
www.thedfg.org

**British Films**
www.britfilms.com

**Irish Film & TV Network**
www.iftn.ie

**The Jerwood Charity**
www.jerwood.org

**The Wellcome Trust**
www.wellcome.ac.uk

**Irish Film Institute**
www.irishfilm.ie

**Irish Film Board**
www.irishfilmboard.ie

project as the BBC is responsible for everything that it broadcasts, so we will always retain editorial control over what we show.

**Q – Have you noticed a change in documentary filmmaking in the UK over the last few years?**

**Jo –** The changes in technology for both filmmaking and distribution has totally changed the way that documentaries are made and seen, but I believe that there is still a major role for broadcasters to play.

**Q – What advice would you offer documentary filmmakers?**

**Jo –** To be bold, ambitious and to keep the story they want to tell really clear in their own minds. I'd also like to give some practical advice and remind filmmakers to read any contract carefully and to always, always ask if they're in any doubt about anything. It is common sense, but so much money and time are wasted because it gets overlooked.

*Q – How would you define British documentaries in terms of the rest of the world?*

**Simon** – It's very passionate. It's very socially and politically minded. It's popular. It's well made. It's commercial. It's amongst the very best. It's a tremendous privilege to be working in commissioning in this country. Brit programs abroad are doing really well, too. Just look at *Undercover Boss* achieving the sorts of success that it did. The fascination of a well-honed format has not gone away and the commercial and creative possibilities for programs are encouraging. We have continued to do well in the feature documentary world as well.

*Q – What kind of docs is Channel 4 looking for?*

**Simon** – I'd say that the things that I'm looking for have changed significantly. Back when we last spoke I was doing a lot of single documentaries. And over the last few years I have been looking after the channel's documentary series portfolio. So I have been commissioning series for the last couple of years. Trying to do big scale popular returning series that looks at British life and offer it up in a way that gets ratings and reputation. We're all driven at Channel 4 to achieve those two things at once. We want to get that sweet spot.

*Q – Are one off documentaries slowly dwindling away?*

**Simon** – No. They are here to stay. Funnily enough, the bigger your series becomes, the more of your schedule you occupy with your big returning series. You have to be assiduous to vary your schedule with the best stand out documentary. We have an incredible run of true stories, which goes on and on bringing the best international films to our audiences on More 4. *Cutting Edge* continues to be important for our audience, which is our flagship 9 o'clock documentary strand.

*Q – What would you say you wouldn't be interested in?*

---

 www.channel4.com

**Simon** – Long-winded, history, Eskimos fishing up in the frozen wasteland types. Channel 4 is a ruthlessly contemporary broadcaster that's got its finger on the pulse of young, upwardly mobile, smart, free thinking Britain. While we do international subjects, we'd do them with an eye on what they say about us. We aren't interested in things that have been done before. There's a word that's used in TV commissioning: reheat. We talk about reheating things. We don't want to give an audience the same thing from last year and then warm it up and expect them to enjoy it as they did previously. We want stuff that stands outs and is fresh and experimental. *7 Days* did very well for us. It was a hybrid between a TV show and an online social media experience and it was incredibly satisfying to work on and very popular online.

*Q – How else has the internet and social media affected what you do?*

**Simon** – Two things. Just picking up again on the *7 Days* point, we created an online space where contributors could update people regularly of what they were doing and the audience could interact with them and influence their lives. That couldn't have been done a few years ago. We've also seen a phenomenon in the UK with Twitter. People use it a lot to state what they think about TV shows as those programs go out and creating a virtual community of fans. They are maniacal about it so it's in the forefront of our minds about what kinds of people are out there waiting for our programming. It helps us focus much more on the kinds of audience members that we deal with and construct programs that will speak directly to them.

*Q – But frequently the consumer's appetite moves faster than the ability to make product to satisfy it. So the trend is over by the time the show is on the air. How do you reconcile that issue?*

**Simon** – That's an interesting question. What I would say is that we have been experimenting with a type of programming that we call *Crunching Time*. We crunch time. Traditional documentaries have been made over a year, a year and a half or longer by a single camera operator. Some of the stuff we do, we film only over a month in various key institutions like hospitals, maternity wards, family homes, hotels and model agencies. But we've done that with thirty to seventy cameras. So we have the sense of 70 people filming over four weeks. And as long as you are curious about the space you are in and you think it is something your audience will value and you have good people making those programs, you can get an extraordinary wealth of material from this new way of filming. We call it using a multi-camera rig. When *Big Brother* started to lose its luster, we began pioneering on how we could use the technology that allowed *Big Brother* to exist and transferred that to a real world documentary space. Consequently, some of the programs that we have in development film over as little as one day. We might shoot in a prestigious London emergency room. So we put seventy cameras in there and each story is what happens over one day in that ward.

**Q – Your director must have seven sets of eyes!**

**Simon** – They certainly have to have their wits about them. We experiment with making television shows where most of it is filmed over a period of time and then is ready to transmit, but you leave a little space within the episode for contemporary actuality or information. So we are thinking much more about the present day impact that our programs can and should make.

**Q – How could someone approach you with an idea?**

**Simon** – One idea per email. Keep it simple, let me know what the headline is and if I'm interested we'll sit down and thrash it out together. I also like it when I get an idea from someone I haven't worked with before as long as I know that they are good and I've seen their work and admired it. Or they come in on the back of someone that I know is good. But people can come up to the front door and knock on it with an idea that they believe in. They don't have to have a track record with the channel in order for me to pay attention to them. But you do have to work harder to get noticed if you don't have a relationship with us. Those that are our regular suppliers so to speak have a circle of trust with us and it takes awhile for that trust to build up. Ideas generally don't walk in through the front door fully formed. They require conversations in order to bring them life. Part of our job here is to be as available as we can to as many people as we can in order to breathe life into the things that they are passionate about. But as with any job, you have to be careful with how you spend your time. You have to spend time with those that you think can transform the audience's relationship with the brand.

**Q – Do you only take HD at this point?**

**Simon** – As with most broadcasters, we are moving more towards that way.

**Q – What are the common mistakes that you see filmmakers make?**

**Simon** – Not asking the question that the audience would ask if they were there with contributor. It's usually because they fear losing access to the protagonist in the film. Some filmmakers feel they have to be the protagonist's friend. They have a duty to be respectful, but their key role is to establish the truth of what's going on in that situation. Sometimes being direct and assertive with a contributor will lead to a better film as well as let the contributor feel like they have shared or told their story.

**Q – What advice would you give a new filmmaker?**

**Simon** – Give people a real ballache about your idea and continue to go on about it if you believe in it. But there will come a point where in every relationship the opportunity for that idea to turn into a film will be gone. You have to realize when that moment has come so you can move onto the next project.

*Q – What kind of documentaries are you looking for to program for DR ?*

**Mette –** We are always looking for strong narratives in most genres. We have weekly current affairs stands both on DR 1 Horisont and DR 2 called DR 2 Global, daily history, weekly science, human interest stories and our weekly feature documentary strand *Dokumania* going out every Tuesday at 9pm. For DR K we look for art, architecture, music, history and for DRHD, both fascinating average person stories as well as beautiful HD productions. MAMA we are looking for youth content.

*Q – As a broadcaster, do ratings come into play on the choice of documentary?*

**Mette –** It's a balance, but we show some eight hundred titles a year, so some we do to ensure big ratings and some make sure we reflect the interest and trends of society as well to educate the public on what's happening in the world.

*Q – How do filmmakers pitch their ideas to you?*

**Mette –** One page is fine as the first contact, including track record and other partners involved. We welcome proposals from Denmark and worldwide. I do invest in new filmmakers, but they must have some shot material behind them. Sometimes I'd suggest for a new filmmaker to team up with a more experienced producer or someone we've worked with before, but it really depends on the story and the investment etc.

*Q – Do you fully fund productions and/or do you work with certain partners as a co-production?*

**Mette –** We fully fund most Danish production and co-produce with anybody from anywhere in the world if they have a great story. But we have been very succesful co-producing Danish productions in recent years. I actually enjoy working with new partners

 **www.dr.dk**

## ESSENTIAL TELEVISION STATISTICS (ETS)

ETS tracks transmissions of your film in over 30 countries around the world.

ETS can give you number of broadcasts per country, on what channel at what time so you can monitor licenses and collect fees if broadcasters are in violation of the license. If they run it more times than they are allowed or longer than the license, then they owe you money.

ETS can get audience ratings of certain broadcasters to help with your marketing.

www.etstv.com

to try and create something fresh once in a while. In general, the filmmaker doesn't retain editorial control.

**Q – How long is the process of putting together finance for a film once it's got the greenlight?**

**Mette –** If we fully finance, it can happen very quickly. If I help getting the finance in place, it's difficult to say but it can take from one month to one year. Some broadcasters take several months just to make the contract even though the project has been editorially agreed.

**Q – Have you noticed a change in the style/form of documentary filmmaking in Denmark and Europe over the last few years?**

**Mette –** There seems to be more of a variety of storytelling. The biggest challenge for me is to let the filmmakers keep their intention but also to make sure that the story is coherent, well documented and of course with a strong premise.

**Q – Are there more opportunities for co-productions now than there were a few years ago?**

**Mette –** I don't think so. I recently heard from a distributor that there are only 20 broadcasters who can do co-pro. I also heard that most commissioning editors around the pitching forums are not decision makers and cannot invest in films. But still a lot of

# HELPFUL SCANDINAVIAN WEBSITES

**Arctic**
**Barents Euro Arcitic Film Commission**
*www.barentsinfo.org*

**Finland**
**Finnish Film Foundation**
*www.ses.fi*

**Promotion Center for Audiovisual Culture**
*www.kopiosto.fi*

**Iceland**
**Icelandic Film Fund**
*www.iff.is*

**Association of Icelandic Producers**
*www.producers.is*

**Norway**
**Norweigian Film Institute**
*www.nfi.no*

**Norwegian Film and TV Producers Assoc.**
*www.produsentforeningen.no*

**Norwegian Film Commission**
*www.norwegianfilm.com*

**The North Norwegian Film Centre**
*www.nnfs.no*

**Sweden**
**Swedish Film Institute**
*www.sfi.se*

**Oresond Film Commission**
*www.oresundfilm.com*

films are being made.

*Q – Has social media played a part in how you promote a film or how you find films to license? If so, how?*

**Mette** – We try but it's only now that I find it's becoming successful. Our film *Dark Side of Chocolate* had 1 million hits after the NDR/ARD screening in Germany.

*Q – What common mistakes have you noticed with European documentary filmmakers?*

**Mette** – I feel a lot of filmmakers do not have the viewers in mind. A lot of films are very internal focused and a lot of energy is put into form over content. There is so much happening in the world today and so much to try to figure out. I wish more had a desire to understand the world.

*Q – What advice would you give a documentary filmmaker?*

**Mette** – Be brave and trust your instinct, research the market, know who to have as partners. Be brave enough to say no, if the editorial style of a broadcaster does not fit your style.

**Q – What is your job?**

*Philippa* – I own and run Cinephil, which is a sales agency based in Tel Aviv we distribute and co-produce documentary films around the world. Our films come from the Middle East and the rest of the world. If we co-produce we support filmmakers by either raising finance for their film or by putting them in contact with someone who can. We follow through till the completion of production, acting either as co-producers or executive producers and when the film is completed as sales agents distributing the documentary worldwide.

**Q – Being an Israeli company, can you distribute to the Muslim countries easily?**

*Philippa* – Not directly. If we want to distribute to Lebanon, Syria, Iran etc, we find a way. There often is a will and sincere interest from cultural organizations and television programmers in these countries. Further, currently approximately half our films are international and we don't deprive our clients/filmmakers of the Arab world television.

**Q – Do you work with Palestinian filmmakers?**

*Philippa* – We're happy to work with Palestinian filmmakers and assist as we do with other filmmakers. We have an open door policy to any Palestinian. Having said that, at this stage many Palestinians follow the 'normalization' understanding which states that life in the West Bank and Gaza or the occupied Palestinian Territories is not normal, therefore they are not Interested in normal connections or relations with Israelis (who do lead a normal life...) We respect this notion, and are willing to work within its restrictions.

**Q – Is a Palestinian film considered foreign or domestic if they come to you?**

*Philippa* – If they're a Palestinian living in Israel, then it's domestic. If they live in the

---

 info@cinephil.co.il           www.cinephil.co.il

West Bank or Palestinian Territories, they're foreign. This has no relevance when selling films around the world. It doesn't matter how their film is funded if made by a Palestinian – it's basically a Palestinian film. If a Palestinian lives within Israel and has an Israeli ID, then they're entitled to all the funding and the privileges that we are entitled to. That means an Israeli broadcaster and an Israeli Film Fund can (and do) finance them. If they are from Ramallah or Jenin for instance, then they aren't because they're citizens of what is or is about to be Palestine. But really, we don't sell it as an Israeli film or a Palestinian film. We sell it as a film that we love, one we've chosen to work with.

**Q – What kind of films are you looking for?**

**Philippa** – At Cinephil we look for films that we feel we can work with, that will reach a real public internationally on any platform. We only take films we can relate to emotionally and intellectually and like them especially if they're pushing at least one boundary. We like smart films, funny films and films that can move us even if a topic has been told more than once.

**Q – What are the types of documentaries that sell well around the world?**

**Philippa** – Current affairs - with an edge, good stories, great filmmaking, scoops. There is less space on broadcast television for the small local stories, for human interest stories. If films are going to travel well, they need to be 'big' in content and often in form. Some examples of such films: *Thieves By Law* by Shasha Gentlev about the Russian Mafia - an untold story with unprecedented access meant that we sold all over the world. *Precious Life* by Shlomi Eldar was short listed for the Academy Awards this year and a Festival hit worldwide, with theatrical releases all over the globe. From HBO in the US is the incredible story of a baby from Gaza who is treated in an Israeli hospital and survives against all odds. Tom Freidman from *The New York Times* reviewed the film *Steal This Movie* and it resulted in outstanding interest. The film was on the world's agenda for weeks.

**Q – Is cobbling together lots of different funders the common way documentaries are financed in Israel?**

**Philippa** – The most common way is to get money from TV. And TV is obliged by the state regulator to put up significant funds. They have quotas that they have to meet for local filmmaking. An Israeli filmmaker can get up to $85,000 from an Israeli broadcaster. A second stop would be the Film Funds - funded by the Film Council, which is funded by the government and television fees. There are two big documentary funds and a bunch of smaller ones. One can receive up to $60,000 from these funds usually. So that's approximately $150,000 to make a film, a reasonable sum considering the size of Israel.

**Q – What would you never do?**

**Philippa** – I try not to take documentaries that will only play locally or in one territory.

I like it when films transcend borders. That said, the slots for creative documentaries are often limited and sometimes docs have great topics or are too slow or hard to comprehend beyond specific territories. These may do better in film festivals than on TV. This is true the other way around too, we've had films that work very well on TV but are not innovative, creative or perhaps sophisticated enough in the eyes of the festival programmers.

*Q – What are most films that you see shot on?*

*Philippa* – Nowadays we've all entered the HD era. Digi betas are finished. Once again there's been a real shift in format and 3D is lurking around the corner.

*Q – Does it matter to you if the primary language of the film is English, Hebrew, Arabic or some other?*

*Philippa* – It doesn't matter to me at all. Many of our films are not English speaking films. But, language barriers are not easier today. In the US, broadcasters are not happy to show films that don't speak English. On the one hand, it's not smart to 'force' a protagonist to speak a language they don't feel comfortable in the result is artificial, distant. On the other hand English does open doors. We still stick to the original language and believe in authentic/real storytelling.

*Q – How is the documentary industry fairing in Israel these days?*

*Philippa* – It's doing well. Israeli films are still very well represented in the Festival circuit, and are well sold worldwide.

### Q – Have you come across any censorship in your part of the world?

*Philippa* – There's an important Palestinian artist who lives here called Muhammad Bakri who made a film titled *Jenin* that was censored, which was painful. Bakri is like the John Wayne of the Middle East and he made a film about the massacre that happened in Jenin. The film wasn't well received by the Israelis. Now he has made a film called *Since You've Been Gone*, which talks about his experiences with *Jenin* and the censorship he endured. It was a dark moment in our culture.

### Q – Why was it censored?

*Philippa* – The Censor thought that he wasn't accurate about what happened in Jenin, that the film misrepresented the reality in Jenin. And most Israelis believe that there was no massacre there. He was implying there was one. Finally, it was allowed to be shown in the cinemateques in Israel, who supported him all along regardless of the negative attacks he received.

### Q – Do you or your filmmakers have problems producing and selling some of your more politically charged films?

*Philippa* – I haven't come across anyone who wouldn't take a film because it's of a certain topic or content. I have come across people saying that they have too many films from the Middle East. There is certainly Holocaust fatigue. Also my personal understanding of the political situation is often the same as many of the Europeans I work with - which makes everything much simpler.

### Q – What kind of deal can a filmmaker expect from Cinephil?

*Philippa* – If you come to me with an idea on a piece of paper, and if I fall for the project, the first thing I'll want to know is your wish list. I want to know your goals and priorities. Sandi Dubowski for instance had a dream to get the whole world to see and discuss his *Trembling Before G-D* which is about gay men and women within the ultra-orthodox Jewish community. That was the priority - and that determined the distribution strategy. Generally speaking, we work on percentage so if we don't succeed, we don't make any money. Cinephil takes less of a percentage for a development project, and more if the film is complete. This is due to the fact that the funds for the projects are for the making of the films. The money for completed films is usually profits. In Europe the earlier the broadcasters join a project, the larger their contribution of funding is going to be. At first sight this goes against one's sense - why would you pay more for paper than for a completed film. But the higher fee is really for a tailored made suit, which will fully fit the needs of a broadcaster - even if it means that the filmmakers will need to make more than one version. Getting in early enables broadcasters to influence the film. Further,

1. Stay Cool! Don't get angry with the situation - always try to smile and appear friendly.

2. Ask the authorities to notify your nearest embassy or consulate. Under international agreements, you DO have the right to speak to an official from your embassy. If denied, be persistent.

3. Once they're informed, your country's officials should visit you and advise you of your rights according to local laws. They can help you get in touch with your family and friends.

4. Your official should help you find legal representation. There's not much else they can do other than monitor the situation to ensure there's no abuse. If you go to trial, they will monitor it to make sure it is a lawful one.

5. Remember, you are subject to foriegn laws overseas and have no rights of your home country. Trials are conducted in the language of that country.

most broadcasters will be interested in a backend in return for the larger investment - or a small section of the films equity. Sales agent rates for a completed film are the standard 70/30% split. We rarely give advances or money guarantees.

*Q – What would you consider a big budget documentary co-production?*

*Philippa –* $750,000 to $1 million.

*Q – What is the theatrical distribution landscape in Israel like?*

*Philippa –* It's an unhealthy environment where two or three companies own, distribute, and sometimes produce the films. They own approximately 80% of the market place. This vertical integration works against the smaller films, and as a result there are very few independent distributors in Israel. Every now and then a documentary will do exceptionally well in the cinemas, recently a film titled Land of Genesis by Moshe Alpert portraying Israeli nature in a creative and narrative way excited local audiences attracting more than 100,000 viewers. That's an outstanding number in Israeli terms.

*Q – How about the other Middle Eastern countries?*

*Philippa –* Egypt has a great cinema culture. We used to get Egyptian films on TV when I was growing up, back in the days when we only had one public channel. But I am not sure how the cinema system works there now after the revolution. I do know that there are serious attempts to introduce art house cinema to the Egyptian public. It's hard for us to work with Egyptians. I know that the Royal Jordanian Commission is successfully developing their cinema scene. Today Dubai, Abu-Dabi and Doha have incredible film festivals and platforms to encourage young and emerging filmmakers from the region - unfortunately, most of the time this excludes Israelis. On a personal level we are happy to work with anyone in the Middle East, and we have very good relations with our neighbors.

*Q – Are the Muslim countries more open to co-productions with Israel?*

*Philippa* – Unfortunately only Jordan is open. Again on a personal level things are very different - there's much curiosity and interest on all sides, and great friendships.

*Q – What are the important film festivals and markets in the Middle East?*

*Philippa* – In Israel, there's one festival which is 100% documentary: Doc Aviv in Tel Aviv in May. Then there are two big film festivals in Jerusalem in July and one in Haifa. The Haifa Film Festival is open to our neighbors. Films from the region, predominantly North Africa, are presented there. The Jerusalem Film Festival has an open door for all, especially Palestinians - though this is a little harder currently under the Palestinian 'normalization' boycott - promoting human rights. There is a new festival in Sderot on the border with Gaza which is garnering good interest from serious curators worldwide. There's a great film festival in Beirut. I don't think there's one in Jordan. In July 2011, the first ever Palestinian Cultural/Film Festival took place in Jenin.

*Q – What are the common mistakes that you see documentary filmmakers make?*

*Philippa* – Many filmmakers don't think about the distribution of their film when they start making it. They should be asking themselves why they're making their film and for whom? Think about using websites and other grass oots efforts to get their film out into the world, or to raise financing via the net. Take the trouble to take stills - so simple, very rare! If there are no stills, how are you going to promote the film when the day comes to get it out into the world? Clear music rights before you leave

## WHAT TO DO IF ARRESTED OVERSEAS

6. Some under developed countries might have certain officials who will expect bribery, but remember one "gratuity" can lead to many more!

7. Showing official looking documents can help, but be sure not to push these in front of any anti-government "terrorist" types.

8. BEFORE you go to a specific country to film, contact that country's local embassy in your country to find out about filming restrictions. Once in-country, you should check in with your embassy.

9. Also remember that certain things we take for granted are not so in foreign countries. For instance, you could be held without bail for 28 days or even more before seeing a judge.

10. Certain prescription drugs in your country may not be considered legal elsewhere, which could lead to a serious problem that carries a death penalty. ALWAYS check with the emabassies of the countries you'll be visiting before you leave .

## HELPFUL AFRICAN WEBSITES

**Africa Film and TV**
www.africafilmtv.com

**African Film Commission**
www.africanfilmcommission.org

**Cape Town Tourism**
www.tourismcapetown.co.za

**Cape Town Film Commission**
www.capefilmcommission.co.za

**Durban Film Office**
www.durbanfilmoffice.com

**FESPACO**
www.fespaco.bf

**Film Contact**
www.filmcontact.com/africa

**Connect Unganda**
www.connectuganda.com

**French Institute**
www.ifas.org.za

**Gauteng Film Office**
www.gautengfilm.co.za

**Kenya Film Commission**
www.kenyafilmcommission.com

**Tangier Film Locations (Morocco)**
www.tangierfilmlocations.com

**Namibian Film Commission**
www.namibia-film-commission.com

**National Arts Council**
www.nfvf.co.za

**Lagos Film Office**
www.lagosfilmoffice.com

**Pan African Arts Organization**
www.panafricanarts.org.dpaff.htm

**Sithengi Film & TV Market**
www.sithengi.co.za

**South Africa Development Fund**
www.southafrica-newyork-net/sadf.htm

**S. African Nat. Film and Video Found.**
www.nfvf.co.za

**South African Comm. for Developement**
www.sacod.org.za

**SABC**
www.sabc.co.za

**Zanzibar Film Festival**
www.ziff.org/ziff

**Zimmedia Film and Video**
www.zimmedia.com

**SA Film**
www.safilm.co.za

you leave the editing suite. Working with sales agents today has become a different process. Filmmakers should be a part of the distribution of their film - there are so many outlets and options out there - on and off the net. Co-operation with a professional and experienced sales agent will maximize a films' potential. Digital rights, whihc are still largely an unknown, need careful attention and step by step planning. I wouldn't go it alone. It 's very complicated and requires the expertise of a sales agent.

*Q – What advice would you give new documentary filmmakers?*

*Philippa* – The scene is tougher these days. The options and platforms are greater, and the funding, though more varied, also harder to get. But there is plenty of  space for wonderful films! If you've a great story tell it! If you've got what it takes to make one of these wonderful films about a small town somewhere with a riveting story, outstanding characters, unbelievable access, great photography and moving moments, then there's a lot of gratification on its way to you. It will be you who open people's minds and hearts. It will be you who can make a difference, informing and entertaining simultaneously regardless of the medium the film is then presented on.

**Q – What is the state of documentary filmmaking in Thailand?**

*Thunska* –Thai documentary used to be about traveling, environment conservation, antiques or celebrities but nowadays they're about the history of the big guns of the Royal Thai Air Force, environmental concern, and bitter and sorrowful lives of the poor. In 2004, a TV program was launched, *Kon-Kon-Kon (People & People)*, which told sorrowful stories of ordinary people. Also, there was *Tum-Pid-Yah-Pler (You Better Watch Out)* that presented social problems like school kids' fighting and gay prostitutes. There's been a breakout of reality TV, with programs like *Academy Fantasia*, but these shows have all been designed as a brand-new form of entertainment just for businesses. However there was a really interesting documentary made in 1975, *Kum-Ma-Korn-Ying-Ha-Ra (Female Laborers of Hara)*, directed by Jon Ungphakorn, which was about a group of female laborers in Hara's jeans factory that usurped the factory because their wage was depreciated. Since then, there hasn't been anything powerful like it.

**Q – How does this compare with the rest of your neighboring Southeast Asian countries?**

*Thunska* – Documentaries in my neighboring countries have much more variety. In Cambodia, Rithy Pahn made a documentary called *The Land of Wondering Soul*, which is about laborers who set underground fiber optics cable for communication networks such as TV channels or the internet while there are still bombs buried in some areas. That country is really not yet ready for that technology because it has just recovered from war. In Singapore, there is *Moving House* by Tan Pin Pin, which tells a story of cemeteries surrendered to the government because of excessive population. This reflects a Singapore policy that seems to be able to handle any issues on the surface, but never anything deeper that will really have an affect on the people. So in these countries, documentaries are driven by the filmmaker's personal interest in certain issues, rather than doing it just for money.

---

f  www.facebook.com/pages/Thunska-Pansittivorakul

**Q – How are most Thai documentaries funded and what are their budgets?**

*Thunska* – It depends on the kind of documentary. If it's a documentary for TV broadcast, or for education in organizations, the fund is either from that organization or the company or TV station will sponsor it. If not, it's often personal funding. My first feature documentary, *Voodoo Girls* was made with my own money. When it was shown in America, Modern Films contacted me and offered finance for *Happy Berry*, and also some monies for my next documentary, *Futon*. But more than 80% is financed by myself and almost 15% is from Office of Contemporary Art and Culture, Ministry of Culture. It's interesting because this is the first film that the Ministry of Culture has approved for funding. This year, I just finished my experimental documentary feature, *The Terrorists*. The film looks at the crack down on protesters in Bangkok in 2010. I got an investment from Jürgen Brüning Filmproduktion. German investor, Jürgen Brüning is the producer of *Bruce LaBruce* and we met when I showed him my film *Reincarnate* at the Rotterdam Film Festival. What's frustrating is that the government, who were not elected democratically, try to control the people, so they support only the films that support their views. I don't, so I can't get any budget from them. My previous film *This Is Under Quarantine* was banned in a festival in Bangkok. The reason for the ban was to preserve national security.

**Q – Are co-productions big in Thailand?**

*Thunska* – Not many people care to fund independent documentary. In fact I'd say, almost none.

**Q – Is there a particular type of subject matter that is more successful than others in Thailand?**

*Thunska* – Overly successful documentaries don't really exist in Thailand. There was a documentary called *Innocent* that got theatrical runs, but the tickets were sold for charity. The film is about taking poor students from the north to the sea. It stirred up the trend of going to see this film as a benevolent activity. But whenever "documentary" is mentioned, people find it boring and end up going to see an entertaining fiction film. So they don't pay much attention. In 2009, we had *Agrarian Utopia* by Uruphong Raksasad, which was a very interesting documentary. This film only screened in one theater for two weeks in Bangkok but won loads of awards both in Thailand and internationally. The film is about a farmer's family and depicts the beautiful nature of Thailand.

**Q – Do all docs get theatrical runs in Thailand?**

*Thunska* – Including *Innocent*, there have been only a handful of documentaries that have come out theatrically. One was *Crying Tiger*, which is about the hard lives of people from the northeastern region who have to go and work in Bangkok. This film was not as successful as it should have been. It's earnings were so slight that the company never considered investing in documentary ever again.

**Q – How important is the DVD market? Is piracy a big problem?**

**Thunska –** It's a problem and it's not. Film companies think people don't go to the cinema because of piracy. The reality is that no one pirates Thai movies because Thai films have small audiences. DVD piracy for international films offers more variety than theatrical cinemas. So film viewers who want to see different things like documentaries tend to get them via pirate DVDs.

**Q – Are there any film organizations where people who want to shoot in Thailand can go to get advice?**

**Thunska –** There's not much. But The Tourism Authority of Thailand a few years ago invited tourists to send in their travel videos of Thailand and they converted them into webisodes. Since then they commissioned a film called *Hearing The Sunshine By Amazing Thailand* which chronicles a few people traveling across the country. We have the Thailand Film Office who are more about bringing foreign movie units to Thailand. That causes a new problem. Whenever a foreign movie unit comes here, Thai crew and service providers such as lights and cameras, flourish because they're offered better wages. Due to that, sometimes Thai movie units have to go on hold because everyone mobilizes to reinforce the foreign movie unit.

**Q – Does censorship appear in Thailand?**

**Thunska –** Thailand is quite unique. We operate everything under a moral frame. This means anything that doesn't fit within our culture, would not be accepted by society. Some things that seem to be strict are actually loose, while some things that seem to be loose are strict and not allowed. For example, we have TV campaigns against women wearing spaghetti-strapped tops but they're all wearing them. We don't support prostitute legalization, but it is widely known that prostitutes populate here more than anywhere else in Asia. It affects our censorship policy. On TV, we don't use vulgarism, we don't kiss, and we don't drink or smoke. Whenever we do, there will be a mosaic screen on those alcohol bottles. Even when we put our feet on a table, it is against our gracious culture, so there will be mosaic screen on those feet too. This also happens in cinemas. Sexual images like nudity in Thai films would be censored while it is ok in foreign films. We are highly sensitive in sexual issues more than violence. Films with gunshots, head explosions, blood splashes are not censored. They are however most watchful on sex. Once, I made a short film, *Sigh*, which has male nudity. It was shown in a short film competition in The 3rd Bangkok Film Festival. A year later, this same film was asked to screen in a Thai Film Festival in Hong Kong, but it was banned by the Thai embassy there. And another year later, *Voodoo Girls* was banned by the Bangkok International Film Festival because of nudity and vulgarity used by women in the film. They said it would build a bad image of Thai women. The government claims that they've changed their rating system but they still have a high ban rate showing that filmmakers should not tell something that the government doesn't want the world to know.

**Q – What does documentary filmmaking mean to you?**

*Thunska* – For me, documentary filmmaking should be for the filmmaker's interest, rather than other reasons, and it should present the social situation beyond the concept under society obligations. It should not be for profit or popularity, but instead made by the genuine interest of filmmakers. For example, I'm interested in Bangkok teenagers. Most films are made to please adults, no rude words, no love in school, while teenagers in our current society are not following the old life frames. I focus on presenting state of

**TRAVELING IN UNDERDEVELOPED COUNTRIES**

7. Have on you at all times a list of contacts that could help you if problems arise. Your nearest embassy, a local organization that supports your film and the Peace Corp would be good ones to have.

8. If your project is charitable you may be able to request, several months in advance, a complementary high clearance rental car from a rental agency.

9. Pack mosquito spray/oils/nets, First Aid kit, Pepto-Bismol, water purification tablets and candy.

10. Take a quick course in the language of the country you're visiting - Rosetta Stone is good for this. Also a basic first aid course would be prudent, too.

11. Cash. Take bills large and small. It may be the only way you can pay for anything. Or get out of a bad situation.

12. Make sure you have all your official documents on you including letters of any high up officials in that particular country.

# HELPFUL ASIAN WEBSITES

**Japan**
**Japanese Film Commission**
www.japanfc.org

**Sapporo Film Commission**
www.plaza-sapporo.or.jp/fc

**Sendai Miyagi Film Commission**
www.sendaimiyagi-fc.jp

**Nagoya Location Nav**
www.ncvb.or.jp/location

**Osaka Film Council**
www.osaka-fc.jp

**Kobe Film Office**
www.kobefilm.jp

**Hiroshima Film Commission**
www.nfdcorp.com
www.fc.hcvb.city.hiroshima.jp

**Fukuoka Film Commission**
www.fukuoka-film.com

**Himjei Film Commission**
www.city.himeji.lg.jp

**Okinawa Film Office**
filmoffice.ocvb.or.jp

**South Korea**
**Busan Film Commission**
www.bfc.or.kr

**Indoneisa**
**Bali Film Commission**
www.balifilm.com

**Hong Kong**
**Hong Kong Film Services Office (TELA**
www.fso-createhk.gov/hk

**Thailand**
**Thailand Film Office**
www.thailandfilmoffice.org

**Thailand Film Foundation**
www.thaifilm.com

**Tourism Authority of Thailand**
www.tourismthailand.org

**India**
**National Film Development Corp.**

**Singapore**
**Singapore Film Commission**
www.sfc.org.sg

**Eastern Russia**
**Vladivostok Film Commission**
www.vfc.ru

**Taiwan**
**Taipei Film Commission**
www.taipeifilmcommission.org

**Seoul Film Commission**
www.seoulfc.or.fc

affairs, rather than judging their behaviors whether they are right or wrong.

*Q – What are the common mistakes that you see documentary filmmakers make?*

*Thunska –* Uniformity and being too strict under social obligations.

*Q – What advice would you give a new documentary filmmaker?*

*Thunska –* Thai filmmakers these days often premeditate about how to make films that get awards or how to attract viewers. For me, I'm interested only in what I'm interested in! You have to ask yourself about the message you want to deliver, how you're interested in that issue, rather than worry whether you will get an audience or an award or not.

MEXICO
ELENA FONTES
AMBULANTE

**Q – What is Ambulante Org?**

*Elena* – We are a non profit organization focused on producing, distributing and exhibiting documentaries in Mexico, as well as helping market them abroad. We were set up in 2005 by Mexican actors and filmmakers Gael Garcia Bernal, Diego Luna and Pablo Cruz.

**Q – What is the Documentary Film Festival Ambulante?**

*Elena* – Ambulante is a traveling documentary film festival, held in collaboration with the Mexican production company, Canana; Cinepolis, a leading movie theater chain in Mexico; and the Morelia International Film Festival. It brings in a selection of 80 groundbreaking documentary films from around the world to more than 100 venues located in 12 regions across the country.

When we launched in 2005, it was extremely rare to find documentaries in theaters or even art house venues, and there were only about 3 or 4 film festivals in Mexico, which only took place in the large cities. But today we play in theater multiplexes, parking lots, plazas, art house theaters, school auditoriums, peripheral communities and correctional facilities. The audience has grown to over 68,000. Our last festival had over 1000 events from Q&As, round table discussions, conferences, workshops and outdoor events with more than 100 guest filmmakers, industry professionals, academic and NGO representatives.

**Q – What is the Gucci Ambulante Fund?**

*Elena* – It's a fund that offers grants to Mexican filmmakers that amount to $30,000 USD for post production expenses.

---

 www.ambulante.co.mx   twitter.com/Ambulante

 www.facebook.com/pages/Ambulante-Gira-de-Documentales

*Q – What is The Guadalajara Visionary Campus?*

*Elena* – It's a training program for Mexican Documentary filmmakers that we set up in collaboration with the Berlin Talent Campus and the Guadalajara International Film Festival. We carry out between 5 to 10 documentary training workshops year round, and across different regions in Mexico and Central America.

*Q – And 'Beyond Ambulante'?*

*Elena* – This is our new project that aims to train indigenous organizations in documentary filmmaking and bring their work to the global film industry. This came about due to our aim to establish important partnerships with a wide range of non profit organizations working mainly in the field of human rights, and to encourage and promote the use of documentary as an advocacy tool.

*Q – How do you help in distribution at home and marketing films abroad?*

*Elena* – We have taken a selection of Mexican documentaries to over ten countries in the past three years, where we've promoted them and established partnerships with distribution companies to market the films in Mexican territory in theaters, DVD, TV and VOD.

*Q – What is the documentary filmmaking scene like in Mexico?*

*Elena* – It's become very active. There's been a significant rise of documentaries made each year and several have garnered important awards in festivals around the world, such as *Presumed Guilty* by Roberto Hernandez, Layda Negrete and Geoffrey Smith, *My Life Inside* by Lucia Gaja, *The General* by Natalia Almada, *Shakespeare and Victor Hugo's Intimacies* by Yulene Olaizola and *Those Who Remain* by Juan Carlos Rulfo and Carlos Hagerman.

Unfortunately the increased enthusiasm for filmmaking hasn't met adequate institutional support. There's no solid infrastructure or system for funding and distribution. Mexico's film culture is extremely self-referential and rarely looks to international resources or partnerships. There's no significant practice of documentary sales to broadcast entities and existing state and academic support systems are limited, generating limited financial rewards. So as long as this lack of distribution infrastructure and potential funding sources, doc filmmakers will continue to face challenges in Mexico. However due to filmmaking technology becoming more accessible, there's been an increase in production with those who previously had no access to express their identities, interests, and stories.

New technology also offers possibility of self-distribution, and distribution on new platforms that is no longer dependent on traditional models or on the current funding schemes. Filmmakers are now taking advantage of social media like Facebook, Twitter and blogs to target new audiences, develop their marketing and distribution strategies, and even to raise funds for their films. Digital screens also facilitate the theatrical release of documentaries that couldn't make it to a 35mm print. Some films have been released simultaneously online, VOD and in theaters successfully, such as the film *Revolucion* produced by Canana which comprised of ten shorts from ten Mexican directors.

**Q – *Are there many government-funding schemes or grant organizations within Mexico that documentary filmmakers can apply to?***

*Elena* – About 86% of funding schemes and grants for documentaries are provided by public institutions, such as the Mexican Film Institute (IMCINE). IMCINE has been extremely active and is offering grants for development, production and post-production specifically directed to documentaries. Public funding, however, largely depends on politics, and on the current party in power, so there is no continuity for film production funding. There are no regulatory commissions that would guarantee continuous funding throughout the years, regardless of the government in place.

The Mexican Film Institute has also been a also a key entity in lobbying for an important tax incentive that is now in place, through which companies can deduct a percentage of their taxes if they invest in film production. The regulatory mechanism still has many loopholes, but in general, it has played a significant role in sparking national production for both fiction and documentary films, on behalf of the private sector. Public broadcasters, such as TV UNAM, Channel 22 and Canal Once are now increasing their funding for independent documentary productions. Documentary filmmakers here in Mexico can also apply to international funds such as The MacArthur Foundation, Hubert Bals. Jan Vrijman, Ford Foundation, although few filmmakers take advantage of these available resources.

A few of the major festivals offer funding as well (Morelia International Film Festival-FICM Guadalajara International Film Festival -FICG) usually through partner organizations outside of Mexico. Overall, however, there is a pressure to produce content that can be exported and exhibited internationally, and this affects the criteria for developing treatments for documentaries.

**Q – *What is distribution like for documentaries in Mexico?***

*Elena* – In Mexico, screen space in theatres is dominated by the large studio productions from the U.S, and about 98% of television airspace is controlled by two major broadcasting groups, Televisa and TV Azteca, which mostly produce and screen their own content. This severely limits the nature of the visual content that is available for the wider audience. There are approximately 4,500 screens in Mexico, 86% owned by 3 major multiplex chains, and 91% of screen space continues to be occupied by Hollywood studio productions. A single ticket amounts to 78% of the minimum daily wage, which limits access to a large portion of the population.

Only 2% of theatrical releases are documentary films. Nevertheless, this year, Cinepolis, the largest theater chain in Mexico, and our founding partner set a historical distribution precedent. They decided to directly distribute the documentary *Presumed Guilty*, raising $8 million at the box office, and attracting over one million spectators in the first couple of weeks of the release. I'm sure that this will spark more interest on behalf of distributors to market documentary films. Some of the larger festivals have also begun to incorporate a market structure for independent films to promote international sales, such as the market of the Guadalajara Film Festival, and more documentaries are being distributed now in VOD and online platforms.

The growing availability of new platforms and technologies is playing an important role in terms of exhibition and distribution, and I believe that they will soon become the primary market for documentaries in Mexico, due to their ability to target specific audiences, as well as their accessibility, compared to other exhibition platforms. Moreover, documentary film festivals have begun to proliferate across the country successfully, so there's also a proven and growing young audience interest in documentary films. 64% of our own audience is between 15 and 24 years old.

### Q – What is the biggest problem for documentaries in Mexico?

*Elena* – Lack of distribution for theatrical distribution. Hollywood studios still largely control it and our broadcasters do not play a significant role in distribution. There's a lack of funding for independent film. And there's a lack of training opportunities for documentary filmmakers. Film schools are concentrated in a few large cities, and are unable to meet the demand for training.

### Q – What is the biggest problem or challenges facing Mexican/Latin American documentary filmmakers today?

*Elena* – There is an extremely limited class of professional documentary producers in Mexico and Latin America, who are aware of the major funding and exhibition patterns of world documentary culture, or possess the professional skills to fund and finish market-ready documentaries. Many documentary filmmakers "produce" for themselves, or are supported by assigned officers of a university program. This is different from a professional producer class within Mexico, who would form the chief interface to the world market. Surely, directors can be effective producers for themselves, but a talent for producing does not naturally flow from a directorial talent. It's a matter of training and experience, and I believe that this lack of training and experience is the biggest problem now facing Mexican and Latin American documentary filmmakers today.

### Q – What advice would you offer a new documentary filmmaker?

*Elena* – I would advise filmmakers to be conscious of the issues that affect their current surroundings - to be aware of the kind of audiences they want to reach out to, and when selecting a subject for their documentary, to ask themselves why they want to make this film and why their selected subject is important at that point in time - who they are making

# MEXICO, CENTRAL & SOUTH AMERICAN FILM WEBSITES

**Mexico**
**Instituto Mexicano de Cinematografia (IMCINE)**
www.imcine.gob.mx

**TV Azteca**
www.tvazteca.com

**Comision Nacional de Filmaciones**
www.conafilm.org.mx

**TV UNAM**
www.tvunam.unam.mx

**Costa Rica**
**Costa Rica Production Serivices**
www.costaricaproductionservices.com

**Uruguay**
**Emerge Film Solutions**
www.emergefilmssolutions.com

**Argentina**
**Cine Ojo Films & Video**
www.cineojo.com.ar

**Argentina Film Commission**
www.filcom.arg.ar

**Medoza Film Commission**
www.filmcom.gov.ar

**Comision Argentina de Film.**
www.caf.gov.ar

**Bolivia**
**APCOB**
www.apcob.org.bo/videos

**Venezuela**
**Venezuela Film Commission**
www.diatriba.net/
venezuelafilmcommisiom

**Brazil**
**Amazon Film Commission**
www.amazonsfilm.com.br

**Brazil Film Commission**
www.minasfilmcommission.com

**Minas Gerais**
www.cultura.mg.gov.br

**Bureau De Cinema Do Ceara**
Tel: 55-85-244-4549

**Chile**
**ChileCine**
www.chilecine.cl

**Planet Vivo**
www.planetvivo.org

**Latin American Confernece of Audiovisual and Cinematographic Authroities**
www.cinecaaci.com

this film for, etc.

Because the distribution market in Mexico is not going to change that quickly, I would also recommend them to take advantage of all available resources, and all the available technologies and platforms that can now be used for fundraising, outreach, and distribution.

I would also advise them to watch as many films as they can from all over the world to enrich their visual references, and to try to go to as many pitching forums, training programs, and markets to develop the necessary skills and practice to be able to reach out to other international markets in terms of funding and distribution. Finally, I would advise them not to be afraid of making more personal and experimental documentaries, and at the risk of sounding cliché, I would say, be creative and experiment, grab a camera, get out there.

AUSTRALIA

JOHN GODFREY

SBS

**Q – What kind of documentaries does SBS look for?**

*John –* The key word for SBS documentaries is distinctive. That is documentary content that feels like it's distinctly SBS, and that you can only get on SBS both in subject and form. If a documentary feels it could be commissioned by another channel here in Australia, such as ABC or feels it fits into their schedule, we won't commission it. If it feels like we're not doing it first, we're not going to do it. We are seeking content that is creatively ambitious in subject and form and will be talked about and memorable. Firstly, everything we do at SBS Docs must be clearly seeded in our charger. It's absolutely crucial that ideas demonstrate how they explore Australian multicultural issues, whatever the documentary genre – be it science, history, contemporary social issues.

The second is our commissioning values which we see as an equation. Charter + Commissioning Values = Distinctive content. Our Commissioning Values are Provoke Debate, Push Boundaries, Surprise Audiences and Inspire Change. We picked these values as ones that define SBS docs as different to anyone else in the Australian broadcast landscape, because we want to be known for ideas that other broadcasters wouldn't consider, to take risks other broadcasters wouldn't - we want to get our documentaries talked about.

**Q – Do you only commission Australian filmmakers?**

*John –* We are only able to commission Australian filmmakers, but that doesn't mean we can't work with international producers. International filmmakers/producers can form partnerships with Australian production companies.

**Q – What are you not interested in?**

*John –* We don't commission arts, natural history and documentaries that don't have

---

 **www.sbs.com.au**

significant Australian content. Acquisitions buy international stories, and we commission Australian stories. We don't as a rule, commission feature documentaries, and we don't commission half hour docs, as we don't have any half hour documentary slots.

### Q – As a broadcaster, do ratings dictate what kind of topics you commission?

*John* – Any broadcaster who tells you that they don't want as big an audience as possible for their documentaries is lying. So of course, ratings matter, but that doesn't mean they dictate what you commission. Filmmakers should aspire to as broad an audience as possible, so that means choosing certain subjects and taking certain approaches should be part of their thinking, as well as avoiding certain subjects and certain approaches to filming.

### Q – How do filmmakers pitch their ideas to you?

*John* – I'd encourage them to first read our website to find out it is we are looking to commission. I would then ask them to send proposals in the mail, but it doesn't have to be a fully developed proposal. It could be anything from a couple of pages depending on what the idea is. I think filmmakers often spend too much time, energy and money on researching and developing a project that is so far away from what we are looking for that I wish people would have contacted me at an earlier stage.

### Q – Do you take proposals from new documentary filmmakers or do they have to have a certain amount of experience behind them?

*John* – Yes, I'll accept proposals from new documentary filmmakers. However, they will only get commissioned if they are working with an experienced producer, an experienced editor and DP. One of the most accomplished single documentaries I have commissioned was by a first-time filmmaker, but that is because they were working with, and listening to, one of Australia's best producers, finest editors and top DPs.

### Q – What makes a proposal stand out to you?

*John* – The quality of the story, strength of the characters, the creative ambition – but more importantly the headline. The one-line synopsis in the proposal should grab you by the scruff of the neck and make you want to read it and want you to see it on screen.

### Q – Do you welcome trailers or samples of work as part of a proposal?

*John* – I welcome trailers, and think they are essential for any character-based documentary so a judgment can be made on the strength of the character. However, they aren't essential. Having said that, they have on occasion tipped the balance in deciding whether to go forward with a project. If I am unfamiliar with a filmmaker's work, then samples of work can help too.

**Q – Do you fully fund productions?**

**John –** In short, no. Our limited resources mean that we rely on the national funding agency, Screen Australia, to contribute funds to documentaries.

**Q – Do you offer pre-sales for license?**

**John –** Yes. We mostly offer a license agreement in the form of a pre-sale. Sometimes we'll offer a license agreement and some investment for things of a larger budget. Frequently, SBS Content Sales will give some money as a Distribution Advance or for DVD rights. Our license agreements usually last for 4 runs over 5 years.

**Q – What are the kind of budgets that you work with?**

**John –** It depends on the type of documentary it is. At the lower end you'd have small observational documentaries that could be around $350,000-$400,000, and at the upper end you'd have high end science or history that could be $600,000-$700,000

**Q – Do you do acquisitions?**

**John –** Our limited resources means that the vast majority of our schedule is acquisitions, but it's not my department. Ben Nguyen looks after documentary acquisitions.

**Q – Can an independent producer approach you with a finished program?**

**John –** No, they should approach Ben Nguyen.

**Q – What is the Indigenous Protocol?**

**John –** The SBS Charter tasks us with exploring Australia's multicultural society and increasing awareness of the diversity of cultures, and an important part of this is indigenous documentaries. The Indigenous Protocols are how we engage with filmmakers and how filmmakers engage with indigenous communities. It's just a set of protocols to ensure that indigenous culture is being honored and the stories are being told in a way that is suitable for that community. So in other words, people's rights are not being trampled on.

"The one-line synopsis in the proposal should grab you by the scruff of the neck."

**Q – How long does the process take to put the finance together once you've green lit a project?**

*John –* It varies and depends on the project, but because the funding process involves the national funding body Screen Australia, and also usually the state funding bodies, then their application and decision deadlines determine how long things take. International deals can take the producer over a year depending on how many international presales the producer needs. If it is a domestic idea and we really want to do it, we may not wait for state funding deadlines, and try and push it through as quickly as possible. This could be a matter of a month or two.

*Q – How has social media changed what you do?*

*John –* New emerging platforms, such as social media are becoming increasingly important to our distribution, audience and marketing. SBS On Demand has just been launched, which is a free video service that lets you watch full episodes, clips and live streams of some of SBS programs, and SBS programs are available on iTunes. A recent three-part series *Go Back To Where You Came From* dramatically illustrated the growing importance of social media. A series that put six Australians on an asylum-seeker's boat and sent them on a reverse journey from Australia to refugee camps in Africa and Asia became a social media phenomenon. The program trended worldwide on Twitter during the first night of broadcast. Across the series there were a total of 42,000 tweets for the #goback hashtag. These tweets had a potential exposure of 2.6 million people. A post campaign evaluation survey amongst people 18-34 in metro areas found that 15% of respondents had seen *Go Back To Where You Came From* mentioned in social media, with the biggest volume on Facebook. For some this was a key driver for viewing. A total of 2.9 million people tuned into *Go Back To Where You Came From* nationally across SBS ONE first runs and SBS TWO repeats, and there were 221,000 unique browsers who visited the SBS website across June. A total of 310,000 videos were viewed, including 198,000 full episode catch ups, the highest of any SBS series to date.

*Q – Do you do feature length documentaries?*

*John –* As a general rule, we don't commission feature length documentaries, but there are of course exceptions when we want to make a documentary more of an event. One example is *The Tall Man* which is screening at the Toronto Film Festival and will be broadcast in early 2012. Based on the Walkley-Award winning book, *The Tall Man* by Chloe Hooper, is the story of the death in custody of indigenous man Cameron Doomadgee on Palm Island and is directed by Tony Krawitz and produced by Blackfella Films who produced the award-winning landmark history SBS series *First Australians*. It is a significant film which will initiate a national discussion about an important issue, and the feature length format turns it into more of an event. The main problem for us is scheduling feature length docs in prime time, as there are only certain times of the year where the slots are freed up.

*Q – Are documentaries playing in the cinema more and more in Australia?*

*John –* There hasn't been any noticeable trend. One unusual thing is that *Mrs. Carey's*

# HELPFUL AUSTRALIAN & NEW ZEALAND WEBSITES

### Australia

**Australian Film Commission**
www.afc.gov.au

**Australian Documentary Forum**
www.ozdox.com.au

**Australian International Doc. Conf.**
www.aidc.com.au

**Pacific Film and TV Commission**
www.pftc.com.au

**Film Australia**
www.filmaust.com.au

**Film Finance Corporation**
www.flc.gov.au

**Screen Hub**
www.screenhub.com.au

**Screen Network Australia**
www.screennetwork.com

**Northern Territory Film Office**
www.nt.gove.au/nreta/arts/ntfo/grants

**Screen West**
www.screenwest.com.au

**Film Victoria**
www.film.vic.gov.au

**South Australian Film Corp.**
www.safilm.com.au

### New Zealand

**The New Zealand Documentary Conf.**
www.docnzfestival.com

**Film New Zealand**
www.filmnz.co.nz

**Maori in Film, Video and TV**
www.ngaahowakaari.com

**Film South New Zealand**
www.filmsouth.com

**Film Wellington**
www.filmwellington.com

**TVNZ**
http://tvnz.co.nz

**NZ Film Archive**
www.filmarchive.org.nz

**Screen Production and Devel. Association**
www.spada.co.nz

**Asia New Zealand Film Found. Trust**
www.anzfft.org.nz

**Open Door**
www.opendoor.net.nz

**New Zealand Film and TV School**
www.filmschool.org.nz

**New Zealand Film Academy**
www.nzfilmacademy.com

*Concert*, the story of a Sydney girls' school music director preparing her students for a concert at the Opera House, took everybody by surprise by becoming the 2nd highest grossing Australian documentary of all time earning $1m in the first 10 weeks. *The Tall Man* will be released theatrically in Australia, too.

**Q – What common mistakes do you see documentary filmmakers make?**

**John –** Structure is the most common issue I come across, and understanding how to best progress the story with narrative/character development.

**Q – What advice would you give a new documentary filmmaker?**

**John –** Study the broadcaster's schedule and website of whomever you are pitching to, to make sure you know what they commission, what they don't commission and what they are currently looking for.

### Q – What is Mercury Media?

*Tim* – Mercury specializes in the distribution of high quality documentaries to cinema, DVD, television, in-flights and on-demand broadband channels. We supply TV and increasingly IPTV platforms: iTunes/Love Film/Amazon/Blink Box/Enabled TV and will be working with a number of global newspaper brands.

### Q – What is the market like globally these days for documentary films?

*Tim* - Generally healthy but there's definitely a preference for quality over quantity. There are generally a number of channels in each geographic market who have an appetite for docs. But it is the VOD market which is now beginning to explode. Newspapers in the UK like The Independent and The Guardian are beginning to mix text based journalism with docs to create a fantastic new digital media mix.

### Q – Do broadcasters around the world have an appetite for content not specifically pertaining to their own country?

*Tim* – Absolutely. The world is inter-connected albeit culturally distinct.

### Q – What format does better around the world?

*Tim* – Films should always be shot in full HD and delivered to distributors on a hard drive with separated audio tracks, graphic elements and in both texted and textless. They need to conform to broadcast standards. If you don't know what these are, then find out before you shoot a frame.

### Q – Are there any genres that sell better than others?

---

 **www.mercurymedia.org**

*Tim* – Yes, Current Affairs, History, Music & Arts and Contemporary Global Lifestyle Issues.

**Q – Does a film have to be in English for you to pick it up?**

*Tim* – We pick up films in any language and the filmmaker supplies it in English as well as the local language.

**Q –'Are there any territories that are more open to purchasing documentaries than others?**

*Tim* - Not particularly. Though countries with their own developed production sector are more likely to favor local producers e.g. Germany, UK, USA, France, Spain. That said, great films will always stand out.

**Q – What are the markets like for documentaries in continents such as South America, the Middle East and Africa?**

*Tim* – The market for docs in South America is thriving: HBO and Fox have good appetites as do many of the local channels. The Middle East is growing with Al Jazeera Doc Channel, Al Arabiya and Alhura all in the market. Asia is steady. Africa remains challenging. South Africa was a good market. Now it is difficult - SABC is bankrupt and whilst there probably will be a viable market sometime only one person I know is making a go of it - Hannelie Backer. Africa is challenging because the license fees paid are uneconomic to service.

**Q – Does piracy have an affect on your sales to any particular country?**

*Tim* – No, piracy is not particularly an issue in the doc world - it is sometimes difficult getting an audience in the first place. I was frankly pleased that one of my films was for sale at the base camp of Mt. Everest for a dollar! That said it is a huge issue for broader entertainment genres. It is up to VOD sites to come up with innovative ways to deliver the best docs in the highest quality at an affordable cost.

**Q – Do you ever come across any censorship issues and does it relate more to any particular country than others?**

*Tim* – If a film won't work in a particular country because of cultural constraints they won't buy it. Clearly a particular country might really like a film but need to edit it to fit a slot length or perhaps because of sexual content. This is particularly true of airlines.

Producers need to understand that buyers have to be allowed to edit films to make them work for their audience - and if they are lairy about that then their film won't be acquired.

**Q – What is Joiningthedocs.tv?**

**Tim** – Joiningthedocs.tv (JTD) is a pay-per-view or subscription platform for docs which integrates trailers on producers websites, trailers embedded/shared in Facebook and in British newspapers like *The Independent* or *The Guardian* with a core hub which streams the films directly onto users devices. Be they tablets, enabled TV's or good old fashioned PC's.

Uniquely if you embed a trailer on your site, you are paid 20% of any directly resulting purchase (less tax), thus you are incentivized to encourage your fan base to purchase. Additionally producers of films on the site get a net 50% of the back end revenue too. Films cost just $2.00 or £2.00 and subscriptions start at £10.

We have directors like Ken Loach and Kim Longinotto contributing films as well as Festival winners and hidden gems. It is a really smart way for films to be seen in an environment where viewers want to see them.

**Q – *When you take on a documentary, do you act like a sales agent - take off expenses, then take your commission?***

**Tim** – We are not a sales agent - we are a distributor. We physically supply the films to the end user in the format they require. This is a particularly skilled activity since the needs of clients vary enormously and require individual editing and duplication efforts.

Unlike our competitors, we don't charge marketing costs. That is our investment in your film. We take a 30% commission. Also we report quarterly and pay within 14 days of invoice. We understand that your share of the licence fee is your money, that you need it and timely payment is a hallmark of the Mercury difference.

**Q – *What do you think of the global theatrical market for documentary films?***

**Tim** – The global theatrical market is illusory! 30% of the films we take on get some 'semi-theatric' exposure but unless you have *Senna, Exit Through The Gift Shop* or *Mrs Carey's Concert*, the marketing costs of a theatrical release will normally swallow up any additional income you might make through TV, DVD etc. With the advent of VOD - a film now has to be really special to justify theatrical exhibition. The truth is that with the exception of Michael Moore, Greenwald, Alex Gibney, and their ilk, theatrical distribution is for many directors an expensive ego driven vanity exercise.

**Q – *Is there anything such as presales in the documentary world?***

**Tim** – Occasionally but it has to be very special, offer unique access and must be offered by a proven team. If you can bring me exclusive access to Obama or Strauss-Kahn then let's talk!

**Q – *What tips can you give filmmakers to make their projects appeal to a global***

*audience?*

*Tim* – Choose a global subject of global appeal, have a counter-intuitive approach and tells us something we don't know. Above all, understand it has to be entertaining.

### Q – Do you handle one off documentaries or must they be series driven?

*Tim* – Generally, Mercury focuses on one off's but we are doing some series. Do understand we were sent over 900 docs in the last year and just 30 got selected for global distribution. It is hugely competitive to win a Mercury distribution contract. Buyers know that the Mercury brand is synonymous with quality and it is a huge task maintaining and improving our offerings each year but that is what we strive to do.

### Q – For a series, is there a number of episodes that people would prefer?

*Tim* – It's not possible to answer this as each case is different but three one hours can work well if the material can sustain - as this becomes promotable.

### Q – What are the common mistakes you think filmmakers make?

*Tim* – That they should be filmmakers - seriously filmmaking is not for the faint hearted. Remember you're making your film for an audience, and length doesn't equal satisfaction. On a practical level avoid commercial music, get release forms signed and have a basic knowledge of fair use/fair dealing when using material which isn't yours.

### Q – What advice would you give a new documentary filmmaker?

*Tim* – Plan for post before you shoot!, Don't borrow money, Understand that for 99% of you film-making is a lifestyle choice not a career, so enjoy the process and celebrate your success's however they may come to you.

# CHAPTER EIGHT
# PRODUCTION

## THE DOCUMENTARY
## FILMMAKERS HANDBOOK

*Q – Did you always produce documentaries?*

*Agi –* I didn't do any documentaries. I started as a sales rep bringing French films to the US. Then I started producing my own feature films, but was having trouble getting them made. One night, I met Stacy Peralta at a party. I didn't know much about him other than he had been a famous skater. But then I saw the Spin magazine article about Dogtown and the Z-Boys. I knew the Vans people because I had a snowboarding feature project in development and I was trying to get them to put money into it. I called Vans and asked them if they wanted to invest in a documentary. I had another company who said they were interested and they had similar demographics, but they fell out. Vans said they would finance the whole thing in order to help me out because they had seen me work hard. If you're passionate and work hard people are going to want to work with and help you. They didn't give us a lot of money, but they gave us total creative control. Jay Wilson, the head of Vans didn't even look at a cut. I said, *"Jay, you have to come in and take a look."* He got there and said, *"You look tired. I'm taking you to lunch."* And he still never saw the cut. He totally trusted us.

*Q – Was it easier to get things going after Dogtown & Z-Boys?*

*Agi –* People started calling me back. It really was a calling card. I'd get a call a week with someone saying they had a project just like *Dogtown & Z-Boys.* So I would ask them what the story was and they didn't have one. They didn't understand that concept wasn't enough. I'd explain that skateboarding has a core audience, but beyond that no one really knows about it. I didn't know skating, but I know that Madison Avenue designers were designing skate clothing. When you have a wider audience you need to stay true to the core, but you try to find a way to make it appealing cross-culturally. Skating, snowboarding and surfing appeal to people who don't do it. So really do your homework. When we were doing press, some of the journalists had never seen the film. How can you ask questions that way? It is the same thing with producing. You have to know whom you're talking to and ask intelligent questions if you want them to help you.

---

 www.agiorsi.com

**Q – What are you looking for when you're coming up with a new documentary film idea?**

*Agi* – A documentary is much harder than a feature. For investors, I do warn them – we have an idea, a concept and a vision, but until you do your interviews, you really don't know what will happen. We thought one person would be the main story, but they weren't. But you have an idea and you have to write a treatment. A documentary is always made up of people who have interesting stories and then you have to know how to tell it. So your interviews are crucial and because we shoot film, not tape, you have to lead them into what you want. They cannot go on and on. You have to find the sound bites.

**Q – Do you transcribe your footage?**

*Agi* – Yes. We hire people to do that. With Stacy, he makes a notebook out of the transcripts and then he writes the scripts. And while he's doing all of that, my job is to do research and bring in the visuals that Paul Crowder, our editor, needs. Then Stacy and Paul find a real interesting way to tell the story. I think that's why our films have been so successful. I had a project with Steven Spielberg and he was in two or three of our meetings. He said, *"You want to make sure that anything the audience sees, they haven't seen before. If they have, they will click off."* I think that's a problem for a lot of documentary filmmakers. Sometimes we'll do a whole act and if it doesn't work, we have to start all over again.

**Q – Do you deal with any of the nuts and bolts of the business side of the filmmaking?**

*Agi* – Yes. I like to write the checks. I guess I'm an entrepreneur at heart. I don't use payroll as I like to keep as much money in the coffer and on the screen. One reason to use payroll is that they include worker's comp. Instead, you can go to the state, which isn't that bureaucratic, and fill

## AGI'S FILMS

**No Room For Rockstars**
*(2011)*

**Lost Angels: Skid Row Is My Home** *(2010)*

**The Achievers: The Story of the Lebowski Fans**
*(2009)*

**Amazing Journey: The Story of The Who** *(2007)*

**Pipeline Masters** *(2006)*

**Once in a Lifetime: The Extraordinary Story of the New York Cosmos** *(2006)*

**Riding Giants** *(2004)*

**Dogtown and Z-Boys**
*(2001)*

225

out the paperwork. You can call them on the phone for help. It's not expensive and you get money back at the end if you've gone the whole year and not filed enough claims to use it all. Then you need to have E&O insurance, which is expensive. It used to be $10,000 and now it may be more like $15,000. You need it. You can't get a distribution deal without it.

**Q – Do you have to get E&O for each individual show or can you run several productions with one policy?**

**Agi** – You can do that for TV shows, but you can't for documentaries. So for each one, add $15,000 to the budget. They have different polices that are 1 year, 3 years and 5 years and it doesn't start until you have your first showing. So if you think you're going to get into Sundance, then you'll prepare your insurance agent to start on a certain date in January. That means you will have to have a financial backer ready to pay that $15,000. You don't need to clear your music for festival screenings, I try to clear all the stock footage or at least let them know you are going to be working with them. But it's always best to not show it in public without insurance.

**Q – Is that something you can get once you have a deal?**

**Agi** – Yes. But you have to have it in your budget from the outset.

**Q – What are some of the tricky parts of clearing footage?**

**Agi** – Well, with festivals you're always cutting until the last minute. For Sundance, you find out around Thanksgiving and it has to be done by late January. You try to get at least an online so you have to find people who are willing to work late hours around Christmas and New Years. So we don't clear all the stock footage, but we try to make sure that no one is going to have a problem with us using it. After the festival, we like to have a public screening of what is not the final cut and through audience reaction at various screenings to see what needs to be tweaked. If a distributor wants it right there and then, and they want you to make all sorts of cuts that you don't want to make you can tell them no. But you make the cuts you want to make.

When Pitching:
"Get into the room and don't leave anything behind. They could show it to someone else and misrepresent it."

**Q – What should documentary producers think about when doing interviews?**

**Agi** – You have to do your research and as the producer you want to facilitate that by getting all the information. You want to meet the person, but don't have them start telling you stories because you want it fresh.

**Q – Do you get your interviewees to sign releases?**

## PRODUCTION BINDERS

The key to a successful production is being organized. A production binder will do the trick. So get an good, old-fashioned 3-ring one and label the dividers. Here are some suggested categories.

Releases Legal

Interview Questions

Subject list and contacts

Location Information

Production Schedule

Delivery Requirements

Archival footage contacts

Insurance information

Deal points

Crew list and contacts

Funder Contacts

Corrspondence

Local Hospitals and Police

Editing Notes/Footage Log

Voice over drafts

Shot list

**Agi** – Yes. You try and get it before the interview, but sometimes it doesn't happen until after. If you're shooting in a public place or a nightclub or something, then you want to put a sign on a door saying, *"Anyone entering here can be filmed."* Then you put the date and the name of the project and you have your cameraman shoot it because you won't be able to get everyone to sign that release. And then you have to get permission from the owner of the place – a location release. Unfortunately, we have trusted people we knew like in *Dogtown* where we had someone say they would sign a release after an interview and then they started getting funny. *"I'll get my lawyer to look at it. Oh, I lost it. I'll meet you for lunch and then I'll sign it."* Then he stood us up. Never signed it, although he gave us two interviews and then he sued. E&O covers it, but it's an expense you don't want your financial backer to have.

**Q – If they've agreed to be interviewed and you film it, isn't that good enough?**

**Agi** – Not unless they say so on camera. It's a delicate balance when you have known a person all your life. I wouldn't do that again. I might interview them, but until they sign, I might prepare everybody to not use the interview. Usually they are playing a game with you so you have to be wary of it and have a game plan.

**Q – Are they usually asking for money?**

**Agi** – Oh, it's all sorts of weird dysfunctional psychology. Dysfunctional people. And there are a lot of them around. And sometimes they make the most interesting characters.

Usually money does not pass hands for interviews in documentaries. But we do like to pay whatever we can out of the budget. It's good will. And there's no set rate.

**Q – What if you film on a beach, do you still have to put notices up?**

**Agi** – You are supposed to get location permits. We try to avoid public places. We would shoot at someone's house, so it's their beach. But if you're a student filmmaker or you say you are, you can take that risk.

**Q – Do you make the schedule?**

**Agi** – Yes. I do the shooting and post-production schedules. You don't want to do more than two interviews a day because it's exhausting mentally for the director. You want to scout the locations as much as possible. Maybe scout in the morning and shoot in the afternoon. The way we do our meals is that I go out and buy it. I rent a van for transportation. I have worked on big commercials and they have trailers and all of that – that's not for me. That's all so time consuming, just like payroll. But know whom you're going to interview and they will co-operate. You will have your "A" interviews and your "B" interviews. Our documentaries are complicated because we have so many different elements – we use Super 16mm film to shoot and the stock footage comes in on all sorts of video formats and Super 8mm. So our post-production budget is always high. If you're planning on going to film-out, then you have to prepare to go to 24 fps instead of 30 fps. So you have to consider all that technology. Then you have to consider going HD in the lab. So if you're shooting on Beta, which is 30 fps, then you're going to have to go to 24fps HD so you have to have people who understand that.

**Q – Do you shoot PAL ot NTSC, or is that not relevant?**

**Agi** – We don't have to worry about that because

we shoot film. But our stock footage on *Once In A Lifetime*, we like to get on PAL. And because a lot of it was from the BBC, we were able to do that. There's a process called Slow PAL, which is a process that takes the 25fps to 24fps, but not everybody does that. They slow it down 4% and it's so much better.

**Q – Is there anything to know about working with labs or other technological aspects?**

**Agi** – It's really important to get people who understand what you are doing. I work with different companies and they're so big you need to establish a relationship with someone in tech. Don't just talk to your salesperson. Go over to the company and meet the tech and see if they have some sort of interest in your project.

**Q – How much time do you schedule for filming an interview?**

**Agi** – An hour. Then we always budget for a second and maybe a third interview. So we do the first interview and Paul will start cutting. We might get two thirds of the way done with the film and realize that we've taken a different turn. So we might need another interview. We never set aside a week to interview people. If you have ten people that you need to interview and some live in Hawaii or Oregon, you try to group them together in one place. You try to get deals with airlines, though that's tough to get. If you go business class you can take more bags and it's worth it because it's like $150 to upgrade and you get to take twice as many bags. If you don't, you might pay $150 for every extra bag! Just make sure that they're an airline that does upgrades. The other thing that you can do with the airlines is ask them to waive their requirements.

**Q – What's the standard crew that you use?**

**Agi** – It's very small because we want people to be comfortable. We didn't use grips and gaffers in *Dogtown* but we did in *Riding Giants* and subsequent films. So one grip, one gaffer, one camera assistant, sound and a sound assistant, I get an assistant if it is local, the director and me. That's it.

**Q – What makes a good documentary crew?**

**Agi** – We want them to co-operate and not say, *"Oh, I am the grip, I can't be a gaffer. I am a sound assistant, I can't pick that up."* That's why we like to buy a lot of good will. We like to get people who are into the subject as they will work for less money. We give them a per diem. We mostly shoot non-union. Or I should say, the crew is DGA, but we can get waivers because it's lower budget. You don't need to have an AD and we couldn't because that would be too many people. All the guilds do want indie and doc members so they have these low budget agreements to work with them.

**Q – Do you have contracts with your crew?**

**Agi** – No. It's usually just a day hire. Although, on this last film with Studio Canal, they informed us when we were turning in our deliverables that they needed a "work for hire" on everybody, which I never used. That says that you were hired to do this job and you have no rights to it so you won't sue. Most people don't use it because if they did get a part of the film, they would have a contract stipulating so. It kind of pissed our crew off to go back and ask them to sign it. And it pissed us off because it took a lot of time. I was working with executive producers who had no experience and were very difficult. If you are working for a company or studio, you should ask to see the delivery requirements when you do your budget.

**Q – Any tips on paying people?**

**Agi** – Pay them right away. That's a great thing to negotiate rates with because a lot of people have to turn in an invoice or go through payroll and it takes awhile. I like to pay them on the day or the next day.

*Q – Any tips when putting together a budget?*

*Agi* – We don't use PA's, but we do use messengers so I like to budget a lot for that. I like to put meals in as that's good will. I like to put entertainment in as well. So you pad it a little bit and that's where you can go when you need extra money for something. Post-production, you always need to budget more because things come up. Also I know how much of a budget my funder is willing to give and so I make my budget for what I think I can do it for, then pad a little bit and see where I am. In our films, we put in a lot in for music and stock footage – especially for stock footage expenses like ordering tapes. For music, people forget that you have to go out and buy CDs. You should put a little more in for transfers. We have our own decks for duplication, so we still put in for bays and since we don't have to actually charge then I can pad there a little bit. We put in a lot for graphics and titles because they make a difference.

*Q – How do you find out how much things cost?*

*Agi* – I just go back to my previous budgets and see how much I really spent. So you could look at a friend's budget on a comparable film and do the same. Then there's the old stand by of calling around and getting quotes from vendors.

*Q – How do you get good deals from rental houses and vendors?*

*Agi* – Most of my crew owns their equipment. But once again, you take whatever your subject is and look at the vendors. The sound facility that just won an Academy Award, they have a guy who they are mentoring who is a skater! So they're going to want to work with me. Always try to get to the top person and try to get them to help you out. With our sound we worked with Dane Tracks who won an Academy Award for *The Matrix*. They asked us how much we had in the budget for post sound and we had nothing. So we made a deal – if we

## NEGOTIATING GOOD DEALS

*9. Offer screen credit or product placement to help reduce the budget. Many businesses not related to the film industry will warm to the idea of being part of a movie.*

*10. Be a comparative shopper. Call various places to get the best price.*

*11. Go into a negotiation with a top dollar amount you will pay. You can always use the car buying "walk out" ploy if the vendor cannot meet your price.*

*12. Shoot in states like Oregon that have no sales tax, or Louisiana that offer rebates on sales taxes.*

*13. Always ask for discount. If you can't get it, try to get something thrown in for free.*

*14. Thank you gifts, such as a bottle of liquor or premiere tickets, go a long way.*

*15. Make sure you get all quotes in writing. This will help avoid any misunderstanding and make it harder for the company or individual to retract their offer.*

get a distributor then we'll pay you what you should get, which I did negotiate down a bit. And I did pay. They sent me a letter saying I was the first person who ever paid. So when I went to them with my next film, they worked with us. So be really direct and open. You are dealing with businesses and they need to, not necessarily make money on you, but if you can bring them something that covers their overhead and helps people they are mentoring, that's a way to do it. And if you think you're going to be high profile and are going to be interviewed by the news or magazines, you can say that we will always mention them.

**Q – Is it hard to do if you don't have a track record like you did with Dogtown?**

**Agi** – No. On *Dogtown*, I called the Jimi Hendrix people and nobody knew who we were. We said that we didn't have any money, but we could send them Vans shoes. And they said OK. They wanted shoes! The richer people are, the more into it they are. So if you really believe in what you're doing and you're not bullshitting people, they'll respond.

**Q – How do you go about raising money?**

**Agi** – Well, with *Dogtown* it was a niche market and Vans was right in there. They had the first skate shoe and when I called and said Stacy Peralta was the director – they said, *"Stacy was our first sponsored skater. He was responsible at 16."* And when I told them he had been directing TV for ten years, they were in. The whole cost of the film was less than what they would spend on one commercial. They got a lot of bang for their buck, but I was dealing with a very creative person in Jay Wilson. And what I've found in my whole career is that if you go to the top, they're not afraid to spend money. They're not going to say no because they're afraid of losing their jobs if they say yes. I had to talk Jay into taking a producer's credit – that's the kind of person you want. And if you aren't dealing with the top person and you're not getting anywhere, as long as it's not stepping on toes, you can try calling someone else there and find a rapport. My agent told me this a long time ago, *"When you go into pitch, find out what they want and what they are about and don't pitch them something that they are not going to be interested in. Because the next time you call they're not going to be as open."* Also, you don't want to waste their time. Make sure to be nice to the assistant because that person may be an executive some day. And they may be able to give you an insight into whom to call.

"Make sure to be nice to the assistant. That person may be an executive someday."

**Q – What is important to put into a proposal?**

**Agi** – It depends on the project, but try not to send too much. Try and get into the room and don't leave anything behind. They could show it to someone else and misrepresent it. If they have to show their boss, just say that you will come back and show it to them. Get them to call your representation if you have some. And if someone isn't interested, then don't push things.

**Q – Any tips on dealing with distributors?**

**Agi** – You want to make sure that the trailer is representative of your film. Same goes for artwork. Get them to send you mock ups and if you don't think that it's right, see if you can get some money to do it yourself. We are very fortunate because our genre is something that we know more about than they do and they want us on their side.

**Q – How about advice on dealing with lawyers?**

**Agi** – Get a good one and get all your contracts and releases airtight. Try to establish a relationship with one to the point of being a friend so you can call them at midnight if things go horribly wrong.

**Q – What are things to think about should things go wrong during production?**

**Agi** – I always try to have a personal rapport with crew and the subjects so I can explain what we're doing from the start. With crew, I say that there are only three of us and if they're going to be difficult, don't hire them if they can't work the way you are working. Be open. Also if the police come and you don't have a permit, be very apologetic and plead ignorance. It's a lot easier to do when you don't have big cameras. Be aware that they can confiscate your equipment. I'm not sure about your footage.

**Q – What are the most common mistakes that documentary filmmakers make?**

**Agi** – They don't choose good interview subjects and they don't realize how important it is. Interviews should be intimate. And you don't want it to be all over the place. It's OK to get different backgrounds, but you want to pick that intimate angle so it doesn't get too busy. We don't do cinema verite because we find it distracting and you don't get that intimacy. You don't get their eyes. If it's an action film then you don't want too much of the sport or else it becomes sport porn. You need to have story, feeling and drama.

**Q – What advice would you give a new documentary filmmaker?**

**Agi** – Develop relationships with people and bring the right project to the right person and don't bug them. Make them want to talk to you. Asking people for advice makes them want to help you.

*Q – What do you discuss with a director before a shoot?*

*Melissa* – We normally discuss what the doc is about. They usually have a script of where the documentary is headed. Then we discuss the style, composition, framing, eyelines, lighting, what kind of camera we are going to shoot on – that kind of thing. On the actual shoot days, we discuss the scene and what they want to get from it.

*Q – What do you show to the director before you start rolling?*

*Melissa* – On set I have a monitor set up next to the camera for the director. While I am lighting the scene they are looking at how I'm lighting it. Usually, we don't have a lot of time so we have to be pretty quick. I have someone sit in as the subject and then have the director make adjustments before we bring in the actual person. In cinema vérité, I usually work with people where I have a trust with them. If it's a situation where we can't have a monitor then they are right next to me directing me as to what to get.

*Q – How do you coordinate movement if you're hardwired to an audio person?*

*Melissa* – Most situations call for wireless nowadays. If we are having frequency issues on set then we will hardwire. But most of the time it is wireless lavs being used. Booms are normally hardwired. Normally, the audio person is behind the cameraperson so they see where we're going and they can move with us and we're not bumping into each other. The worst thing that can happen is that you're tethered to the soundman, they aren't watching where you are going and they tug on the camera and mess up the shot. The other thing is to make sure that they don't end up in the shot. But nowadays, most situations call for wireless so they are off behind us well out of the way. The other thing we discuss is time code. For shooting B roll or a one-camera situation, I will record run and start with hour one. And if it's a multi-camera situation then we will do time of day and JAM sync the cameras together. Then we will do a slate or a hand clap so that all the cameras are in sync for post.

*Q – What is JAM sync?*

*Melissa* – It's when you come out of time code out of one camera, usually the A camera, and then you go into time code on camera B or camera C. So that way they are all matching time of day in the time code.

*Q – What format is most prevalent today and what would you recommend for a beginner?*

*Melissa* – For a theatrical release, I recommend shooting 1080i/24p. I usually shoot true HD, which is 1920 x 1080. It's the easiest way to finish on film. If you are releasing to the web, then most people shoot 720p as it takes up a lot less storage space. More people are shooting HD these days than film. I like the feel of 24p because it's more movie like to me. It's got a jittery motion that feels more like film. Right now, the Panasonic HPX-500 is a good camera to shoot with. I like where all the switches and menu settings are. It's shoulder mounted which is better for your back. It shoots on P2 cards and can hold four so you can shoot up to four hours of HD without swapping them out which is great for documentary.

*Q – 30 frames per second gives you sharper images than 24. Is there ever a time when you would want that?*

*Melissa* – Personal taste. It would be easier to edit 30. I do a lot of my own editing on documentaries because of budgetary constraints. When I shoot 1080/24p and I am editing in Final Cut Pro, I have to do something called a reverse telecine. So I normally edit in a 23.98 timeline in order to deal with the 24p. Otherwise I am going to have stuttering in the motion. In fact, I think the newer versions of FCP may even do this conversion automatically.

*Q – With the use of DSLRs now, what are some of the pros and cons?*

*Melissa* – The two most common now are the 5D and 7D and they are different. The 5D has a much larger sensor and it's more equivalent to shooting anamorphic or 65mm film. Because the sensor is so large, it has a very shallow depth of field. So where I would normally shoot at f-stop 2.8 on a HD camera, on a 5D I would shoot at a 5.6 or even an f-8 in order to increase the depth of field. It's very hard to pull focus, especially for documentary where you are not measuring the distances and you are eyeballing it. With the 7D the sensor is smaller, so you don't have a lot of the focus issues that you have with the 5D. You have more options for video because that camera was designed more for video. With the 7D, you also have some frame rate selections that you don't have with the 5D. But with both cameras it's hard to keep a nice steady shot because the cameras are so small. It helps to have a brace of some kind like the ones made by Red Rock. I don't recommend changing the iris as you shoot because you can see it switch. It's not a smooth transition. Both cameras can overheat if you leave them on too long and for long interviews that can be an issue. But a big plus with the cameras is that for relatively little money you can shoot true HD.

**Q – What about audio and lenses?**

**Melissa** – Most people are handling the audio with Zoom recorders. The H2 or the H4 are really good. You would do a hand clap when you start and there's a program in post called Pluralize that recognizes the wavelengths and matches the wavelengths from the Zoom to the camera without using time code.

**Q – What would be a good basic light kit to have for a doc?**

**Melissa** – If electricity is not an issue, then I think having an Arri kit is very handy. A 1K with a Chimera and 300 and a 650 for a kicker. And then some smaller units for fill or to light the background are very handy. I also like using a Gekko ring light that works in zones. So if I am working on the fly and I don't have a lot of time to put up a lot of lights, I can get away with the Gekko and turn off a zone to create a shadow towards the camera. It also produces a nice ring in the eyes. If I am doing an interview outside, I like using Flexfills for bounce. If I am going to a place that doesn't have a lot of electricity, then I like to use the ring light because it can be AC or DC powered. Nila lights are good too. They are stackable LED lights. They can be as big or as small as you want and they are dimable. China balls are good too. They are soft and even and relatively low wattage.

**Q – What is a good workflow for managing the media once you've shot it?**

**Melissa** – Mostly I deal with P2 cards rather than tape. I download the footage off the P2

## WORKING WITH CHILDREN

Don't patronize children. Talk to them like adults or they will turn off.

Children don't have long attention spans so keep your questions simple and short.

Children get tired and hungry easily. Be prepared for short sessions and mood swings.

Some children are shy so giving them a prop to play with can open them up. Sometimes it helps to let them use the camera for a while.

You must get a release from the child's parent or guardian in order to use the interview.

With older children, be prepared for them to say the most intimate things right away. Sometimes they may see you as a confessor.

---

cards to one main drive and two back up drives to be safe. I store the back ups and use the main for editing. I always check my footage and make sure it opens up in the editing software, such as using Log and Transfer in Final Cut Pro, before I delete the P2 cards. If I am dealing with tape, I use Log and Capture in FCP when I am back home after the shoot it over. I store the original tapes back at home and don't touch them.

**Q – Have you ever been in an ethical situation where you want to turn off the camera instead of shooting?**

*Melissa* – Yes. For me filming impoverished people is tough. Part of me feels like I am taking advantage of this person. Often times, the answer is no, it's just unsettling. I feel that when I look through the lens it acts like a buffer. If you need to get the shot, it helps when you are looking through the camera because it's like an alternative reality. In doc, the rule of thumb is that you never turn off the camera because you are going to miss something.

**Q – Many times you are shooting people that are not used to cameras. What are some good tips on how to relax them?**

*Melissa* – Usually I turn the tally light off on my camera so people don't know when I am shooting and when I am not. That really helps. When people think they aren't being filmed, that's when they are the most off the cuff and genuine. But generally, the longer you keep the camera rolling and the longer you interview somebody, the more they are going to forget that it's there.

*Q – Are there any practical pitfalls one needs to think about when shooting HD?*

*Melissa* – I like to shoot fairly wide open – like a 2.2 to 2.8 in order to have less depth of field. And I often use an Ace Black Frost filter in order to cut down the harshness of HD. HD can tend to exaggerate the pores in people's skin, it's so detailed.

*Q – What are some tricks to getting smooth shots?*

*Melissa* – When I am shooting 24p, I'm careful not to pan or tilt too quickly because it can look jagged. So I do those slow. When I am shooting with the DSLRs, it's handy to have the Red Rock system so you can do nice smooth hand held shots. Those cameras are tricky because they're so lightweight. You have to add weight to them to get a smooth shots. Tracking shots without using dollies can still be done. The old school method is to use a wheelchair. You could drive slowly by in a car.

*Q – Zooming and quick panning are sort of looked down upon these days in feature films. Is it the same for documentary?*

*Melissa* – It's way more forgiving in a doc. As long as you have a subject that is intriguing and enraptures your audience, they don't notice any of that stuff. You could have poor lighting and out of focus shots, and people will still like it if your subject is interesting. It's more about getting the information across in documentaries. However, you should always try to do your best to limit those things.

*Q – As a DP, are you thinking about the storytelling of your shots such as wide shots and close ups?*

*Melissa* – I always discuss that style before hand. Just like in a narrative film, you have to discuss when to use close ups, medium shots and wide shots. I save my close ups for the emotion such as when people are crying or getting to the importance of a subject. Otherwise, it's better to stick to medium shots for interviews and also good to have wide establishing shots.

"In doc, the rule of thumb is that you never turn off the camera because you are going to miss something."

*Q – What are the common mistakes you see filmmakers make?*

*Melissa* – People who don't put any planning into their documentaries. Some people think because they're shooting video, they don't have to think about style or filters or lightning. And in my opinion it's always best to make things look as good as possible. Young filmmakers sometimes forget about all the tools they have even on a limited budget.

*Q – What advice would you give a new documentary filmmaker?*

*Melissa* – Business sense. Get your money up front as you won't make any money on the back end. Also figure out a way to make money other than documentary filmmaking because it usually takes a long time to make them and sometimes the best projects don't have money associated with them. I'm a union cameraperson, so that's how I do it.

**Q – What is the IMAX format and how does it work?**

*Greg* – In IMAX filmmaking you shoot 70mm film where the frame is 10 times larger than 35mm. That big frame is then projected with a million dollar projector onto a gigantic screen 80 feet tall and 100 feet wide that the audience sits very close to. The reason that these films are so engaging and fun is that the images give you a sense of being there. The IMAX projector is so amazing. Every film frame is pin registered and the celluloid is blown flat against a piece of glass so that you have absolute perfect sharpness edge to edge and in the center. No 35mm projector comes even close to that. So when you're sitting really close, you get a completely filled peripheral view. The effect is stunning. I saw my first IMAX theater film in 1974 at the World's Fair in Spokane, and I'm still mesmerized and awestruck by the experience today. In fact, what's interesting is that an IMAX theater audience doesn't really equate the IMAX experience with other films. They equate it more with other real experiences like a roller coaster ride or a trip to the edge of the Grand Canyon. That's why the most popular of the films have been the true-life adventures. They have enraptured millions of people and grossed lots of money.

The most attended IMAX theater film was our first IMAX Theatre film, *To Fly,* which has been seen by over 100 million people. But our film *Everest* is the highest grossing IMAX theater film to date with a worldwide box office gross of more than $150 million. When I made my first film there were only four IMAX theaters and today there are more than 500.

**Q – How is making an IMAX theater documentary different from a regular documentary?**

*Greg* – You use different ways of writing, directing and shooting. And the result is different. You have a different audience. The films are shorter – usually 40-50 minutes in length. My company owns four cameras, all of our lenses, dollies, cranes, helicopter mounts, etc, so we are able to go out into the field with our team and make one of these specialized films efficiently. We try not to repeat the same mistake twice. We try to test

---

 info@macgillivrayfreemanfilms.com   www.macgillivrayfreemanfilms.com

the limits creatively. We try to utilize advanced technology. For example, our film *Greece: Secrets Of The Past* has the most extensive single CGI sequence that's ever been done in a large format film. That one shot, over four minutes in length, required two years of work.

**Q – IMAX theater films seem to go places other documentaries cannot in order to get that visceral experience.**

**Greg** – That's really important. Obviously, we're running out of some of those places since so many IMAX theater films have been done. So we do a lot of research. I do a lot of reading and subscribe to about 40 different magazines. I'm continually looking for new locations, subject matter and things that I think the audience would be interested in and would work well artistically in a large format. With these films, you don't want to do just a conventional drama like *The King's Speech* or *Jane Eyre*. It wouldn't benefit that much from the format. In fact, it might even subtract from it.. While dramatic features are compelling on a storytelling level, our films are compelling on a visceral, visual and emotional level. What we have been trying to do since *To The Limit* was released in 1989 is to engage more with our characters. Develop more richly etched character stories. And we did well with that film and *The Living Sea, Storm Chasers* and *Everest*. And the films of this decade, *Dolphins, Coral Reef Adventure* and the like, all engage with stories that are wrapped around very interesting people. With *Everest*, it was naturally riveting because it was a life and death struggle. The same thing is true with *Hurricane on the Bayou*. It's about Katrina and has four characters in New Orleans. It's very emotional as it's a story of perseverance, redemption, music and the richness of culture. And our new film, *To The Arctic*, is a touching story about a polar bear family struggling to survive in the changing Arctic environment.

**Q – With the personal approach, has the length of the IMAX theater film gotten longer?**

**Greg** – I'd love to make a film that's even longer. Artistically, it would allow me to do more character development and story telling. But the IMAX theaters need a film that's less than 45 minutes in length so they can show it every hour on the hour. They want 10-13 shows a day. The theater owners tell me that if I make a film that's longer, they'll be less apt to run it. It's harder to do, but you can tell a pretty compelling story in 45 minutes. Winston Churchill said, *"If you want me to make a minute and half speech, it will take two weeks to prepare. If I do a speech that is half an hour long, I could do it right now."* And that's the way I always feel. You have to choose every word, image, piece of music carefully. You don't have a lot of time to mess around and take side journeys.

**Q – How different is the structure to a regular documentary?**

**Greg** – The conventional beginning, middle and end structure is pretty much what you have to grasp in an IMAX theater film. But you can go in different directions. You just don't have a lot of time to go in different directions. Sometimes we start with flashbacks,

1. Remember that you are a guest in someone's home or office and you and your crew must act like guests. Be courteous and clean up after yourselves.

2. Be aware of sound issues like running refrigerators, air conditioners, airplane flight paths, traffic, etc. Scout out the location on the same day of the week at the same time to get a feel for the place.

3. Check out any lighting issues that may come up – or lack of lighting issues.

4. Many docs are shot outside, so check the weather forecast and then protect the equipment and yourself.

5. Try to avoid places that require permits to shoot in like beaches. If you want the beach in the background, try to shoot at a place that looks out onto a beach.

6. Cell phone/internet coverage. Is there access?

7. Insurance. Need it for traveling. For the actual location, keep your crew small and you probably won't need it for most locations.

historical elements, change tenses. We can even do fantasy sequences.

**Q – What kind of documentaries is an IMAX theater film best suited?**

**Greg** – True-life adventures are the best. People want to visit someplace and experience something that they perhaps can't get to. Films that are fiction, even if they're really good fiction, aren't as interesting because you lose the component of truth. When an audience comes to an IMAX theater film, they think they're going to see something that's completely factual and truthful and has been vetted by ten different experts. In a fictional film, the audience has to suspend their disbelief and get into the story. So the the most expensive of our fictional films was *Wings Of Courage*, directed by Jean Jacques Arnaud. It wasn't popular with the public partly because it was fiction. They'd say, *"It was a pretty good story, but it wasn't as good as The Bear."* That was another of his films. They compare it to another fiction film, not an IMAX theater film. Certainly, if we were to do our New Orleans film as a fictional film, I can assure you it wouldn't be as good as a film like *Crash*. You don't want to compete with something that has ten times the budget and expertise behind it. Our films are in the $5 million budget range, so it's difficult to compete with films with higher budgets.

**Q – I've read that the experience is so visceral with an IMAX theater film that when people watched The Coral Reef Adventure, their body temperatures actually dropped.**

**Greg** – There have been those reactions. People sometimes feel nausea with films that involve flying. The vertigo reaction is common when you do a shot at the edge of a cliff. So it's true that the experience is different than seeing a conventional movie. You have to understand how the audience appreciates the medium in order to make a good IMAX theater film. It's rare for a first time director to understand it well enough to make a good film.

*Q – IMAX films also tend to go to dangerous places and situations.*

**Greg** – True. I've almost been killed a couple of times. One time was in Palau when I was shooting from a small airplane and one was in an underwater scene that I was filming for a surfing sequence. Danger is something that you manage. Proper filmmaking technique, no matter what format you are working in, requires that you manage safety issues. I lost my partner in a helicopter crash during the filming of a TV commercial 30 years ago. So the way that we manage safety issues is very carefully. We rarely get a scratch on our sets. We always go slowly when there's an exposure of risk. Going too fast or being so budget driven that you are doing things foolishly or cheaply or unsafely is just something we would never do.

*Q – What are the challenges of shooting with an IMAX camera?*

**Greg** – The challenges are akin to shooting the first Technicolor films which were done with a three strip camera - they weighed a huge amount. Or to shooting the first sound images with the cameras in 1929. The cameras are big and bulky. Add sound dampening and they become even bigger. Put them on a crane and they are even more giant. So it's lugging equipment, planning ahead even more so than a 35mm shoot. Our heaviest cameras weigh about 200 lbs. It's a specialized camera that shoots high-speed slow motion – 100 fps. Our lightest camera is 25 lbs., it only shoots a minute and half of film, but you can mount it on a hang glider, a kayak, a Steadicam or you can hold it. Our customary sound camera that we use is about 100 lbs. and it runs almost silently so we can run sync sound very easily.

The real trick with IMAX filmmaking is that you want to shoot wider than you would in any other format. Far wider. 100% wider and sometimes 200% wider. And you want each shot to last longer so that the audiences can orient themselves. Then their own

## LOCATION TIPS

8. Check to see if there is power at the location for recharging batteries, etc.

9. Aesthetics – does the location work visually for your film?

10. Accessibility – do you need a car? A four-wheel drive truck? Donkey? Knowing this will affect what equipment you can take.

11. Make sure your crew knows how to get to and from the location. Draw them maps in Powerpoint and attach it to the call sheet.

12. Let your crew know where ammenities such as ATMs, gas, food and hospitals are.

13. If you are in a foreign country, have someone with you who knows the culture and knows the language.

14. Get a location release wherever you go.

vision zooms into the subjects and gets captivated by the environment. Moving the camera is a very important thing. You don't want to move the camera sideways too much with a standard dolly. You want to move it forward and backward so that you feel in the space. Try walking and then look sideways as you are walking. You're continually compelled to look forward. Same thing in IMAX. You want to look forward. It took us a long time to understand that. It's harder to do sound work and do the directing work with IMAX simply because the director has to be further away from the subject. There's a lot more space around the subject so you can't cheat things and you can't cut from one character to the other like you can with a normal feature film. You can't film a conversation with over the shoulder shots and cut between them. In IMAX, that would drive you nuts. You have to shoot a conversation in a two shot and you cut your chances of getting a good performance 50%. The struggles are all worth it, though, because if you make a good IMAX theater film, the audience will show up in big numbers and love the experience. It's not feature filmmaking or really documentary filmmaking. It's something completely different. I see myself in this very strange branch of filmmaking doing these highly technical motion pictures on a limited budget.

**Q – Who finances your films?**

**Greg** - Well, believe it or not we are true guerilla filmmakers as most of our films have been financed by our own company. We're completely independent of Hollywood or any other groups or companies. I solely own this company, which has been in operation for 40 years now. We decide what subjects to do and hire writers to get the scripts correct. We do our own marketing, publicity and distribution and essentially try to be a mini, mini, studio in Laguna Beach, CA. We release a film a year and we're always working on at least three or four films at a time. Business people like it because with only 300 IMAX theaters it's something that you can get your arms around and understand and get to know the people in it really well. You form all these great friendships because we are supplying films to these theaters every year. And they're great to work with because most of them are directors of museums and have a doctorate in geology, astronomy or physics and then they run a museum – wow, what a fascinating person to talk to.

**Q – How does the sound camera work?**

**Greg** – We have one sound camera that runs quiet perfectly in sync with the recorders. We record to either a digital recorder or a Nagra running in sync with the camera.

**Q – Do you light many of your films?**

**Greg** – Oh, yes. We have tons of lights. Huge HMI packages that we take on location. You need high contrast with IMAX so it looks super crisp, Sometimes we have trouble getting the lights in places. When we were in Russia shooting the Bolshoi Ballet, we made arrangements to work through Gorky Film Studio and utilize all their lighting. It was all at least 40 years old. We had to eventually bring over one light of our own. But the classic thing was working with all their technicians who were true pros, but had been working with antiquated equipment. They knew all the quirks of the lights. They knew which ones had to be jiggled a certain way. It was so much fun to work with them. On that shoot, we must have had 100 lights working to light that big stage. They were performing *Giselle* with 30 dancers in these beautiful white flowing costumes through smoke. It just looked beautiful. But we had to get a lot of light on the stage because we shot most of it in slow motion. You plan all these things out like you would a conventional Hollywood film.

**Q – How difficult was it to film on Everest?**

**Greg** – On *Everest*, we had a base camp and all we used were small lights. Then, battery operated lights on the mountain. The more character oriented shots I did later on in cold climates so that I could recreate the moment but have more control over the lighting.

**Q – What are some of the more unusual places that you have taken the camera?**

**Greg** – One of the big achievements in *Coral Reef Adventure* was going 350 feet deep, which is well beyond conventional diving equipment. We did 26 dives that deep to do a sequence that lasts two and half minutes. Getting the camera to the top of Mount Everest was a challenge. It had to be lightweight and work at 40 degrees below zero. We had to hire and train a five-person Sherpa team to carry the pieces of the camera up the mountain. I have mounted the camera on jet dragsters and really strange things like the luge, a bobsled, a pair of skis, a surfboard, a hang glider, a rubber raft down a rapid, all kinds of aircraft. We have put the camera on a base jumper and a skydiver. We did this amazing sequence with a sky surfer. That took us two and a half months to plan.

**Q – Presumably the cameras are very robust.**

**Greg** – You do have calamities with the cameras. We have one that's sort of our rough and ready camera, which we are taking to the Alps. It'll be in a crash box and sit in the path of an avalanche. Essentially, that camera is triggered remotely by radio control. But then you have radio transmitters to locate the camera after the avalanche passes.

**Q – How long is the production period for an IMAX theater film?**

**Greg** – The actual shooting period is not too much different than a regular feature film, which is about two to three months. There are times we have shot nine months to a year if we wanted something like spring and winter shots. Sometimes we work with multiple crews. We shot the Greece film in eleven days because we had three crews working concurrently. We had a limited time and permits were hard to come by.

**Q – How much footage is in a magazine?**

**Greg** – The film magazines on the regular cameras are about 1000 feet, which is about

3 minutes. And the smaller camera, is 500 feet or a minute and a half. We end up shooting about 150,000 feet on any film so our shooting ration is about 20:1. On *Coral Reef Adventure* we shot more film than anyone has ever shot for an IMAX theater film. We shot over 100 miles of film. It takes two people about a minute and a half to reload a magazine.

**Q – How careful must you be to not get dirt on the lens?**

**Greg** – Technically, you must be perfect. I was lucky to be trained by Stanley Kubrick so it comes second nature to me now. You check your lenses with columniation tests, film tests for sharpness and color. Distortion. You have to have a carefully checked set of lenses every time you go out. The camera is checked every time you go out for steadiness and flatness, sharpness, breathing quality. You are working at the highest level of perfection – far more precise than 35mm.

**Q – When it comes to editing, is it the standard editing process as on a regular film?**

**Greg** – Pretty much. What we do that's different is that we do a lot of projection. We edit on the Avid and then we match the 35mm work prints to that Avid edit and then watch them in a projection booth on a big screen. We sit close to the screen so that we get close to the IMAX experience and then we go back and re-cut. So you continually go back and forth between the two and that has provided us with the best results.

**Q – How would a new filmmaker who wants to get into IMAX filmmaking go about doing it?**

**Greg** – It's not easy. The best thing is to learn how to make films first in cheaper formats. Start with video, then 16mm, then 35mm so that by the time you are ready to do an IMAX theatre film, you're completely aware of lighting, camera usage, editing and writing, so that you are not wasting time and money. Having said all that, you have to prove yourself as a visual filmmaker. If you're really good at drama, you probably aren't suited for an IMAX filmmaking career. But if you're good visually, and there're probably 20 people I can count off that are, then it may be for you.

### Q – Does digital have an impact on IMAX?

**Greg** – Yes. We use digital all the time for special effects and titling. And in the future we will use it more for image capture. I kind of suspect that digital projection being comparable for IMAX theatre films will be a long time coming. Just because there are not enough IMAX theaters for someone to put up the R&D money to make it happen. I can see us capturing studio images digitally very soon. I have to look at it as a tool that allows me to do things that I haven't done before.

### Q – What advice would you give a new filmmaker?

**Greg** – Never give up on your dream. If you have a desire to make IMAX theater films, never give up on that quest. It's a sensational experience to make one of these films and see it with an audience. It's so immersive that the audience reacts to it in a wide, broad way. And you can see that joy and thrill in their faces. That's the reward. Especially when I watch a bunch of children watching it. I showed a film in Chicago and a teacher came up to me afterwards and told me that taking his students to this film was one of the most rewarding experiences in his whole teaching year. He said that many of the kids will never have the joy of being in that environment or taking an airplane trip like you do in the film and seeing their world from above. That in terms of instruction is far more important than learning how to divide long fractions. On another note, the films, in a way, preserve the wonders of our world and teach people conservation. These kinds of rewards don't make you a lot of money, but they're the reasons I do what I do.

## WORKING FROM HOME

7. Have a safe, dry, stable place to store your tapes and hard drives.

8. Set up an editing station separate from your main computer. Don't hook it up to the internet. This way viruses can't get to it and you can rent it out to make extra cash.

9. Make sure your workspace is separate from your living space. This way you have a place to meet with clients, investors or subjects that feels more professional. Also some tax laws require you having a separate space in order to get deductions.

10. Friends and family might assume that because you work at home you are free anytime - not true! You end up working longer and on weekends so set them straight.

11. Keep your receipts in a safe place so you can claim them at tax time.

12. Keep your office as clean as possible. There's nothing that stifles creativity and productivity more than a cluttered workspace.

**Q – What do you think makes good documentary sound?**

*Giovanni* – The ability to hear and understand every single line of dialogue. And also so that one gets a good idea of what the environment is like where and when they filmed a scene. Something you should let your readers know is that the procedure for gathering sound is a collection of tiny little, almost imperceptible elements that all come together. It's very tricky to put this process into specific words.

**Q – What kind of gear would you choose to get those results?**

*Giovanni* – I would prefer always a boom pole with a microphone on it rather than a wireless microphone. Although, we often film in very noisy environments and we are obliged to use wireless microphones. And sometimes it's good to find a good balance between these two elements: wireless and boom. A trend I see today in documentary is to put a wireless on each character if you have enough money to afford it. Never the less, this is an incomplete way of taking sound. A wireless microphone cuts out a huge amount of the reality that is taking place outside its sound sphere.

**Q – What do you like to talk to the director about before each shoot?**

*Giovanni* – Ideally, I would like to know him or her as a person. And then I would like to hear his or her explanation of his point of view about a specific situation and get to know the human beings that we are going to be filming. It could be five minutes, two minutes, but some kind of orientation is always helpful. Also it would be important to refine those ideas over the course of the day and tailor fit it to what is happening in front of the camera. And most important, I would like the trust of the director. A lot of new directors, and some of the older ones, don't understand this. Sound mixers have had a long history of dismissal from the creative process and it's very, very sad event. A lot of mixers have developed a real body of solutions for solving problems. It would be a great contribution to our art, if the directors would be aware of what we do and all of the things we can bring to the production.

*Q – What do you like to speak to the DP about since you are so intimately involved?*

*Giovanni –* I like to observe the body motion of a cameraperson and try to fit within that precise approach to filming. First, I try not to get in their way! I try to figure out what is the preferential frame size that the camera is using and try to stay out of it – especially if I am using the boom. If I am totally free from the camera, meaning I am wireless, I simply stay back. But I have to tell you that a very important creative element in my creative process comes from the emotional involvement of the sound mixer, and it is missed in a totally wireless set up. Booming allows for very little mistakes and is very gratifying because I am emotionally involved.

*Q – What gear would you recommend for a low budget filmmaker?*

*Giovanni –* Again, the boom. But I know that many new filmmakers cannot afford that approach so the only option is to buy one or two inexpensive wireless mics and connect those right to the video camera and accept whatever comes with that solution. There's nothing wrong with that basic setup for creating the beginning of an exciting soundtrack for a documentary.

*Q – How do you make people, who aren't used to being filmed, comfortable?*

*Giovanni –* I'm Italian so I have an accent plus a quirky sense of humor - so that helps! Sometimes you just put the radio mic on a person and then stay back in quietness. Sometimes just exchanging a few lines explaining what you are doing to the person or introducing yourself to the person can help.

*Q – What do you usually record to these days and what's a good workflow for the media?*

*Giovanni –* We record on a storage media that entails compact flash (CF) and SD cards mostly. This approach has resolved a lot of the problems that used to happen with the old media. These formats have become very stable, but not infallible, and it's very easy with the available software to download the files almost all the time without any loss. I use a compact flash recorder. I own several types of recorders, some domestic and some Japanese. Some with timecode, some without. The sound quality is very good, but not perfect. I'm nostalgic for analog tape. Digital recording has just not matched its quality. It's like painting: watercolors and oil.

As for workflow, sometimes I only record right to the compact flash drive without having to go to an analog recorder. On a more professional shoot, I can record to an internal hard drive recorder as well as an outside compact flash recorder. One of the great variables of most compact flash is battery power. How long will I be able to power my set up? The other is storage capacity. How much can I actually record? Plus we have to factor in the many different sampling rates versus sound/amibence reslotuion ratio.

## GETTING GOOD SOUND

*1. Hire the best sound recordist you can.*

*2. When looking for locations, bear the sound in mind. Traffic, planes and air conditioning units are your enemies. Most natural sounds can be covered up and disguised in post-production.*

*3. Make sure to record a few minutes of "room tone" in each of your locations so your editors can cover their edits.*

*4. A heavy atmosphere track can cover many natural sound problems.*

*5. Avoid using lots of wireless mics as the frequencies can interfere with one another. Also, you are relying on the fact that batteries are not going to give out.*

*6. Your final mix should be done in a studio that handles feature films as opposed to TV programs or news. While these other studios may be cheaper, you will not get the best-shaped sound and end up in the more expensive suite anyway.*

So the equation is pretty varied. But for a low budget filmmaker, quality pro-sumer recorders are adequate. They are reliable, too. What makes one better from another are the chips that convert the analog signal of the microphone to digital format of the recorder.

**Q – Does shooting on a DSLR present any unique challenges for you?**

**Giovanni –** The most difficult thing is being able to deliver sound to an extremely small device that is extremely compact and hardly sound friendly and in the hands of a camera operator who has different priorities then that of the sound mixer. It's always labor intensive in any case to record usable sound directly to any of these still camera devices. The challenge involved in this approach are all the personal dynamics and the human interactions of the various crew members. That is to say being able to blend together and being able to work patiently with devices that are very small or with people who don't have a lot of patience. The best way to shoot with DSLR cameras is to record everything to a separate digital recorder and use a slate to sync - going back to what we call double system recording just like we used to do with film. It's funny. We've walked so far into the future only to go back to the beginning of our history.

**Q – How do you deal with wind and other sound issues?**

**Giovanni –** I always have a windscreen on all my microphones. I have created my own windscreens because what was available a few years ago wasn't very good. Now there are some good ones, but they're very expensive and heavy. When it comes to fabrics of the clothes that people are wearing, a little bit of creativity or as we'd say in Italian, "spirit of observation," can become relevant. Above all, what is important is the phyical positioning of the microphone on the person who is speaking. Where would I put it? Where would I tape it? Is it visible? Those are the choices I have to make. Recently, I had to film a Baptism, and I had the Godfather was not wearing a jacket. I took for granted that I could put a wireless on him and hide the cable. I found myself pretty soon having to rewire him right in the middle of the ceremony and damning myself for not having a little more forethought. Mistakes happen everyday and we should always be very forgiving with ourselves.

**Q – Do you ever get involved in the sound design or sound effects?**

**Giovanni –** Not really. I've recorded sound effects many times, but I'm really a location sound technician. And I don't endorse location sound mixers sitting at a desk and fiddling with programs. I see that as the job of the editor. They are two very different jobs – like being a barber and a cobbler. I don't like to mix them.

**Q – What are the common mistakes you see filmmakers make?**

**Giovanni –** Thinking that what we do on location is something that can be re-created in post-production. Or that the totality of our creation is concentrated on this tiny little thing with glass in front of it called the camera. It's always this big deal with the camera. It's much more than all of that. It's the whole thing. It's you, me, the camera, the recorder, the dog, the background, the talent, the weather – everything has to do with everything. I also believe a lot in the creativity within the movies could come through sound. A lot can be suggested with the creative use of sound in a movie. If you take away the sound element on any TV show or documentary you will have pretty boring series of pictures. The sound can carry many different powerful elements that the visual component doesn't have. Sound makes the viewer think and feel in different ways than the visual.

**Q – What advice would you give a new filmmaker?**

## GETTING GOOD SOUND

*7. Get the mic as close to the subject as possible, maybe 12-18 inches from their mouth. For stationary interviews mic from above with a boom.*

*8. Anticipate from where your subjects are going or coming. Someone may come into a room while you are shooting something else – you need to be able to get that.*

*9. Use people's bodies to shield noise.*

*10. Always use a shock mount for camera mounted mics.*

*11. Use a mic high pass filter to get rid of handling noise.*

*12. Invest in a good pair of headphones so you can tell when something goes wrong!*

*13. Wind is your worst enemy. Stay out of it at all costs. If you have to be in it, shield the microphone as much as possible.*

*14. ONLY use a camera's onboard mic if it is the difference between getting a shot or missing it forever.*

## SHOOTING OVERSEAS

1. Check the weather!

2. Always have petty cash on hand for bribes and last minute fixes.

3. Hire a fixer who knows the local customs, vendors and language.

4. Find a local doctor or dentist that speaks your language.

5. Talk to a local film commission who can supply you with maps, location photos, hotel brochures and other helpful things.

6. Check to see if you need any immunizations in order to travel in that country.

7. Check for poltical unrest or terrorist activity so you are prepared.

8. Find out if the country takes US carnets.

9. Inform your insurers of where you are going to make sure your insurance covers you. If not, have them help you find a local insurance agent and take out full coverage.

10. Set up a Fed Ex/UPS account when you get there.

11. See if you need to set up a separate company and get a local bank account to pay crew.

12. Hire local crew if you can and pay them promptly. They can be de facto fixers.

13. Make sure everyone has a current passport that will not expire during production.

14. Meet with local authorities to find out what filming permits are needed.

15. ALWAYS have a hand on your expensive gear. It WILL get stolen otherwise.

16. Bring extra hard drives to back up your footage and make copies.

17. Make sure you have the right power adapters.

18. Find out if the country is PAL, NTSC or SEACAM so you can playback video properly.

*Giovanni* – Open your ears and follow your heart. As a director, you should never think that you are more knowledgable than the rest of your crew. The best people I've met in my experience are those that know very well when to listen and when to talk. For myself, I always try to remember those that came before and inspire me. For me, it was people like Alan Barker, Trent Wilson, my mentor and Cathy Alexander, a great classical music recording engineer. I spent a lot of time with these people and it helped inform the person I am today. I think that any new filmmakers would benefit a lot from doing the same with their own chosen "elders."

Something that should never be overlooked is the unique contribution we bring to the art of recording sound on location. It should be understood and cherished as the precious beginning - the backbone of any soundtrack. I understand and am aware that these can be very big words for what we do in an age when a movie audience is presented frequently with the multitude of unnecessary, complex, loud sounds recorded and recreated artificially on a Foley stage in an editing room. Indeed, there are a lot of things that are added later that never existed at the time of recording. This could lead a rookie director to understand the role of the audio mixer as an ordinary and tolerated dialogue collector. Once a director has committed to understanding what a soundman does, there are whole different ranges of results that can be achieved.

**Q – It seems that no matter what country or culture you're in, you get really relaxed interviews.**

Ian – The thing is that you have to put yourself in their shoes. Especially in the remote places that we go, most people haven't seen telly. There's that huge void between them and me. Me, too, when I saw a documentary, I thought it was just one guy with a camera. And when I tell people that there's a whole crew of five, they almost feel cheated. A good documentary or show is when you can make it look like it runs so easily. But really it's a lot of people working hard to get it to look like that.

**Q – Any tips on making the interviewee feel comfortable?**

Ian – Some of the stuff we do is set up and a lot of it isn't. Some of those people have never been on camera before and when you have one shoved in your face, it's intimidating and scary. You know that they're the one with the amazing story, so you want it to come over the best way it can. Usually, I will chat to the person beforehand, talking about normal things and not looking at the camera. Just pretending it isn't there. You can also relax them by telling stupid jokes and if they don't like something, they can say stop. There's no pressure. And then you chat and usually they almost forget the camera is there. I tell them to not even think about what they're going to say. Because the reason that we're talking to someone is because they have done something amazing or it's about their life. So they don't have to prepare anything. I don't need a list of questions. I'm going to plug them with question after question so they're not going to have time to think about it or worry about the camera. Also, if they feel their answer has not come over clearly enough, I tell them not to worry and we'll do it again.

**Q – What are the problems with interviewees that you've faced?**

Ian – Sometimes the people that you think are easy to chat to completely freeze when the camera is there. Or the funniest thing is you go to a blacksmith's and it's all rustic everywhere and rundown – like something out of *Lord Of The Rings*. And then you go down the next day to film and they've vaccuumed it, made it clean and the guy's wearing a suit. He's aware that he's showing off his place.

 www.pilotguides.com/tv_shows/globe_trekker

*Q – You come across all sorts of cultures and languages. The one thing that seems to bring down all the barriers is humor. Are you conscious of using it?*

*Ian* – Of course. Telling a joke relaxes people automatically. Humor is the best thing for that in anything like getting a point across or defusing something or just at the end of the day, getting on with people. There's no difference between that person in Mongolia and the one down at the local pub. It's just you chatting and you either get on or you don't, that's life. There's a tendency when traveling to be overpatronizing or overhumble, which is just as bad as someone who is arrogant.

*Q – Are there any special qualities that a documentary or TV presenter should have?*

*Ian* – I think the main ability is about being honest with it because people aren't mugs and they know if you're not being honest. But then sometimes I know there are documentaries where people question and question and wait for the person to say something and say, *"Right, we got it."* The scary thing is the 80% of it is in the editing. The way I say one sentence can be cut between anything and made to be ten completely different emotions. It's frightening. Sometimes it worries me that some film crews take advantage of people who let them film them. Because, even the news has a slant to it and has been cut with a slant to it. Just because it's a documentary people think that it must be true. No. No. No. No. No. You almost have to watch them more because you forget there's hours of editing for that. For a travel program as a host, you can't do anything but be yourself. The viewers aren't stupid. They know if you lie. They know you're making it up if you say, *"That cockroach tasted lovely!"* You almost want to tap into that thing of when the viewer is sitting there, you have to think how they would feel. I'll be talking to some guy and he's a lunatic. I'll then turn to the camera and say, *"This guy is a nutter!"* And when you're sitting there you say, *"Thank God you said it because we are all thinking it."*

*Q – Have you ever had a bad experience in a country when filming?*

*Ian* – Yes. But with filming the show, if you have a really shitty day, you're doing it for three weeks and the next day could be phenomenal. You have to remember that you're also judging a country through filming. Baja California was a nightmare because it was a textbook of everything that could go wrong with filming. We went there at the wrong time of year and the light was flat. All the cameras broke and had to be sent to Mexico City. We only went there because there was this amazing festival in La Paz, which turned out to be village fete in a parking lot. It was so barren. There's no indigenous culture or history. It was a nightmare. There was another time where I was mugged traveling in the streets of Morocco. That's the worst. You realize how vulnerable you are. But also that's why I love Morocco! Even when you're getting mugged you can haggle the price down! I swear to God that's true. The guy goes, *"Give me 100 and I'll let you go."* I said, *"I'll give you 60" "80."* Then I haggled him down to 75. Luckily I had change on me. I probably could have gotten change as well. But I never wanted to go back to Morocco again and it's a sad thing when one thing can completely screw your vision up of a country. So when I got this job, one of my first programs was bloody Morocco. I couldn't believe it! The best job in the world and now I have to go back to Morocco. But after two days, it was heaven.

**Q – How do you choose your interviewees? Do you do a lot of research beforehand?**

*Ian* – Yes. Because it's six months real traveling condensed into two and half weeks, you have to know when to go, when the festivals are. You have to have a rough idea of who you're going to interview. So the producer will go out there for two weeks and try to pinpoint people. And then a director will go a week later and write a script. And then we'll come out, rip the script up and start again. About 50% of it is spontaneous. It has to be or else it wouldn't work.

**Q – How big are your crews?**

*Ian* – Five people. Me, camera and sound, a producer and director. Plus we usually have a fixer, who can sort things out on the ground from the country and a driver. The fixer is usually someone who knows people like the head herdsman or the guy who trains the eagles. And if they don't, they'll go find them.

**Q – Do you always use the same crew?**

*Ian* – No. You have to use different crews or you'll go insane. I can't even go around London for three days with my mates without us driving each other mad. Imagine three weeks away. Oi!

**Q – How important is it to have the right team on board when filming?**

*Ian* – Oh, God, yeah. There might be incredible things going on all the time in incredible places with incredible people, but your crew might be a couple of assholes. It doesn't happen that much. Every now and again it has been a nightmare. Like in Tunisia and Libya, this director was an asswipe. I couldn't work with him. Bizarre as after doing this for seven years, you realize how vulnerable you are. I lost all my confidence. It was like the first job I did.

**Q – Can you choose with whom you work?**

*Ian* – To a certain degree. I try to work with people that I've worked with before. But it doesn't matter if there are new people. And there has to be new people to freshen it up. They bring new ideas to it. If it were the same director, then after three or four programs, the thing would be identical. You wouldn't even be aware that you were slipping into patterns of where to stay or what to do.

**Q – You also shoot some Super 8mm as well, right?**

*Ian* – Yeah. And we have a small back up digital camera to go along with the Digibeta. I love those small cameras because you can really get in there even though the quality is not as good. Sound is a bit of a hassle as well. But soon, you'll be using a matchbox and half the people will be unemployed. And with HD, it's frightening. But that's why I like working with big crews because everyone is concentrating on their job. Then you get the best because you're not doubling up and losing quality. These days we're struggling to even make them because every broadcaster wants them cheaper, but of the same quality.

**Q – How may times a year do you go off and shoot a program?**

*Ian* – At the beginning, it was about six or seven months. Not all at the same time or else you would go insane. Now I only do about two months maybe three.

**Q – Sometimes on the show you have to eat really weird stuff like sheep's eyes. How do you deal with that?**

*Ian* – In a way, you have to just swallow it! Literally! It's not going to kill you. And whether the camera is on or not, in those situations you have to try anyway. And most of the people are not going to be offended. They know that you have never eaten that kind of rubbish in your life. They're almost chuckling to themselves. But if you're in a small village in Morocco and they're giving you lamb and that's what they eat, then that's more likely to cause offense if you don't like it. You just have to chew, chew, chew.

**Q – What is the worst thing that you've had to taste?**

*Ian* – A cockroach. That was in Cambodia. I had to spit that out on camera. But probably if you served that up and you didn't know what it was, it probably wouldn't taste too bad. But because you have that thing coming toward you and it's just a cockroach that you have down in your fridge, it's a different ball game. I used to be a vegetarian before I did the program since I was thirteen. And that was one of the hardest things about doing the program - knowing that I would have to eat the meat!

1. Relax your interviewees by telling jokes or talking about non-subject issues.

2. Don't schedule more than two or three interviews a day so that you stay fresh.

3. Keep your subject from saying things in pre-interviews. It's hard to recapture that magic in the second go around.

4. Be honest with your subjects and they will open up to you.

5. Keep eye contact. This keeps your subject engaged, so don't look through your notes while they are talking.

6. Don't speak while your subject is speaking. Active listening is good for day to day conversations, but it will wreak havoc in your edit sessions if your voice is there.

7. For more formal interviews, have your subject repeat the questions as part of their answer.

*Q – What are the some of the risks involved when doing travel documentaries such as dealing with unstable political situations?*

*Ian* – We haven't had much trouble because we do research on that. But things do crop up. Stupid things. Like in Haiti where we're driving in government vehicles and the crowds are on the streets at midnight. Any crowd situation can be a bit scary. Other shows we've got caught up in a couple of riots and stuff like that. *Globetrekker* isn't politically motivated and only skims the surface. We only give you a taste of the country. And I don't want to go to a country that is potentially volatile anyway. It's only a lighthearted travel program. I'm not going to die making television.

*Q – Have you had any weird situations with animals?*

*Ian* – That's a bit personal, don't you think?! I got stung by a two-inch size ant that hurt like hell. That was in Guiana. They said we wouldn't see any wildlife. That was when I put my hammock on a tree that these ants were going up. And of course at night, I put my hand on it. They had these fingers coming out of their abdomen. I had to put my finger in a cup of water for a couple of hours. Also, we went to Katmandu to film in a monkey temple. The director stepped on a baby monkey. These things are big and could rip you to shreds in a couple of minutes. Ten of them are snorting at you. The director's hiding behind me and they're grabbing my trousers to get to him because they know it's him. A monkey jumped out of a tree and onto the back of his trousers and took a little bite. He's only been filming for two hours and the director's already been bit up the ass by a monkey. He's like, *"It's OK. It didn't cut the skin."* Then he looks down and there's blood everywhere. We took him to the hospital and got rabies jabs. He was alright, but he was a jinx, that guy. In Madagascar, he fell down a sewer walking back while he was doing a shot. He also got mugged in Rio on the beach while snogging some girl.

*Q – Do you have any advice about taking equipment into foreign countries?*

*Ian* – Keep your bloody eye on it.

*Q – Do you take it on the plane with you or do you put it in the cargo hold?*

*Ian* – God, no, we couldn't cart it all. What we take on the plane is the rushes (dailies), the tapes, the cameras and the sound equipment. I've had stuff nicked in Sweden in a posh five star hotel. It doesn't matter where you are. You have to keep your eye on it. We've had a $20,000 lens nicked in Uzbekistan from the back of the van. We get back and there are a bunch of fourteen-year-old kids waiting for us asking us how much we are going to buy it back for. They didn't know what it was, but we had to give them $200 to get it back.

*Q – Have you ever had any delays in getting things in and out of countries?*

*Ian* – Oh, God yeah. In Syria, they wanted to go through all of our tapes to make sure there wasn't anything bad on them. But I think even they got bored of looking at them. I would. Forty tapes at a half hour each of me yakking on. It was more protocol really. But there were times when your kit doesn't turn up. So we're waiting in the airport for 24 hours and going mad because we're losing days. But then the kit turns up and we've lost a day and we're buggered.

*Q – Do you do the voice over in the country?*

*Ian* – No. We do it in London. You have to cut the whole thing up to know where anything comes in. I hate voice over. If you listen to my voice over it sounds like a different person is reading it.

*Q – Do you write it?*

*Ian* – No. The voiceover has to be right because it is facts and figures. It's not a personal journal, the voice over. It's more information lead.

*Q – Do you sit down with them and go over it?*

*Ian* – Not really. They're picking up information all along. They know roughly what they want to say in that

## INTERVIEW TIPS

8. Try not to be too encumbered by people and equipment when interviewing. It's intimidating otherwise.

9. If a subject is lying to you or being difficult, you can confront them on it as long as you know you're right.

10. Don't speak too much. It's not your question that is important – it's their answer. Also it's a human reaction to fill in silences so they might give you more if you keep your mouth shut.

11. Don't ask yes or no questions. Pat answers make for boring interviews.

12. Ask your interviewees how they felt during the events you are chronicling. This will get, literally, to the heart of the answer.

13. Do your research before you interview anyone. They will respect you more (and give better answers) if they know you took the time to learn about them or their field. And they will know!

14. Have water nearby in case you or your interviewee's mouth gets dry.

segment. People ask me if I go into the edit room. Who wants the bloody presenter in the edit room? Worst nightmare for anyone. And that's not my job. I don't know what the director's vision is.

**Q – How much footage do you end up with on a three-week shoot?**

*Ian* – Some directors squirt, and squirt and squirt and then try to patch it together in the edit suite. The one we did on Alaska, I think we had 17 half hour tapes, which is the shortest ever. That's only eight and a half hours for a one-hour show. So that's extraordinary. Because when you're interviewing someone, I'll be chatting to someone to get stuff and you're going to use a minute or less in the program. Sometimes we'll come back with 40 hours of tape, which is crazy.

**Q – How long is the actual post period?**

*Ian* – When they come back they have three weeks to edit.

**Q – Do the producers pick up any indigenous music to put in the program?**

*Ian* – Oh, yeah. They have some great composers who put it all together.

**Q – Do you have any advice for a travel documentarian?**

*Ian* – The worst crime is a lack of imagination and a lack of flexibility. When you're traveling you cannot be rigid because you can't control situations. You can't be rigid to your script. You might write a beautiful script and no one turns up. You have to be in a state of flexibility or you're going to be shafted and everyone is going to be on each other's nerves. You have to have the balls and the experience to say, *"That's crap. Let's try to do something else."* They're the best directors for me. We went to a festival where there were four Peskies with a top hat and a feather coming out. They were coming up to the camera making noises and going backwards and forwards. And I was saying, *"Am I jaded? Have I seen too much? Or is this bollocks?"* No, this is bollocks and they're just taking the piss and I couldn't stop laughing. You can get into that when you're abroad. You have to have patient like you've never had to be. Forget filming, just the logistics of traveling. That's why most of the people on this are people who have done a lot of traveling. But then again, sometimes the spontaneity of someone who's never done it before is exciting.

### Q – Is there anything you would tell people to avoid?

*Ian* – Hippie travelers. Avoid them like the plague! I always travel with a hippie baseball bat wherever I go just to clear them out! Those dirty, crusties that sit in the corner and tell me that they're the only ones really experienced in the country. We're all fake and they're all real. They're so free. That one cracks me up because they're the tightest group you're ever going to meet. They've got such a long list of criteria that you have to fit before they'll talk to you. What pisses me off is that they're running on the mysticism that people won't challenge them because it's Mr. Jones on the corner. No, he's an arrogant wanker. I've actually heard one of them say that they were just as poor as the locals. That's an insult. They're there because they are the new middle class rich colonials. And their money will last a hell of a lot longer. They drive me insane. In reality, 95% of the people on this Earth couldn't even dream about stepping on an airplane. So if you can travel, you are rich. So have the balls to say that you are rich and lucky.

### Q – You must meet some amazing characters when you do your shows?

*Ian* – You are humbled every time. We were walking around the back of a town in Mongolia and this guy comes out of a shitty little garage covered in oil. We started chatting and he has four degrees in metallurgy, speaks seven languages and is working for two pence an hour. And I'm walking around in my stupid shorts and I can't even speak English properly. Or the A-bomb victim who survived Nagasaki. It's a once in a lifetime thing to meet these people. Every single job, I thank my lucky stars that I'm on it. I cannot believe that I do this. If you do the trips that I have done you will talk about it and bore people senseless until the day you die. I have done 55 of them. I'm the ultimate travel story bore. I have no friends left. No, not really.

**Q – Without insurance, what problems could befall a filmmaker or producer?**

*Kent* – About a year ago a props person running an errand lost control of his car and crashed headfirst into a mother and two children. The medical bills alone ran over a million dollars. A grip truck recently skidded off the side of a mountain road and crashed totaling not only the truck but all the equipment. During a multi-million dollar production the lead actor developed cancer and could not continue shooting. Without insurance the responsibility for these devastating financial losses would have fallen directly on the production company.

Insurance takes your individual risk, quantifies a premium for it, pools that premium with others and then pays for agreed upon losses. For a relatively small amount of premium the insurance company assumes risk and protects the assets of the production company and the film.

**Q – Is this why all equipment rental houses require insurance?**

*Kent* – Yes. And they not only require that you have equipment coverage, but they also want the production company to have liability cover. They want to know that if their equipment is damaged it will be repaired or replaced. And they also want to know that if you drop the camera and break someone's foot that your insurance will pay the physically injured person for their medical bills and pain and suffering.

**Q – How much money should a producer set aside for insurance?**

*Kent* – It's impossible to say without knowing what the budget, script and where the production is being shot. A movie with a $20 million budget will of course pay more for insurance than a movie with a budget of $100,000. Generally the larger the production the less the percent cost of insurance is to the overall budget. A movie with a lot of stunts or dangerous or difficult activity will probably pay more for the insurance than one that is

---

 kent@tvdco.com       www.tvdco.com

without such risks. Also a film shooting in a third world country is usually deemed more risky then one shot in Los Angeles or New York. Some producers project 1% to 3% of their budget to insurance but that is an extremely rough guess especially at the lower budget levels where the insurance company has minimum premiums. It is best to check with an experienced production insurance broker who can understand your shoot, know the going rates the insurance carriers are presently charging and give you an honest projection.

*Q – Say you have a documentary at $100,000 with a two-person crew that is going to be shot entirely in the US and in no dangerous or bizarre situations.*

*Kent* – There's still many things that would need to be known such as how much equipment you would need and if we are to cover the worker's compensation. Let's suppose your shoot is less than 60 days and has no stunts or pyros. For a short term liability policy, only you could pay as little as $500 and with more coverages (workers compensation and a producers package) and a longer term you could pay $10,000.

*Q – When should a producer approach you and what should they give you?*

*Kent* – Once the production looks fairly solid, one of the first phone calls an experienced producer will make is to his insurance broker. The broker can help the producer project a reasonable premium for the budget and then get an actual quote from one or more insurance carriers. Usually the larger and more complicated the shoot, the longer is needed to get the actual quotes.

*Q – What are the lengths of short-term and long-term policies?*

*Kent* – You can get as short term for one day or up to two months. A long term policy usually lasts one year.

*Q – What are the main differences between what a documentary filmmaker and a narrative filmmaker might need for insurance?*

*Kent* – One of the things is cast insurance. Unlike a feature film, documentaries usually don't have a group of actors that are instrumental to the film. Cast cover reimburses the production company in case a declared actor or director gets sick or dies and causes a loss to the production company.

*Q – How does general liability work?*

*Kent* – Liability is insurance that provides coverage should the production company cause injury or damage to the public. Suppose a PA running an errand to the prop house is distracted by a cell phone call and ends up rear ending a car at a stop light. Liability cover would pay for the repair of the rear ended car as well as any injury to the person or persons in the car.

**Q – What other kinds of insurance would be good to have for a documentary film?**

*Kent* – Worker's comp. It's required by law. It is the law in most all States that you have to have worker's compensation cover for all people (employees, independent contractors and volunteers) to whom you give direction unless they are covered by workers compensation elsewhere. Documentarians can usually get this cover through their insurance broker, a payroll service or from a State Worker's Compensation Fund.

The other major policy is the Producer's Policy. This multifaceted policy covers your film, tape or digital work should it be damaged or destroyed or the image is damaged in filming or processing. It also covers your equipment, props, sets and wardrobe. The policy also has" extra expense" so that if any of your equipment fails you can redo the shoot. Third party property damage protects you if you damage a location at which you are shooting. If you're shooting abroad you need foreign liability and foreign worker's compensation. Errors and omissions protects you if you inadvertently libel or slander someone.

**Q – When should you get E&O insurance?**

*Kent* – Tricky question. If you're making a movie and it's bonded or banked, they require Errors and Omissions cover at the start of principal photography. There's risk right away. Someone reads about the film in the newspaper or believes that you stold their idea and can file a claim. However, most documentarians get the cover when they make their deal with their distributor.

**Q – Does E&O cover music clearance and licensing problems?**

*Kent* – That's what it's all about - script, music, film clips – all those things have to be cleared. Most E&O insurance companies will require a lawyer to review the releases. I've seen several movies get made and sadly they could not get distributed because they didn't do the right clearance work. For instance they shoot underage kids in compromising situations – that might make a great movie, but they are minors and you need a sophisticated lawyer to help you obtain the proper releases.

There is a new aspect to documentaries and that is "fair use". Provided you meet certain requirements it is possible to provide content in film without the permission of the creator. It is suggested you call a specialist E&O broker when dealing with this issue as they can guide you to qualified lawyers whose clearance work in this area is acceptable to the insurance carriers.

**Q – Are there any tips for reducing risk so that you don't cause damages?**

*Kent* – Common sense should prevail. If you are a low budget producer and you're going to shoot in a mansion, don't let anyone with a car that leaks oil park in the driveway. Look at the sets environment, walk through it and think you can NOT damage it.

If you're moving a lot of equipment and the house has brick steps, have your carpenters put some wood over the steps or find a different route. Put matting on nice floors. Fence off easily damaged areas and don't walk across grass and create paths. If you damage the grass or anything else at a fancy home the owner is going to want the damage fixed.

**Q – Is there anything else about worker's comp we should know?**

**Kent** – The only person who can legally exclude themselves from cover is an owner of a production company. Excluding the owner can save money because there are minimums and maximums premiums for owners worker's compensation.

**Q – What if you buy a car for a production?**

**Kent** – It needs to be covered separately than if you're going to rent a car. Usually it's not great to buy a car if you can rent it instead. It's a bit more expensive.

**Q – What's a deductible?**

**Kent** – When you get a policy, you basically partner with the insurance company and the first hit, the first money paid in a loss is yours. The insurance company wants you to be responsible and know that loses hurt financially – it hurts them and you. You have to pay a certain amount out before your insurance policy kicks in – that's a deductible.

**Q – How does one submit a claim and what is the process after that?**

**Kent** – First of all when you get a claim, let your insurance broker know right away so that the people who can verify the claim can easily be contacted. Just call up or send an email and file a claim. Describe the who, what, when, where and how of the claim. The broker will then send you some official paperwork or you will receive a call from the claims adjustor of the insurance company. The adjustor will ask you questions to verify the claim and then will try to establish the value of the loss through documentation.

When you get a claim, it's a frightening situation because as a producer you are afraid you're going to lose money, not finish your project or claimants will threaten you. Co-operate with the claims adjustor and tell the truth because professional investigators will generally find the truth out anyway in their investigation. They've seen it all before. An adjustors job in liability situations is to protect you from claims against you. They establish the value of such losses and are knowledgeable about the legal standards for settlement.

You can also have a loss that the insurance is obligated to pay you (i.e. cast loss or damage to your film). Often the frustration for the producer comes in the insurance company requiring specific documentation on the value of the claim before they will pay for the loss. The insurance company will want to see all the specifice invoices and relevant contracts. Producers are often overworked and in great turmoil in the aftermath of a claim and quickly grow impatient with the need for documentation. It is often wise in the larger claims to hire an accountant or someone knowledgeable in putting claims together to assist in gathering the necessary documentation.

If you run into trouble with the claims adjustor call your broker he may be able to help resolve issues with the carrier or make sense to you why you might not be being paid for something.

**Q – How long does it take to turn around a claim?**

**Kent** – That depends on how large and how complicated the claim is. A simple production car backing into a vacant vehicle may be settled in a few days whereas the death of a lead actor in a large motion picture could take many months. Simplistically it should take as long as qualifying the claim as something that is covered under the policy and the insurance company accepting the documentation that proves the specific value of the claim.

**Q – Is there anything that you won't cover?**

**Kent** – Some things are not insurable. Such as whether you make a profit or not. Purposeful activity (i.e. driving a car into a wall) would not be covered.

**Q – What if you're shooting wild animals, underwater or in dangerous parts of the world?**

**Kent** – Elements of danger effect the policy and the premiums. Let's take the most important part – the people. Worker's compensation is related to what country you're in and for how long and what the individual Is doing. Each country has a rating as to how dangerous it is and some countries like Cuba, the insurance carriers will not cover people because of laws in the USA. Some countries are at war or in revolution and the carriers won't write workers compensation in those countries or if they do they will have very high rates because of the danger.

If you are shooting underwater that is dangerous but if you are shooting Great White sharks underwater that is even more dangerous. Insurance companies generally want more premium for greater risk. If you are using wild animals the carriers will want to know how the public and your crew will be protected and how experienceed the handlers are. The better the controls and the more experienceed the handlers the less risk and the less premium will be charged. Anything out of the normal that could be dangerous should be discussed with your broker.

*Q – Is there anything people from other countries need to know about if they are coming to the United States to shoot?*

*Kent* – First, if you already have insurance in place abroad you need to check with your production insurance broker in your home country to what coverages are transferable to the USA. Often the Producers Policy (cast, negative and faulty etc) may extend to the USA but you will be required to obtain the legally required local workers compensation for Americans, and liability and auto liability cover here in the USA. Depending on the country you are from and the insurers you are using vendors may not feel secure with your insurance and request that you also obtain local equipment and/or props, set and wardrobe cover. Many times a foreign producer will hire a production services company and that local company will provide the local insurance as part of their services. Otherwise you call an American broker experienceed in the field, explain your needs and he/she should be able to provide you with the proper cover as long as you have a presence and an address in the USA.

*Q – Any other tips for saving money on insurance and still being properly covered?*

*Kent* – There are some organizations that advertise themselves as setting up insurance deals for film producers. Some of these are quite legitimate, others aren't. Some of these illegal companies are quite attractive because they are cheap. You can't rent insurance. You either want to  buy insurance directly from a licensed broker or hire a production company to be actively involved  in producing and shooting your film. Generally, you can't protect your filming  activities on someone else's policy unless they are contracted and truly involved in your production. Otherwise, thinking you have insurance could be a dangerous illusion and you may find out that you don't have coverage.

Another trick to the innocent producer is that a distributor may say they have a cheap E&O policy a producer can use, but in some of those cases all the insurance covers is the distributor and not the producer. The distributor gets the naïve producer to pay for his

# INSURANCE TYPES

### NEGATIVE FILM AND VIDEOTAPE
*Direct physical loss, damage or destruction of raw film or tape stock, exposed film (developed or undeveloped), recorded videotape, sound tracks and tapes and software.*

### FAULTY STOCK, CAMERA AND PROCESSING
*Covers loss, damage or destruction of raw/exposed/recorded film or tape stock, sound tracks and tapes, caused by or resulting from fogging or the use of faulty materials; faulty sound equipment; faulty developing; faulty editing or faulty processing; and accidental erasure of videotape recordings.*

### MISCELLANEOUS EQUIPMENT
*Covers against risks of direct physical loss, damage or destruction to cameras, camera equipment, sound, lighting (including breakage of globes) and grip equipment, owned by or rented to the production company.*

### PROPERTY DAMAGE LIABILITY
*Pays for damage or destruction of property of others while the property is in the care, custody or control of the production company.*

### ERRORS AND OMISSIONS
*Covers legal liability and defense against lawsuits alleging unauthorized use of title, format, ideas, characters, plots, plagiarism, unfair competition or piracy. Also protects for alleged libel, slander, defamation of character or invasion of privacy.*

### WORKERS' COMPENSATION
*Coverage provides medical, disability or death benefits to any cast or crew member who becomes injured in the course of their employment. Coverage usually applies on a 24 hour per day basis whenever employees are on location away from their homes.*

### COMMERCIAL GENERAL LIABILITY
*Protects the production company against claims for Bodily Injury or Property Damage Liability arising out of operations in connection with filming activity. This coverage will be required prior to filming on most location sites requiring filming permits.*

### BUSINESS AUTO POLICY
*Protects all non-owned adn hired vehicles. Includes picture cars and prod. vehicles.*

cover and the producer has no cover of his own. That is a dangerous place to be when to "begin" to defend such a claim can cost in the neighborhood of $40,000-$60,000.

*Q – What common mistakes do you see documentary filmmakers make?*

*Kent* – Not taking insurance seriously. Seeing it as an obstacle, not as help. Your insurance broker is there to help you stay out of trouble and protect you if you do get in trouble. We are your armor but you need to understand your policies and their limits.

*Q – What advice would you give a new documentary filmmaker?*

*Kent* – Focus on two aspects – the creative aspects of course, but also the reality aspects like insurance. It is hard dealing with individuals that are very scattered. You have to focus on what you're doing both creatively and in the real world in order to sustain your vision. You have to use your right brain and your left brain. I wish you all the best and great success in your projects. You are all courageous!

**Q – When should a documentary filmmaker approach you?**

**Larry** – As soon as possible. Once they know what they're shooting on, how many frames per second, what aspect ratio they're shooting and what their deliverables are down the road. Just keep things in mind when you start. You're not going to shoot a 2:35 movie if your deliverable is full frame TV. Remember you can't go back and it's a big blow up to get a full frame version from a 2:35 ratio.

**Q – What things should a filmmaker think about if they shoot on a film format?**

**Larry** – Do they want to use the film as an intermediate or do they want to use the film as a final deliverable? Meaning if they shot 16mm or 35mm, they can put sound on it and then they have a finished film. If they shot Super 16mm, that's just an intermediate step because you cannot put sound on Super 16mm. Let's say you shot Super 16mm. That has an aspect ratio of 1:66 to get the whole image of the Super 16mm or you can do a 1:77 aspect to match HD. If you plan to project this film, then you want to frame your shots for 1:85 aspect. So you really want to keep in mind proper framing.

**Q – And if you're shooting and editing HD?**

**Larry** – Let's start with 24 frames versus 30 frames because that's what a lot of people are shooting these days. If they shoot at 24, do they shoot with advanced pull down or do they shoot normal pull down? The answer to that is what editorial box are you going to be using. For instance, Final Cut Pro cannot take out a normal 3:2 pull down upon digitizing. It can only take out the advanced pull down. Whereas, the Avid can take out both. What looks better in my opinion is to use normal pull down because even if you are shooting at 24, the tape is recording at 29.97. Normal pull down looks like any other 24 frame

 **www.mega-playground.com**

telecine transfer. You don't see as much stutter as you do with advanced pull down. We also recommend editing at 24 if possible and if you use Final Cut, use Cinema Tools to convert to a 24-frame sequence. Editing at 24fps gives a 1:1 frame relationship if you are going to go out to film.

*Q – What is normal pull down and advanced pull down?*

*Larry* – Normal pulldown utilizes the same 2:3 or 3:2 pulldown cadence long used to transfer 24fps film to NTSC video. The first 24p frame is written to two fields of 60i video, the next is written to three, the next to two, and the next to three again. Advanced pulldown uses a 2:3:3:2 pulldown cadence to stuff 24 frames into 60 fields. It creates 1 dummy frame every 5 frames to get from 24p to 60i

*Q – What about framing your shots for how you're going to watch the film?*

*Larry* – Now you can shoot 4x3 and on some cameras you can shoot 16x9. But be careful about choosing a video camera to shoot 16x9. You can do a true anamorphic 16x9 or there are some lower end prosumer cameras that do a squeeze 16x9. The camera stretches the images and softens it dramatically. You want your camera to do the former. If you're going to shoot 4x3 and you know it's going to be a film-out down the road, you want to frame for 1:85 and keep the full frame safe of booms and lights. In post you can reposition your images up and down and make them safe for 1:85. il you do not frame for 1:85 and you have booms and other unwanted things in the shot, it's going to cost you more money down the line to get them out.

*Q – Can a 16x9 anamorphic lens give you the picture that you want?*

*Larry* – The only problem with that is that are you keeping in mind what you actually see in the lens? Your video-out might look one way versus how it is going to be recorded. You might have a 16x9 anamorphic lens, but then you are going to have a lot of vignetting on the side. Then you're going to have to blow up your film 12%-14% to get rid of the vignetting from the camera, especially if you zoom out all the way.

*Q – When would you suggest someone shoot PAL versus NTSC?*

*Larry* – The only caveat with PAL is your sound because a lot of American sound houses want their sound at 29.97 and their Pro Tools systems are set up for NTSC and not to handle PAL, so you have to do a conversion of your picture to match against to get your sound in sync. If you do a film-out on PAL, most facilities will just keep everything at 25 fps and let the projector slow it down to 24 fps. 99% of the time that's fine, but music and maybe comedy timing can get thrown off.

*Q – What are the various kinds of HD?*

*Larry* – There's two kinds. There's 1280x720 or 1920x1080. In HD, you aren't paying for

# SHOOTING HD

With so many inexpensive cameras around, there's no excuse not to shoot HD. It is the industry standard now and you can always downcovert to SD if need be.

Feed your sound directly into the camera if possible. If you're shooting on a DSLR it's best to record sound separately and use a slate to sync picture and sound.

Never overexpose or underexpose as this limits your ability to grade the image later.

Use the very best format you can get your hands on. Start with HDCam, then DVCproHD, then HDV.

More important than format is the camera and the lenses. Invest in some good glass and rent a good camera and you will be in good shape.

If you shoot with a DSLR, you may need to "transcode" the footage as some editing systems can't handle their codecs (FCP can't handle H.264 well). This will take extra time and storage space to convert the files to something usable.

If you plan to do green/blue screen, don't shoot HDV. HDCam and DVCproHD have better color sampling and make better matte with compositing.

Do your final online with professionals, not at home, unless you are a professional.

Plan a post-production route where you can be editing within hours of ejecting a tape or transfering off your cards. Don't put this off until after the shoot!

If you decide to back up your audio on hard drive or compact flash, use Time of Day timecode so they are exactly the same. Match the recording levels as well.

Shooting HD requires a lot of storage. Multiple terabyte external disks will be necessary if you don't have a RAID (redundant array of independent disks).

If your project uses a lot of slow motion, shoot on a camera that supports true slow motion. If you can't afford it, then shoot at 1080i as the interlacing with give some extra information that will look like film when slowed down on the computer.

the developing and prep of film, but what you are paying for is downconverts to standard definition. You shoot HDCam, but in the edit bay or on your computer at home, you're not going to have a $150,000-$200,000 HD deck to load your footage. So you have to downconvert your tape to DV to digitize. You will also be paying for sync and layback as you would in film. The other kind is HDV, whether it's Sony, Panasonic, JVC or Cannon. It's an MPEG stream. If you shoot at 30 fps, you can just ingest it right into you Final Cut Pro and away you go. But most filmmakers don't want to shoot at 30fps because they think 24fps looks more filmic. Of course, if you shoot tapeless then you don't have to worry about the downconverting.

**Q – Is HDV true HD?**

**Larry** – It's lower resolution. There's a hell of a lot more compression. It's not frame based – odd and even fields, progressive versus interlaced. It's an MPEG stream. It's not HD in reference to a true 1920x1080. It's a prosumer version of HD.

**Q – Does PAL, NTSC or SEACAM mean anything in the HD world?**

**Larry** – There is a 1080/50 which transcodes back to 25 fps, which is PAL. But those three formats are Standard Definition TV formats.

**Q – What are the differences between progressive and interlaced scans in HD?**

**Larry** – When we talk about HD, field based HD – an interlaced image has two fields of video. There is motion between the two. So if your hand moves from point A to point B, you'd see physical motion between field 1 and field 2. A progressive frame or 1080 psf, which is partially segmented frames. That means field 1 and field 2 are identical and when those two fields are combined they become a progressive image. A progressive image is cleaner as you don't have the interlacing motion artifacts that you have between field 1 and field 2. However, if you are shooting sports or something with high motion, you want that interlacing because with 60 fields instead of 30, there is more information that can be captured. The motion looks cleaner and smoother.

**Q – Is there anything special to think about when dealing with audio in HD?**

**Larry** – Audio likes even pairings. For instance, if you're shooting at 24 frames per second, record your audio at 30. If you are shooting at 23.98, record the audio at 29.97. So if you're shooting with a 1080, 23.98 system, record your audio at 29.97.

**Q – Is DSLR camera footage difficult for you to handle?**

**Larry** – As long as you can open the footage in Quicktime Pro and the frames per second rate that you want to use is set correctly, it works fine. Those cameras generally shoot H.264 media, which is a compression codec. It allows you to change the data rate and if you do that it actually changes the frames per second. So instead of 23.98

fps it will be something like 23.24 fps. We get stuff from XDCAM, P2 – a lot of tapeless material we utilize now. Here's the big thing - even though you can mix and match resolutions, you want to stay in one format. If the majority of your footage is 24 fps, then you want to stay 24 fps. Even though you can mix and match in the editing timeline, that option is not always the best. You get artifacting and playback issues among other things.

**Q – Is there a way that a filmmaker can avoid this situation?**

**Larry** – Your first decision is: what is your majority of your footage? If most of it is 30 interlaced video material, then cut everything at 30 fps. If most of your footage is film or 24p video, then cut everything at 24 frames. To split the difference, what is helpful is cut your sequence, run everything at 30 fps because that is what the tape is going to be running at, then when you are done, make two sequences. Put all your 30fps video originated material on a higher timeline in your editing program and put your 24 fps film stuff on a lower timeline. Then differentiate between your 30i and your 24-frame video material. Only do this after your locked picture. One thing, if you're seeing something that goes from 24fps to 30 fps and you think you want to dissolve – don't. Keep is as a cut.

**Q – How long does a film blow up from HD take and how much does it cost?**

**Larry** – A 90-minute film normally takes about a week. Cost is simply supply and demand. When there used to be 3 or 4 houses that used to do this, it was a lot higher than it is now. It's still an expensive process depending on the length of your film. If it's coming from HD the nice thing is that HD's aspect ratio is 1:77 and you are blowing up to 1:85. It's not a big jump. You don't have to worry about dropping the heads as if it were 4x3 full frame material. So how it looks on HD is how it will look on film. You have to re-color correct for film because of the contrast and the color spectrum, but that is about it.

**Q – What is telecine?**

**Larry** – It's taking your film-originated material and putting on a machine that transfers the film originated material to video for you to work with. When it passes through the color corrector, you have several options. You can do a one light transfer, which means one light of information is passed across the image and it's transferred onto tape. It looks flat. You can also do a best light or also known as scene to scene which allows you to go in and tweak the color and make things sharper. That gives you a cleaner, pristine and prettier picture for your daily transfers. At this time you can sync the audio in the suite, or you can lay it down silent and sync it later. The telecine process is when the 2:3 pull down is inserted to get 24-frame film to 30 frames of video.

**Q – Can you fix anything that is out of focus in telecine?**

**Larry** – No. You can fix underexposed and overexposed. There are softening filters, but that is not the job of the telecine process on the first pass. The process is to give a visual representation of how the DP shot the film. So if you put in a lot of enhancements and color and bring up everything that looks underexposed, the DP doesn't correct anything, and so he cannot make it better during production. So the first thing you want to do is put up a chip chart and determine how the image was captured. After editorial if there are things you want to clean up you go into the telecine suite for a second time and do a pass for tape-to-tape color correction. You can add enhancement, different masks to the image to brighten things up or darken them. You can do something called power windows where you want to make the upper corner darker and keep everything else less, or you can change the color of someone's shirt. But you don't want to spend money doing that on your initial transfers.

**Q – Is there anything you can do by playing around with frame rates?**

**Larry –** If you did overcrank or undercrank your film, you could always transfer it at a different rate like 18 frames or 16 frames – but you would do that going back to the film and then to tape, not once you already have it on tape. If you shoot slow motion and then transfer it at a faster film rate like 16, it would look faster.

**Q – Are titles and opticals part of the HD world or are they a thing of the past?**

**Larry –** In the HD world, your resolution is 1920 x 1080. For a film-out or tape to tape, you are creating 2k files. We still do 2k files for end rolls or intricate title design work, but blowing up HD to 2k versus doing a 2k titles and lower thirds, there's not much difference. But then at the same time, if you're doing a very intricate title design, you want to work at 2k so you don't lose any of the information.

**Q – Are there any rules of thumb about what looks good and bad with titles?**

**Larry –** What looks bad on HD looks bad on film. You don't want to use a lot of edgy fonts. If you do use a serif font, you want to make sure it's visible against the background.

**Q – What is pan and scan and does that matter in the HD world?**

**Larry –** Yes. Normally for TV deliverables, they're going to want a full frame master. Even the HD that is simulcast over the air, unless it is available in widescreen, is going to be 4x3 pillared HD. That means if you have 16x9 HD, you have to make a 4x3 full frame master. The easiest way to do this is a center extraction. Statistically 70% of the film can be corrected this way. For the other 30% of the film you have to do a pan and scan to get the actors in or the points of interest on the edges of the frame into view. The cost of it is mostly editorial time. For a 90-minute film, it takes 6-8 hours to do depending on how far apart the points of interests are.

**Q – What should one think about when doing animation or motion control?**

**Larry –** The nice thing about animation is a second is a second is a second. No matter what you originate on 25, 24 or 30 frames, going out to film doesn't matter – a second, is a second is a second. The only caveat on that is you want to make sure that speed of the animation it to your liking. Motion control cameras are going to be recording film and running at 24 fps. Think of it as if you were shooting regular film footage. Or if you are doing an After Effects program, what do I render my animation out to? If you are shooting HD, what you need to render at is 1920 x 1080 at 23.98 or 720p, but you should also render out a lower resolution draft so you can see how it plays.

**Q – Are there any ways to get deals from a lab?**

*Larry* – Sure. The more things you do at one facility, the cheaper those things become. It's also good to stay in one facility as much as you can because if there are problems, it's easier to trace them.

**Q – Are there any new technologies that are coming down the line?**

*Larry* – There are going to me a lot more CMOS (complimentary metail-oxide-semiconductor) based cameras out there. Hopefully down the line their shutter speeds will better handle panning shots and tilts. People are shooting now with the Canon 5D and 7D and they think it's a film camera. They move the camera and it tears the image and it stutters horribly. So that will probably get better. Also very shortly, there will no longer be tape for recording and archiving. Everything will be file based, which on my end will be a nightmare. That's because with tape there is a standard. With files, even when some tells you exactly what format it needs to be in, there will be growing pains to get that file into the right size to playback on different servers. It will save the filmmaker money because they will be able to output out of their system a file for screening or even a finished file if they have a computer fast enough. But different theaters and networks will and do have different broadcast formats. Even now, one file that's right for one network is not the same for another. Whereas if the networks all use HDCam SR tape to air, that's what you have to do. But once it goes tapeless, one network might say they want a Quicktime with MPEG-4 compression where another might say they want AVC-Intra100. So it's going to be a little confusing for people when doing their deliverables. Plus file sizes are huge! We are going to get to the point where people are uploading and downloading there movies onto the net. How are we going to do that in a timely manner?

### Q – Have upload and download speeds gotten any better?

**Larry** – It's whatever the net will handle. You might be able to get a 15MB or 20MB download, but somewhere along the pipeline it might be only 1MB. Down the road there will definitely be streaming sites – media sites that handle file transfers and that is what the networks will have to do.

### Q – Any differences in color correction over the years?

**Larry** – People used to work in 2K file structure or a lot of standard def, which is 601 color space. Now everything is HD and we're at 709 color space, which is larger so there's more latitude for coloring. On the high end, some films are colored using HDR or high dynamic range, which uses a large gamma structure and you can really push the envelope in your coloring capabilities. And like everything else, a lot of the hardware is now software based, which makes things less expensive.

### Q – What are the common mistakes you see filmmakers make?

**Larry** – Definitely the frame rate issue. And then they don't get post involved earlier in the process. Then sometimes they use options that they shouldn't. Just because your camera has the ability to do a Cinemode or to color something, you are limiting what can be done down the road. So if you use a cinema filter on your camera and it makes things grainy, dark and contrast-y. Then down the road while cutting it, you want to open it up and make it lighter because it's too dark. Well, you've already crushed the image and it's going to be harder if not impossible to bring that up because you made the adjustment in the camera. The same thing goes for programs like Color in Final Cut Pro. The first thing I do when I get something to color correct is remove all the color correction that's been done already. If they've pushed the envelope as far as it can go with color, then you might not be able to bring it back if you leave it there. Now, if they say, *"This is the look that we are going for,"* that can be helpful because now I have target.

### Q – What advice would you give a new filmmaker?

**Larry** – Concentrate on writing and concentrate on the story. If you cannot reshoot, then spend the money on the best camera with the best lens you can.

THE EDITOR

ENAT SIDI

**Q – What attracts you to certain projects?**

**Enat** – One is, of course, subject matter. Two, is the filmmaker – their vision, their style. When you work in feature length documentary, you work together with the director for really long periods and for me, there should be a certain chemistry. I have to say that most of the directors I have worked with have become my friends.

**Q – When you start the process with a director, what are some of the things you hope they convey to you?**

**Enat** – We start with a dialogue of what the film is about and who the characters are. I like to know the topics the filmmakers are interested in fleshing out and their overall vision for the film. Is it going to be cinema vérité? Are there going to be interviews? How many hours did they shoot? What is the budget of the film? What is the editing schedule? These are some of the initial conversations I have with the directors.

**Q – Do you prefer to have the director with you the whole time or do you like to do a cut by yourself and then present it to them?**

**Enat** –The first thing I do is screen the footage. It's extremely important for an editor to retain and absorb the material. You need to have plenty of time to do that. I know that a lot of filmmakers get their footage transcribed and that can be important, but personally I like to work with the footage that is in front of me. So viewing is the first thing I do. You can do it with the director or by yourself, but with an increased shooting ratio, as a result of digital filmmaking, and the limits of budget, you find that you have to divide the task. When I start viewing, I select by marking footage and note my first response to it, as this is the point where my reaction to the material is most fresh. So, I really try to be aware of that. It could take many weeks of viewing before you actually start editing. When I start the assembly of scenes, I'd say that I prefer to be alone in the edit.

**Q – What's your approach when you start editing?**

*Enat* – When I start to assemble scenes, the director and I will meet to screen the cuts on a bi-weekly basis and take notes. I never really think a scene is done until it is part of a structure. I tend to leave my edits loose and it stays that way until the architecture of the film is more apparent. Once there's a structure, then you can adjust and refine the scene accordingly.

**Q – Do you think about creating characters first or assembling a story structure first?**

*Enat* –The performance and emotion of characters dictates a scene for me. I watch the material and observe what stories are emerging. I look for moments in a scene interesting to me and start to build from there. I'm looking for drama and for things I respond to emotionally. I think it's integral for establishing pace and rhythm as well as developing a character.

**Q – When do you like to come onto a project?**

*Enat* – As early as possible. I'm currently working with Rachel Grady and Heidi Ewing on their next film. The edit informs the shooting that's still taking place. We are able to sketch out characters and scenes and can come up with ideas for additional shooting.

**Q – Is there anything a director or producer could do to make your job easier?**

*Enat* – Understanding the story that's taking place and observing it will deliver meaningful and compelling material. When emotion is captured it guides me to tell a powerful story. Keep in mind, images help tell the story. They are more than just B-roll. I like the shots to linger so I can establish the right pace and rhythm of a scene.

**Q – Given the switch of shooting on cards instead of tape, is it harder to keep footage organized?**

*Enat* – It's different. When you transfer from solid state cards into the editing software, you get file names from the camera that are just strings of numbers. You have to be careful when organizing

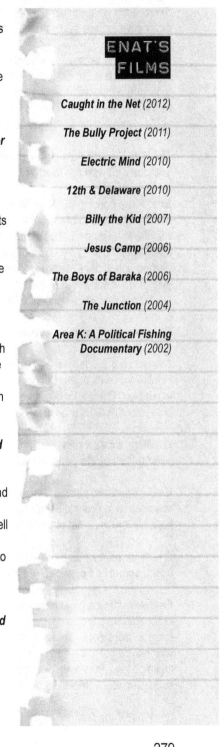

**ENAT'S FILMS**

*Caught in the Net* (2012)

*The Bully Project* (2011)

*Electric Mind* (2010)

*12th & Delaware* (2010)

*Billy the Kid* (2007)

*Jesus Camp* (2006)

*The Boys of Baraka* (2006)

*The Junction* (2004)

*Area K: A Political Fishing Documentary* (2002)

the media so that you're doing it in a way that makes sense to you - whether it's with a descriptive logging system or naming bins by scene or character.

Also, now that filmmakers are shooting on DSLRs, like the Canon 5D and 7D, and are using external audio devices to record sound, there's an extra step of sycning the audio to picture. While we have powerful tools today that analyze the waveforms to sync the material automatically, a drawback to these cameras is the lack of timecode. So when you're syncing your audio, your sequence becomes your source.

*Q – With the DSLR cameras, do you have to do any additional converting before you can edit with the footage?*

*Enat* – The popular DSLR cameras today are using the H.264 codec which is a highly compressed web format but it's not great for editing. So before we can start to edit with the footage, it must be transcoded to a more robust file type, such as the Apple Intermediate Codec if you're working in Final Cut Pro. Although Final Cut is good at dealing with various media in mixed formats, if you really want to avoid glitches, the best thing to do is convert all your media to the same file format and it should be done to all the footage before bringing into Final Cut.

*Q – Does it matter which editing software that you use?*

*Enat* –To me, no. It's just a tool. For me it's merely an adjustment period. If I work on a Final Cut project for three years and then go to an Avid project, I might need a few days to readjust. Overall, though, I would say that Avid has stronger media management tools, but I've certainly finished plenty of feature length documentaries on Final Cut Pro.

*Q – Many times filmmakers fall in love with their footage and won't cut things that need to be cut. Do you have any tips for filmmakers on seeing the larger picture?*

*Enat* – It will take place over time. You cannot kill your babies in the beginning. It's helpful to screen rough cuts to people who were not involved with the film. By the end you will hopefully arrive at that place where you will make those difficult decisions.

*Q – As an editor you have a lot of power over how a character will be portrayed or how a scene will play out. Are there any ethical issues in this regard?*

*Enat* – We have a great responsibility to the characters in a film. These are real people with which we are dealing. I went to a screening of a film on which I consulted and the subjects were in the theater. In the film, there is a funeral scene of the subject's son. As it played out, I realized they were about to relive this intimate moment in front of all these people. They were extremely emotional. Usually we try to screen the film with the subjects in a private setting before it's seen in public.

*Q – What if the family had freaked out at the scene during the intimate screening*

## TRACK LAYING

Documentary films often neglect the quality of the sound, which is strange because docs rely on sound and dialogue more than fiction films to convey their messages. It's time consuming, but a little know how in post can make your film pop.

**Narration** - Make sure it's been recorded crisp and clean. Be careful where it comes in - you don't want it fighting a music cue.

**Audio Track**s - Hopefully your sound recordist did his/her job and you don't have to use subtitles. In an interview, put each interviewee on a separate track so that the mixer can easily access each. However, there are times when a plane will fly overhead or a dog won't stop barking. You can only hope your mixer can reduce the noise.

**Music** - Background or featured music. Again, make sure it's not competing with your audio and narration. Think of when it's good to be silent.

**Sound Effects** - Rare in docs. But you might want to add something to enhance comedy or punch up some animation. Sound Effects downloads or CDs are good sources of high quality stereo recordings of anything you can imagine.

**Foley** - Recreation of movements is rare in docs. The main exception would be docu-drama.

**Spot Efffects** - subject and story driven sounds, so again rare in docs. More likely in docu-dramas.

**Ambiance** - continuous background sound/room tone that appears throughout the film. This should be recorded on set and can help your mixer cover up edit points around that annoying noise mentioned eariler. Can also be used to create a score for your film if you are clever.

You can track sound with any editing system these days and be 100% digital. You will need a quiet space, a good computer, good amplifier and speakers and a high quality microphone. Best of all Avid and Final Cut Pro export OMF.

*and wanted it removed? How do you mitigate that?*

**Enat** – It's really a director's decision. My responsibility is to stay as close to the truth of the material as possible. There's a difference between telling the truth and showing the truth. Showing the truth is not being able to cut anything. Telling the truth is translating moments into effective images and sounds most appropriate to the telling of the story.

*Q – What are your thoughts on music?*

**Enat** – Music helps to create a mood and atmosphere – a sense of space. Sometimes I will use music and then remove it as I sketch out the scene. But I will say this, I don't like to use music as a decoration. It's another element just like the image or the sound that helps complete the story. It's great to find a composer early on in the process and collaborate. Working with temp is tricky. Finding instrumental versions of the right tone can be tedious and costly. If you get too attached to the temp music, you either have to clear the rights or your composer will have to create something of a similar feel.

*Q – Do you help the director decide what kind of music should be in the score?*

**Enat** – It's a collaboration but the main direction for the composer comes from the director. Once we find the composer I will work very close with that person. It's a back-and-forth process where I send them cuts and notes and they compose to picture.

*Q – Do you supervise the sound mix?*

**Enat** – As I edit, I layer different sound elements already prepping for the sound editing and mix. I'm probably the person who knows the film as intimately as possible. If it's possible, I'll always sit-in on a sound mix.

*Q – What are some tips for working with bad production sound?*

**Enat** – There's not a lot of tips. Make it your number one priority to record it properly on location. It's as important as picture. If the sound editor and the sound mixer can't fix it, then there's nothing I can do. In cases of bad audio, if it's important to the story, we keep it. Sometimes we see the use of subtitling. That's one way of getting around it, I guess.

*Q – One trap filmmakers fall into, is not knowing when to stop editing...*

**Enat** – It's never done. It's just taken away from you! I've watched films I did six years ago and there are still things I would want to do to them!

*Q – Can you speak as to whether one should or should not edit their own film?*

**Enat** – Obviously, there are some individuals who can do it all. An editor is your first filter. When you're out in the field during production, there are a lot of things that affect your sensors, like the emotion in a situation, or how hard it was to get a certain shot. An editor that wasn't on location, doesn't have the same attachments. They're once removed from the production process allowing them to approach the material in a fresh way.

*Q – What are the common mistakes that documentary filmmakers make?*

*Enat* – When we go to see a fiction film, we don't expect to be told what we're about to see. We get engaged in the story, drama, action and emotion. Sometimes there's this feeling in documentary that you need to know what the story is before you've even started. I think we have to approach documentary films in a similar way to fiction films. Build a sense of drama and don't spoon feed the audience.

*Q – What advice would you give a new filmmaker?*

*Enat* – In a documentary, there's no script so the great challenge is finding the structure. There might be rules in editing a film such as what makes a good or a bad cut but all of this is highly subjective. I don't think there's a recipe for making a unique film or there's one way of telling a story. Editing is an eagerness to experiment and explore and a certain level of intuition.

*Q – How different is composing for documentary films versus narrative films?*

**Miriam** – In non-fiction, or documentaries, I feel more responsibility to the subjects because they are real. But, just like fiction films, docs tell stories about characters - drama, comedy, action, mystery, etc. The director and content determine the tone of the film, so I don't think there are any hard rules. And actually, documentaries have really opened up, in terms of craft and style, since the days I first started. So it's about finding what works for each film more than anything else. But there are some challenges specific to docs.

*Q – What are some of those challenges?*

**Miriam** – In any score, music helps engage the viewer emotionally, highlight certain moments, support the themes, and move the story along. Quite often in docs, in addition to scoring scenes, music is used to pull together a variety of material illustrating the narrative – archival, interviews, B-roll, narration. Sometimes this requires strong themes, other times, a non-intrusive bed. The challenge is to keep it musically interesting - to continue to grow the music so it's not static or boring. And yet, it has to be somewhat transparent so that viewers are not distracted from what they need to absorb. It can be tricky to write music that doesn't compete with voice over or a powerful interview and yet keep the story emotional, interesting, and energized. One good thing for composers is that the rules of thumb for using music in docs has changed. Now there really are no rules of thumb! Well – I do have one rule of thumb – in addition to serving the film and filmmaker, my score must have musical integrity and work for me.

*Q – When we last spoke you said that the digital process means that filmmakers can bring you on earlier. Is that still true?*

**Miriam** – Yes, more than ever. I think filmmakers realize that bringing the composer on

---

 **www.miriamcutler.com**       **mir.cut@verzion.net**

earlier can inform the editing process and help them craft the film with music in a more integrated way, instead of as an afterthought. Sometimes music can take their film to a different place than they expected. Coming later to the process, the composer also brings a set of fresh eyes so I can sometimes make a suggestion that the director and editor may not think of. Also, I'm always tuning in to the emotional narrative rather than individual shots or moments.

A big part of the overall change is that you have generations of filmmakers coming up now that didn't start in analog. So they don't have an awareness of the old ways of doing things. Instead, they have access to tremendous amounts of data which can be updated, moved around, and stored in an unrestrictive way.

*Q – Have the new technologies made writing and mixing music longer or shorter?*

*Miriam* – Much like filmmakers, I'm always hungry to try all the innovative gear and software that come out. The system that I have is stable and then I add the new stuff and things slow down because there's a learning curve, or I must make adjustments when integrating new software or gadgets. And software compatibility issues always arise. As for length, it's like when computers came out and people thought we'd have a three-day work week because they allow us to do more. No, we just cram more into the week. So now I am expected to do more because of the power of my system. Technology never shortens the time – it just makes more things possible. And because of this, it may add more time. It's a kind of circular cycle.

*Q – How has the technological aspect of what you do changed with the digital revolution?*

*Miriam* – The biggest tech update is that FTP servers are commonplace. Even when working with people in LA where I live, we don't get together anymore. We send things over FTP. You can send huge files that way – whole films even. Now anytime there's any minor change in a scene, I can get a new copy within minutes. This creates a constant forward motion. Or if there's a problem in the mix, they can call or email me and I can fix it and upload it in real time. It's more labor intensive, but in the end, we're working more in real time. In terms of delivery, I upload scores now. 48K broadcast .wav files seem to be the standard. I haven't made CDs or DVDs in years. Another amazing development is the vast amount of material available on iTunes and other digital music download sites. I used to have to drive all over town to find copies of music I needed for reference or source, then buy the recording and digitize it. Now – I can access musical resources and help filmmakers find great temp scores very quickly online.

*Q – Do you use MP3s anymore?*

*Miriam* – They're good for the working process because they upload and download quickly.

## TEMP MUSIC

While you are editing, you will want to put some kind of music track down to set tone, find pacing and liven up dead spots before you have actual score. Music editors call this "tracking." At this point any music is fair game. You don't have to pay royalties.

Many film festivals will accept temp music in your submission for entry. But you will need a festival license to actually screen it. Get your score done beforehand.

Temp music has a big trap. You can fall in love wth it. Now you MUST have that Rolling Stones song or else a scene won't work in your mind. And creating sound alike score just feels hollow. Unless you have deep pockets or good relations in the music industry, get past the separation anxiety.

Temp music can serve another purpose - it can give your composer an idea of what you want in a specific area..

**Q – What are some things a director can do to jump start your imagination?**

**Miriam** – Most of the time I like to see the film and talk about it with them. If they have specific music ideas or tastes, I want to know what they are. I need to know if they're truly open to all ideas or if they have preconceived notions.  Spending time talking to the filmmaker is crucial, whether in the same room or remotely,  so I can understand their goals, taste, style.  I can't emphasize this enough – filmmakers - the more you participate in the scoring process, the more likely you are to get the score that meets your goals.  So make time to give your composer the input and feedback needed.

One thing that's different than the last time we spoke is that I'm not in such a rush to go through the whole film. If we spot the first half hour of the film, then that's plenty for me. When we come across ideas that we're in agreement on, then we build on those ideas. So I might really concentrate a lot on the first fifteen minutes of the film in order to get that right. We'll then know the role the music will play in the film, begin to develop a cohesive structure and approach for the score. Plus it's an opportunity to get my communication down with the director and editor and it makes it much easier to work on the rest of the film. And that's especially important because  as the film gets closer to completion there are more and more demands on the director's time. So it's often over the phone, email, or on Skype.  In fact, now it's even possible for the director to see my screen as well as my face while we're talking (and vice versa).

**Q – It seems so much more immediate this way.**

*Miriam* – Yes. And that's great because you can get close to one another without being in the same room. Time constraints of life and work in the 21st century seem to make it more and more difficult to get together in person. Also, some filmmakers are more comfortable reviewing my music with their team in the comfort of their edit room, experiencing the score in their own space without me being there. Then when they've had time to absorb the material, can come back to me to discuss it cohesively. Sometimes when you are in the room together they are afraid to say what they think or they aren't sure what to say. Or they just need time to live with the new ideas. But of course, many directors thrive on the personal contact. I'm good either way – as long as they participate in the process.

*Q – Would you say a good budget for a fully funded feature doc for a composer would be $15,000 to $30,000?*

*Miriam* – Yes. Live musicians make the music much better and add production value. The score will feel more emotional and organic. But filmmakers need to understand the process and support it. Using players adds costs and takes more time. Recording live can easily add 2-3 weeks of work to my already heavy workload. Musicians are paid by the hour. Then there's music preparation services, a score mixer, sometimes studio assistants to help. So you can see how it can become complex. To pull it off, it takes a lot of careful planning and there isn't much room for error. Many of my colleagues aren't using live musicians just for these reasons. But I'm here to tell you that it is doable with a filmmakers support. That means proper budgeting and scheduling. Depending on the number of live musicians, a decent budget should be no less than $20,000 for a feature doc and of course can go much higher.

*Q – Do you agree that wall-to-wall music comes about because directors are insecure? Except for specific occasions?*

*Miriam* – Sure. I still agree with that. There are many ways of creating a soundscape for the film – and music is one of them. I won't rule out an occasional situation where wall to wall music may be the most effective way to do it, but generally that just waters down the effect of the score, and often it is just plain annoying to the audience.

*Q – How has what you need from the director physically, changed?*

*Miriam* – There's no tape anymore. There are not even DVDs anymore. They send me QuickTime files with window burn time code and ideally, split audio tracks. For some reason, it is sometimes hard to get a proper dub from the editors - I think there are issues in both Final Cut Pro and Avid which complicate this. But it's well worth the trouble  as it gives the team a common reference point and allows us to be frame specific when discussing a cue or working with spotting notes. I can't stress enough the necessity of clear and accurate communication between filmmakers and composers. The better it is, the more fun and satisfying the scoring process.

*Q – Do you need to have your audio split?*

*Miriam* – I love it when it's split. It's saves time and is very helpful. If you have your music and your production sound on the same track, I can't turn off the music to just hear the production sound. So what good is that? And at the same time, if I want to use the music as a reference it's way more convenient and time saving to have it right there on the QT. If they can't do a split track, then I say give me two versions of the film: one with music and one without.

*Q – Are there any differences in what you do when you working on a web project?*

*Miriam* – Usually there is a quick turnaround time and the budgets are low. No one is investing in high quality audio or video for the web, but a lot more people may see it. It's going to have lower resolution and fidelity isn't as much of an issue. The quality can't be better than an MP3. This is a situation where it may be advantageous to license something from my library rather than spending time creating new music.

*Q – Does shooting on HD or any other high end format affect you in any way?*

*Miriam* – Not yet. So far I'm just getting Quicktime files. My digital audio workstation can differentiate between HD, drop frame, and non-drop frame. But so far, I haven't had to use my HD setting – the film mixer seems to handle that part of it after I turn in the score.

*Q – Do you go to the final mix?*

*Miriam* – If I have time and I'm invited, then I love going to the film mix. It's exciting to hear all the elements come together, and in a collaborative environment, a composer can add a lot to the overall sound concept. While many mixers are fantastic at mixing, they may not quite understand all the possibilities for how the music can enhance the film or help fix audio problems. They may not be aware of how much planning and effort went into a certain cue to achieve a particular effect. So it's good to be there to support the filmmakers as they share these ideas.

> I often suggest that the music be approached in the context of the story structure; if you drew an emotional arc over the whole film, what would that look like?

*Q – Is it important to know about music when speaking to a composer?*

*Miriam* – It helps, but if you can tell us what you want emotionally from a scene, it's much more effective. I often suggest that the music be approached in the context of the story structure; if you drew an emotional arc over the whole film, what would that look like? Then think of the arc of each Act, or possibly the arc of a character.

Although, it might be useful if there were a

## SOUND FX LIBRARIES

**Hollywood Edge**
www.hollywoodedge.com

**The Sound Effects Library**
www.sound-effects-library.com

**Creative Sound Design**
www.sonicstudios.com

**Soungle**
www.soungle.com

**Digital Juice**
www.digitaljuice.com

**Power FX**
www.powerfx.com

**Sound Dogs**
www.sounddogs.com

**Sound Effects**
www.soundeffects.com

**The Recordist**
www.therecordist.com

**Hanna Barbera Sound Effects Library**
www.sound-ideas.com

**JRT Music**
www.jrtmusic.com

**Omni Music**
www.omnimusic.com

standardized schedule of concepts that directors could have to make communication faster, and directing the composer more efficient. Usually, each filmmaker and I develop our own vocabulary, unique to his or her film. But as a rule of thumb, I always tell directors to think of music as punctuation – parenthesis, period, comma, underline, exclamation point! Music can be used the same way to bring out something in a film. It can also make a slow section feel faster, and rushed section feel calmer, bring a dull scene to life, suggest a feeling that isn't obvious onscreen, give the audience permission to laugh, create a sense of irony, and so much more. I think every cue should have to justify its existence, and if it's not needed, should be removed. We have total control over what we put in a film – why not use it!?

### Q – What are the common mistakes that you see filmmakers make?

*Miriam* – Not being realistic or informed about the cost and time required to create a proper score. They need to think about the music while making the initial film budget so they can plan realistically for their score. If you want an orchestra, $15,000 isn't going to cut it. And the amount of time needs to be realistic. Do your research – talk to other filmmakers, find out about scores you like and what was involved costwise, timewise, etc. Find out about composers and how they were to work with. Also, plan ahead - we get booked up because we work on things for two to three months. Got to book us early. Plus - people often underestimate the amount of time it takes to edit a film and this can throw a wrench in your schedule down the line as you get into other aspects of post production. You can't set arbitrary deadlines or else it won't be good. You've been working on a film for four years, why rush the post process?

## MUSIC LIBRARIES

You can either order CDs from these places or download MP3/AIFF files from their websites. You must pay for licenses (sync, mechanical, performance rights) depending on what you plan to do with the music.

**FirstCom Music, Inc.**
www.firstcom.com

**Global Graffiti**
www.globalgraffiti.com

**Killer Tracks**
www.killertracks.com

**Promusic, Inc.**
www.promusic-inc.com

**Sonic Licensing**
www.soniclicensing.com

**DeWolfe Music Library, Inc.**
www.dewolfemusic.com

**www.lapostmusic.com**
LA Post Music

**Pond5**
www.pond5.com

**APM**
www.apmmusic.com

**Getty Images**
www.gettyimages.com/music

**Stock Music**
www.stockmusic.net

**All Music Library**
www.allmusiclibrary.com

**OBT Music**
www.obtmusic.com

**Royalty Free Music Library**
www.royaltyfreemusiclibrary.com

**The Music Case**
www.themusicase.com

**Fresh Music**
www.freshmusic.com

**Aircarft Music Library**
www.aircraftmusiclibrary.com

**Extreme Music**
www.extrememusic.com

**Studio Cutz**
www.studiocutz.com

**Konsonant**
www.konsonant.com

*Q – What advice would you give a new filmmaker?*

*Miriam* – My advice is to just follow your heart. The world is in the mess it is because there are too many people not following their hearts. They try and control everything and buy up all the artists. I'm disappointed that artists aren't leading the way more; most of us spend too much time being bummed out about things rather than inspiring people. To me, documentary filmmakers are like a beacon. They are inspiring us to keep caring. So I say, stick with it! Stay independent! For all our sake!

**Q – What is the job of the re-recording mixer?**

**Mark –** The re-recording mixer is responsible for the finished soundtrack of the film. He takes the edited sounds – dialogue, music and effects – and blends them together to tell the sonic story of the movie. There's no "right or wrong" in the execution of this, only basic principles, conventions and personal taste.

**Q – What are the main differences between how a documentary film and a narrative film are mixed?**

**Mark –** Because of the "guerilla" nature of most documentary filmmaking, the primary difference between mixing is in the condition of the production track – the sound recorded when the picture was being shot. Usually these tracks are noisier and more inconsistent than those recorded under the relatively controlled circumstances of a narrative film. Therefore, they require more attention to make them intelligible and smooth. In addition, you usually don't have sound effects and Foley tracks in documentary mixes.

**Q – What materials do you need for the final mix?**

**Mark –** I'm normally provided with a set of sound "tracks" which contain all of the sounds that will appear in the final mix. They've been edited for their proper synchronization to picture and grouped together according to whether they're dialogue, music or sound effects. The mixer then views these tracks while watching the picture, and adjusts each of the sounds through a mixing console.

**Q – Can you do a proper mix with home editing software?**

**Mark –** Yes, in the same way that you can completely mess up a mix with a million-dollar console. It's not so much about the equipment as it is about the mixer. The principles of good mixing far outweigh the technical side, because sonic quality has improved so greatly in the past 20 years. But that having been said, most home editing software is tedious to use considering there are literally thousands of adjustments to be made to

## THE FINAL MIX

This is when all your music, dialogue, sound effects, room tone, ADR and Foley are mixed into one. It's exciting because your documentary will leap into life.

Sound studios are expensive. Make sure all your creative decisions are made and you know what the problem areas are so you don't waste time.

Mix in stereo. Docs rarely benefit from a surround mix.

It's possible to mix a doc in 3-5 days with your Music and Effects (M&E) track. Don't let the mixers persuade you into 3 weeks.

You can use atmosphere/room tone tracks to cover lots of problems. And the filters they have these days can even take out air conditioning hum and traffic.

produce a finished track. If you're doing these one by one with a mouse and keyboard, it will take quite a long time, and you'll find it difficult to get a "flow" going. That's why consoles and control surfaces are so important.

**Q – Is there any kind of paperwork a filmmaker or producer should be aware of in terms of the sound mix?**

**Mark –** Other than the payroll check? Seriously, there was a time when the console was filled with "cue sheets" telling where all of the sounds could be located, according to the sync and also the track layout. That's all been made obsolete because of digital audio workstation playback, where all the tracks are easily viewed on computer monitors.

**Q – Are there any main differences in terms of the mix between films that were shot on film versus video or that are going to end up on film or video?**

**Mark –** How the picture originated – film or video – is much less important to the mix than how it will be viewed. If it plays in a theater as a film presentation, the audience will be much further from the loudspeakers than they will in a typical home video presentation. In addition, a movie theater's sound system, especially if it's THX, will offer a wider dynamic range and frequency response than a home system. For these reasons, adjustments are sometimes made in the mix to compensate for these limitations, if the primary venue is to be video.

**Q – How many people are present at the mix?**

# POST-PRODUCTION SOUND

1. Make sure that recorded the best production sound you could. This will reduce subtitling and ADR.

2. Put your interviewee's voices on separate tracks so your re-recording mixer can se their levels oncefor each track instead of having to move up and down as each person speaks.

3. Put effects on a separate track from your dialouge and music. Same goes for Foley.

4. A good ambience track will act like filler in the cracks, smoothing over edits.

5. Emphasize any sound effects if necessary to add to an existing effect but also to cover any natural sound problems.

6. Your tracks should compliment each other, not compete. Don't put loud music over voice over.

7. Too much music can make an audience "music deaf." Know where to place music and when to keep it quiet.

**Mark** – I've had anywhere from zero to twenty or more. Sometimes it's just the director, or the picture editor or sound supervisor. At other times it's a full house with all the related parties. There's no rule here, except that the more people who get to offer their opinion, the longer the mix will take. It tends to work best when one person is clearly in charge and has the final say as to the myriad of decisions encountered in a mix.

### Q – What is a pre-mix?

**Mark** – A pre-mix is a step done before the final mix where individual dialogue or sound effects, sometimes music are isolated, adjusted and smoothed out before combining them with the other elements of the mix. This allows you to devote attention to problems within those tracks before the conflagration of the final mix takes place. I call the pre-mix "picking fly specks out of pepper." It's a pains-taking process that usually drives everyone but the mixer crazy. Sometimes him, too.

### Q – How much should you use surround sound?

**Mark** – Whatever is appropriate to your film. What's important to keep in mind, however, is that the surround speakers are a sound "field," not point-source monitors like the front speakers. That means the same sound comes out of multiple speakers in the surrounds. That makes it good for ambiences and reverbs and music, but less appropriate for say, a voice – unless you want somewhat of a disembodied effect. My feeling is that if a sound from the surrounds makes you turn around, then it's probably a mistake because it will take you out of the picture - unless that's your intended effect. In general, I like to use the surrounds to "fill the room," but in an unobtrusive way.

### Q – Is it common for documentary films to be

*over-scored and do composers come to the mix?*

*Mark* – The amount of music in a film is a personal choice, and if that's the intention of the filmmaker, then who's to say it's right or wrong? My only feeling is that if you become aware of the music, then something isn't completely right. In fact, if a sound mix is completely successful, you won't be aware of any of it at all. You'll just love the moods and emotions of the film. Composers do sometimes come to the mix, and I've had it be both a boon and a bane. It's great if they're able to illuminate something that's not obvious in their tracks – but it can also be difficult if they're not able to keep in mind that their music is just one of the elements that go into making a soundtrack. The tendency is to want to hear all the nuances and that's simply not always possible or even desirable when combined with dialogue and sound effects.

*Q – What are the common tools you use?*

*Mark* – Pro Tools is usually involved in most of my work in some form or another. More often than not I am mixing on control surfaces that directly manipulate Pro Tools – Pro Control, Control 24, D-Command and ICON. The advantages of these systems over conventional console mixing are huge in that the automation and processing are part of the session and can easily be taken from system to system, edited or manipulated in ways that were not possible until now.

*Q – Do you do the M&E mix?*

*Mark* – I sometimes do, but frequently that is assigned to a separate effects mixer.

*Q – Do you normally do Foley on a documentary film?*

*Mark* – Foley is usually involved in some form or another if only to fill in missing production

## POST-PRODUCTION SOUND

*8. Taking out your score when you have interviews couldbe jarring, so think about fading down and keeping it in.*

*9. Silence can create great tension.*

*10. If you need to edit music, cut on the beat. In some instances, a cross fade will do just fine.*

*11. Get to know your dubbing mixer so you can talk about the kind of sound and effects you want. Defer to their opinion if you are in doubt.*

*12. If you are aiming for a theaterical release, then mix in a studio that does feature films.*

*13. Make sure you have enough money to pay the re-recording studio. You don't want them keeping your tapes/hard drives hostage.*

*14. If you planb to track lay yourself, don't underestimate how much time it will take.*

*15. Work out how you are going to get your audio to the mix. OMF is usually the best way.*

effects. If a fully filled M&E is required, than a complete Foley pass needs to be done. For documentaries, this isn't usually the case – they tend to be sub-titled more than dubbed.

**Q – Is there anything a filmmaker can do to make your job easier?**

**Mark** – Having a clear vision of what he wants in his soundtrack and being consistent in that vision is most helpful. Barring that, an open mind is also a great asset. Mixes are collaborative efforts – but they benefit most from having a unified vision.

**Q – How much time should one budget for the final mix? How do you get good rates?**

**Mark** – Attempting to mix a feature-length documentary in anything less than a week is bound to lead to serious compromises. Extra time spent in the mix room leads to further levels of refinement and detail. It can also alleviate a bit of the stress on the mixer who has to make every minute count. The best way to find a good rate is to do an "all in" package. That is, have the same company do your sound editorial, Foley, ADR, mix, etc. so that they can discount your rate. It can also eliminate finger pointing if there are any problems. Also, beware of getting caught up in bidding wars while shopping your product to different facilities for bids. There just isn't that much fat to trim in the sound business these days. You may think you got a great deal when you found the studio that would do it for half, but the problem comes when that product you thought you were getting for less is really less of a product. A company that has a significantly lower sound bid than others, is without a doubt, planning on delivering that Mercedes without a steering wheel or tires.

**Q – Have there been any changes in the way things are done in the sound business in the past few years?**

**Mark** – It's as if two sides of the proverbial "cheap/fast/good" triangle have been removed. Sound companies are now working with less money and time and still expected to deliver the same high-quality product. There have been technological advances that have allowed the accomplishment of some of this, to be sure. For the most part, however, those developments have been exploited to save money, delay locked-picture deadlines and reduce the sound package time frames, rather than make the process less stressful or produce a better product.

"I call the pre-mix 'picking fly specks out of pepper.' It's a painstaking process that usually drives everyone but the mixer crazy."

**Q – When should a filmmaker approach you?**

**Mark** – Usually I'm contacted when the picture is close to being "locked" and the attention shifts from picture to sound.

*Q – What are the common mistakes you see documentary filmmakers make?*

*Mark –* Not giving enough attention to the hiring of the production sound mixer. This very difficult job requires an experienced and creative professional to deal with the impossible situations that will likely be dealt him. And his tracks will almost certainly be the centerpiece of the final mix. If the voices are off-mic and buried in noise, there's virtually nothing the re-recording mixer can do to fix it. And nothing brands a film as less-than-professional than poorly recorded voices. Spend the money on the production mixer – it will be well worth it.

*Q – What advice would you give a new documentary filmmaker?*

*Mark –* That in spite of the fact that mixing can be a stressful and intense experience - don't forget to have some fun along the way. There's a reason we all do this instead of sitting in cubicles, counting beans.

# CHAPTER NINE
# FILM FESTIVALS

**FULL FRAME**
**NORTH CAROLINA, USA**

**SADIE TILLERY**

### Q – What kind of films do you program?

*Sadie* – We program documentary films, both shorts and features and many in between. We're fortunate because we have the opportunity to showcase films that may seem "atypical" in length. For example 50 or 60 minute films, perhaps cut for television, that may not have the same theatrical opportunities as traditional features but we find affecting. We look for films that are visually striking. Films that are emotionally poignant. Films that are intellectually stimulating. Films that stretch the boundaries of what we might expect a documentary to be, even. It's usually a combination of these impressions that contributes to our programming a particular film.

### Q – What wouldn't you program?

*Sadie* – I've made an effort to remain open to some 'techniques' that are sometimes frowned upon, for example ambiguous reenactments or staging. In my experience, I've found that hard and fast rules about what is or isn't a documentary are really in the eyes of the particular viewer. Sometimes there is controversy over films we end up programming because whether something rings false or true is incredibly subjective. So, I don't have a firm rule about what we wouldn't program.

However, I don't respond positively to films that feel careless or rushed, and I tend to be less drawn to works that dictate or preach a particular viewpoint or idea to the viewer. That said, there are always exceptions, and I think there are places for those films, but it's not necessarily the type of work we are looking to program at Full Frame.

### Q – How does your selection process work?

*Sadie* – We have a carefully chosen team of 20 Selection Committee members that review submissions with us and meet throughout the season to discuss feedback. The

---

 info@fullframefest.org        www.fullframefest.org

300

Selection Committee makes recommendations to a smaller Programming Committee that takes their feedback into consideration and selects and schedules the final slate.

**Q – Are the people who select the films staff?**

**Sadie** – Several staff participate on the Selection and Programming Committees, but the majority are professionals from other backgrounds and organizations who generously volunteer their time.

**Q – What kind of formats can you project?**

**Sadie** – Full Frame projects HDCam, Digibeta and Beta SP, along with 35mm and 16mm.

**Q – What are the Full Frame Fellows?**

**Sadie** – We invite students from around the country to attend the festival as Fellows. Festival passes are offered to Fellows at a discount. During the four days of the festival, participating students have the opportunity to attend screenings and panels. Fellows also enjoy private master classes with filmmakers. Previously, we've hosted sessions with DA Pennebaker and Chris Hegedus, Steve James and Peter Gilbert, Marshall Curry, Albert Maysles, Rachel Grady and Heidi Ewing, and James Longley, among others.

**Q – What kind of panels do you like to program?**

**Sadie** – We have a variety of panels around filmmaking and around themes presented in various films. We select a guest curator to organize a program of films around a particular topic for our Thematic Program. In turn, we feature a conversation around the Thematic Program each year.

There are also a number of panels that directly follow screenings, such as our Center Frame events, that feature longer discussions with subjects and filmmakers. We want Full Frame to be an arena where filmmakers can come together to discuss the form, and our panels are organized with that goal in mind.

**Q – How can a filmmaker make the most of a festival or prepare for a festival?**

**Sadie** – Have an idea of what type of festival you are about to attend. At Full Frame, even though we only screen films once, it's great when filmmakers can come for the entire festival, and make time to attend other screenings, parties and panels. We offer an intimate festival setting; all venues are within a one block radius. So it's easy to meet other filmmakers and industry members, but you have to be here to make the most of what Full Frame has to offer.

We don't schedule meeting opportunities for filmmakers, so perhaps it's even more important for filmmakers to attend festival events and make the most of interacting within the community we build for four days.

**Q – What can a filmmaker do to make their screening go well?**

**Sadie** – In Full Frame's case, outreach helps and participating with our press team is key. But I would say the single most important thing is to follow all deadlines and instructions. That way the Festival has the tools required to ensure the screening is a success.

**Q – What kind of publicity materials should people bring to a festival?**

**Sadie** – Posters are effective. Audiences seem to snag postcards, too. We request those materials in advance, and take on hanging all posters around the festival site. It's one less thing for filmmakers to do when they arrive, and by doing it in advance all is set by the time audiences arrive first thing Thursday morning.

**Q – Have you seen any publicity styles that are effective at getting people to a documentary screening?**

**Sadie** – I think making links between a topic and a potential attendance group is key. Getting the word out about the overall festival and particular themes represented helps us build an audience. There is plenty of content at the festival that appeals to filmgoers who may not be immediately charmed by the idea of an all documentary festival. Facebook and Twitter are important resources for building audiences.

*Q – What distributors come to the festival and do you put them together with the filmmakers?*

*Sadie* – Representatives from various distributors often attend, including Magnolia Pictures, HBO Documentary Films, A&E IndieFilms, Oscilloscope Laboratories, and others. We do not set up individual meetings, but the atmosphere at Full Frame is so intimate that it's very easy to make connections and meet industry professionals organically.

*Q – What are the common mistakes that you see filmmakers make?*

*Sadie* – I think perpetuating misinformation is an overall problem. Being unresponsive or uncertain of what formats are available, is problematic. It's very important to read all materials, and be upfront about needs, limitations, and expectations.

*Q – What advice would you give a filmmaker regarding festivals?*

*Sadie* – Follow instructions, be courteous of the process, and don't give up if you don't get in. Having to say 'no' is a big part of programming. It's not personal, and sometimes it's not even an indication that a filmmaker's project is flawed. At the end of the day only so many films can be scheduled. But just as there are more and more films made these days, there also are more and more festivals.

**IDFA**
**AMSTERDAM**
**MARTIJN TE PAS**

*Q – What are you looking for in the documentaries that you program at IDFA?*

*Martijn* – Creative documentaries of any length completed after August 1st of the previous year. We look for a great variety of styles, genres, lengths and content. We also select hybrid, interactive, cross media and New Media projects.

*Q – Must all the documentaries have social relevance?*

*Martijn* – No, pure cinematic or experimental works are also shown at IDFA.

*Q – What are your screening formats? Do you screen HD?*

*Martijn* – We screen HDcam, Digibeta, Betacam-SP, 16mm and 35mm. All other formats have to be discussed with the program department prior to the festival.

*Q – Is there a fee to apply to the festival and what is the process of selecting films?*

*Martijn* – There is no fee required for entry. All films entered are viewed by professionals in the documentary field. The final selection is made at the beginning of October. Films entered at the first deadline, May 1st may have to wait till then to get a final answer. This is also the case for films entered for the second deadline, August 1st.

*Q – What are the competition programs and awards that are offered?*

*Martijn* – First is the IDFA Competition for Feature-Length Documentary. Fifteen feature-length documentaries compete in this category for the VPRO IDFA Award for Best Feature-Length Documentary. The prize is a sculpture and 12,500 Euros. In addition, the jury may grant a Special Jury Award. Then there is the IDFA Competition for Mid-Length Documentary where sixteen documentaries shorter than 60 minutes compete. The award

---

 www.idfa.nl

 http://twitter.com/IDFA

 www.facebook.com/idfa.nl

is a sculpture and a cash prize of 10,000 Euros, provided by Dutch broadcaster NTR. NTR Television will also buy and broadcast the winning film. We also have the IDFA Competition for Dutch Documentary where seventeen documentaries compete for a sculpture and a cash prize of 5,000 Euros.

*Q – How can a filmmaker make the most of the Festival; for both those attending with films or those visiting the festival?*

*Martijn* – Inclusion with a project in the FORUM is very effective but it's good to visit IDFA with new projects anyway. The attendance of possible funders or co-producers makes for good networking opportunities for filmmakers and other professionals. IDFA and Docs for Sale offer the possibility to watch new films and documentary classics. IDFA features a lot of panels and discussions and attending filmmakers will participate in Q&A's after the screenings of their films.

*Q – Do you provide publicists for the invited filmmakers?*

*Martijn* – All films are available for the press to view either online with a special press account prior to the festival, in industry screenings during the festival or at the press center. At the press center journalists can set up interviews with filmmakers and posters of films are distributed during the festival. TV programs do like to screen clips of films screened at IDFA, so it's always good to send clips on DVD (final cut, no trailer). If filmmakers prefer to work with a private publicist, our press department can always suggest and recommend people.

*Q – Do you pay for the airfare and accommodation of invited filmmakers?*

*Martijn* – The filmmakers with a film in one of the competitive sections and the reflecting images program are offered 4 nights hotel by the festival. For filmmakers with films in other IDFA programs the festival offers 3 or 4 nights. IDFA does not offer accommodation for Dutch filmmakers with a film in the festival program. Occasionally IDFA is prepared to bear part of the travel costs of filmmakers with a film in the program.

*Q – Have you noticed a trend in the documentaries that you've been screening in the last few years?*

*Martijn* – The trend is going towards hybrid, interactive, cross media and New Media projects, using multi platforms and actively engaging with - and finding new audiences.

*Q – What is DocLab?*

*Martijn* – IDFA DocLab is the new media program of the International Documentary Film Festival Amsterdam. Since 2008, IDFA DocLab showcases the many new and unexpected forms of documentary storytelling made possible by digital technology and the internet. In a few years, the program has become a unique platform for transmedia

## FESTIVAL DO'S AND DON'TS

*Do research on festivals before you start to submit. What kind of films they program? When do they program? Who attends them? What resources do they have available?*

*Do be mindful of entry fees. Sometimes you will find one that is free, but most likely they will be between $25 and $50. Don't enter a festival that is over this amount.*

*Do budget for your stay at a festival. Hotels, food and transportation can add up. Get a bunch of friends together and pack one hotel room. Makes for great stories.*

*Do not pay to be part of the festival program. You should be included since they have chosen you to be in the festival. In fact, some festivals will pay YOU to screen the film.*

*Do get your social media and digital content going. Blog that you got into a festival, blog from the festival and take video of being there for content on your website. This engages your audience and makes them more likely to buy your film or support your next one.*

*Do advertise your film yourself. Bring press kits, DVD copies, flyers, posters, hats and anything else you can slap the name of your film on. Be creative - if your documentary is about cowboys, dress one of your friends up as a cowboy and have him walk through the festival handing out flyers.*

*Do bring as many of your subjects along as possible. Great for your Q & A events.*

*Do get a publicist, but ONLY if you are going to be at one of the larger festivals.*

*Do make sure to get your publicity materials to the festival headquarters as soon as possible so they can create their program.*

*Do schmooze with the festival operators. They know where the free food, booze and parties are. But don't monopolize their time, either.*

*Do not freak out if the projector blows up or the sound drops out of your film. Remain calm and professional. Usually it is a volunteer running the projector with very little training.*

*Do not stay too far away from the festival center. The pace of most film festivals, especially the larger ones, is draining. Having to drive half an hour or more to your hotel at the end of the night just sucks.*

documentary and multimedia projects, ranging from web series to interactive webdocs, live performance and media art. Every year at IDFA in November, IDFA DocLab presents a series of Live Cinema Events, installations, workshops and industry panels. Throughout the year, IDFA DocLab maintains an online project archive and organises guest programs at other festivals (such as SXSW) and new events, such as Photo-Stories.org. Many of the projects that premiered at IDFA DocLab have gone on to win Webbies, Digital Emmies and other awards. These include *GazaSderot* and *Prison Valley* by Alexandre Brachet / Upian, *Interview Project* by Austin Lynch and *Welcome to Pine Point* and *Highrise* by the National Film Board of Canada.

**Q – What common mistakes have you seen by filmmakers that could be avoided?**

*Martijn* – Don't send too many work-in-progress tapes. Make sure you can deliver the film in time for the festival dates and then decide to apply or not. Sometimes it's better to work on the film a bit more then to rush things and send a preview tape that doesn't give a good impression of the final film. Make sure you send enough information along with the preview tapes. It does make a positive difference if a synopsis, biography and some background information are included in the application.

**Q – What advice would you give a documentary filmmaker who's attending the festival?**

*Martijn* – See as many films as possible and meet as many people as possible. Attending IDFA can be exhausting but as most of the decision makers and creative people in the documentary field are present it can be a truly inspiring experience.

IDFA'S
JAN VRIJMAN FUND
ISABEL ARRATE

**Q – What is this fund and why was it set up?**

*Isabel* – The Fund supports documentary filmmakers living in developing countries. Our aim is to help develop and preserve an independent film climate in countries where because of political or economical reasons the production of documentaries is difficult. We do this by supporting documentary film projects but also by supporting or collaborating with festivals in developing countries.

**Q – How do applicants apply and what are you looking for?**

*Isabel* – We look for creative documentaries. There are no requirements concerning themes or length. Projects are selected twice a year. The deadlines are always 1 February and 1 June. We've three different categories for documentary film applications and a 4th category for festival or workshops proposals. To apply it's necessary to fill out the online entry form, and send the required materials by email, courier or regular mail. All materials have to be in our office on the day of the deadline at the latest. So not postmarked the day of the deadline. On our website there is an extended list of the materials to send in.

**Q – What does IDFA consider a developing country?**

*Isabel* – Each year the Organisation of Econonic Co-operation and Development publishes the so-called DAC-list, listing the countries that receive Official Developing Assistance. The countries are listed according to the income per capita. As one of our main financiers is the Dutch Ministery of Foreign Affairs we follow the official policy they have for development aid.

**Q – Can a producer from a non-developing country who's teamed up with a producer/filmmaker from a developing country, apply?**

---

 www.idfa.nl/industry/markets-funding/vrijman-fund

*Isabel* – Only if there's a co-production agreement between two production companies, one in the developing country and the other in the non-developing country. The director has to be a citizen of and live in a developing country. Besides this, the application has to be done by the producer in the developing country and if the project is selected, the contract with the fund will be with this producer. A general requirement of the fund is that a contribution from the fund has to be spent in a developing country.

### Q – Must all applications be in English?

*Isabel* – Yes. We only make exceptions for applications from French-speaking Africa.

### Q – What do you require to accompany the producer's application?

*Isabel* – An application doesn't necessarily have to be done by a producer. It can be a director that isn't attached to a registered production company. When sending a project it is best to read the regulations on the IDFA website, especially the Jan Vrijman Fund page where we have a section with frequently asked questions that helps to clarify the requirements.

### Q – How much money can one get from the Fund?

*Isabel* – It depends on the category. For script development we give a maximum of 5,000 Euros, for post or production a maximum of 17,500 Euros, for other categories like festival applications and workshops a maximum of 15,000 Euros.

**IDFA FORUM**

**DAAN VERMEULEN**

### Q – What is the Forum?

*Daan* – The Forum's aim is to bring together independent producers/filmmakers and commissioning editors, distributors and other financiers to collaborate in the financing of new high quality documentary films. Over three days, this aim is reached by matchmaking the participants in seven-minute pitching sessions, round table discussions, individual meetings and by providing networking opportunities at organised social events, screening facilities, catalogues and guides. It was set up in 1993 with this specific aim and also to create a network of documentary professionals throughout Europe, which didn't exist back then. Now, the Forum has become Europe's largest gathering of independent documentary producers and directors, television commissioning editors and other financiers.

### Q – What is the criteria to get into the Forum?

*Daan* – With the creative documentary as its point of departure, the Forum provides the opportunity for independent producers to submit projects in all stages of financing. The Forum looks for traditional linear documentaries as well as multiplatform interactive projects. We select up to 50 projects from around 450 applications.

The Forum has two pitch categories, each one characterized by a separate pitch setup and formal entry requirements. For the Central Pitch category, a project has to have at least 25% of the total budget financed, but no more than 75%. In addition, at least one broadcaster or film institute has to commit itself financially to the project. The formal criteria for the Round Table Pitch category are less stringent. Projects submitted are not required to have any financing in place nor any commitment from a broadcaster or film institute. Only up to 15% of the projects in the selection are non-European. The Forum is partly funded by the European Union's MEDIA Program, which means we have to focus on the European audiovisual industy. You'll find detailed information on the selection

www.idfa.nl/industry/markets-funding/the_forum

criteria on our website.

**Q – How does one submit to the Forum?**

*Daan* – The entry form is available online from July until September. We also need copies of letters of commitment or contracts from broadcasters already attached to the project. Also, a synopsis, a project description, a budget and biographies of both director and producer. If available, we like to receive visual material as well, like a trailer, a showreel or previous work.

**Q – What are you looking for in the documentary projects?**

*Daan* – The projects need to have an international scope, meaning that the project should potentially interest broadcasters from different countries. The Round Table category offers a platform to a bundle of projects within the same genre.

**Q – What is the pitch workshop? How much is divided into pitching, networking and meetings?**

*Daan* – Each pitch team has 7 minutes to pitch their project followed by 8 minutes of Q&A with the panel of commissioning editors. In the Central Pitch category, the project is presented to 26 commissioning editors. Projects pitched in the Round Table category are pitched to about 10 potentially interested commissioning editors. The pitch sessions are presided over by one or two moderators. They do the introductions, stimulate the discussions after each pitch and are there to support the pitch teams.

In the afternoons, the pitch teams have pre-arranged, one-on-one meetings with commissioning editors and other financiers. For the other participants, the Forum organizes panel discussions with leading professionals. The Forum offers all participants plenty of networking opportunities as well by organizing opening and closing drinks, daily lunches and a daily cocktail hour (for all professionals attending IDFA). To prepare the producers and filmmakers, and to improve the quality of the pitches at the Forum, we organize a pitch workshop together with the European Documentary Network (EDN) on the Sunday prior to the Forum (the Forum is Monday through Wednesday). The pitch teams try out their pitch on a panel of experts and get feedback. In addition, the pitch trainers gives general advice on the presentations. Participating in the workshop isn't obligatory.

**Q – When pitching, is it advisable to have a trailer to show?**

*Daan* – We strongly encourage producers with projects to accompany their verbal pitch with a trailer as it will give potential financiers an impression of what the end product will look like. However, if you feel like the trailer will be a disadvantage then a producer could decide to not show it.

*Q – Do you help introduce the attendees to commissioning editors/broadcasters?*

*Daan* – We have two matchmakers on staff that helps with introductions. They also give advice on which broadcasters best to contact for a specific project. In addition, there is one staff member in charge of the one-on-one meetings and available for introduction.

*Q – Do the same commissioning editors and broadcasters attend the Forum each year?*

*Daan* – For many commissioning editors the Forum is a fixed item in November with about 110 of them attending each year. Each year we also welcome a few new faces. In recent years quite a few commissioning editors interested in crossplatform documentaries have become welcome additions to the already attending group of commissioning editors.

*Q – Are the consultants that you have at the Forum for individual meetings, all on the distribution side of the business, or are any from any other field of the documentary filmmaking process?*

*Daan* – These consultants are not limited to the distribution side of the business. Participants can ask these international experts, who have backgrounds ranging from sales to interactive production, about subjects as varied as distribution, sales, marketing, cross-media, use of archives, etc.

*Q – How can the Forum help new documentary filmmakers and producers?*

*Daan* – The Forum has a unique setup in which public pitches are accompanied by individual follow-up meetings. If your project is selected to be pitched, you'll have the attention of a large number of commissioning editors and other financiers at once. For a filmmaker or producer that's new to the international market, this is advantageous because you not only pitch your new project, you also present yourself and your company. In the individual meetings afterwards, producers with projects can discuss their project with interested commissioning editors in more detail. Especially if you do a great pitch, people will remember you. As a result, it will be easier to get meetings with broadcasters and financiers afterwards not only here in Amsterdam but also at other markets where you do follow-up meetings. The Forum is not only an indispensable documentary market for producers pitching projects, but also for other professionals attending as observers. The public pitches enable all professionals attending to stay up-to-date with the latest market developments.

*Q – Can anyone attend and be an observer to see how the Forum works?*

*Daan* – Yes, every producer is welcome to attend the Forum as an observer. It's restricted however to one person per company. Also, we receive more observer applications each year than there are seats, so we have to do a selection. And, like with

## MAIN INTERNATIONAL DOC MARKETS

**Australian International Documentary Conference, Australia**: *Offers a unique mix of masterclasses, lively panels and informal meetings offer countless networking opportunities. You can apply for the pitching forums, submit your documentary to the videotheque and much more.* **www.aidc.com.au**

**The European Film Market, Berlin**: *The business component of the Berlin International Film Festival. Running alongside, and requiring separate accreditation is The Berlinale Co-Production Market .* **www.berlinale.de**

**Thessaloniki Doc Market, Thesaloniki, Greece:** *Takes place alongside the film festival and for the five days scheduled is devoted to intensive screenings, participation in the festival activities and facilitation of meetings and negotiations.* **www.filmfestival.gr/docfestival/uk**

**MIPDOC – Cannes, France:** *Held two days before MIPTV, MIPDOC brings together industry leaders in creation, development and financing to debate the hot issues affecting the production and distribution of documentary programming.* **www.mipdoc.com**

**East Silver Doc Market – Prague, Czech Republic:** *Gathers key European buyers, distributors and festival program directors. This forum allows access to difficult to find films from Central and Eastern Europe.* **www.eastsilver.net**

**The Documentary Forum, Hot Docs – Toronto, Canada:** *A unique presentation forum that assists independent documentary producers from around the world and their market partners raise co-financing from the international marketplace.* **www.hotdocs.ca**

**The IFP Market, New York, USA:** *The IFP Market is a great networking opportunity attracting 1500 filmmakers, screenwriters, distributors, television and home video acquisition executives, domestic and international buyers, agents, managers, development execs, and festival programmers from the U.S. and abroad.* **www.ifp.org**

**The Asian Film Market, Pusan, South Korea:** *Takes place alongside the Pusan International Film Festival. The market hopes to act as a bridge between the Asian film community and the world.* **www.asianfilmmarket.org**

**Docs For Sale – IDFA, Amsterdam:** *An internationally-oriented documentary market offering a limited number of selected documentaries.* **www.idfa.nl/dfs_content.asp**

313

the projects, we take more European than non-European observers.

**Q – How much does one have to pay to either attend the Forum or to be an observer?**

**Daan** – The observer fee is €310 excl. VAT (€368,90 incl. VAT) per person. The project fee differs per category: €400 excl. VAT (€ 478 incl. VAT) for a Round Table Pitch, €535 excl. VAT (€636,65 incl. VAT) for a Central Pitch. The project fees are for two people. Both fees include access to the pitching sessions, the lunches and the Forum receptions. All participants also get the Forum catalogue, the Industry Guide, the EDN Financing Guide as well as access to as to the other festival venues.

**Q – How can producers get the most out of their Forum experience?**

**Daan** – Before pitching a project here, it's a good idea to first attend the Forum as an observer to find out how it works. Not ony do producers get to know some of the people, but they are also able to gain up-to-date market knowledge and get familiar with what the potential financiers are looking for. It's important to approach the right broadcasters with your project. Don't approach a broadcaster with an arts slot with a sports documentary for example! Finally, be well prepared. Even if you're not selected to pitch your project, make sure you have a short pitch ready for informal meetings you have here, even for that very brief chance meeting during the coffee break!

**Q – How would you describe the state of the European documentary market,**

314

*particularly in the last few years where documentaries have been doing well financially at the box office?*

**Daan** – The documentary genre has been enjoying great appreciation in recent years. At Cannes, the Danish documentary *Armadillo*, pitched at the Forum in 2009, won a prestigious prize. Nonetheless, in this economic climate, the financing of creative documentaries has become more difficult as budgets of European public television stations are shrinking. Yet the main financier for documentaries in Europe is still television, and of course national funding mechanisms.

*Q – What are the common mistakes you see documentary filmmakers doing?*

**Daan** – Keep in mind that pitching your project at the Forum is an investment in not just this particular project, but also in those to come. Even if you don't receive immediate funding, be aware that commissioning editors are aware of your project and do follow-ups with these potential financiers as the project develops. Use the 8-minute Q&A as moment of feedback, try to have as many commissioning editors as possible make a comment, and use the follow-up one-on-one meetings for further discussion.

*Q – What advice would you give a documentary filmmaker?*

**Daan** – Observe the public pitches carefully and become familiar with what commissioning editors are looking for. Then approach the right commissioning editors for your particular project.

SILVERDOCS
MARYLAND, USA

SKY SITNEY

**Q – How is SilverDocs different from other film festivals?**

*Sky* – It's an exclusively documentary film festival. Discovery Channel is our founding sponsor and we're a program of The American Film Institute. One thing that is unique about us is that we're located in Silver Spring, MD outside of Washington DC. Many of the films we screen have social or political messages and are presented in an environment where leading policy makers who have the power to enact change are in the audiences.

**Q – What do you look for when you are programming films?**

*Sky* – I would say a confident artistic vision. It's harder for documentaries to achieve this than fiction films because the director can't control everything while they are shooting. But when I see a film unfold that has been crafted with intention and with integrity; that's when I get excited. It's a bit elusive, this concept of artistic vision, but it's the key component to the most successful and poignant documentaries.

**Q – What is something you wouldn't program?**

*Sky* – We stay away from films that are obviously a TV sensibility – like reality TV ideas. Even though reality TV is non-fiction, it isn't the same thing as a documentary film.

**Q – How does one apply for SilverDocs?**

*Sky* – Anyone can apply. We have some parameters as to what is eligible but that has largely to do with when the film was made, how long it has been on the circuit, if it has played locally already – things of that nature. But to apply you can either go to our website and download a paper application or use the system Withoutabox where you can

---

 **info@silverdocs.com**      **www.silverdocs.com**

 **http://twitter.com/silverdocs**

do an online application.

**Q – You host a Documentary Conference. What can a filmmaker expect from it?**

*Sky* – We have the International Documentary Conference, which is the largest of its kind. Over 1000 industry professionals participate in master classes, panels and pitching forums and works-in-progress screenings. It's a nice companion to the over 100 ecclectic documentaries we screen. We try to make it accessible to filmmakers of all levels of experience so the subjects discussed there are important to all. For example, we do fundraising panels or master classes on directing so they can improve their craft. Last year we did a master class with Steve James who did *Hoop Dreams* and *Stevie*. We do editing, music composition, distribution or transmedia. Some panels will be basic for first timers and others are more advanced so mid-career filmmakers aren't being left behind.

We also have The Good Pitch where we select eight projects from a call for entries that all had a social message. The audience watches the filmmakers pitch their ideas to a wide swath of funders from broadcasters to NGO groups. Pitching is an art form so to see those at the top of their game do it, is very beneficial.

**Q – Do you have to apply specially for the Conference?**

*Sky* – Any filmmaker who has a film accepted in SilverDocs gets a badge for the Conference. We encourage those from the general public to participate as well, but they have to buy a pass.

**Q – What is Silver Sessions?**

*Sky* – Those are forty-five to fifty, 12-on-1 mini-panels with an industry professional. It gives someone the chance to have an intimate meeting where the filmmaker can hear from that professional what they are looking for and how to navigate the terrain they represent. It's not easy for a first timer to get a meeting with the senior acquisitions person at HBO, so these sessions provide that opportunity. Filmmakers in the festival get a free pass and everyone else needs to buy one.

**Q – What is School Docs?**

*Sky* – In 2008, we created a two-day, sub-program of the conference that taps into the classroom as an arena to screen documentaries. It started out as a way to educate educators on how to adapt to the 21st century classroom by using the documentary as a teaching tool. But it morphed into a way to explain to filmmakers how to tap into an underutilized revenue stream. So filmmakers learn how they can translate their films to the educational market. For example, they may make teaching tools that go along with their film.

**Q – What format can people screen at your festival?**

## FILM FESTIVAL NECESSITIES

*Get your airfare, rental car and accommodations squared away early. See if the festival has any deals on these.*

*Save some cash so you can have fun and relax.*

*Make business cards.*

*Get your website updated and get a video camera/still camera ready for content.*

*Create a press kit for media outlets. Include your EPK in it. If you can have all of these things downloadable from your website, even better.*

*Make a trailer of your film for your press kit.*

*Bring some nice clothers for any parties you might attend.*

*Keep your cell phone charged and on. But be careful of international roaming charges.*

*Have a next project to talk about.*

*Hire a publicist for the larger festivals if you can afford it. If you can't, call all the media outlets before you go and see if you can arrange interviews.*

**Sky** – We are lucky that the festival is housed in one of the most advanced theaters in the country – the AFI-Silver Theater. We can screen everything from 16mm to 70mm in film to all kinds of digital mediums like Digibeta, Beta SP and HD. We never screen DVDs because we pride ourselves on the high quality exhibition.

### Q – Do you do shorts?

**Sky** – They are a very strong part of our festival. We have one of the most robust shorts programs in the country. We show about forty-five shorts a year. We even have noon-time, lunch-time programs that are free.

### Q – With the rise of social networking and digital filmmaking, what do you think a filmmaker should be doing in those areas when it comes to their film and going to festivals?

**Sky** – Years ago when a filmmaker got into a festival they had to rely on a grass roots style of marketing. Get there early. Put up flyers everywhere. But with Facebook and Twitter, so much of that can be accomplished beforehand. These days it's assumed that a filmmaker will have a website for their film. It wasn't that way a few years ago. I don't think that after putting all your money into a doc that you have to make an expensive website, but there should be some consideration of what it looks like. And sites like Jimdo can be very inexpensive. There are tools that can aggregate contacts so you can generate a mailing list based by zip code. That way you can target segments of your fan base so that someone in Chicago isn't getting that extra email that is meant for those in Miami. It makes your marketing so specific and powerful. The festival can do some marketing for you, but the most successful films are the ones where the filmmaker collaborates and understands how to market using these tools.

**Q – What should a filmmaker do to be prepared for a film festival publicity-wise?**

**Sky** – Good question. Certainly bring some DVDs but don't hand them out to everyone. You don't want it to seem like you are creating some kind of public forum for the film. You want the distributors to feel like they have something exclusive. Also many of these key industry professionals simply won't be able to get to your screening, so having a DVD so they can watch it in their hotel room or after the festival is a good idea. You should also be of the mindset that your best calling card is yourself. So learn how to engage with the community and remember this: the people that might be the most important to you might not be the people in power at that moment. The other filmmakers in the festivals may be profoundly important collaborators down the road.

**Q – What trends are you seeing in distribution from your end? Are more platforms showing up at festivals like iTunes?**

**Sky** – A few years ago there was this track that everyone wanted to do. Get a high profile festival launch at Sundance or Toronto and then move onto a robust festival circuit that could be more selective. And that would lead to a theatrical release by someone like Magnolia and then a broadcast release. Now I have noticed that the time window for all of this has collapsed significantly. Films can premiere at a festival and the same week they can be in theaters. With the dwindling of theatrical releases and fewer distributors, I see more self-distribution. So people might go to a festival and then straight afterwards release the film on Vimeo or an On Demand channel.

**Q – Any examples of films that have been successful that way?**

**Sky** – Race To Nowhere has screened that way. It feels like it's screening every single day! It's

## FILM FESTIVAL NECESSITIES

Meet as many people as possible. Get their business cards!

Create a buzz for your film. Pass out flyers and postcards. Get your subjects and friends to help you.

If you can afford it, throw a party for your film.

Talk to everyone about where the parties are and then crash them!

Take lots of pictures and video for your website.

Blog! Tweet! Update!

The film festival office will usually have some free food and drink if you're on a budget.

Hand out promos to jounralists and distributors.

Follow up with everyone you meet.

Don't sign any contracts at the festival unless you have your reps present.

Collect all press and reviews.

Support the other doc filmmakers at the festival by going to their screenings.

HAVE FUN!!!

319

# STILLS & IMAGE

*You need one iconic image for your posters, DVD box, postcards and website that captures the essence of your film. This image is 90% of the reason why people decide to see a film at a festival.*

*Hire a professional photographer with a great camera. High resolution is a MUST!*

*Get pictures of the director and of your primary subjects in action.*

*Your publicist is going to want 10-15 good shots. Put them on your website in a media section at full resolution for easy downloading.*

*Make sure you include the right to use these photos in the talent release document.*

*Get all your elements together before you start creating. That includes doing a MS Word version of your credits so you can check spelling. Last thing you want is to print 500 posters and have typos!*

*Use Adobe Photoshop to clean up your images or enhance them. These images are in pixels or dots so as you blow them up, the quality deteriorates. That's why high resolution masters are essential.*

*Use Adobe Illustrator or similar to handle your graphics. These are vector based programs so edges will look clean and sharp no matter how big you make them. But vectors art is that it can't be used for photo realistic images. You need Photoshop for that.*

*To make the final document (poster, postcard, etc.) combine these elements (photos and graphics) into a layout program like Adobe InDesign (used to make this book!) Quark is another good program. Mac or PC doesn't matter, just stay in one format throughout.*

*Get everything printed professionally. So burn the files to DVD or put them on a flash drive and take them down to the best place you can find. Flash drives are great to carry around with you in case you ever need to off load to someone's computer in a pinch.*

*Many online printers are very good. Ask them for samples and they will send them to you. If they look OK, go for it! Just remember they are usually printing them in China, India or some other place like that.*

a film about the education system, but it's the antithesis of *Waiting For Superman.* It makes the argument that school is too rigorous and demanding in some ways. I know it's been screening in churches and schools. I doubt a distributor would have had the time, passion and wherewithal to do this alternative model. I think it took someone dedicated and passionate about their film to do this.

**Q – What are the common mistakes that you see filmmakers make?**

**Sky** – In terms of the submission process, we get DVDs that are empty, aren't burned correctly or are scratched so we can't play them. Some times people aren't looking at the rules – we get fiction films sometimes. If a film is not accepted into a festival, I sometimes get very hostile responses. You know, one would hope this is not a one time only filmmaker, so why would you burn bridges like that? Graciousness is remembered, but hostility is remembered more. Remember, we have to turn down a lot of good work because we just can't screen them all. So don't get discouraged.

**Q – What advice would you give a new documentary filmmaker?**

**Sky** – This might sound corny, but remember that making a film is a journey. Don't be so fixated on what success means or to have a predetermined notion of what will happen. Allow for the possibility of surprise and trust what happens down the line could yield some new relationships and collaborations that could have profound impact later.

*Q – What is your job?*

*Caroline* – I'm a senior programmer of the Sundance Film Festival. I'm a member of the core programming team, responsible for selecting which feature length films are ultimately included in the festival program.

*Q – How does the selection process work for documentary films?*

*Caroline* – Everyone is welcome to submit their new films to us for consideration. It's our job to find the gems, so we take all submissions very seriously. Films may be submitted from mid-June to mid-September each year. Filmmakers should go online to our website to check annual deadlines. Every film is watched twice at Sundance. In the first round, we have excellent pre-screeners who watch and write coverage on every film (the way narrative screenplays get covered by production companies and studios). In round two, one of the programmers then screens the film. It's our job to evaluate each film, both on its own merits and in the context of the many, many other films we've reviewed in our time.

Our curatorial philosophy is this. We believe programming is not about personal taste, but about evaluating whether a film is succeeding on its own terms. Thus we work closely as a collaborative team and employ a process of group discussion and debate to reach our decisions. We understand how difficult it is to make a film, so we're always looking for a positive angle. If a programmer identifies something special in a film, that programmer will then share it with his or her colleagues on the programming team. Let's say it's me that's excited by this film: I'm first going to pass it to the colleague whom I think will like it best. And they'll then pass it on to the next person, and so on. So I'm in effect building support for it, or at least making everyone aware of it, so even if my colleagues disagree with my opinion, the film will be discussed rigorously. During this process, the film goes

---

 www.sundance.org/festival  www.facebook.com/sundance

 http://twitter.com/sundancefest

up on the proverbial Board. The Board is our list of films that at least one person on the team strongly believes should be considered for the Festival. Films on the Board are discussed and debated on at least a weekly basis.

*Q – When do you start cutting the list down to the final set?*

*Caroline* – After an ongoing process of debate over the course of many months, we make our final decisions at the end of November, right after Thanksgiving.

*Q – What gets you excited about a film that makes you want to include it in the program?*

*Caroline* – Describing what makes us want to program a film is an eternally elusive prospect, because every film is different. Every film sets its own distinct terms. The question is, does the film live up to these terms? Does it fulfill its vision? Does it accomplish what it sets out to do? Our task as programmers is to determine: what is this film trying to do? And then to evaluate it on its own standard. So if a film is trying to be a dark psychological thriller, I must evaluate it as such. If it's experimenting with form, I don't hold it up to the conventions of a more formally mainstream film. Our job is to be open to excellence, innovation, and vision in all genres and styles, and in all kinds of story telling. We believe the best film programmer is the eclectic programmer, able to appreciate and evaluate a full range of work.

With documentary, as with all films, we're open to any stylistic approach or story. There can be a film on a fresh topic we've never seen examined before, and even if the execution is rough, that's a film we're still going to consider carefully. Or sometimes the material is more familiar, but the filmmaker has a special point of view, unique access to the subject matter or a special, highly innovative artistry with the material, and that can elevate the film. Or a filmmaker might be formally experimenting in a way that particularly resonates with the content, and that can get us excited. At the same time, we might also champion a more conventional documentary if it's executed consummately.

*Q – Is there anything you would never program?*

*Caroline* – Nope. One of the definitions of the programming profession is to be open to anything and remain elastic in terms of our taste. It's important not to have preconceived notions of what's acceptable or what works in a documentary. Because you never know – people are always blazing new frontiers in all different ways, both formally and in subject matter. The truth is we never know what constitutes a "Sundance" film until we see it.

*Q – How important is the first five to ten minutes of a documentary film in terms of getting you excited?*

*Caroline* – A film doesn't need a flashy hook to grab my attention. I'm always going to stick with a film for a significant amount of time to get a sense of where the story is going.

323

Otherwise how can I evaluate it properly? Besides, some feature documentaries really take their time. I'm reminded of *Into Great Silence*, which screened in our World Cinema Documentary Competition, and won a Special Jury Prize. It's a quiet, spare film about the monks of Chartreuse who take a vow of silence. It takes its time and unfolds without dialogue, which is exactly the right tone and pace for the subject matter, because it sends us into a meditative space so we can more keenly observe and understand the monks' world. So as a programmer, it's my job to be open to that aesthetic.

*Q – Once a documentary gets into Sundance, what's the process at that point?*

*Caroline* – There's a flurry of activity as filmmakers immediately connect with the different Sundance departments such as our press office, our guest services office and print shipping department. The programming team is here to offer advice and to help filmmakers strategize how they can maximize the festival. We hold orientations for the filmmakers in Los Angeles and New York, where we explain what to expect, how to navigate the Festival, and most importantly urge them to have a good time and not stress out! Some filmmakers will retain a sales agent or publicist as well to field interest from buyers and press.

*Q – Is there anything filmmakers should have ready to go?*

*Caroline* – More and more in the documentary arena, with the democratization of digital tools, and as viewers' appetites for non-fiction grow, filmmakers are taking charge of their films' audience engagement campaigns. We're seeing filmmakers begin to build audiences early in a film's life instead of through through community partnerships, social networking, even through the fundraising process itself. It behooves documentarians to hatch and implement these grassroots marketing strategies from the start. A loyal circle of followers, active organizational partners, and a web presence will be invaluable in the distribution phase of their films.

On another, purely pragmatic note, you can never have too many good still photographs. The photograph speaks volumes about the film and is in some ways the most important tool in marketing a film to the press and future audiences. So during the shoot, I highly recommend that filmmakers hire a still photographer not just for one or two days, but for five, seven or ten days so they can really capture moments that will ultimately become the key images with which to engage viewers.

*Q – Who writes up the blurb of the film for your program?*

*Caroline* – The programmers write the program notes. These are designed to give the audience a picture of what to expect, style-wise and story-wise, from the film. At the same time the notes give us programmers a chance to wax poetic about what we admire about a particular movie.

*Q – Do you have a preferred projection format?*

*Caroline* – We can accommodate 35mm, 16mm and HDCam. Sundance led the way with digital projection. Well over half the films at the Festival are now projected on HD.

*Q – What are the various programs that Sundance has for documentary films?*

*Caroline* – Sundance has a major commitment to documentary cinema and has since the beginning. The core of the Festival is four competitions - each comprised of 16 films. And unlike any other festival in the world, two of these are documentary competitions. There's the U.S. Documentary Competition and the World Documentary Competition. There's also a new section called Documentary Premieres designed to showcase the work of more veteran documentarians. Documentaries often appear in our New Frontier and Midnight sections as well.

*Q – Does Sundance program documentary shorts?*

*Caroline* – Absolutely. Every year we play 75-80 shorts in the festival and there are always documentaries among them. We usually have a shorts program dedicated to documentaries. And then there are also documentary shorts that play prior to features. There are so many great ones that come through.

*Q – Do you talk to the Sundance Labs when looking for films and do you discuss your program with the Sundance Channel to promote distribution?*

*Caroline* – We collaborate and work closely, but we don't have influence over each other's decisions. So if I talk to Cara Mertes or Rahdi Taylor about a documentary project that I really hope they'll consider for the Sundance Documentary Fund or Lab, I can share my enthusiasm, but it's not my decision. And likewise, if they recommend a film they're supporting to the festival, I'm going to take that very seriously. But they cannot make the final decision. It's a nice check and balance. We sometimes share ideas with the Sundance Channel as well, but certainly don't directly influence their programming.

**Q – Do you find that most of the docs in your programs are self-funded or do they have some sort of financial backing?**

*Caroline* – It's a mix of private equity, broadcast deals, foundation grants, charitable donations, and corporate funding. Many filmmakers end up self-financing at least part of their documentaries because often they have to generate a sample reel on their own before outside funders will jump on board. It remains to be seen how significant a role crowdfunding will play in documentary financing.

**Q – How about on the international side?**

*Caroline* – The Europeans have a lot wider basis of public and broadcast funding for documentary, so there is a higher percentage there of films with formal funding behind them and much less reliance on equity and charitable funding.

**Q – Do the broadcasters lobby you to include their films?**

*Caroline* – We're certainly in touch with key people at the broadcasting companies. We welcome recommendations from colleagues we respect. That doesn't mean that if someone suggests something to us we're necessarily going to show it. A recommended film doesn't become any more important than a film we've never heard of that comes in without any personal "connection" to Sundance. Each film still has to speak for itself.

**Q – Do you ever solicit films from filmmakers?**

*Caroline* – We're always reaching out to filmmakers, producers and companies to see what they have in the pipeline. We keep careful tracking lists and we check in on films that we know are in the finishing stages. On the international front, because we are dealing with the whole world and there are so many countries each with their own national cinemas and output of product, we do a lot of outreach work with sales agents, film commissions, production companies, and filmmakers. That said, we're always especially excited and delighted when we find great films that come to us without any prior connection.

**Q – What are the common mistakes that you see documentary filmmakers make?**

*Caroline* – Filmmakers often underestimate the time needed to edit a documentary and end up submitting their films to us before they're fully cooked. The truth is there aren't any shortcuts when you're chiseling structure and story out of hours and hours of footage. My advice is, budget for ample editing time, schedule in break days to gain new perspective, and be rigorous: seek advice and counsel from smart colleagues, figure out what your film is about in its juicy core of meaning and make that course through the film's DNA, study other relevant films.

*Q – What advice would you give a new documentary filmmaker?*

*Caroline* – It's tremendously difficult, perhaps even impossible, to make a living as a documentary filmmaker, so be realistic, but don't take your eyes off the prize. If you've got a story to tell, do not be deterred.

**Q – What does a producer's rep do as opposed to a sales agent?**

*Josh* – We represent producers with a primary focus on selling domestic theatrical rights to get the best possible deals on their behalf. Sales agents work on selling the rights to various territories around the world but often not North America.

**Q – What are you looking for in a film that makes you want to represent it?**

*Josh* – We are looking for something new that we haven't seen before. It's always exciting when it's different and unique in either the topic or the filmmaking style. An example of that is a film we took on to represent recently called *Scene of the Crime*, which was at The Full Frame Film Festival and ended up winning the grand jury prize. The spine of that film is an interrogation. The filmmakers got the rights to utilize a ten hour interrogation of a suspect. The film then goes back and forth to see the POV of various people connected to the process. So we saw the POV of the lawyers, the police officers and the jury members. It seemed really fresh to me. I don't remember ever seeing anything like it. It's very emotional and immediate.

**Q – When is the best time for a filmmaker to approach a producer's rep?**

*Josh* – In any calendar year, pretty much anytime except around the big festivals like Sundance or Toronto. If the Sundance Film Festival is about to happen and your film didn't get into that festival, that is not usually the best time to approach a producer's rep but sometimes a gem can be discovered so there are no hard and fast rules. July is a slow month for us because there aren't many festivals happening but it's also a time when we try to wrap up deals from Tribeca, Cannes and other festivals and it's a time when we are primarily gearing up for Toronto in the fall.

---

 **www.submarine.com**

*Q – Do you prefer to see completed films or will you look at works-in-progress?*

*Josh* – We will look at almost anything although we won't look at a written proposal. But if someone has a three minute demo reel, that's fine, too. The best advice I have is that you should come to us when you feel your project is really strong. We sometimes see films that get to us too early. An example of that is *Catfish*. We saw it before it was invited to Sundance and before they brought on an executive producer who gave them substantial notes that made the film closer to what it was when it premiered. When we saw it we thought there was something fascinating there, but it was perhaps a little uncooked and the narrative was not in focus at that early stage.

*Q – Do you help filmmakers strategize festival releases and distribution sales?*

*Josh* – Yes. Any producer's rep working today has to be able to negotiate the film festival maze but our focus would of course be on the festivals that are more specifically focused on sales. The same goes for figuring out the best distribution model to use – that's our bread and butter. But yes, we can help with the film festival launch so bringing us on early and making us part of that conversation can be helpful to the end result of what you are trying to achieve.

*Q – Do you ever help find financing for documentary films?*

*Josh* – We do, but it's not our primary mandate. For certain projects we feel strongly about or feel a strong personal connection to we may come on board to serve that function but usually we come onto the scene once a film is more or less close to be finished – perhaps at a rough cut stage.

*Q – What can a filmmaker do to make their film more visible?*

*Josh* – Well, sometimes we don't want the film to be visible. We want to hold it back and build industry interest prior to a festival. Then we might release a short teaser so the community can get a sense of it and excited by the film. Other times we want a lot of awareness so we will have the filmmaker start a Facebook page if they haven't already created one. We will get them on Twitter to raise awareness. We have them connect with grass roots organizations that have some kind of investment in the topic of the film.

*Q – In our last interview, you said your fee was about 15%. Is that still true?*

*Josh* – Our fee is different for each film. Sometimes it's 12.5%, sometimes it's 10% and sometimes we do 15%. We rarely go below 10%. When we handle direct international sales on behalf of a film it can be 15-20%.

*Q – Do you help filmmakers navigate deliverables?*

*Josh* – Generally, we don't handle delivery on behalf of producers and filmmakers. We don't know what kind of clearances or material they have so it can be a slippery slope. If we are involved in the film at an early stage, for instance with a film like Andrew Rossi's *Page One*, then we may get involved in assisting with delivery because we were involved in the production process.

**Q – Is there something a filmmaker can do to help make a film visible at a festival?**

*Josh* – When we sold *Page One* at Sundance, David Carr and Brian Stelter from *The New York Times*, who are subjects in the film, happened to be there. They were great spokespeople for the film and that really helped having them at the Q&A sessions after the film played. The year before we were at Sundance with Joan Rivers. Between our team, her team and both our publicists we were able to make a lot of noise. If you can't afford publicists, then leveraging the support of those in the community that your film speaks to can be a powerful tool.

**Q – Does shooting on HD effect how you do business in any way?**

*Josh* – Not really because almost all films are shot on a version of it these days. The point of entry into HD cameras is so affordable now.

**Q – What is the state of distribution right now for documentaries?**

*Josh* – The world of distribution that we are in right now is fairly complicated in terms of splitting rights and figuring out digital windows such as streaming rights and VOD rights. It's especially crucial for docs where you might have sold the TV window in order to get financing to make the film and then you have to figure out how to handle the rest of it. It becomes very complicated and you should hire someone who lives and breathes it every day to help you sort it out.

*Q – How does distribution and worldwide rights work with the global portal of the internet?*

*Josh* – There is usually language in most contracts that states that until there is a geo-filtering technology that can keep films exclusive to certain territories, internet exploitation is prohibited. Once a film is officially streaming on the internet, you are really far down the windows of exploitation and not too worried about it. If it's streaming in one country and still in a first window, such as TV, in another, then that can be a problem unless it is territorially restricted.

*Q – What are the common mistakes that you see documentary filmmakers make?*

*Josh* – The biggest issue is that filmmakers don't get the correct level of clearances for their archival material. And sometimes they don't have releases from all their subjects. Also many first time filmmakers are blissfully unaware how incredibly expensive music can be. They stick a Beatles song in a temp mix and hope the distributor falls in love with that song and will pay for it to be included. That almost never happens.

*Q – What advice would you give a new documentary filmmaker?*

*Josh* – Understand why you want to do this. If your goal is to be rich and famous, then being a documentary filmmaker isn't the right path for you. If you're passionate about certain stories and want to tell them, then you're on the right track. Also take some time to learn the craft. We see some good films where the camera and sound work is really rough. If the director and his team had just taken more care to get sound, framing and lighting just right it may have elevated the film to another level. More than anything be true to yourself and tell a story you actually care about.

*Q – What does a publicist do?*

**David** – We implement press strategies for films. This includes looking at all angles that would be hot topics for press to cover. We work with the filmmakers, the producers, the sales reps, the distributor and the entire team to ensure that we can position the films correctly and get maximum press coverage and marketing on the project. And I also pitch journalists to write features or reviews on films that are going into theatrical, broadcast or film festivals.

*Q – When is a good time for a filmmaker to approach you?*

**David** – Usually I get approached right as they are finishing their film and they want to set up a film festival strategy. Or they will call me when they get into a major film festival like Sundance, Tribeca, Toronto, Berlin or South by Southwest. Once the film is picked up, we are approached by the distributor to work on publicity and marketing.

*Q – Do you help them create the image of the film?*

**David** – What I do is listen to the vision of the director. Then we look at the film and see which images would be the best to give out to the press. We look at their current press kit and help them edit the various sections like the filmmaker's notes. It's an important part because it allows journalists who don't have access to the filmmaker to look through the notes and see what the point of view of the filmmakers was in terms of making the film. With photos, we try to find that iconic one that says what the film is or that will show up in print. So for *Super Size Me*, the photo was always the one with Morgan Spurlock's mouth stuffed with french fries. For *Mad Hot Ballroom*, it was always the two kids dancing on the street with the city of New York behind them. The photos for *Being Elmo* are with Kevin Clash, who the movie is about, with Elmo right by his side.

*Q – Is it important for the director to take pictures of the filmmaking process?*

---

 dmagdael@tcdm-associates.com     www.tcdm-associates.com

**David** – First we would want a headshot of the director. Then a shot of the filmmaker on set with either the subjects or the camera. That always makes for a good action photo. Then what is most important and often missed is we need a set of amazing photos from the film that we can present to the press to use in articles and coverage. Having photos from the film and the set are VERY IMPORTANT and should be considered during filming. However, if this is impossible we can possibly get screen grabs. Although, that is not the best, but it can work.

## Q – How do you charge for your services?

**David** – For a festival, we charge a flat fee. For a large festival like Sundance, you're looking to pay fees for a strong publicist anywhere between $10,000-$15,000. If you want to do a festival run, then every agency is going to be different about how they are going to handle that. For us, we'd come to an agreement about how much work would be done over say those three to four months and come up with a fee structure.

## Q – When you sign a filmmaker, what's the first strategy session like?

**David** – First and foremost, we have to love the film as much as the filmmaker. We have to bring as much passion to the table as the filmmaker does because we are going to be positioning that film to journalists and to the public. Personally, it has to move me or be something that I've never seen before.

Then we would sit down with the filmmaker and discuss with them what their objective of the film is. What do they want the audience to take away after viewing the film? Why is the film important to them? Why did they make it? Then the third thing we discuss is the distribution objective of the filmmaker. Do they want theatrical or broadcast? Fourth, we like to meet with the producers and the sales rep so that we know when they have a world premiere, what that press is going to be geared towards. We want to get audience buzz on a film possibly so the journalists will want to go see and review it. At the end of the day, it's about the strategy and planning how we need to market and promote the film to the press and public.

## Q – Has the format of the press kit changed at all over the last few years?

**David** – I think it's pretty much the same – a Word document or a PDF. What's changed is how you get the information out. Every film should have a website, a Facebook fan page and the press kit should be on both areas. Do you need to have a Twitter account? It depends on what the film is. You want to make sure you can have downloadable pictures as well as the press kit. You could have clips on there too. Do you need to cut a trailer? Not necessarily. If you have the time and resources to do so, then it's up to you. Most of the companies that pick up your film will cut their own trailer. And they can be a minute or a minute and a half long. But what I really need are four clips that run sixty seconds long that we can use to get you on radio and TV. In these four clips, there

*This should be detailed enough so that a journalist could write about your film without seeing it. Put it on your website for easy downloading*

**Cover:** *Film title, contact details, press quotes, any awads won and perhaps a good still image or symbol that represents the film.*

**Synopsis:** *The plot of the film. Pop in a few pictures to spice it up. Don't give away the ending.*

**Cast & Crew List:** *Bios of main subjects and crew members. Have photos of each for easy indentification.*

**Production Notes:** *The story of how the film got made - where, when, why and how.*

**Reviews:** *Good ones only!*

**Credits:** *Full credit list without bios. Many media outlets require this now.*

**Miscellenous:** *Anything else that the press needs to write about your film like a glossary of industry terms.*

cannot be anyone doing drugs, we shy away from profanity as well as nudity. So when you're on a show and they say, *"Let's go to your clip,"* you want that clip to be able to get people excited to say they want to see it.

**Q – So the electronic press kit (EPK) is still going strong these days.**

**David** – I think it is.

**Q – Has the format changed at all? It used to be on Beta SP tape.**

**David** – Beta SP still works some places. Some stations will play DVDs. One thing that's changed is you can put your clips up on Vimeo or an FTP site and then the station can download them. That's great because I don't have to FedEx them as much anymore. Radio stations like DVDs. I only use CDs for sending photos these days and to be honest, it's so much better to have high res photos on your website or Facebook page so people can download them as they need them. Some festivals will put parts of your press kit up on their websites for you these days.

**Q – What are the other parts of the press kit that people should create?**

**David** – We need a filmmaker bio and a characters bio. Character bios can be up to a page, but I would keep them to a paragraph. You should do a bio for the editor and if you have any special crew such as a well-known composer. You want a page long synopsis of the film plot.

You want to have filmmaker notes that are two or three pages. And when you do your filmmaker notes you need to answer a few questions. First, you want to answer how you found the subject. Two, why did you make this film? And three, what do you want the audience to take away from the film about the subject matter? Then you want to have an anecdote about the making of the film that's interesting. Maybe you started shooting and then something happened that changed the whole production process.

Something else that has changed is that journalists want a full credit list – up to four pages long. If the composer or producer is someone they know or if the DP shoots something incredible, they want to have the credit list to refer to. They even want the thank you section in case there's someone of note in there. Just remember that the press kit is a tool for the journalists to use should they not have access to you. Write it with that in mind.

**Q – Are there some publicity items that filmmakers can create which they may think are expensive, but in fact, aren't?**

**David** – You should have a theatrical poster. It should be thirty inches by forty inches. You want to present your film as a real movie and posters help that. You should put them up wherever the film screens and wherever people buy tickets. The other question that comes up is post cards. It gives you presence and they don't cost very much, so if you can make them, it can't hurt. The other thing that might not be expensive but you might not really need is schwag. You have to decide if you need key chains, buttons or tee shirts. For some films like *Being Elmo* it makes sense. To extend the experience of the film, the filmmakers purchased Elmo iPhone covers that had the screening times on it. Another thing that was popular at Sundance was buttons that you could put on your lanyard. That way as people are walking around, you have a presence. But don't get caught up in schwag. Only do it if it makes sense and if you have the money.

**Q – What pointers would you give for dealing with the press during an interview?**

**David** – Speak from your heart and tell the truth. What I like to do is do a "media training" session with the filmmakers and the subjects of the film and go over what questions most likely will be asked. And we also tell them that now their film is in a large festival that people are going to start calling

## THE EPK

*The Electronic Press Kit is used for TV, radio and web media outlets.*

*Include 3-4, one minute clips of your film that don't give away the ending.*

*Shoot a behind the scenes/ making of the doc. Shoot on HD and interview the director, producer and main subjects on why they choose to make the film.*

*Use music from the film as the score for the behind the scenes section.*

*Find a quiet room with a nice background to shoot EPK interviews. You can use simple three point lighting schemes and a lavaliere microphone.*

*Make DVD copies for your publicist if you have one. Put it on your website or on an FTP site, so journalists can access it easily.*

*Make sure your interviewees repeat the question in their answer for easier editing. (What is your role in Gasland? My role on Gasland was…)*

*State the name of the film often.*

*1. You are never off the record with the press. If you don't want something printed, don't say it.*

*2. You will be asked the same questions over and over again. Be prepared with concise, intelligent, humorous or profound responses.*

*3. If you're being recorded, pause before answering. This will give the editor a clear editing point.*

*4. Answer the question with the question in the answer. For example: "What was working with an elephant like? " is answered, "Working with an elephant was amazing..."*

*5. Say the name of your film as many times as you can. Try to avoid referring to the movie as "the film" or "the project". If people don't know what it is called they won't go see it.*

*6. You may avoid answering confrontational questions, especially if the reporter has a grudge against you. Politely decline to answer or shift the conversation back to the film itself.*

them. We prefer that the filmmakers send all media inquiries over to us as the publicists to clear everything out. We also want to discuss any sensitive issues and/or topics for the filmmaker and subject ahead of time. We want them to be as comfortable as possible. I don't want them to feel ambushed. We don't "spin" or create answers because your reality is your reality. And if a journalist doesn't agree with you, it doesn't matter. This is your truth of the story.

**Q – Can you ever have too much publicity at the wrong time?**

**David** – Yes and that's why you work out a strategy. Something may happen when the filmmaker or the subject are suddenly thrust into the spotlight. If that happens, then we deal with it in a strategic way. But normally, we try to plan the publicity so that it coincides with a festival or whatever the film's distribution pattern will be.

What's different these days is that things happen so fast. Someone says something on Twitter to the internet universe and it gets picked up really quickly. We are living in a time where everything is "breaking news." One of my clients, doc filmmaker Morgan Spurlock, has a Twitter account and tweets regularly. I "follow" his Twitter feed so that I can monitor anything that comes up of which I should be aware.

**Q – What do you do when something goes wrong and you have to do damage control?**

**David** – In those situations, we try to get all the facts and respond to the problem as strategically and quickly as possible. We need to know the facts of what really happened. For example, If there's a situation where the filmmaker or the subject has to apologize, then we work with them to develop a strategy of how to deal with this and try to do this in a timely manner. People who try to hide things seem to always get discovered. And the more you keep people in limbo the more they will start to make up their own minds. Get the facts, come up with a strategy and if need be, come out with a statement. It's all very tricky and you want the situation to be handled swiftly, efficiently and effectively.

### Q – What are the common mistakes you see filmmakers make?

**David** – The biggest common mistake I see happen doc filmmakers is when they don't embrace their subjects of the film they just made. They forget that they are the conduit by which the public now sees the lives or issues of their film's subject. Your subject is the subject of your movie. It is the subject of your film that is going to make your film stand out and be ahead of the pack. And if you embrace that notion, it will only be a win win situation for you and your film.

Patience is also something one needs to consider. The other thing is worrying too much about getting into Sundance. It's OK if you don't. There are other avenues these days for getting your film seen and to get a sale. South by Southwest has really come up in the last few years. Slamdance is another very viable option. Their programming has gotten better and better and the documentaries are usually through the roof. And don't forget about Hot Docs. You also have Tribeca, LA Film Fest, New Directors New Films, Seattle International, San Francisco International, Palm Springs and other regional festivals that are fast becoming important in finding your audience and getting the film out there to press and buyers.

### Q – What advice would you give a new filmmaker?

**David** – Go out and make your project. If you fail, it's OK. Pick yourself up and try again. There are too many people who run around saying they have a project and they never do finish it. If being a filmmaker is the thing that lights the fire in your gut, then own it and do it. FINISH THAT FILM!!!!!

## HANDLING THE PRESS

7. Always have your publicity stuff on you – press pack, EPK, stills, posters, etc. Business cards, too, so they spell your name correctly.

8. Telling good, relevant stories is always better than giving boring standard information.

9. Make sure you know how long the interview will last so you can get the maximum amount of information out.

10. The interviewer may want you to say something particular or in a particular way. Indulge them as long as they are accurate!

11. Always be complimentary of other filmmakers and their work and others with whom you have worked.

12. Avoid talking about the budget of your film unless it was truly a remarkable feat such as you made it for $7,000 generated by having medical experiments done to you.

13. If you are setting up the interviews, do it early. Most magazineshave 3-4 month lead times. Online media is much more nimble.

# GLOBAL FILM FESTIVAL CHART

## JANUARY

**Sundance Film Festival**
Park City, Utah, USA
www.sundance.org

**Slamdance Int. Film Festival**
Park City, Utah, USA
www.slamdance.com

**Rotterdam Film Festival**
Rotterdam, The Netherlands
www.filmfestivalrotterdam.com

**Goteborg Film Festival**
Goteborg, Sweden
www.giff.se

## FEBRUARY

**Berlin Film Festival**
Berlin, Germany
www.berlinale.de

**Jamison Dublin Int. Fest.**
Dublin, Ireland
www.jdiff.com

**Mumbai Int. Film Fest. for Doc. Short and Animation**
Mumbai, India
www.miffindia.in

**Bangkok Int. Film Festival**
Bangkok, Thailand
www.bangkokfilm.org

## MARCH

**It's All True International Documentary Film Festival**
Sao Paulo, Brazil
www.itsalltrue.com.br

**Thessaloniki Doc. Festival**
Thessaloniki, Greece
http://tdf.filmfestival.gr

**South by Southwest**
Austin, Texas, USA
www.sxsw.com

**Amnesty Int. Film Festival**
Several Cities
www.amnestyfilmfest.ca

**Chicago Int. Doc. Film Fest.**
Chicago, USA
www.chicagodocfestival.org

**London Lesb. & Gay Fest**
London, UK
www.llgff.org.uk

## APRIL

**Full Frame Doc. Film Fest.**
Durham, North Carolina, USA
www.fullframefest.org

**San Francisco Int. Film Fest.**
San Francisco, USA
www.sffs.org

**Munich Doc. Film Festival**
Munich, Germany
www.dokfest-muenchen.de

**Hot Docs**
Toronto, Canada
www.hotdocs.ca

**One World Human Rights**
Prague, Czech Republic
www.oneworld.cz

**African Diaspora Film Fest.**
New York, USA
www.nyaadiff.org

**Hong Kong Intl. Film Fest.**
Hong Kong
www.hkiff.org.hk

**Doc Aviv**
Tel Aviv, Israel
www.docaviv.co.il

## MAY

**DocFest**
New York, USA
www.docfest.org

**Seattle Int. Film Festival**
Seattle, USA
www.siff.net

**Tribeca Film Festival**
New York, USA
www.tribecafilm.com

**Doxa Doc. Film Festival**
Vancouver, Canada
www.doxafestival.ca

**Hollywood Doc. Film Fest.**
Los Angeles, USA
www.hollywoodawards.com

**Melbourne Int. Film Fest.**
Melbourne, Australia
www.miff.com.au

**London Int. Film Festival**
London, UK
www.lff.org.uk

## JUNE

**Human Rights Watch International Film Festival**
New York, USA
www.hrw.org/iff

**SilverDocs**
Silver Spring, Maryland, USA
www.silverdocs.com

**Florida Film Festival**
Florida, USA
www.floridafilmfest.com

**Sydney Film Festival**
Sydney, Australia
www.sydneyfilmfestival.org

**Hollywood Black Film Fest.**
Laos Angeles USA
www.hbff.org

## JULY

**Encounters Doc. Film Fest.**
Cape Town, South Africa
www.encounters.co.za

**Karlovy Vary Int. Film Fest.**
Karlovy Vary, Czech Republic
www.iffkv.cz

**Message to Man**
St. Petersburg, Russia
www.message-to-man.spb.ru

**Jerusalem Film Festival**
Jerusalem, Israel
www.jff.org.il

**AUGUST**
**Edinburgh Int. Film Festival**
Edinburgh, Scotland
www.edfilmfest.org.uk

**Haifa Film Festival**
Haifa, Israel
www.haifaff.co.il

**SEPTEMBER**
**Taiwan Int. Doc. Festival**
Taipei, Taiwan
www.tiff.org.tw

**DocNZ: New Zealand**
New Zealand
www.docnzfestival.com

**QueerDOC**
Sydney, Australia
www.queerscreen.com.au

**Raindance Film Festival**
London, UK
www.raindance.co.org

**Jackson Hole Wildlife Film Festival**
Wyoming, USA
www.jhfestival.org

**Vancouver Int. Film Festival**
Vancouver, USA
www.viff.org

**OCTOBER**
**Sao Paulo Int. Film Festival**
Sao Paulo, Brazil
www.mostra.org

**Yamagata Int. Doc. Film Fest.**
Yamagata, Japan
www.yidff.jp

**Sheffield Int. Doc. Film Fest.**
Sheffield, England
www.sidf.co.uk

**Hot Springs Doc. Film Fest.**
Arkansas, USA
www.hsdfi.org

**UN Assoc. Film Festival**
www.unaff.org

**Ukranian Doc. Film Festival**
Kyiv, Ukraine
www.molodist.com

**AFI/LA Int. Film Festival**
Los Angeles, USA
www.afifest.com

**Pusan Int. Film Festival**
Pusan, South Korea
www.piff.kr

**Int. Leipzig Fest. for Doc. and Animated Film**
Leipzig, Germany
www.dok-leipzig.de

**Jihlava Int. Doc. Film Fest.**
Jihlava, Czech Republic
www.dokument-festival.cz

**Abu Dhabi Film Festival**
Abu Dhanbi, UAE
www.abudhabifilmfestival.ae

**NOVEMBER**
**IDFA – Amsterdam**
The Netherlands
www.idfa.nl

**Montreal Int. Doc. Film Fest.**
Montreal, Canada
www.ridm.qc.ca

**Beirut Int. Doc. Film Festival**
Beirut, Lebanon
www.docudays.com

**Int. Film Fest. of Barcelona**
Barcelona, Spain
www.alternativa.cccb.org

**Int. Fest. of Doc./Bilbao**
Bilbao, Spain
www.zinebi.com

**Stockholm Int. Film Fest.**
Stockholm, Sweden
www.stockholmfilmfestival.se

**DECEMBER**
**Cairo Film Festival**
Cairo, Egypt
www.cairofilmfest.org

# CHAPTER TEN
# SALES AND DISTRIBUTION

## THE DOCUMENTARY
## FILMMAKERS HANDBOOK

THE SALES REP

JAN ROFEKAMP
FILMS TRANSIT

## Q – What is Films Transit?

*Jan* – We sell licenses and rights of documentary films for people to use them in certain media worldwide. We operate out of Montreal, Canada and have an office in New York, which Diana Holtzberg runs. Lots of these media are broadcasters as the market for documentaries is primarily a broadcast market. If you look at the world map, there are about two hundred sovereign states and about forty to forty-five buy the type of documentaries that we're interested in, which are mainly political, social and cultural documentaries. Why only these countries? Because they're the countries with a tradition of some kind of public broadcasting, and it has always been public broadcasters that buy these docs. Overall, broadcasters account for 75% of the sales and 25% is other media - theatrical, educational, festivals, the DVD market and increasingly the new media: Internet stream and/or download, all kinds of forms of VOD, etc.

## Q – You said you like social, political and cultural documentaries. What makes for a good one that you would take on?

*Jan* – Don't forget that buyers, after having bought a film, have to 'sell' that film to their audiences, whether this in the cinema, or on dvd or on the small screen. What we increasingly hear from buyers is that it's important that the viewers in a country can relate to the subject matter. It has to be told in a way that no matter where it comes from, people all over can relate to it. The buyers ask themselves the crucial question: why does my audience HAVE to see this film? You as a producer should ask yourself the same question. If you or we have a very good answer to that question, half the work is done.

So what are the subjects that are on top of the priority list? Subjects that people think about. Subjects that are on top of peoples' minds. These are things that translate. Films with a certain relevance. Then they have to be decently made. There has to be some kind of a filmmaker signature. There are a lot of sales agents out there that will sell whatever they can get their hands on that seems commercial. Many of these films

 janrofekamp@filmtransit.com     www.filmtransit.com

are what you would not call significant filmmaking. They last 52 minutes, they have a beginning, middle and an end and they are bland. They may do well because of the subject matter, but it's nothing special, they do not have an impact, nor do they change people's thinking. I like to have films that are just a little special. Films that will make you remember them.

We have two specialties as well. We're always interested in documentaries about cinema. And we are always interested in a quirky film about sex. But a film that has something to say.

### Q – What would you not be interested in?

*Jan –* There's a whole slew of what we call factual entertainment: pretty blandly made films on science, history, food, travel , etc. You know them: image, interviewee, statistic, image, interviewee – a very simple way of filmmaking. There's a lot of docs on exploration. Every single millimeter of the world has been explored - more than once.And every animal has been filmed more than once. Every time you put on channels like these you see sharks or tigers. I'm not interested in that. I'm not interested in sports unless it's a social issue about sports. There have been some stories about soccer in different parts of the world, which are quite significant. The market has a hard time with short films, which is sad. It's not that people don't like shorts; there's just no economics in them. We'll occasionally take on a short because we like it. Whenever we meet a buyer, we show it and they usually buy it, but for very little money. Classical music, dance, opera I'm not interested in because there are  well functioning infrastructures for people to co-produce with each other and where buyers for these genres meet each other.

### Q – Does it matter these days what format a documentary is shot on?

*Jan –* It has to be digital. It has to be 16x9. And today it has to be HD. I heard someone say, *"If your film is in HD you can do broadcast, if you don't have HD, you can only do on-line."*

### Q – What are some other reasons that documentary films don't sell?

*Jan –* The biggest problem we face is the overwhelming number of documentary filmmakers out there. Almost anything has been 'done,' almost any subject has been touched. I hear of great films and a day later I hear of a film on the same subject, sometimes even with the same protagonists.

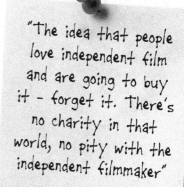

*"The idea that people love independent film and are going to buy it - forget it. There's no charity in that world, no pity with the independent filmmaker"*

You can ask yourself the question, *"But how different is a tenth film about homeless people?"*

1. Consider the viability of your film as a salesman - would I want this film and if not, why?

2. Style counts in doc, but not as much as content. If your story is great and the information satisfies the built in audience, you have a shot at selling it.

3. Sales people are tough negotiators. They will want long sales times from you with high commissions and expenses paid. Advances are rare these days. Try to get them to reduce something so that you get a better deal.

4. Try to keep either some territories or platforms for yourself to sell in case your sales agent messes you about. This way you can do a direct sale and keep all the money for yourself.

5. Alongside your actual film, a distributor will want deliverables - technical things needed for the broadcast. Your sales agent will get you a list of what's needed and guide you through the creation process.

Or how different is a film on homelessness from the USA, the UK or from Finland? How different is a tenth film about the Middle East issues? Anyone who is looking for their next subject matter has to think twice. Not just twice because someone else may have done it already, but how can I do it differently? Whenever I do courses or workshops, I always say the moment before you start making a film, you have to do a lot of research and find out if your subject matter is appropriate for a documentary. Maybe it is better to a 20-minute item.

### Q – Should filmmakers always try to make feature length documentaries?

**Jan -** A feature documentary has a lot of advantages and a lot of disadvantages. Maybe it's a subject that's better for an hour format. Now you get into the real crucial issues that filmmakers have to think about. If you make a feature documentary, you have to have a story that starts somewhere and goes somewhere. It has to have a beginning of a story that develops all the way to the end. If you don't have that and instead do something observational where you just follow someone, that's not a structure. The other thing is if you desperately want to do a feature doc, we're increasingly finding that broadcasters don't want them. It's not an issue for DVD. It's not an issue for festivals. But it is for broadcasters. There are less and less slots in prime time for long format documentaries. And with the exception of places like The Sundance Channel, ARTE, the BBC, documentaries aren't a priority. Even the Germans, the Belgians and the Fins, they do pay attention to documentaries, but it isn't a priority. That translates into practical issues. If you go to the market with a feature length doc, you'll almost never get it into prime time. It will have to air after 11PM or midnight. If you make an hour version of your film and everyone likes you film, you can get a 9PM or 10PM screening. That's a choice filmmakers have to make while in production. Increasingly, we're cutting down films that were once feature length films. Filmmakers always say they don't want to cut it down because it is too hard or it costs too much and why don't we see if we can sell it as a feature. It is not a good idea anymore. But we think they have no choice and might as well start thinking about this during their production process.

**Q – How important are film festivals to selling documentaries and which are the important ones for documentaries?**

**Jan –** Festivals are very important. There's a big distinction between how it works in the US and the rest of the world. In the US. we have figured out that if you literally plug your film into the twelve key festivals such as Tribeca, Seattle, Denver, Full Frame, Hamptons and SXSW, you'll get a cumulative effect. It means that the film comes floating to the surface and the chances of you making a deal in the US are pretty high. There's a lot of DVD interest for documentaries in the US. Overall there are about three thousand film festivals. But there are only 4 that we call launch pads: Berlin, Sundance, Toronto and Amsterdam – those are the launch pads for feature docs. Once you have done that, I'd say there about 35 to 40 key festivals in the world. Sydney and Melbourne, Yamagata in Japan, DocPoint in Finland, the Stockholm Film Festival, The Munich Dokumentary Fest, Rio, DocsBarcelona, Nyon, It's all True in Brazil, Hong Kong, Encounters in South Africa etc. are part of these 35 to 40 key festivals. If you don't have a deal yet in these countries, you can try to get one there. If you do have a deal, then the distributor can use the film festival as a national launch pad. This is what our strategy is all about: launch pads and key festivals. We do the US. We do the launch pads. We create a strategy for the key festivals, but hand that over to the filmmakers we work with. The producers have to do the work there, but we tell them exactly what to do. Beyond that, there're a zillion other festivals and we don't want to know about them unless it's a nice vacation trip. We also need to have some fun sometimes. The market is not big enough

## SALES AGENT TIPS

6. Try not to state how much the budget of your film is. It might lead to low ball offers.

7. Attending a big doc film market will give you a good idea of what you sales agent is doing. These are not creative, they are all buisness.

8. At film markets, look to see which companies buy docs like yours and approach them.

9. Get a performance clause in your sales agent agreement so that if they aren't delivering, you can get your film back and move to someone else.

10. Cap their expenses! Otherwise you will never see any money from your film.

11. Be tough from day one. Demand reports and payment on time and as agreed. You will not tolerate complacency. And if you make yourself a nuisance, which is within your rights, you may get what you want.

12. You don't have to go with a sales agent from your country. Go with the one tha best for you or offers you the best deal.

*1. Ask yourself what interests you need to protect and are they sufficiently protected.*

*2. Do you have any existing contractual obligations to other people? Are you going to be in breach of those existing contractual obligations?*

*3. What are your liabilities in this agreement and if things go wrong, what are you liable for? Look out for clauses which make you personally liable even though you may be contracting through a company i.e. a personal guarantee for a loan which is being made to your company?*

*4. Is the agreement reasonable and within your power to deliver?*

*5. If you are required under the agreement to do something, ask to change any reference to your using your 'best endeavors' to 'reasonable endeavors'.*

*6. If you are providing your own original work or any intellectual property owned by you under the terms of the agreement, what happens if the project does not go ahead? Do you have the chance to regain or repurchase your property?*

to soak up all the documentaries that are made. So people have to make selections and they select the films that they like or have heard of. So we want all of our films to pop up in all those key festivals in order to create a reputation for them.

**Q – What are the important film markets to attend?**

**Jan –** All of the bigger festivals have some kind of facility that allows people to do a bit of business. That's very good. But there are a couple of broadcast only markets, which are MIP-COM and MIP-TV. In the broadcast world, these are musts. They are not easy to operate because they're huge. Ten years ago, people would walk by and make an appointment and everyone was cool about everything. Now seven weeks before the festival, people start e-mailing their appointments. The only way it works is to go there with an agenda. If you go there just to take a look, you'll get lost. You'll leave town screaming. If you have an agenda with appointments, it makes a lot of sense because people have time for you, they are in the mood and they're concentrating. Then there are the film markets – Berlin, Cannes, Sundance and Toronto. My assessment is that the people that go to these markets are primarily fiction film buyers. People say that now there's a lot more interest in theatrical documentaries – it's still very fragile. If during a year or two there are no major worldwide documentary theatrical hits, the interest fades away. The broadcast markets are very clear. The film markets are very trend sensitive. One big difference that we see between now and 15 years ago, is that 15 years ago if you went to a market screening for a high profile documentary, none of the theatrical and DVD people would show up. Now they do show up. It doesn't mean that they will buy, but they're going to see the films.

**Q – Does it make a difference in the deal if you sell a film at or after a market?**

*Jan* – I'm not so sure. I think it's important to grab the opportunity at the festival if there's interest. The trick after the festival is to solidify the interest and get them to sign on the dotted line. Filmmakers have to realize that in the broadcast world where most documentaries go, the decision to buy is a decision based on content. Everywhere outside of that, theatrical, internet, DVD a decision is made by recent experience or the question: can we make money on it? All decisions are based on calculations, in DVD: how much units can we turn? They figure out how much it will take in the first month and then at three months and six months. The idea that people love an independent film and are going to buy it – forget it. There's no charity in that world, no pity with the independent filmmaker.

### Q – Which window of sale usually generates the most revenue?

*Jan* – It's either the surprise at the beginning where someone offers you $300,000 for an all media deal worldwide, or it is long-term broadcast revenue. Somewhere in the middle are the smaller theatrical distributors, the DVD or New Media people, the educational people. Here the percentages that go back to the filmmaker are not great, also the deductible costs sometimes are a little vague - be careful here! Broadcast sales are very clear: you sell, you get paid. Any other media deals where advances or guarantees come into place and where revenue is shared, are tricky as there is little or no control over what happens in the books of the distributor and there are very few mechanisms to control revenue reports. There are only a few countries in the world that have a state operated control system for box office and home entertainment. France is one. It's very, very easy for someone who is very, very far away from you to monkey with the figures. There are a lot of respectable people out there but most of them are just in the business to make money and 'deductible distribution costs' is the one vague area where people get the short end of the stick.

## 10 THINGS TO LOOK FOR IN AGREEMENTS

7. If you're due to receive any royalties or profit share under the agreement, make sure that the other party has an obligation to collect in any revenue derived from the film or project, that they must show you their books and you have the right to audit those books. Check also your share of Net Profits (as defined in the agreement) is as agreed i.e. are you receiving a share of the Producer's net profits or a share of all net profits?

8. What are the possible sources of income from the project and are all those sources being exploited? If so, are you getting a fair share of that income?

9. What sort of controls do you have over the conduct of the other party? What happens if they are in default of their promises?

10. Remember that if the agreement is being provided by the other side, the terms will be very much in their favor. This does not mean that they are necessarily trying to stitch you up, this is just business.

**Q – You mentioned new media like cell phones, do you think those will become viable revenue sources?**

*Jan* – The new media are definitely there today, but if they will ever become a reliable revenue source for the documentaries that you and I like, I am not sure. The problem is that when you make a TV sale, you sell the right for broadcast in ONE country for ONE relative high amount and once that broadcast has happened, you get paid. In the new media world, your film gets thrown out there and the number of 'clicks', being people who watch, will determine the money you eventually get. It is like the traditional channels: theatrical and DVD; you are, in the end, dependent on the consumers picking up your film, whether it is viewing, streaming or owning/downloading. The more 'clicks,' the more money, very few 'clicks' is very little money. The consumer has a million choices in the new world…where among all of this is your film?

**Q – What about piracy?**

*Jan* – I don't believe that the scale on which 'our films' are being pirated is very big. The pirates concentrate on what the masses want: movies, sports, porn, music - we have come to understand that the masses don't want our films. But piracy does exist and it is annoying, especially when it is out in the open and it blocks other deals. People will say, *"It's already on the internet!"* Amazon and Ebay also trouble the waters for one can buy a US import DVD in the UK on Amazon UK and that is legally not permitted, but no one does anything to stop it.

**Q – When do you like to be approached by a filmmaker?**

*Jan* – There are three stages. The idea stage, just before the fine cut and of course a completed film. We really like before the fine cut because it's really important how you start your film in the broadcast world and a lot of documentary filmmakers don't have a clue about that. So they start their film with something very slow and a buyer has already turned it off. The beginning of a film must make you want to see the rest.

"Filmmakers need to have flexibility to create sometimes even two or more versions of their film."

**Q – Do you ever fund a documentary film?**

*Jan* – We have, but we don't have a lot of money. We may help out if a filmmaker can get bridge financing if he's getting a subsidy in two months from somewhere. Or in the last stages before a film gets released, we can help there.

**Q – If you find something that you want to take on, what kind of deal can the filmmaker expect?**

*Jan* – We have a standard contract that many say

is the best in the business. It's a 30% commission and very few deductible costs. The next step is to get the contract signed and then determine where the film starts. If it's for broadcast, then it will start at the next broadcast market. If it is a feature doc that may have theatrical or strong festival potential, we will be looking for a major film festival start such as Sundance, Berlin, Toronto or IDFA.

*Q – What are common mistakes that you see documentary filmmakers make?*

*Jan* – Submitting unfinished films to a major film festival. Bad mistake. You better call them and ask for an extension of the deadline. The other one is not thinking of other formats while you are in production. Filmmakers need to have flexibility to create sometimes even two or more versions of their film, maybe one for domestic use and one for export.

*Q – What advice would you give a new documentary filmmaker?*

*Jan* – The most important thing is not to work completely alone and to be open to advice and be active in seeking advice. One thing we have found is that filmmakers have very little access to strategic information like how to submit to film festivals. So learn from each other, phone your colleagues, talk to them at festivals. Other filmmakers' experiences are very important.

**Q – Is Magnolia still doing mostly theatrical or has that changed?**

*Eamonn* – Theatrical has gotten tougher for independent films in general. A lot of those companies have gone out of business. The economics of the independent world were just askew. Now people are doing things on a smarter financial basis and new distribution patterns have emerged such as VOD. We're able to distribute films more efficiently than we have in the past.

**Q – What is Magnolia looking for these days?**

*Eamonn* – Well crafted documentaries with a strong aesthetic. With HD cameras being so affordable these days, it's a bit easier to achieve. We also like films that don't preach and don't feel like you are taking your medicine to watch them.

**Q – Are film festivals still important places for you to find films?**

*Eamonn* – I would say so. The big three of Toronto, Cannes and Sundance are very important. But there's also Tribeca and South by Southwest, and smaller fests too. And if you are in competition in the festival, that can help, but it's definitely not the only way we pick up films.

**Q – Have the deals that filmmakers get in either advances, length of term or rights taken, changed much?**

*Eamonn* – Not so much. Most of the time television stations fund documentaries so there are a lot of bifurcated rights. We'll take theatrical and DVD and another company will take TV. Some sales agents can make more money selling off all the parts bit by bit. Like the film *Man on Wire*, the filmmakers got it commissioned by Discovery Channel. Discovery kept the television rights and we did it theatrically. Though interestingly it never played

 **www.magpictures.com**

on Discovery. I don't know why. The advances part though has changed. Back then we were doing advances of mid six figures or so and now we mostly don't do that. We pay smaller monies upfront or we might give no advance and a more generous back end. On *Elliot Spitzer,* they got a very advantageous back end and the producer made a very substantial amount of money on it. And of course, we still like to recoup expenses before we pay out revenue share.

*Q – Are documentaries still palatable to theater owners?*

*Eamonn* – No question. There has been a rebound in the documentary market since that lull period. *Man on Wire* came out and did $3 million. *Food, Inc.* came out and did $4.5 million. *September Issue* came out and did a lot of business. I think we are in an era where if something catches the imagination of the audience, be it a fiction film or a doc, it can go viral very quickly. You can get it out to a large group of people and it takes on a life of its own. Social media has enhanced the ability for word of mouth.

*Q – Is social media something you do with the filmmaker or are they left to do it themselves?*

*Eamonn* – No. No. We work with them. It's a very important part of our outreach. The best thing a filmmaker can do is to make themselves available to do it. And we love listening to a filmmaker's input. They know the material better than anyone. And if it's about a specific group or subject, then they've spent time in that world and any contacts they have made are very important. We will try to market back to that world.

*Q – Do you build websites for the film?*

*Eamonn* – Yes we do. We have a dedicated executive who does online outreach, which includes a web presence as well as doing social media like Facebook and Twitter.

*Q – Has the DVD market changed or contracted at all?*

*Eamonn* – A little. It's subject matter related. But we have done extraordinarily well. We have a number of documentary titles that have sold over six figures in units. *Jesus Camp* and *Man on Wire* did well. *Food, Inc.* has done over four hundred thousand units. I think it was the number ten best selling DVD on Amazon all of that year. But there's no question that the DVD market in general, especially the rental market, has been down.

*Q – Digital distribution has always been a big deal for you. So how has VOD faired with you?*

*Eamonn* – It's a huge deal. It's a platform that just keeps on getting better. Interestingly enough, docs don't do that well on VOD. They do better theatrically and on DVD. It may be because DVDs are more old school and the people that watch docs tend to skew older. The older audience may still be adapting to VOD. There have been some strong exceptions though, and I think as the VOD audience accelerates, performance across all types of films will improve.

**Q – How do the deals for DVD and VOD differ from theatrical and TV?**

*Eamonn* – With DVD, you have a product and you sell it. With VOD, we have a better revenue share than theatrical.

**Q – Are clearances still a major problem for you?**

*Eamonn* – In some respects, but in the last five years or so people have gotten much more sophisticated about clearing copyrighted material. It's rare that someone will turn up with a low budget documentary without the clearances sorted out. That kind of naiveté has mostly gone away.

**Q – Do you need the film to be shot on HD?**

*Eamonn* – Not to accept it. But with HD cameras being so cheap to own or rent these days, it's becoming what everybody does.

**Q – Can you make decisions on works in progress or do you need a finished film?**

*Eamonn* – If something was really compelling we might go for it. We have no hard and fast rules here.

**Q – Do you do international sales?**

*Eamonn* – We sell a lot of documentaries to the foreign market. We do well with it. One thing to be careful of is that if you have an American political documentary, it will be a tough sell in other countries. Whereas something like *Cocaine Cowboys*, which is more of a crime saga, did very well in foreign.

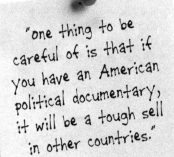

"one thing to be careful of is that if you have an American political documentary, it will be a tough sell in other countries."

**Q – Do you sell all the rights together when doing foreign?**

*Eamonn* – Yes in the vast majority of cases. Many countries don't have a theatrical market for docs so selling all rights together is the way to go.

**Q – Has marketing changed at all?**

*Eamonn* – In the independent world, more and more these days your subject matter is going to determine how it's going to do. It's short synopsis driven. It's more logline driven.

## SALES & DISTRIBUTION AGREEMENT TIPS

1. Make sure that you, the filmmaker, still own the copyright of the film.

2. Clarify the territory and platforms of the distributor. (i.e. domestic TV rights)

3. Limit the length of the distribution agreement. TV can be 2-3 years, DVD can be longer. Each time an agreement expires, they renegotiate and that means more money to you.

4. Make sure that license fee is clearly stated and the schedule of payments is fixed. Try to get as much of your fee up front as possible. They may not pay you the balance until after the license expires.

5. Sub Distributor Fees should be paid by the distributor, not you.

6. Taxes should be taken out of gross receipts, not net.

7. Errors and Omissions insurance - you will need it. Make sure you know how much coverage you require.

8. Limit distributor editing rights to that of censorship requirements only. Larger distributors may not give you this right.

9. Get the right to have input on the marketing campaign.

10. Find out who will make the trailer. This could be a hidden expense for you.

11. Release window: get the distributor to commit to release the film within a reasonable time frame.

12. Audit rights - you must have the right to check their books. And your statements must come on time.

13. Make sure the rights of the film revert back to the filmmaker if the distribution company goes out of business or becomes insolvent.

14. Indemnity: make sure you receive reimbursement for losses incurred as a result of distributor's breach of contract, violation of third party rights and for any changes or additions to the film.

*15. Termination Clause: if the distributor defaults on its contractual obligations, the filmmaker has the right to end the agreement.*

*16. Arbitration Clause: any disagreements will be solved through binding arbitration. Try to get these hearings as close to you geographically as possible.*

*17. Filmmaker Warranties: your statement that says you can enter into this agreement freely and there are no third party rights that are being infringed by the filmmaker.*

*18. No cross-collateralization: when a sales agent offsets the expenses and losses of their other films against your profits. Avoid at all costs!*

*19. Filmmaker Default: The distributor should give the filmmaker 14 days written notice of any alleged default by the filmmaker and an additional 10-14 days to fix the default before taking any enforcing action.*

*20. Late Payments/Lien: All monies due and payable to the filmmaker should be held in a trust by the distributor for the filmmaker and the filmmaker should be deemed to have a lien on the filmmaker's share of the revnue. The distributor should pay interest on any amounts past due.*

*21. Schedule of Minimums: a list of what a sales agent minimumly thinks they can sell a film platform for in a given territory. The filmmaker will give the sales agent proxy to trigger any deal where the amounts are equal or more than the minimum. Any deal that is under the minimum requires the filmmaker's consent. This schedule should be provided to the filmmaker by the sales agent at the beginning of working together.*

*22. If you can, try to keep the rights to sell your film off your website directly. It's a good revenue stream.*

People want to be able to see the poster in their minds sort of like how they do it with studio fiction films now. Unfortunately, it's become harder for great substance to triumph over difficult marketing. The marketing department really has gotten more power in the decision-making.

*Q – What are the common mistakes that you see filmmakers make?*

*Eamonn* – I think that if you use a template to make your film, it will suffer. So if you do a competition doc and you just hit all the same beats as other films, it will feel like something you've already seen. You need to approach your film from a fresh angle.

*Q – What advice would you give to a new documentary filmmaker?*

*Eamonn* – Make sure you have a back up plan. People don't get rich from making documentary films. Also look for stories that are compelling and work well in a short synopsis. And then again, in spite of what I've said, you have to follow your obsessions. Just be realistic about them.

**Q – What is Docurama and New Video?**

*April* – Docurama Films has been discovering and distributing award-winning non-fiction films for more than 10 years, beginning in 1999 with the first documentary to ever be distributed on DVD, D.A. Pennebaker's *Bob Dylan: Dont Look Back*. Docurama's catalog of more than 250 titles features an array of topics covering performing and visual arts, history, politics, the environment, ethnic and gender interests, including *The Wild Parrots of Telegraph Hill, Andy Goldsworthy: Rivers and Tides* and the 2011 Oscar®-nominated film, *Gasland*, among many others. We're the only label dedicated exclusively to documentaries in the home entertainment marketplace. New Video is our other label that also distributes a few documentary titles through partnerships with Arthouse Films and Tribeca Films.

**Q – What do you attribute to the explosion of documentaries in the last few years?**

*April* – Popular Sundance, Toronto and SXSW documentary categories; stalwart and new doc festivals – niche category fests: SilverDocs, Stranger than Fiction, DOC NYC, True/False, Hot Docs; more opportunities on cable, e.g. HBO, Documentary Channel, True TV, PBS; increased interest in "reality" programming, albeit in need of higher quality. I also think as the category has grown, people have come to realize it's as varied as narrative film in terms of subject and style.

**Q – Do you only do the DVD market?**

*April* – New Video has been in the DVD business for twenty years, but we are also the world's largest independent digital video distributor, providing over ten thousand hours of film and television to download and streaming platforms, including iTunes, Hulu, YouTube, Netflix, Xbox, Playstation and Amazon. We also service cable VOD. All of these distribution outlets are available for our documentary titles, including possible

 www.docurama.com           www.newvideo.com

theatrical and TV distribution, depending on what rights we have.

**Q – What kind of documentary does Docurama look for?**

*April* – Potential for grassroots marketing; good critical praise and word-of-mouth praise, cause-related, i.e. opportunistic, newsworthy or widely popular topics. Or a film that can build a profile throughout a sustained release schedule such as festival, theatrical, public screenings, VOD, DVD, digital and broadcast.

**Q – How important is the DVD market to documentary films?**

*April* – Important. Most audiences will see your documentary in their living room or on their personal device. In the ancillary market, the physical DVD market is still the strongest for marketing and publicizing documentary film – the mechanism is still firmly in place for traditional campaigns, special sales opportunities, etc. It is more challenging to get press for a pure digital release. We often analyze strong digital sales for potential DVD releases. Digital platforms give filmmakers more opportunities for audiences to find the film, especially with the shrinking of the retail landscape in recent years. However, digital audiences are more comfortable paying less for streaming or subscription services, resulting in a downward pricing pressure on film titles. We strategize how best to exploit the film across all platforms.

**Q – What kind of deal can a filmmaker expect from Docurama?**

*April* – We structure deals in a variety of ways. We do royalty deals, distribution deals, 50/50 deals; it really depends on the sales potential for the film and the risks involved to achieve that. Our deals last typically between five to seven years. We do sometimes offer advances, but that varies based on the title.

**Q – What do you mean by 'the risks involved'?**

*April* – In a royalty deal, the filmmaker gets a percentage, say 20%, from the first dollar of revenue. In that situation we are assuming all the risk in terms of the outlay of money to produce the DVD. In a distribution deal, which is most common, New Video fronts all of the costs, then we recoup those costs from the revenue, take a 25% distribution fee, and flow through all remaining revenue to the filmmaker. So there's potential, if a title scales, for the filmmaker to bring in significantly more in a distribution deal or 50/50 deal (in which New Video splits the revenue 50/50 rather than taking a distribution fee), though it means recouping costs before

"Podcasts, viral videos, Facebook ad campaigns, etc. These offer amazing opportunities for creative, cost-effective marketing."

## TEST SCREENINGS

seeing that money.

**Q – Do you do international as well as domestic?**

**April** – Yes. Our focus is English-speaking territories. Distributing digitally in these other territories is easier than on DVD, but we have an international team that specializes in physical distribution internationally.

**Q – Do you interact with the filmmaker on the artwork and deliverables?**

**April** – We like to work closely with the filmmaker, understanding that the filmmaker really knows their film best, while we understand the marketplace. We like to start with the art that's been used for theatrical or other exposure, if that exists, but our marketing and sales teams weigh in as well to ensure that it successfully markets the film at retail. Similarly, we look to the filmmaker to advise on what bonus materials would really support the film, but also offer guidance based on our experience.

**Q – What elements do you want from the filmmaker when you put the DVD together?**

**April** – Everything available! We like to have all materials that exist that we can work with for art, promotion, PR. If the film's already had a theatrical, it's very helpful to be looped in on all of the marketing and publicity that's happened so far, so we can go about it strategically. Aside from bonus materials, we also look for additional footage that could be used promotionally, whether it be for getting an exclusive in or featuring it on "Free on iTunes" or the Amazon order page. A good trailer is invaluable for promotion, iTunes and VOD. And of course contacts for outreach—we like working as closely as possible with the filmmakers to be sure we can leverage all of the supporters of the film to promote the release. New Video has an affiliate program that offers a referral fee to organizations that host a link to the product page, so we find that's a great way to encourage support from them while giving them an incentive.

*Q – Do you want an HD master?*

*April* – Our preference is digibeta or HDCam for DVD and digital. We've released a couple of our bestsellers on Blu-ray, but don't automatically release on Blu-ray at this point, as it's more expensive and time-consuming, without the same market saturation as DVD.

*Q – Is there anything about closed captioning or other languages they need to know?*

*April* – If closed captions or subtitles exist, we like to include them, but they're not required for DVD or digital. VOD does require captioning or subtitles.

*Q – Do you do the authoring?*

*April* – Yes, we author in-house and also work with some outside authoring houses.

*Q – What kind of marketing and publicity do you do for your releases?*

*April* – When developing marketing plans for new titles, we try to follow four main guidelines: schedule the multi-platform release with an eye to the theatrical release, holidays and promotional opportunities, awards, and information gleaned from the target or niche audience for the film; collaborate as much as possible with the theatrical marketing and PR teams, if possible, to capitalize on their market and media research; partner with organizations who can help broaden the film's audience through their constituencies, e.g. museums, art galleries, music venues, libraries, cultural centers, etc; exchange product for advertising, contests, giveaways, etc.

More recently, social networking and digital

## TEST SCREENINGS

6. Create a questionnaire and ask them to fill in answers. Do this before you get into a group discussion in order to avoid "group think."

7. Have a freeform discussion at the end of the screening and ask questions about things you suspect are problems. But don't lead your audience to answers.

8. Your studio or distributor may require a test screening of their own so they know how to market it. This will be with a complete unknown group in your target audience from all walks of life.

9. This can be a harsh environment for directors and producers. Don't let subjects attend unless they are on your advisory board and can help spot problems.

10. If one person mentions an issue, it may or may not be an important problem. If most of the group mentions the same problem, then you HAVE to address it.

## GOING UNDER

1. Make a deal. If you owe more than you can afford, offer to pay then half or even less to settle the bill. But you will have to pay then and there.

2. Try to get on a payment plan.

3. Most people don't want to force you to go bust. They will work with you usually.

4. If you do want to go into insolvency, then let them push you into it. They'll have to pay the liquidator or receiver rather than you.

5. If you go into liquidation, you will have to supply all your books and records and they will be scrutinized. Make sure you didn't do anything illegal or undeclared.

6. If serious negligence/fraud is discovered, you will be barred from running a company again.

7. Make sure you made the film under a company and not personally. This way they can't come after your home, car or tools of trade.

8. Always talk to your creditors. It makes them feel like you aren't hiding.

9. Seek legal advice immediately.

10. Bankruptcy stays on your credit report for 7 years. But you can always start over!

marketing has become a crucial strategy for marketing our titles, as these are the best, most effective tools for reaching and growing target audiences and "fans." Podcasts, viral videos, Facebook ad campaigns, etc. These offer amazing opportunities for creative, cost-effective marketing.

As for press, we have a dedicated in-house media relations person who kicks-off each title with the filmmakers to determine where their film lies in the publicity landscape and where the best press opportunities would be. We sometimes hire publicity specialists to leverage niche press. If budget allows, event and screening publicity helps promote films via electronic media.

### Q – Can a filmmaker approach you directly?

*April* – Sure. Our acquisitions team sources films from festivals, agents and other avenues, but it's certainly fine to send us a screener for consideration directly. It just may take a little while for us to respond.

### Q – What are the common mistakes that you see documentary filmmakers make?

*April* – I think the biggest mistake is not looking at your film's release comprehensively. Looking at the theatrical or broadcast or DVD+digital release in a vacuum often means you'll miss out on some opportunities. If you lock in your broadcast before addressing other rights, you may find that you've effectively eliminated any opportunity for VOD, as VOD needs a window before broadcast. Or perhaps there's a big lag between your theatrical run and your ancillary exploitation, so any buzz you created during the run has disappeared by the time you're releasing on home video. The goal is to look at the entire life of your film, including festival screenings, theatrical, grassroots screenings, VOD, DVD, digital and broadcast. If you do split the rights, work closely with your distribution partners to make sure everything is being timed and windowed in the best way. And keep building the profile for your film – our most successful films begin building it in the theatrical and it just keeps snowballing through every platform, building on itself.

**Q – What advice would you give a new documentary filmmaker?**

*April* – Filmmaking is an art form and filmmakers are artists. Like all creative endeavors, a film is about communicating. Taking elements such as a target audience into consideration affords you the opportunity to reach a wider audience. It doesn't mean you have to alter or compromise your film. However, keeping in mind your target audience, the best ways to best position the film in a landscape overflowing with other films competing for the same audience creates the best chance of your work reaching and influencing other people. It's important – and not a compromise – to be honest with yourself from the outset about what you want to achieve – who, and honestly, how many you want to reach with your message or ideas.

*Q – Your organization focuses on documentaries as a teaching medium, so who does your library reach?*

**Cynthia** – DER's mission is to cultivate community engagement with the peoples and cultures of the world. Our programs reach millions of individuals each year through broadcast, film festivals and classrooms throughout the world. We sell directly to educational institutions worldwide including an extensive sub-distribution network throughout Asia. We address the need for tolerance and understanding of people who are different than ourselves. This need is universal and more evident in today's global political, social and cultural climate than ever before. Underlying the diversity of the films is the conviction that documentary and ethnographic films can broaden and alter preconceptions of marginalized and underrepresented peoples and cultures within the United States' population and abroad. We also maintain an archive of historical significance and public interest.

*Q – Do you handle the US K-12 grade school market?*

**Cynthia** – While K-12 has historically not been our focus market, we've made workshop presentations to help educators develop ways to utilize our collection in schools. As an example, the head teacher at the Moccasin Community Day School requested video donations to be used by their disadvantaged student body. We donated programs from our collection that feature young people dealing with socio-economic and cultural problems in a wide range of environments throughout the world. In exchange, we asked that the students write essays in response to the films. Submissions were judged and the winning students were allowed to pick a title of their choice from the DER film collection. We used the Moccasin Community Day School Project as a model for the development of a multicultural media workshop for schools and communities struggling with poverty

---

 docued@der.com       www.der.org

 www.facebook.com/docued

and ethnic diversity. We've made strides in reaching teachers at the K-12 level through workshops and presentations on integrating global issues in curriculum. We have made curriculum and study guide material available as free downloadable PDF files off our web site. We're also starting to offer free programs via Google Video.

*Q – Do you deal with museum distribution?*

*Cynthia* – We work with museums in two ways; first many museums rent or buy films from us for their film programs and screenings. Second, they also license footage from our archive that is often integrated in their exhibitions.

*Q – What kind of documentaries are you looking for with regards to your distribution library?*

*Cynthia* – While we come from a strong cinema vérité tradition, we've broadened our interests to include many other stylistic approaches to documentary storytelling such as experimental and animation. What we look for are programs where the esthetic fits the story, where content is king, and where the filmmakers demonstrate a deep commitment to and engagement with their subjects.

*Q – What documentaries aren't you looking for?*

*Cynthia* – Formulaic approaches, wall-to-wall narration, unnecessarily long docs and history.

*Q – What are the best selling lengths for documentaries in your library?*

*Cynthia* – Length does not factor in on popularity or sales. We have best selling shorts as well as full-length features.

*Q – Do you have to become a member of DER to participate in the rental of your films?*

*Cynthia* – No, we aren't a membership organization. We have a tiered pricing structure - institutional with public performance rights, K-12 teachers and Community Colleges, and consumer/home video.

*Q – What kind of deal does the filmmaker receive from DER if their film is included in your library?*

*Cynthia* – We offer royalty based on gross sales from all sources. We do not buy out rights. We have a standard contract that's negotiable. If there's competition for a film that we really want to acquire we'll offer a cash advance on the royalties.

*Q – Do you license any of your films to broadcasters? If so, what kind of deal does*

**Cynthia** – Yes. 50% of gross is our standard. Again, negotiable depending on the circumstances.

**Q – How important is it for the documentary filmmaker to look at the community outreach of their film?**

**Cynthia** – This is becoming essential from most funders POV. It should be a built in component of every filmmaker's business, funding, and distribution plan.

**Q – Can you help find funding or finishing funds for a documentary filmmaker? How successful is the response to the films seeking donations on your website?**

**Cynthia** – Through our role as a fiscal sponsor we currently support the work of 27 independent filmmakers whose subjects range from an examination of Native Alaskan sovereignty within historical, cultural, spiritual and political contexts to *The Mathare Project* where the filmmaker has been living in and documenting life in an orphanage in Kenya over a period of years. As a result of our support, all these projects have raised some funds moving them closer to completion - others have been fully realized.

**Q – Is there a deadline for what is required?**

**Cynthia** – We have a rolling deadline. To initiate an application we require a treatment, ideally two pages, bios of the production team and a budget. A trailer is not required, but previous film work may be requested.

**Q – How important is the internet in today's distribution of documentaries?**

**Cynthia** – Essential! Without the internet, we

## HUMAN RIGHTS ORGANIZATIONS

**Amnesty International**
www.amnesty.org

**Witness**
www.witness.org

**Article 19**
www.article19.org

**Human Rights Video Proj.**
www.humanrightsproject.org

**Doctors Without Borders**
www.doctorswithoutborders.org

**The Innocence Project**
www.innocenceproject.org

**Rights and Democracy**
www.dd-rd.ca

**United Nations Foundation**
www.unfoundation.org

**UNICEF**
www.unicef.org

**UNIFEM**
www.unifem.org

**Human Rights First**
www.humanrightsfirst.org

**The American Red Cross**
www.redcross.com

would have been out of business several years ago.

*Q – How does a filmmaker approach you if they have a film that they'd like to be included in your library?*

*Cynthia* – E-mail is a good start. They should first visit our website to see if they feel their film would be at home with us.

*Q – What common mistakes do you see with documentary filmmakers that could be avoided?*

*Cynthia* – We often get DVD's or other previews for acquisition with no indication of how long is the piece. Also, often there isn't sufficient contact information on the material sent to us.

*Q – What advice would you offer a new documentary filmmaker?*

*Cynthia* – Know whom you are talking to! I hate it when a filmmaker wastes our time by sending us programs that are clearly not anything that would interest us. Do some research before you make that initial contact. Go to a distributor's or funder's web site before you make your first phone call or send an email query to them. People appreciate the fact that you took the time to do this. It also saves everyone time in the end.

**Q – Is there any criteria for the kind of documentaries you show at IFC Center?**

*John* – Because I'm in New York, I have the luxury of being able to program what I think is the best, without having to make any concessions for commercial concerns. If we program films that get support from the press, they might only appeal to a niche audience, but in New York those audiences run pretty deep.

**Q – Do you usually screen the films before you show them?**

*John* – Yes. And that's true with most art house cinemas in New York. You have to think long and hard about what audience a film is going to have. The films we do don't have a lot of P&A dollars behind them so there's a lot of pressure on the film to provide it's own marketing engine to attract audiences without the marketing tools that more mainstream releases get. We spend a lot of time trying to figure out what kind of reviews it will get. What kind of word of mouth is it going to generate? How are we going to get people to come out to it? So looking at the film is the first step in all of this.

**Q – Do you help advertise the film or is that mostly on the filmmaker?**

*John* – It's mostly on the filmmaker, but in New York many theaters do ads in the weeklies and *The New York Times*, which are small and basically list the days programs. But if someone wants to do some display advertising on top of that, that decision and expense is on the filmmaker or distributor.

**Q – Have you seen any special advertising that filmmakers have done that were unique?**

*John* – There are a lot of grass roots promotions that come into play for documentaries

---

 info@ifccenter.com      www.ifccenter.comm

 www.facebook.com/IFCCenter      http://twitter.com/ifccenter

all the time. That goes especially for social issue documentaries that have a core constituency that really cares about those problems. People do special screenings for those groups and then go to places where those people are and hand out postcards and so forth.

### Q – With whom do you usually deal with in getting films into your theater?

*John* – Usually the distributor. We will take on a film from a foreign sales agent when there's no US distribution. In which case we'll do the publicity and marketing of the film ourselves. There are situations when we deal directly with the filmmaker when they have retained the rights and aren't working with a sales agent or a distributor.

### Q – What is the standard deal that you do with a distributor?

*John* – For a new film, we usually do a locked run of one or two weeks. There's always the possibility of holding over beyond that if a film does really well. In terms of revenue, we do the standard New York theater deal which is a 90%/10% split. It's a little more complicated than the deals around the country, but basically the theater will retain a house allowance for a film playing for a week. The house allowance is like rent. After that house allowance, which is sometimes called the "house nut," the payout is 90% to the filmmaker and 10% to the theater. If you don't make the house allowance, then there is a floor of 25% that goes to the filmmaker. And if we did publicity or press screenings, we'd deduct that from the amount that goes to the filmmaker. Also the filmmaker bears part of our directory advertising cost.

### Q – What is common in the rest of the U.S?

*John* – The amount to the filmmaker is based on a flat percentage. It's usually around 35% and there may or may not be expenses taken out of that. For the bigger theaters and the chains it is still based on a percentage, but you might get a sliding deal. So the first week you get 60%, then the second week you get 50%, then 40% and 30% and it goes down as you get further into the run. But unless you are at a firm terms theater, which there aren't a whole lot of, it's basically a negotiation with each theater.

### Q – What is the gap of time between agreeing to run a film and screening it?

*John* – Usually it's about a three to five month window and that's a little longer than it is for most theaters. Sometimes you open a film on Friday and it does worse that expected. On Monday you're already looking for a new film for that next Friday. It doesn't happen much with us because we're tightly booked.

### Q – What is four walling and would you recommend it?

*John* – It's paying a fairly high fee to own all the playtime in a particular auditorium for a week. So you can give a theater $5,000 and you can play your film for a whole schedule and any ticket sales in that week go 100% to you the filmmaker. If you gross more than $5,000, then you did OK. If you gross less, then you lose money. Filmmakers do four walls most often when they can't convince theaters to play a film in a conventional way. It's usually a last resort situation. And if that's your only option, then it might be because your film doesn't belong in a theater based on the marketing tools that you have at that point. The other side of four walling is if you have something heavily branded like *Spike & Mike's Tour of Shorts*, and you know you have a big, predictable audience coming, then you can make a lot of money four walling.

**Q – In the calendar year, are there any dates or times that aren't recommended for opening a documentary film?**

*John* – It used to be a little more complicated. For a long time people wouldn't open small, niche films in the summer because that's when the big Hollywood movies took over. And early December was a bad time because it's just before the Oscar movies come out and everyone is Christmas shopping. Now it's changed where every weekend is a bad weekend to open a little movie because it's so crowded. Even early December now that they've moved the Oscars up, so everything is not clogged up at the end of December. It's all spread out from Thanksgiving on. A small movie opening in the teeth of the Oscar releases is going to have a hard time. But generally, a good week to open your movie is when there are no other movies opening that are going after your audience. And you can't predict that because everything shifts. You can strategize a bit, but you don't want to be defensively shifting your film all over the place.

**Q – When do you start putting trailers for films in theaters and how long are they?**

*John* – A good trailer is between 90 seconds and two minutes. And we'll play a trailer as early as eight weeks prior to the opening. But we'll only play three or four trailers at a time. We give preference to the movies that are playing sooner. So we might get a trailer in and it will have to wait in line until there is room available.

"You usually have one shot to do something for your film, so don't hamper your chances."

**Q – How have documentary films been doing at the box office?**

*John* – Michael Moore's movies have made a big difference in terms of convincing everyone that docs can do big box office. The market place is cyclical. In the 1970's and 1980's there were big docs that did very well. *Woodstock* and *The Last Waltz*, which were music themed and then *Noah's Ark* that did well across the country. Now it seems that the political docs are finding audiences, but it's not really a new thing for docs to find success. We do well with docs. They tend to be more review and word of mouth driven than opening weekend box office numbers driven.

*Q – What kind of film and sound formats can you screen?*

*John* – 35mm, Digital Content Protection (DCP) and nearly all tape formats.

*Q – Has social media helped you publicize your films?*

*John* – It has to a certain extent. At IFC Center, we have our own way of reaching out to the community via Facebook and Twitter. But really, I find social media to be more valuable to the filmmaker to enhance their films visibility, especially with social issue documentaries. They can make their films bigger by reaching the communities that would be interested in their subject.

*Q – Is there anything a documentary filmmaker can do to benefit their screening?*

*John* – Use marketing tools like posters, trailers, postcards, flyers, word of mouth screenings and online campaigns. For people who have made a good documentary, I usually tell them to get a distributor or hire a consultant to advise you through the process. It's a difficult and risky thing to do – for you to take on the marketing of your film alone. You usually only have one shot to do something for your film, so don't hamper your chances. Just make sure the people that you ask help from are experienced.

*Q – What are the common mistakes that you see documentary filmmakers make?*

*John* – A common problem is to not take good on set still photography. It's the most basic of deliverables and it becomes very difficult, especially when your distributor is trying to do things cheaply, to do any marketing materials without good art. So get someone who knows what they're doing and have them take good photos. It makes a big difference.

*Q – What advice would give a new documentary filmmaker?*

*John* – Watch a lot of great documentaries. Spend a lot of time seeing how people have achieved telling really great stories and new ways of telling them. And be in it for the love of filmmaking and because you are in it to tell the story you want to tell. Don't be in it because you want to make a lot of money or have a stable career with it. Your gratification should come from the work itself.

**DIY DISTIBUTION**
**ROBERT GREENWALD**
**BRAVE NEW FILMS**

*Q – Brave New Films has really taken off. The internet seems to have played a huge roll in that.*

*Robert* – Yes. We've moved from using the internet as a way of merely talking to our audience to it actually becoming our primary distribution mechanism. We just passed 55 million views of all of our work online. And of course we are using social media in a robust way. We have a quarter of a million people on Facebook. We are using Twitter. It's been so exciting to see the possibilities expand so rapidly.

*Q – Last time you couldn't really download a movie and watch it. Now that's completely changed and must have helped you tremendously.*

*Robert* – It's not so much the movie downloads, but it's the ability of our short one to two minute videos to get seen and passed around hundreds of thousands of times.

*Q – Why does that work better than say a 15-minute video piece?*

*Robert* – I wouldn't say it's better. It reaches a wider audience because people online and in general have shorter attention spans and are besieged and bombarded with an enormous number of opportunities at every moment of their living and breathing time. So the short pieces will get you the largest number of viewers, but the longer ones have different value. With our *Rethink Afghanistan* films, we did a 2-minute piece to get the widest audience and then we offer an 8 or 10 or a 15-minute piece for those who are really interested and want to invest the time.

*Q – You use social media for publicizing your films. Do you take a different approach when using different types of social media?*

---

info@bravenewfilms.org　　 www.bravenewfilms.org

 www.facebook.com/bravenewfilms　　 www.twitter.com/bravenewfilms

*Robert* – Absolutely. When we first started it was almost exclusively email because the other stuff didn't exist. In email, the subject line is the thing that gets people's attention. But something we changed is that we used to only have a link to the films in the email. Now we put a screen grab of the video in the message to further entice people to go to the film. With Facebook, you need to keep your message really short because people are scrolling through lots of entries – especially if they have a lot of friends. The good thing about Facebook is that it allows you to target specific groups of people very quickly. With Twitter, that's best for letting people know that information is coming. Like there's a new film we're putting up or that I'm going to speaking somewhere.

*Q – You have a lot of different films that tackle lots of different subjects. How do you keep people from getting lost in all that information and choice?*

*Robert* – We segment people and feed them the info they want. Someone who is interested in our healthcare films gets information on that and not our Afghanistan films. This is where Facebook really helps. Once they come to our site and watch the healthcare pieces, they will see that we've drawn a link in the rise of health costs to the war in Afghanistan. Then they will probably check out those films to get more information.

*Q – How do you get people to trust you?*

*Robert* – The internet is great because you can learn a lot about a segment of society so you can speak their language. Then you need to be as transparent as possible. Put up drawings and clips of what you are doing. Show them everything. That way they know you aren't pulling a fast one.

*Q – Is fundraising difficult even for such small documentaries?*

*Robert* – It's always difficult and hard. One change is that we get some funding from grants now, but those have their own challenges.

*Q – What is the future for Brave New Films?*

*Robert* – It's hard to say. Five years ago, I had trouble convincing people that the internet was a good way of disseminating information. Now 12-17 year olds think that email is too slow. So now they text. The key is to have your eyes open and not be afraid of whatever is coming up next.

*Q – What advice you would give a new documentary filmmaker?*

*Robert* – Find a way to make it. Get the price as low as possible. Get your own camera. Steal an editing system. And just go make it. Because the energy that you are going to spend convincing someone else to give you the money sucks the blood and energy away and it turns you into a salesman and not a better filmmaker. So given how cheap the technology is today, just find a way to make it. Even if it's only 10 or 15 minutes long.

*Q – What is Dynamo Player and how did it come about?*

**Rob** – Dynamo is a paid video platform that came about after several years of frustration we felt as producers trying to get film and web video out without a major backer. Dynamo's main feature is the ability to upload a video of any type, set your own price and publish it anywhere online. You set your own access terms, so maybe it's $.99 for six hours or $9.99 for thirty days. You have a wide range of options and you are totally in control. Your viewers can embed it anywhere they like or spread it around on Facebook, use the share buttons to spread the word through Twitter. So it's like many other players online with the exception that with just a few clicks people can pay very easily through Paypal or Amazon, which most people are familiar with.

*Q – How do you differ from Vimeo and YouTube?*

**Rob** – We're open to any kind of producer. We have no entry restrictions and no upfront costs. And aside of not allowing pornography or anything illegal, we are wide open as far as content goes. The other thing is that we are completely platform agnostic. Youtube has a paid content system that they allow some of their partners to use, but it's somewhat limited and it only works with Google Checkout, which is not a very popular payment system. We are happy to use Google Checkout if people want to use it, but we hit well over 90% of the market with Amazon and Paypal. We also really built Dynamo to replace the DVD. DVD sales have been plummeting the last few years and they will continue to do so. We wanted you to have a way to view all the extra content online. You can cut a preview and put up a trailer and you can add unlimited other videos. So you can put in the behind the scenes stuff and the outtakes and the interviews with the filmmakers. You can put in various versions of the film in different languages or with voice overs.

*Q – How does one make all those things stay together? Do you form a channel of*

---

 www.dynamoplayer.com

*some kind?*

**Rob** – All of those videos can be included in a single program for a single price, or you can create separate programs for them. You're totally in control of how you manage your content. With Dynamo, we're really a utility service. So while we do have featured content on our website and will do more of that and provide some destination pages, really Dynamo is a service for filmmakers to do their own promotion and shape the user experience on their own website. Many of the producers we met when we were building the system were frustrated because they had a great website, but they had to click out to some other platform that didn't look that good or sent to a retail site where their viewers were suddenly surrounded by other things to buy. We wanted the producers to have complete control so the priority for us was to let them embed it, adjust the size and the environment of the presentation. Dynamo is not a destination site on its own. Ultimately, it is a tool set to present films in the best way to a particular audience. A lot of our users are documentary filmmakers, but we also have many feature films, educational videos, short comedies and more, each with their own unique audience.

### Q – What kind of formats do you accept?

**Rob** – We accept just about everything. I don't think we've had a video that wouldn't covert. The most common high quality format we see is H.264, hopefully not too large so it can be uploaded in a day. The main limitations come from long upload times from large files. We automatically convert to 1080 HD and a couple of smaller versions for various connection speeds.

### Q – Anything users should know about the audio component?

**Rob** – It's all high quality stereo. I believe 44k is the standard.

### Q – How long of a clip can you upload?

**Rob** – There are no limitations on file size or film length. There are also no restrictions to how many videos you can add to a single program.

### Q – What would you say are good price points for various videos?

**Rob** – For feature films, we really notice a drop off below $1.99 and above $4.99. There's a surprising lack of bargain shopping going on there, especially for documentaries. $.99 seems to signal that it's not worth it. The exception is in short films. Short films need to be $.99 or $1.99. That's their sweet spot. Documentaries

*"Take presentation seriously and put the extra resources in to make sure your website looks clean and crisp."*

do better at higher prices than dramatic films. They do better at $4.99 and above than any other genre can. I think it's because the viewers know what they are getting. They are not sitting back and waiting to be entertained, they have something specific in mind and know they want to see it. Due to that it has a unique value to them. The one exception for high pricing is instructional content. There are high quality instructional videos that do very well at $7.99, $8.99 or $9.99 – largely because someone knows exactly what they are going to get out of it. And those are for longer access periods like a month and people will watch it four or five times.

**Q – How many people can be watching a film at any given time?**

**Rob** – It's unlimited. We're on a global cloud network of servers.

**Q – Do you envelop social media in with the player or is that outside the purview?**

**Rob** – We will do some promotion for films that use Dynamo via our own social networking. But when it comes to the player, we have a share button that immediately converts short URLs for Twitter and Facebook. We will be improving the sharing options over the next few years as Facebook and others improve their platforms. One big feature that we're excited about is the ability to gift a program to a friend. With just a few clicks you can send anyone an access code to watch the film on your dime.

**Q – How do you set up an account and what kind of revenue sharing do you do?**

**Rob** – Just go to the website, sign up and you're ready to go. You can start uploading videos, setting a price and publishing on your site immediately. Everybody gets 70% of every sale automatically. We felt it was very important to give filmmakers a better profit percentage than anything they would find on Amazon or YouTube. It's also on par with the iTunes store. It's also the point in the worst-case scenario that we break even.

*Q – You offer geo-blocking. What is that?*

**Rob** – That allows you to limit where your film is sold either by DVD region, continent or country. So, for example, if you have a deal in a particular country that prohibits you from any online distribution there, you can check off that country and Dynamo won't let people there buy it. We had one occasion where an Australian filmmaker did a premiere online, the film was showing at a film festival there and they had a lot of press for theatrical screenings, but they also wanted to do a simultaneous international release. So outside of Australia, it was available immediately. Within Australia, they had their theatrical push and then opened it up a few weeks later.

*Q – Do you do analytics?*

**Rob** – Sure. We do real time stats and transparent accounting. One of our big frustrations as producers ourselves was having to wait weeks to see your stats and then even more weeks to be paid. With Dynamo, as soon as a payment is made, it goes right into your Dynamo account. When you want to get that cash out, you submit a simple form and it's usually approved within an hour or two. Then it goes right to your Paypal or Amazon account. If the numbers are large enough, then we can cut you a check.

*Q – What are the common mistakes that you see filmmakers make?*

**Rob** – Expecting that the internet will deliver viewers with search terms. They expect that marketing will just happen or that's it's overrated. For independent filmmakers who don't have the marketing and promotional team behind them that a major studio has, a blog isn't enough to get the word out about your film. At some point, someone has to be actively selling the film no matter how good it is.

## GRASS ROOTS DISTRIBUTION

*6. It takes a long time and a lot of effort to self-distribute. You are like a start up business, no one really knows you so you have to spend a lot of time making noise.*

*7. Tweet, Blog and Vlog. Social media is the best way to reach a lot of people really quickly. Go into other blogs and leave comments as well. By doing so, others will check you out to see who is leaving such astute remarks!*

*8. Get into as many film festivals as possible. This is still the best way to connect with the movie going audience and winning some awards gives you more to promote via social media.*

*9. Hire an advisor who is an expert in grass roots marketing.*

*10. For foriegn markets, a sales agent is still the best way to broker the big deals, but increasingly everything else on this list holds true for places far from home. Also work a deal to be able to sell in territories that haven't been sold by them yet.*

# WHEN DISASTER STRIKES

1. Don't avoid legal issues or taking advice to the last minute. Get on them quick.

2. If you think a distributor or sales agent is being dishonest, write them an email or letter. Get increasingly more agressive if they start ignoring you. Copy your attorney.

3. A contract cannot force someone to act correctly. But a good contract has remedies for you to get your money or film back if they are.

4. Try to have your contracts made in your company's name instead of yours. This way you are not personally liable for lawsuits or bankruptcy.

5. Have a distinct paper trail or who owns the copyright of a project so you can defend yourself. Save all your emails and back up your computer hard drive.

6. Have a bankruptcy contingency clause in your agreements stating that if your distributor goes under, the film copyright reverts back to you.

7. Arbitration favors the wealthy. If you can, avoid arbitration and sue them instead.

8.Sometimes the best course of action is to ride out the deal and get your film back. If it's a valuble title, you will still be able to sell it.

9. If you're owed money by a company that goes under, stay on the person's bankruptcy proceedings. People will try to get away with things if they are not checked.

10. Actors and crew cannot take their names off films if they have a contractual obligation to do so.

11. As a last resort, you can get an injunction to stop a film from being released. This is VERY expensive and should only be done if you know you are right and could win a huge settlement.

12. Bankruptcy does offer you an out from your problems, but your credit will be ruined for seven years. So forget getting that mortgage or car loan.

*Q – What advice would you give a new filmmaker?*

*Rob* – My advice when it comes to using any online resource to promote or sell a film is to make it look really good. Take presentation seriously and put the extra resources in to make sure your website looks clean and crisp. Have it designed by someone who has done it before. Then put your film for sale right up front on your website as an impulse purchase. Don't bury it in a store. Make it easy so they can buy it right off the home page with a few easy clicks.

**Q** – *When we last spoke you were talking about a new distribution model that would take hold in the industry. It's not so new anymore as it's more or less the standard. Do you agree?*

**Peter** – What appeared to be coming at the beginning of 2006 has arrived, but the old model hasn't gone away. The traditional distribution path still exists and there are filmmakers who are only aware of that approach. So, the possibility of choosing a hybrid approach isn't even in their minds. There are some people who feel an Old World approach is more appealing to them for several reasons. They feel that it gives their work more legitimacy. The second reason is they don't know anything about distribution so they want experts to come in and do it. And the third reason is that they don't want to be distributors. They want to be filmmakers and they don't want to spend the time even if it means more money. They would rather put their time into their next project. I think all of those are legitimate perspectives. I give filmmakers I consult with a sense of the full spectrum of distribution paths for their movie. Then they can choose where they want to fall on the spectrum. They can decide which avenues they want others to handle (such as foreign sales) and which they want to handle themselves. There are often areas where they have strong relationships or knowledge of the networks and the organizations. Sometimes they hire someone to handle this area and they supervise them. To design a successful strategy for a film, you need to know the options and then decide which ones best fit your film.

**Q** – *What would you recommend first when consulting with a client?*

**Peter** – Step one is to be clear about your goals. I ask clients to tell me their most important goals, which usually include at least one of the following: maximizing revenue, maximizing career, or changing the world. These are not mutually exclusive and there may be others, but it is important to prioritize them. Without a clear sense of your

 peter@peterbroderick.com      www.peterbroderick.com

 www.facebook.com/DistributionRevolution

378

priorities, it's really hard to make decisions. Once you've ranked your most important goals, you can design a strategy customized to your film.

In the Old World of distribution, filmmakers didn't have strategies they just had reactions. This doesn't work anymore because distribution is so much more complex. There are many avenues of domestic distribution and then there's foreign. You need to think about what's going on theatrically. Do I want to have a theatrical release? Am I fine without one? Semi-theatrical screenings - single special event showings on campuses, at museums or in theatres - have become increasingly important. The filmmaker may be there for a discussion or may be on a panel. Experiencing the film at a special event screening is very different from seeing it in a multiplex.

For many filmmakers, semi-theatrical has become more important than theatrical. They get paid rental fees for their films, either a percentage of ticket sales or a flat fee if it's a free screening. If the organization putting on the screening has the resources, they may be able to bring in the filmmakers, cover their travel expenses and pay them an honorarium or a speaker's fee of at least $750 in addition to the rental of the film. Whether the filmmakers are there or not, DVDs can be sold at the screening. If it costs them $1 to make the DVD and they sell it for $20, and they sell eighty copies, that's real money. These semi-theatrical screenings often lead to consumer sales and educational sales afterwards. The most important reason to do semi-theatrical screenings is that they create awareness and exposure that can give a film life. If you're in theaters for a minute, few people will learn about your film. But if it's being shown semi-theatrically across the country to core audiences involved with the issues the film deals with, viewers will tell other people about your film.

### Q – What are the most important avenues after semi-theatrical?

**Peter** – There are many other important avenues including television, retail DVD, digital (which includes iTunes and Hulu), and educational. Direct sale avenues have become super-important. Filmmakers are selling DVDs right from their websites and at screenings. They are also selling downloads and streams directly from their websites. Filmmakers need to retain these rights as well as the rights to sell DVDs from their websites. The profit margins on direct sales are much better, and you get the customer data, which allows you to add each individual to your core personal audience. There is also cable video on demand where people pay $4.99 to watch a movie. If your film's title doesn't begin with A, B, C, or D or a number, you're in trouble because searches are alphabetical and people usually give up after D.

"If a DVD distributor wants to do your movie but won't let you retain the rights to sell DVDs from your website, that's not a deal you should make."

Filmmakers need to decide on the sequence of

all these avenues. They also need to decide whether they will have different versions of their films. If you have a feature documentary, then you're going to need an hour for overseas TV. An hour will also be easier to sell in the educational market. Sometimes a filmmaker makes what she feels is the perfect version of her film and when confronted with the need to cut an hour version, makes something quick and dirty to send overseas. Filmmakers need to be thinking from the beginning of a project what the best hour would be and should edit it simultaneously with the feature length version. Hoping that someday someone will pay you to make the hour is a bad approach. Just plan for multiple versions.

**Q – Would you say it's more beneficial to do the new model yourself and bypass the old method of distribution?**

**Peter** – No. Filmmakers need partners. To do retail video, you need a company that can get it into stores, get it on Amazon and into Netflix. With the digital rights, you need an aggregator or a company like Distribber. With cable VOD, the same thing is true. You can't do that without working with a company. With theatrical, I recommend working with a booker or a service deal company. They have the contacts and the expertise. On their own, filmmakers should sell DVDs, downloads and streams from their websites. They can also do educational sales directly from their websites, but there are some very good educational distributors that specialize in particular areas and have great mailing lists. Filmmakers should assess the possibilities. If they believe they can sell five to six hundred educational copies at $300 each, they have to decide whether to do it themselves or go through a distributor and receive a 30% royalty. If they think they can only sell fifty copies, then I'd recommend using a good educational distributor because it's probably not worth their time. The worst thing that can happen to your educational distribution rights is that they are not exploited when you give all your rights to one company. That company may have no educational distribution experience or capabilities. Filmmakers need to be careful not to give away more rights than a distributor deserves. If a distributor is really good in an area, then that's what you want them to do.

*"You should not make a deal with a company that won't allow you to sell downloads and streams from your website."*

**Q – Is it difficult for a filmmaker to retain certain rights these days? It wasn't so easy a few years ago.**

**Peter** – Things on that front have improved a lot. A few years ago DVD companies thought of it as a zero sum game. They assumed that if a filmmaker sells one hundred DVDs from his website, the company is going to sell one hundred less. Now the more sophisticated companies have realized it's not a zero sum game. If they let a filmmaker sell his movie off his website and he actively promotes the film online, that's going to increase the retail sales of

### START EARLY

All the tools to create amazing marketing materials, to build a professional web presence and to reach consumers, fans, followers and potential collaborators are now freely available. It's not expensive and it's not rocket science. There is no excuse for a shoddy or poorly thought out campaign. Most people who fail to create an amazing marketing campaign do so because they don't start early enough. When they need it, it's a little too late.

Thinking of your key artwork and creating something in Photoshop, building a website and starting a blog, starting a Facebook page and twittering - these are all things you should be doing at the same time you are researching your doc. You need to be an expert in all of these technologies and skills because when you get into production, or close to the release of your film, there just isn't time to get creative. All you can hope to do is to add to or maintain what you already have. Plus, it's too late for a social media campaign at that point anyway.

Remember, it's all what your competitors are doing and they are doing a damn, fine job of it. Audiences won't be interested in your film if they don't know it exists.

the DVD company. It's win-win. These distributors realize that the filmmaker understands his core audiences, has connections to them, and can get their mailing lists. Distributors should think of these filmmakers as partners. They don't have to pay them anything and should just unleash them. If a DVD distributor wants to do your movie but won't let you retain the rights to sell DVDs from your website, that's not a deal you should make. In the digital area where rights are generally non-exclusive, you should not make a deal with a company that won't allow you to sell downloads and streams from your website.

**Q – What about places like Dynamo Player and other affiliates that take a small percentage for giving tools to help you self-distribute?**

**Peter** –There are a number of companies that will enable you to do streams and downloads from your site. Filmmakers shouldn't pay more than 25% and could pay as little as 5%.

**Q – How would you recommend a filmmaker uses social media to promote their film?**

**Peter** – Social media expertise is very important. Not just when a movie is opening theatrically or at a film festival, but in an ongoing way. It's important to have a social media person on your team. Filmmakers need to have a distribution team just like they had a production team.

Some filmmakers think that if they have a Facebook page, they don't need a website, which is completely wrong. They need both and should figure out how they will complement each other. Their website should be dynamic. If it is just a static online press kit, people will come to it once and never return. You need to create something that can potentially have a life of its own. The website should encompass content about the subject of the film outside of the movie itself. This makes it richer and more diverse especially if the filmmaker can harness user-contributed content, which is a very powerful asset.

**Q – What about using a blog as your website?**

**Peter** – It's too easy. With blog software words are primary and images are secondary. One of my clients asked me, *"Do you know what the problem with the web is? Too many words."* I've never forgotten that. People don't use the power of images as much as they could. A website allows you to create whatever look you want. Blogs on websites are easy to overlook among all the other categories. The blog is often in a corner from which it is hard to return to the website. The best websites feature the filmmaker's persona throughout.

**Q – Do people want that?**

**Peter** – Yes. Think about the politics of persona. Kevin Smith, Spike Lee, and David Lynch are filmmakers who have distinct identities. Too many websites just have official bios that give no real sense of the filmmakers. These sites are merely online press kits written in the third person. On the web, people are more supportive of individuals passionately making movies.

### Q – What are the common mistakes that you see with filmmakers these days?

**Peter** – Not showing their movies to strangers while they are making it and getting candid feedback. Applying to festivals too early. When the Sundance deadline comes along, many filmmakers are incapable of resisting the impulse to submit even if their movies are nowhere near ready. The rationale is that *"I have nothing to lose"* but I don't think that's true. They may say, *"By next year I will be way past festivals."* Then a year goes by and their movie is finally done but they've already been rejected. The third mistake is they don't realize that bringing a movie into the world is as hard or harder than making it. You should start reaching out to and building audiences as soon as you begin working on a new film. With crowdfunding, you can get a sense of how interested people will be in your film before you even start production. You can launch a Kickstarter or IndieGoGo campaign. If nobody is enthusiastic, that is likely to be the response when the movie comes out. The fourth mistake is not having a strategy. Without one, you will always be operating at a disadvantage. You need to execute a strategy stage-by-stage. After each stage evaluate what has worked and what hasn't, modify your plan for the next stage. Filmmakers who are nimble can continue to refine their strategies.

### Q – What advice would you give a new documentary filmmaker?

**Peter** – Filmmakers need to understand that things are changing rapidly and make an effort to keep abreast of opportunities. It should be part of their ongoing education. If they have decided to be an independent documentary filmmaker, they must try to do it in a self-sustaining way. The goal is to continue to make movies. To do that, you have to understand this new world of distribution. Hybrid distribution, where you are splitting your rights and retaining the right to do direct sales, allows a filmmaker to have greater control of distribution and to build a core personal audience that she can take with her from film to film.

# CHAPTER ELEVEN
# DOCUMENTARY MASTERS

## THE DOCUMENTARY FILMMAKERS HANDBOOK

**Q – What does documentary film mean to you and what excites you about it?**

*Nick* – It covers an enormous genre of very different films. Some of which have very little to do with one an other. You can lump films like *The Weeping Camel* in with documentaries even though it has nothing to do with documentary at all. So I guess the term is really inadequate and confusing in and of itself. Subsequent terms like cinema vérité or observational filmmaking are slightly more accurate because they define a particular style or approach. I suppose the thing that excites me about them is their rawness and spontaneity and the uncertainness of the interaction between the filmmaker and the subject. Those amazing moments that are completely unique to that form of filmmaking – that only otherwise happen in real life encounters where you're in conversation with someone and/or something quite remarkable and unexpected happens. Fiction tries to imitate that, but very rarely comes up with anything as complex or as amazing. I think documentary encourages filmmakers to be very flexible in their approach. To not go into subjects with a thesis all carefully worked out. They have to be open and on a voyage of discovery themselves and take the audience with them.

**Q – Your style has something of that, as your films tend to be about you making the film as well as whatever your subject matter is.**

*Nick* – That's implicit in any film as the filmmaker goes on a journey. It's just off camera to a greater or lesser extent. Making documentaries is a very intimate relationship between the subject and the filmmaking and the extent that the relationship is successful is completely reflected in the film. That relationship, I feel it's easier to acknowledge it and use it as a very positive structuring device. Sometimes, not always. I think there are certain films that don't require that kind of structure. Films from institutions or films of processes or films of events that have a built in beginning, middle and end don't require another structuring device like the filmmaker telling the story. But if you're doing a film that seemingly has a lot of arbitrary connections and those connections only seem to connect in the filmmaker's mind and require those connections to be made explicit, then

---

 info@nickbroomfield.com     www.nickbroomfield.com

it's very useful to have the presence.

**Q – Do you tell your interviewees that you're going to walk in with the cameras rolling?**

**Nick** – I say that I'm making a home movie and I'm filming everything. If I come in with a film camera rolling, don't be surprised.

**Q – With your style you're able to get things from subjects that they probably wouldn't say in a conventional interview. What tips would you give new documentary filmmakers on interviewing subjects?**

**Nick** – The main thing is not to box the interviewee into a corner and to not make the situation so formal that it's inhibiting. Or in any way to make the interviewee feel inadequate. They can't feel as if they or their house are messy. They have to be made to feel absolutely OK with exactly whom they are, which is exactly what you want for your film. So the main thing is to make people relaxed with you and to enjoy to a certain extent, your presence. I'd say have a very tiny crew. I think the ideal size is two – one on camera and one on sound - and just to get on with it. Don't say too much about what you're doing why you're doing it. You're obviously there to make a film.

**Q – Do you think going in with the camera rolling gets a gut reaction from the subject?**

**Nick** – The initial meeting with people is often the moment at which your first impressions form and those are the strongest. You resort to an almost animal instinct in your judgment of people. It's almost before your intellect has started working. You go on what they're wearing, how they look at you or if they're fat or thin – all these animal things that have nothing to do with their political position. They all influence your reaction to them and indeed, the audience's reaction to them. And as you are taking the audience on a journey that you're involved in, those initial meetings are essential to the audience because they are meeting them for the first time, too. They want to see the houses that they live in and kind of curtains that they have in their windows.

**NICK'S FILMS**

*Sarah Palin: You Betcha!* (2011)

*Ghosts* (2006)

*Aileen: Life and Death of a Serial Killer* (2003)

*Biggie & Tupac* (2002)

*Kurt & Courtney* (1998)

*Fetishes* (1996)

*Heidi Fleiss: Hollywood Madam* (1995)

*Monster in a Box* (1992)

*The Leader, His Driver and His Driver's Wife* (1991)

*Lily Tomlin* (1986)

*Chicken Ranch* (1983)

*Soldier Girls* (1981)

*Q – You don't seem to ask rapid questions. You give them a chance to breathe.*

*Nick* – Maybe that's because I think of them as conversations or interactions. And hopefully you've done enough work where you can be fluid and flexible in the order in which you ask your questions or steer the conversation. Realistically, unless you're structuring the film around one interview, you're only going to cover a couple of main topics. It's very rare, in my films for example, that an interview will last more than three to four minutes. So in that time, you only can cover a couple of things. I prefer to go back and re-interview them on different questions rather than stand them up and ask the same thing, which creates a static feel as you keep going back to the same interview throughout the film. I think maybe your first interview is wide where you're covering lots of different topics and you're getting to know them and you are asking a lot of background stuff, but subsequent interviews become more and more specific and more and more centered around one or two topics.

*Q – When you are recording phone conversations – do you have to tell them that you are doing so?*

*Nick* – I think you're probably supposed to.

*Q – Have interviewees ever said that they refuse to let you use what you shot of them?*

*Nick* – I've never had that problem, but I've occasionally decided to not use footage in order to protect someone.

*Q – Would you suggest that people pay their subjects for interviews, as that sort of proposes a contract that they have agreed to do it?*

*Nick* – If you're taking up a great deal of someone's time and you're invading their house and eating their food, it'd be a customary form of the society we live in that you'd offer them something. But if they're super rich, then you might be insulting them. Most people kind of like to receive something. Not always. But some people feel it's appropriate. It shouldn't be something that would change their objectivity or that they would indeed start telling you things that they wouldn't have or they start to perform and make you happy. You don't want to pay people money as that changes the basis of your relationship.

*Q – Do you need to have clearances for selling the film?*

*Nick* – Yes, you do need to have clearances. And sometimes you need to have clearances so that the people in the film acknowledge that they've in fact given you their permission and that there won't be any argument later. I suppose if you don't have hidden cameras and a big camera is pointing at them, they know you are making a film and they carry on. There's an implicit agreement for them to be filmed. And obviously, if it's someone who's serving in a public capacity like a policeman, schoolteacher or politician, somebody who in a way has sacrificed their private persona because they are fulfilling a public function and as such are accountable. With other people who are very private and you're in their home or whatever, it's appropriate to get a release form them. And also I suppose in terms of Errors and Omissions later, it's generally useful to have releases. Although, I think that everyone would agree that a release is not watertight. If anyone wants to sue you, they'll sue you anyway. It is interesting – every TV station has very different releases. HBO, I remember, were very scornful of the BBC release. The BBC has a different release from Channel 4. No one really agrees as to what a correct release should be. And if you pull out a complicated release that is pages and pages long and people feel they have to read it all and they don't understand the language, it doesn't make your job easy.

**Q – You seem to like lightning in a bottle characters, like Courtney Love. Do you think character first before story in order to get a more personal approach?**

**Nick** – I don't think you start with a character and then find a story. I mean that film was to be a study of Kurt Cobain and it turned into a story of Courtney Love because she was trying to stop the film. So it was the only story I could tell. I think you have to tell a story about what's happening rather than the story you may have originally set out to make. Terreblanche – I did know about him before, but the film was going to be about him and the AWB. He is obviously a very colorful character, but I was more interested in his driver and the driver's wife than I was in Terreblanche.

**Q – You seem to push the interviewees a bit to the point where it seems that your life may be in danger. Do you find that you get more out of them this way?**

**Nick** – I think you're generally on a quest for truth of answers. And I think any filmmaker is in the capacity of an odd father confessor figure. The subjects very much see you that way because you're asking them about their lives and this is their moment of truth. Their moment to define themselves. It gives you the ability to ask questions that you wouldn't do in normal conversations probably. Or certainly in a more blunt fashion. I think it is an acknowledgement of what's going on. Films always make things larger than life, partly because they're seen by so many people and are on a big screen. The mere fact that you study something that has been removed from life and is being shown back produces something that takes on another significance. Asking questions that are more pointed than normal just acknowledges that.

**Q – What do you do when you aren't getting what you want from a subject?**

**Nick** – I remember once with Victoria Sellers who was giving nothing and lying to me, I turned the camera off and said, *"I'm tired of this shit you're giving me. We aren't going to continue unless you start answering some of the questions and telling me the truth."* That had the desired affect. So occasionally I think you have to do that.

**Q – Is there anything you do when you film in terms of trying to get more out of a**

*subject? For example, when the driver in The Driver says something radical and then you say, "I don't understand that. Can you explain further." It digs deeper.*

**Nick** – Yeah. With some of his weird theories, I really don't understand him. I suppose it gives him an opportunity to really express what he's going on about. They are certainly nothing I know about because they're weird theories about the Jews or the Bible. Those things you need explained. Those are genuine questions of not understanding what he's talking about.

**Q – Ethics in documentary filmmaking is a hot debate. How would you advise filmmakers to handle this?**

**Nick** – I think they need to answer their own consciences. When you sit through your own film, do you feel comfortable about certain things that you have done which might not be fair or might not be representative of the situation? That's a very subjective thing. People have a very different ethic about things. I think one wants to get away from there being a McCarthy ethics board documentary. And there have been moments of that which have always been bad times for the form. There can be a slight religious quality to documentary sometimes which can be a little too Puritan.

**Q – Are there any ethical boundaries that you wouldn't cross?**

**Nick** – I'm sure there are plenty. I think all the time you're assessing what you think is appropriate in the same way you do on a day-to-day way of living. You try to do good things that you can justify to yourself. I think it's very important to be aware of the reason you're making the film and what you feel the bigger picture is. That'll justify certain things that you wouldn't be doing otherwise. It's a big responsibility in a way.

**Q – Do you think there is a certain discipline missing today because people aren't shooting film?**

**Nick** – I suppose they will learn that discipline in the cutting room because sooner or later. You have to work out what your story is and how to structure it. And maybe that's more painful when you have shot so much material and have to cut it down.

**Q – What mistakes do you see by documentary filmmakers that can be avoided?**

**Nick** – With myself, there are a couple of films that if I had carried on filming for a couple more weeks, I could've had a really remarkable film. And by not carrying on, I shortchanged the film. That is one really big mistake that one shouldn't repeat.

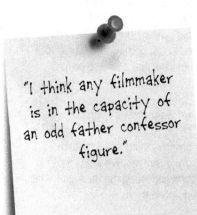

"I think any filmmaker is in the capacity of an odd father confessor figure."

I suppose the other one is in second-guessing oneself. I remember when I was making a film about Lily Tomlin, I never thought she was funny. But everyone else thinks she is funny, so she must be funny. And the film wasn't funny. I should've really listened to my own feelings.

**Q – What advice would you give a new documentary filmmaker?**

**Nick** – If there is a subject that you really want to film, on your first film you just have to go out and make it even without having proper financing. Then use that as your passport to make films that are funded in the future. It might take many months and it is a big gamble. But it's better than sitting around waiting for money that probably will never come.

**Q – What does the term "documentary" mean to you?**

*Barbara* – For me it's about taking the time to go beneath the surface and find the heart of the story. I think documentary filmmakers struggle to create unforgettable and entertaining films that introduce people to characters they might never know. Or show a different side of people that maybe we thought we already knew. I think that documentary films and filmmakers sometimes take you halfway around the world or just to the other side of the tracks. Anyway you go with it, it's a journey that can change you forever. I think what makes this journey possible is the collaboration you have with other directors, camera people, editors, sound people and the subjects of your film.

**Q – Do you think it's important for a documentary filmmaker to go to film school?**

*Barbara* – I didn't go to film school. I learned by doing. I got to work with the Maysles brothers. I got to do sound, editing and got to see how things came together. I just wanted to be out in the field. I wanted to feel it, taste it and be part of it in whatever way I could. I was voracious in learning so that no one could ever say to me you can't do this. I needed to be able to say, *"Yes, you can."*

**Q – What advice would you give a new filmmaker in choosing subject matter?**

*Barbara* – The subject matter you choose is something you're hungry for. It should have a diverse perspective and a story that makes the film come alive and turns the viewer on. Maybe it even fills a void. Something that makes you, as a filmmaker, want to go out into mainstream media, to use every device you possibly can, to make a film that means and says something to you. It makes you laugh or cry. Or the people that you follow are so fascinating that they just jump off the screen.

**Q – How can you get subjects to trust you especially when you are treading on**

 info@cabincreekfilms.com     www.cabincreekfilms.com

*sensitive ground?*

**Barbara** – You have to be real. You have to be true to who you are and put yourself out there as a person, as a filmmaker – be part of whatever you are doing. There are no agendas to go by. I think you just have to be as truthful as you can with your subjects.

### Q – How do you diffuse tense situations with subjects or crewmembers?

**Barbara** – I'm extremely patient and if somebody flares up, I don't take it personally. What I struggle to do is to go underneath who that person is and try to figure out what could've possibly made them flare up. Then I try to go at it around a different corner or from a different perspective. And suddenly everything else will stop and it's about figuring out why they're in that place, whether it's a cameraperson or sound person. I always let them talk and I never come at anyone from a place of anger. I just listen and try to take them in a different direction.

### Q – Are there any ethical boundaries that you feel shouldn't be crossed when making a documentary?

**Barbara** – Not that I want to skirt the issue, but you never know until you're in one. It's difficult to tell you. In Eastern Kentucky, when we were doing *Harlan County*, the issue was trying to stay alive. And trying to stay on that picket line. We're always trying to film in a way that would ensure nothing would happen to anybody on that picket line and to these people that I'd come to know and care about so much. I think it just depends on when you walk into it, what you do and who you are. It's almost like making a documentary film, you can't script how you are going to react, what you're going to say or do.

### Q – When you were on that picket line was the camera acting more like a shield or a red flag to a bull?

**Barbara** – It could've been either one. To me it was a shield and maybe to the strikebreakers it was a red flag. I felt protected because I had my Nagra with a mic and

## BARBARA'S FILMS

*Fight To Live* (2011)

*Woodstock: Then & Now* (2009)

*High School Musical: The Music In You* (2007)

*Shut Up & Sing* (2006)

*Bearing Witness* (2005)

*The Hamptons* (2002)

*My Generation* (2000)

*A Conversation with Gregory Peck* (1999)

*Woodstock '94* (1998)

*Wild Man Blues* (1997)

*American Dream* (1990) - Academy Award™ Winner

*Harlan County USA* (1976) - Academy Award™ Winner

Kevin and Hart had their cameras. While you're recording, you feel safe because you can see and are attuned to everything that's going on. But then the people on the other side were pissed off that we were there and preventing them from doing what they wanted to do.

**Q – How do you deal with dangerous situations like when you were shot at with machine guns when filming?**

*Barbara* – You just have to be in the moment. You don't think about a schedule of things or get out a list of things to do. You just think about survival. If I do this, what will happen in the spur of the moment? It's like a car accident – everything slows down and you sort of go with it and watch it happen.

**Q – Do you have any advice on pitching projects to funders?**

*Barbara* – You need to know what story you want to tell and really do research on the different places that you are pitching. What are the kinds of things that they show? You should tell them something that's within the line of what they're doing, but it's also something they've never heard before. So somehow you're inspiring them to maybe break their own rules or question what they're supposed to be doing. You have to size up whom you are telling it to. Stories are things that we all share together and if you tell them something that you really feel committed to and so vibrant and passionate about, you are going to get them to feel that way. Sheila Nevins, who is the head of programming at HBO, says, *"It may not be what someone says, because in documentaries it takes all different shapes and it goes in all different ways. But if there's passion behind the filmmaker, and if it comes from their heart, I'll probably do it."*

**Q – When a filmmaker starts their project, what are some of the main things they should be talking about? Is it important to think about where it will end up?**

*Barbara* – When I start a project and I have no funding, no distributor, and the only one interested in it is me, I don't think about where it's going to end up. I think about who the people are, what the story is, how we can film it, what the style is, the humor in it, the sadness in it. I think more in those terms.

> "Have a place that's comfortable wherever you are filming so that person blooms and is open."

**Q – What should a filmmaker think about as they sit down to edit their film?**

*Barbara* – When I go into an editing room, and particularly if I have been on location, I keep my mouth shut while the editor is watching. That way he or she can feel what is happening. I always like to sit where I can see their faces and watch where they smile or get bored, I like to see what the editor takes in. Once they have seen it, they can tell me if I don't have something. It makes for a totally even playing field. Editors in documentary films are incredible storytellers and are the people who really help shape these films. They're so important. It has to be someone that you like and respect and someone who is there because they care about the subject matter and the story.

*Q – What common mistakes do you see documentary filmmakers make?*

*Barbara* – I don't know if there are common mistakes because you're not in their editing room. You're not in the field with them. You don't know what they have to work with. You absolutely do the best with what you have. I think as a filmmaker, you can't talk too much. You have to have a place that's comfortable for whoever you are filming so that person blooms and is open. You can't push your agenda on anybody else. That allows them to take it to other places. And they will totally surprise and shock you. It's better than anything you have in your head. So keep quiet and let your characters take the lead.

*Q – What advice would you give a new documentary filmmaker?*

*Barbara* – As a new filmmaker, they are taking on an incredible responsibility when they walk into the world of someone else. Making a documentary brings you closer together and shows our collective human spirit. You need to have a personal responsibility to the people you are filming. It's so important. We have to respect them and their story.

*Q – What lead you to documentary filmmaking?*

**St. Clair** – Basically, it was dissatisfaction with what I saw on TV about the Civil Rights movement. Many of the times they got it wrong about what they said about black people. When I was coming up the media was just about to open up for black people. At the time I thought the height of being a documentary filmmaker was being a producer on a national network like CBS. They had the money, the exposure and the audience. And at the time, they actually did, but they essentially didn't have the truth. Through a series of circumstances American public TV created a series called *Black Journal* and it allowed me a chance to make the films I wanted to make and have an audience; clearly not the audience CBS had, but then people started to look at public TV as a place to get new information, black and white, and then brown and yellow, etc. So though I gripe about it now, public TV was a way for me to start projects.

*Q – Was this at the height of the Civil Rights movement?*

**St. Clair** – It was 1968 and the Civil Rights movement had basically run its course and the Black Power movement was coming in. Black people as a group began to want power to figure out what they wanted to do whether white liberals agreed with them or not. I was able to make films that captured that spirit. And because the power structure didn't really know what we were doing, we could get away with it. That experience still empowers me to this day - the feeling of being able to make a film and have people act on the information you gave to them.

*Q – What was Black Journal?*

**St. Clair** – It was the first black controlled national public TV documentary series. What happened happens a lot in America - white liberals started the idea of a black show. And they said it was to be by, for and of black people. But in fact, of the 32 people on staff, only 11 were African-American. Most of the producers were white. They were very

---

 www.chambamedia.com     www.badwest.org

sincere and had good intentions, but they began to interpret our experience. So we went on strike and literally embarrassed them as liberals. We had press conferences saying they advertised such and such, but this is the reality and they won't give up the power. They backed off, changed the structure and we began to do the work and make the films of the contemporary black social experience in these short documentaries. There were two people who were hosts and then we the producers went out and produced 5 minute to 25 minute film pieces. Sometimes we would have in studio discussions.

**Q – It seems like it was breaking new ground.**

**St. Clair** – It very much was breaking new ground. The only reason they kept us doing it was that we had a great audience. It was African-American based, but then white people began to discover it because they could find out things about their black citizens that no one else was saying. So they tuned in and wrote in saying, *"we didn't know this."*

**Q – How different is documentary filmmaking now from then?**

**St. Clair** – Because it was for TV, it was basically a TV report. You could get fancy a little bit. We usually had one of the two hosts as the narrators and the interviews were mostly on camera interviews. There were some voice-overs, but they thought that was too avant garde. And in fact, if you apply for co-financing from the PBS series *American Experience* today they will send you the same sheet that they adhered to back then. Set up what you are going to say with an expert. Show what they are talking about and then have another expert explain what they've just seen. If you're a documentarian in this country, and you are making a film for American public TV, you have to realize the rest of the world doesn't respect that format. So if you're making a film like that for PBS, you really need to think about alternative versions in terms of being able to sell it. And also if you want to sell it to France for example, who has really good budgets, they're not interested in seeing talking heads speaking English. That means

## ST.CLAIR'S FILMS

*The Visitors (2009)*

*Before They Die! (2008)*

*Twelve Disciples of Nelson Mandela (2006)*

*Dr. Ben (2001)*

*Innocent Until Proven Guilty (1999)*

*John Henrik Clarke: A Great and Mighty Walk (1996)*

*Making "Do The Right Thing" (1989)*

*A Nation of Common Sense (1975)*

*Let the Church Say Amen! (1974)*

*A Piece of the Block (1972)*

*Something to Build On (1971)*

*Ourselves (1971)*

they have to put either a voice over or subtitles, so visually it's easier for them if you have the visuals and have a voice over because they can just put in subtitles. That's a technique that you have to be aware of when you talk co-productions.

## Q – Do you use vérité style?

**St. Clair** – Yes. That was en vogue when I started and I like that. And because we were new, most of the documentaries would have a college professor or some expert, but we at *Black Journal* we'd get articulate people from the community to talk. We called it *The Interior Voice* – the voice from inside the community. That's another technique for filmmakers. I'm not saying one is better than the other, but if you choose to use somebody from the community that you're going to do a film about, let the funders know because that's now a production value. A big difference now is that most funders would like to see the film that you're going to make on paper. In the old days, you could go in and say, *"I have this idea. I'm not sure how it's going to work out. Here are some the elements."* They would say, *"Here's some development money. Go out and let us see what it looks like."* And what they really want now is a producer to come in with that on paper and a five to seven minute trailer. The technology is relatively cheap so you can do that. But it's a difference. I produced a film for HBO on Gordon Parks who was a world famous photographer, they had me go out and film him to see if the camera likes him.

## Q – Have you noticed archival houses charging a lot for clips and not giving in perpetuity lengths anymore?

**St. Clair** – Yes. What I'm encouraging filmmakers to do is make contemporary subject matter that alludes to the past. It reduces the need for archival footage and also the stuff that you create becomes archival footage for the next generation. Then you can sell it and you don't have to be as exploitative as these current houses are. But with the clips now, you can purchase different scales. You can buy it for just domestic TV or just for film festival exposure or both. Or film festival, domestic TV and foreign TV. Or one for domestic theatrical. If you can afford it when you do your budget, you should put in a figure for what they call "buy out." That's for rights to all windows. That way, if somebody wants to buy it for, say, ARTE, you've got it cleared for evertything. And now there's Fair Use, that's a way for people to work that out.

## Q – Is it still possible to make films about Civil Rights in the way that you want to?

**St. Clair** – Advocacy was a valid artistic approach in the Civil Rights days. Now advocacy, especially if it's against something the government is doing, is not big. They don't really like that today because of two things, the power of the government in terms of controlling media and also the compression of the existing media corporations and their closeness with people in the government. The way you can get around that is doing what Robert Greenwald is doing. That's to identify your audience and feed them the information directly. The thing about ethnic material is that it's always under attack. Culturally, this country is run with a Eurocentric sensibility. Oddly enough, myself as a media activist of African American descent, I never find a shortage of material. Frankly, I'd rather there wasn't because it would reflect a better society but the reality is that it's on going and it'll probably be on going. And it's just not ethnicities. Gays, for example, have to think about how their message fits into an increasingly conservative environment.

**Q – Given today's environment of illegal wiretapping, it feels like nothing's really changed from the 1950's.**

*St. Clair* – The hard lesson that I've had to learn and prevents me from burning out is America is a perpetual work-in-progress. There are always new immigrants coming into the country and that upsets the people who are already here. So there's always turmoil. For a documentary filmmaker, that's really good because there's always material. Secondly, there's a class struggle here that no one talks about. The people who own the means of production and the people who work in that structure of production are always in that battle. One of the reasons we always fight the same battles, is because we always approach it as: once it's won, it's done. But that's not true because nobody really looks at it from a class analysis. I curated a special program at the Full Frame Film Festival on class in America. I looked at over 100 films and I'm very disappointed because even in the progressive wing of documentary filmmaking community, the idea of class is shown via ethnic films. They think a poor black person being helped by a white person is a class issue. There are class elements in it, but what I'm hoping for is for more people to incorporate class in their films. That goes for me, too. I'm basically a race man, but I've had to realize that my films are incomplete unless I put in class. There will still be this battle, but at least you will know why and not get as frustrated.

**Q – Do you see a lot of censorship today?**

*St. Clair* – Yes, I do. Two ways. One, it's masked as marketing. They don't say, *"We don't want this material in there."* What they say is, *"Well, there's no audience,"* or *"People won't understand this,"* or *"Our demographics indicate that we don't know who this person is."* For example, there's a guy named Dick Gregory who was a comedian and social activist and I pitched that to several people. They won't say, *"Well, we don't know if we want this black guy critiquing and accusing the government of diminishing the rights of citizens."* What they'll say is, *"Nobody knows who he really is."* The other type of censorship is self-censorship and this is happening more and more. Filmmakers will say they want to make a film about how the government is cheating the citizens of voters. *"Wow, that is going to be hard. Maybe I'll just show one case where one machine didn't work. So I won't indict the system, I will treat it as an individual situation."* That's self-censorship.

**Q – What about Michael Moore?**

*St. Clair* – Spike Lee did the same thing when he came up. He became a showman. He marketed his image as a provocative person. In Spike's case, it was a militant, kick ass filmmaker who speaks the truth on behalf of the black masses, which is what he was. In

Michael Moore's case, it was this fat guy from Michigan who was a working class hero who struggled to tell the truth against this huge structure in America that was trying to screw the white middle class. And he made them laugh every once and awhile. He's very clever.

**Q – Can the documentary community support many filmmakers like that?**

*St. Clair* – No. That's the thing. Part of the way of marketing your film is that you become subject to the understanding of marketing. That's if you have an image, you can only push that image so far because people burn out on it. So either you have to put it out there little by little so that it doesn't or you have to let it go out there, burn out and come up with something new. I don't think the community can support a gimmick or a technique for a long time. The only thing they will support is good information. And even that has to be jazzed up a bit. A good example is *Emmett Till*. It's not a great film, but the information that comes out there is fantastic and in fact, it reopened the case.

**Q – So how would you define the term "documentary"?**

*St. Clair* – I'd have said innovative, journalistically based films, but I can't say that anymore because people are using re-creations and animation. It's always changing. In fact, when I first started making films, the camera work that exists in films and music videos today was considered bad camera work. Point of view, shaky camera, lots of angles – you wouldn't be hired if you brought in stuff like that and now the audience accepts and likes it. I think a good documentary should be of service to the audience. They should feel they have more information that makes them think their lives can be better. And there's a commitment of truth to the information that you bring to your audience. After that, anything else is up for grabs.

**Q – With news in the US being so concerned about ratings, are documentaries one of the last places where someone can find truth?**

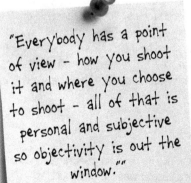

"Everybody has a point of view - how you shoot it and where you choose to shoot - all of that is personal and subjective so objectivity is out the window.""

*St. Clair* – Yes and that's why the documentary has gotten popular in the last half decade. People are getting information from them that they would not get from their regular news broadcast. That's why they're willing to pay for it. People may want sensational docs soon. *Super Size Me* is an example of this. As long as they have a commitment to truth and information to make you live better, then it's good.

**Q – Can you be objective in documentary filmmaking?**

*St. Clair* – That's a myth. And I think people use

that ploy to cool out the truth. *"What you say may be true, but you're not being objective."* Maybe, maybe not, but that's not what I am trying to do. Everybody has a point of view – how you shoot it and whom you choose to shoot – all of that is personal and subjective so objectivity is out the window.

*Q – And with so many points of view, it is difficult to know what is right and wrong.*

*St. Clair – Control Room* explores that. And there's a film called *Desire*. It's about a white woman who follows four teenage girls of different ethnicities in New Orleans pre-Katrina. She puts herself in it and she teaches the four young women to make their own films, which she puts in this documentary. And then she allows herself to be interviewed by them. She's trying to avoid being the boss because she comes from a privileged background. If you come at it that way, it's OK. She says this is good information and at the same times lets me know what their prejudices are.

*Q – In the UK, people can really question the Prime Minister, in the US the President is treated with so much respect he doesn't seem to have any checks.*

*St. Clair –* It's not respect, it's fear. That's where the documentary people jump in fearlessly. Their job is to question them no matter who's there. And that's why Reagan started to cut the funding of institutions to documentary filmmakers. They cut the NEA and the NEH by saying these are the *"hate America people."* I was there for this. The press secretary would call the presidents of networks and say, *"The White House was displeased with this report."*

*Q – What would be the response of the filmmaker to the President?*

*St. Clair – "We can't make this film. I really don't want the White House on my ass because they may instruct the IRS to do an investigation and cause us to explain to our stockholders why the IRS is looking at us."* I'm amazed at the amount of documentaries made given the pressure to stop that line of inquiry. Usually it's the young people who do it. Documentarians have to band together now. You have to have a real posse and everyone has to acknowledge their role.

*Q – How has black documentary making changed over time?*

*St. Clair –* Back then, there was a feeling of overt political commitment and the battle was to get the resources to fill that. Right now, there isn't a political commitment. At best, it's an attempt to rewrite history so that our role is in it. *Emmett Till* and *Gordon Parks* are exactly that – to go back into the past and show another version. One thing that has been achieved is that a black point of view is integral to talking about America. Diversity is a given.

*Q – Do people of different races and socio-economic classes experience film in different ways and how does that affect documentary filmmaking?*

*St. Clair* – Yes. On the race thing, if you grew up as African-American working class, you see how differently the system works for someone who is African-American and middle class. Even though they're still African American, it's at odds with the Euro-centric culture of the country. That comes into play when you pitch to a network or commissioning editor because you have to legitimize the black view. You don't have to do that if it's white. For example, if we talk about slavery then we have to say many years later the working class sees the cars and jewelry as things they were deprived of and now it's seen as achievement. You have to be very clear about what elements you want to put in depending on whom you want to talk to.

## Q – How do you feel about minority programming?

*St. Clair* – At the time, we were so shoved to the side we were thrilled when someone said, *"There must be money set aside for minority programming."* It was an acknowledgment of our existence. Same with Black History month, *"During February we must make sure that information about blacks are on TV."* Good! Now we say, wait a minute. Why just once a year? We're just as American as anyone else. Our sensibilities aren't in the minority. There are more white kids listening to hip-hop now than ever. Some of it is just ignorance because if you confront people on it they say, *"Oh, yeah. You're right."* With *Paul Robeson*, I lost a battle because I wanted it to air during his birthday in April, but they said no – Black History month. It will change. Black basketball style of playing used to be called black basketball, now it's just basketball style.

## Q – What are the biggest challenges in documentary filmmaking?

*St. Clair* – Financing. After that, it's the artistic control of it. And then it's outreach. Getting it to as many people as possible as well as getting it to the people who will benefit the most from the material.

## Q – What tips would you give documentary filmmakers on having long careers?

*St. Clair* – You should really have a group that you talk to and work with. I'd concentrate on engaging with material that you're personally fascinated and attracted to. It's really hard to make a film and sometimes the only thing that keeps you going is your personal interest in the material. Have a good accountant who keeps track of all your bills and can tell you when you're over budget. And whatever you do, publicize. People laugh at me because I send something out every week or two. I'm not NBC and I don't have a publicist. So I have a list of people who work for the papers, who are freelance journalists and the word of mouth people. Don't wait until you finish the film. Each time you accomplish a step, announce it.

## Q – Is the idea of having people around you why you started your organization?

*St. Clair* – Yes. The Black Documentary Collective in New York and The Black

Association of Documentary Filmmakers in Los Angeles. When I started working, I had a whole group of colleagues that I could talk to. But as time went on, some of them fell away – they quit, started teaching or died. When I started doing *Gordon Parks*, I realized in the production meetings that I am the only one from my generation. And I wouldn't be able to talk to anyone about anything and when the production was over, I'd be alone. So I put word out for African American documentary filmmakers to get together so we wouldn't be alone. I would rent a space once a month and people would come. After three months I formed an organization in New York, The Collective and one in LA, West. They're separate and have their own personalities.

**Q – What are the common mistakes that you see documentary filmmakers make?**

**St. Clair** – Accepting as gospel the way things have been done before. In the long run, you may have to retreat to that position, but don't come into HBO or Discovery that way because they may buy some of your new ideas and let you try them. They say they are open to new stuff, so take them up on it. That's one thing I see with the black groups. They're so happy to be working after a lifetime of discrimination that they won't shake it up. And a lot of the time, if it's black material, the networks want to be told what to do.

**Q – What advice would you give to a new documentary filmmaker?**

**St. Clair** – It may sound corny, but you have to really chart out what you want to do because once you do that, you can go anywhere. You're the center of what you want to do. It takes a lot of heart to do that but it is what keeps you going. Go into Discovery and say I just got out of film school and I've got some new shit. What do you think? So self-affirmation, not big headedness, is important because that informs how you approach the money and other people to work with you.

*Author's Note: This interview was conducted in our first edition in 2006. St. Clair unfortunately passed away a year later in 2007. He was a pioneer in the documentary world, as well as life, and will be missed dearly. Please watch his films so we can keep his passion alive.*

*Q – What does "documentary" mean to you?*

**R.J.** – It's a form of storytelling that uses real life and real people to tell true stories. What I learned from D.A. Pennebaker and Chris Hegedus when I did *The War Room* is that cinema vérité, which is the approach to documentary filmmaking that they, I and many have taken, is a form of documentary filmmaking that aspires to all the things that great scripted movies aspire to. As a documentary filmmaker, I go into a situation and observe and film it as clearly as I can. In the post-production process, I work as hard as I can to tell a truthful a story about what I witnessed. Documentary filmmaking isn't objective. I spent time as a journalist and it's not satisfying or possible to me to be objective. But that doesn't mean my obligation to tell the truth is any less than the obligation the journalist has. I combine the story of what I witnessed with the experience I had while witnessing it. So if you look at a film like *A Perfect Candidate*, if you had witnessed the Chuck Robb-Ollie North Senate campaign for an entire year and had filmed it, what you might have seen would've been the exact same thing that I saw, but the film you made would be completely different. And the difference would be the difference between you and me.

*Q – Two of your shows 30 Days and Black And White seem to invoke social change or at least to think about the world around them. Is that important for documentary films?*

**R.J.** – All narrative art gets people to think about the world around them. I'd tell you that I don't consider myself to be an agit-prop filmmaker. I'm exploring things and asking questions. That question might be - what's it like to run a presidential campaign? It might be, how come Oliver North is able to raise $17 million and run for Senate in Virginia when seven years earlier he was about to go to jail for lying to Congress? Or it might be - what's it like for a white male from the Bible belt who believes homosexuality is a sin to spend a month with a gay roommate with whom he might develop a strong friendship? I know there are others who use documentary to pursue social change. For me, it's really about telling stories of real people by asking questions and exploring the answers from

---

 questions@arp.tv

 www.arp.tv

many different angles.

**Q – How is working on a feature length documentary film different from working on a season of TV?**

*R.J.* – Well, film and television have many things in common and many things that are different. One of the things that I learned from Penne is it's important to know what you're doing right from the beginning. In a theatrical environment, your audience has chosen to come see the film. The first thing you do is give them an opportunity to settle into the movie and leave the world behind. TV, which has its own advantages in terms of storytelling and reaching audiences, is very different. Your audience may have made a choice to come to you, but they're constantly conscious of all sorts of other choices that they have. And unless you are working in a premium cable environment or a non-ad supported environment, every 12 minutes or so there's a reason for them to go away. So you're thinking about all sorts of different things in terms of structure — you have to build in what we call act-ins and act-outs.

When you are editing a film that's for theatrical release, it's a very different thing because you aren't working with those built-in breaks and you aren't working with those kinds of constraints. I'm not saying that one is better than the other, only that you're thinking about different things. Among the advantages that television has is the fact that you're far more likely to have all the money you need to make your project, or at least you have a big head start. Whereas if you're making an independent theatrical film, the chances are that you're doing it on maxed-out credit cards or borrowed money from friends and family.

**Q – How are they the same?**

*R.J.* – In both, you always have to be aware that first and foremost the story belongs to the subject and not to you. Lots of things follow from that. If they don't want to be filmed at any given moment, I don't want to be filming them. Why? The story belongs to the subject and not to me. When I'm editing I'm always focused on telling the story as truthfully as possible. Why? Because the story belongs to the subject and not to me. In the field I work very hard to impact the environment that I am in as

R.J.'S FILMS

*The Met Ball* (2010)

*"Hick" Town* (2009)

*Deals on the Bus* (2009)

*The September Issue* (2009)

*Thin* (2006)

*Black, White* (2006)

*30 Days* (2005)

*Bound For Glory* (2005)

*American Candidate* (2004)

*American High* (2000)

*A Perfect Candidate* (1996)

*The War Room* (1993)

minimally as possible. Why? Because the story belongs to the subject and not to me. By the way, one of the greatest misconceptions about cinema vérité filmmaking is that the filmmakers become 'flies on the wall.' Documentary filmmakers are human sized, present and in the room. They don't disappear or fade into the woodwork. What a good filmmaker does is create an environment wherein the subject becomes as comfortable as they would be with a good friend whom they trust. So the most important thing to do when working on these projects, TV or movies, is to earn the trust of your subject. There are many ways to do that and you have to do it every day. The most important way to earn trust is to be who you say you are. You have to tell the truth. To get back to your question – the process of making the television series or the theatrical film is mostly exactly the same. The tools you use – character, narrative, interwoven stories, earning the trust of your subject, combining the experience you witness with the one you have – those are all the same, whether you're working in film or television.

**Q – On American High you gave the kids cameras. Did you train them and is that a good way to earn trust?**

**R.J.** – We worked with them. In getting access to the high school, one of the administrators who I was talking to said, *"What's in it for the kids?"* I said, *"Well, they get to be in the film and they get to work with these filmmakers."* He said, *"OK, but this is a school. What are they going to learn outside of experience?"* That was a damn good question. So I thought, what if they were able to learn something concrete, for instance how to use a camera? Then I realized the way to do it was to give and teach them to use the cameras so that in those moments where the filmmaker isn't present, we can still capture the experience the subject is having. In fact, the subjects will be able to capture it themselves. The filmmaker's not going to be there at 1am when 17-year-old Kaytee Bodle is thinking about a guy she loves. But if Kaytee has a camera and has been taught the principles of composition, angles and lenses and how they can help communicate, then Kaytee can contribute to the story in a way I never could. I found that the texture of the experience and the contribution of this internal monologue added great depth to the stories.

> *"one of the greatest misconceptions about cinema vérité filmmaking is that the filmmakers become "flies on a wall." Documentary filmmakers are human sized and present."*

**Q – What tips would you give new filmmakers on pitching TV executives?**

**R.J.** – Don't pitch TV executives, go out and make a movie. If you're really hell bent on selling a TV idea, and if you have a good idea that you really must make, then I'd consider partnering up with someone with a little more experience. It was extremely valuable to me to work with DA Pennebaker and Chris Hegedus when I was first starting out on *The War Room*; it was equally valuable to partner up with Erwin More, Cheryl Stanley and Brian Medavoy on *American High*. Other than that, I'd say, try to sell ideas that you are truly passionate about and you feel that you need to make. It's always going to be very hard, so if you don't really care about it, it's just not worth it.

**Q – Is it difficult to give up final cut when working for a broadcaster or studio?**

**R.J.** – Not really. I can't think of a single instance where a network or studio has cut behind me, or asked me to change something that I really didn't want to. So really the question is, how difficult is it to take notes from network and studio executives. And the answer is that it's not difficult at all, and in the best cases it can be extremely helpful. You're always going to be getting input during production and post. In a TV environment, hopefully you're working with smart executives whose insight and advice is going to help you. It's always hard to get notes from anyone be it your best friend, your mother or a TV executive. You think you've done it the best you can and done it the right way and someone tells you a scene isn't working – that's hard for anybody to hear. So one of the things you have to learn is how to listen.

When I'm getting notes, I always write everything down. I type as I take notes. I want to make sure that I'm hearing it as clearly as possible. Because sometimes my first reaction is they don't know what they're talking about. But then I give myself a little time to reflect. And on reflection I've got to admit that they're probably right. Even if they don't have the right solution to a problem, they've likely identified an issue that needs to be addressed. To me, anyone who is looking at your work before it's done is a potentially helpful resource. It's an opportunity to make your work better. It's not easy to show your work before it's done. I always say if you look at an unborn child at seven months and you expect it to be cooing, you're going to be disappointed. It's still growing. The same is true of art, and that's why it's hard to show it to people before it's completed. But if you have some friends whom you can trust, you need to show it to them. And you don't even have to ask them about it afterwards, because if you're really honest you can tell what's working and what isn't just by standing in the back of the room and observing. You can tell what's funny and what's boring. You can't avoid the truth when you show it to people.

**Q – Any tips on going from managing perhaps a small three-person crew to several crews and multiple editors on a TV show?**

**R.J.** – That's about managing resources and people. You don't have to know how to do everything, but you do have to know how to get people who know how to do everything. That's what producing is. You get the right team together to solve the problem at hand. The first film I produced was *The War Room*. The first thing I did was call Wendy Ettinger and ask her to produce it with me. She was my friend and

"What a good filmmaker does is create an environment where the subject becomes comfortable as with any good friend that they trust."

I had tremendous respect for her opinion. She also had great access to the resources to get the film made. The next thing we did was go over to DA Pennebaker and Chris Hegedus and asked them to direct the film. That was just good producing.

**Q – Do you usually compensate the subjects for your films and TV shows financially?**

**R.J.** – It depends on the circumstances. When you're making a straight up documentary like *American High* or *Thin*, then no there's no compensation for the subjects. But projects like *Black.White.* where we asked the six family members who participated in it to leave their jobs and homes over a six week period, we gave them a stipend. It wasn't a lot of money – probably not as much as they would have earned in their jobs. But we didn't want them to be unfairly burdened by the fact that they were participating in the show.

**Q – What ethics should filmmakers be thinking about when dealing with sensitive material?**

**R.J.** – Here we go back to the fundamental principles we spoke of earlier: The story belongs to the subject and not to you. You have to be who you say you are and earn the trust of your subject every day. Acting according to these principles is about ethics. We don't film people who don't want to be filmed. We don't lie about who they are and their stories. We don't steal from them. If we don't get a release from them, we don't use the material.

**Q – Have you ever had to deal with censorship or ended up censoring yourself because of TV standards?**

**R.J.** – In a commercial TV environment, the language you can use is restricted, but that's really the only limitation I've faced. Of course, I'm always making choices about what I keep in the cut and what I don't use, but those decisions have to do with telling good, truthful stories, or with other considerations that matter to me.

I remember the first week we were filming *American High* we filmed with a kid for a couple of days and he went home and told his mother about the things he had said while we were filming. Not that it was anything too bad, but he had told some stories. His mom got uncomfortable and he came to us the next day and told us that he didn't want to be part of the project anymore. We said, OK. And he said my Mom's uncomfortable that the tape even exists. We said, *"Here's the tape, it belongs to you. It's your story, not ours."* It was an easy decision to make because of the fundamental principles that we work by. If you've identified these principles, it becomes easy to make decisions in difficult times.

**Q – What advice would give a new documentary filmmaker?**

**R.J.** – My advice to filmmakers is always to make films. Take advantage of the fact that you live in a time where the technology is extremely affordable. Part of being a documentary filmmaker is being resourceful – so go out and get the equipment and tell the stories that you need to tell. It's going to be hard and painful sometimes, but if that's what you want go out and get it. Don't take no for an answer. I always say that no is the pathway to yes – I mean, at least the person saying no is engaging you in conversation! Go out, make your film and have fun. It's an exciting way to live your life and experience the world – embrace it with passion.

KEN BURNS

*Q – What does "documentary" mean to you?*

**Ken** – Documentaries range from cinema vérité to propaganda to history films and to things that seem so stylized that they cross the line into fiction. So to me it's a broad encompassing term of approaches. In the end, it's a fact-based way to get at the truth.

*Q – What is your approach to historical documentaries?*

**Ken** – Ultimately, I'm looking for a good story in American history. But I suppose I have a creed, which is that I'm interested in the power of history. And I'm especially interested in listening to the voices of a true, honest, complicated past, that is unafraid of controversy and tragedy, but I'm equally drawn to those stories that suggest an abiding faith in the human spirit and particularly the unique role this remarkable and often dysfunctional republic seems to play in the positive progress of mankind.

*Q – You take on topics that have large swathes of time. How do you take that mammoth idea and condense it down?*

**Ken** – Unlike most contemporary documentaries, where often someone is telling you what is going on, I would rather show a process of discovery in my films. So our research period never ends. Our scripting never ends. Our filming is less concerned with following the script than it is trying to find the stories in visual material before us. Visual materials being a still photograph, discovery of footage in an archival house, an interview or the cinematography. The script is not some God that directs the shooting and editing. It's a corrigible document that undergoes vast transformations while we assemble the music, sound effects and other first person voices to compliment the visual element.

*Q – Do you find that you write more before, after or during shooting?*

**Ken** – It's a little bit of all that. It may be that we have to write a huge, cumbersome

---

 information@florentinefilms.com   www.florentinefilms.com

document in order to procure some funding. It may well be that a first draft of a script may come well before the end of principal photography. But I like the fact that it doesn't usually come before principal photography because principal photography itself is an extremely elastic and elongated process. It's not like a feature film where you know where you are going for eight weeks. It's interviews spread out over a long period of time – in some cases years. Our *National Parks* film is a huge effort to shoot as many of the parks as possible during all the various seasons from all different angles. Plus we are getting still photographs of the parks that are both specific to the project and generic as well as archival footage. And all the time we are reading and learning stories and following through with comments that were made or pictures that we see or experiences that we have. All of which combine to create this unknowable final project that is so far from the original "yes" that sent us in the direction of its pursuit.

**Q – I've read that you try to keep things from being boring by finding the emotion of the story, "the emotional archaeology."**

**Ken** – That's correct. I had this sort of panic attack after I finished my first film on the *Brooklyn Bridge*. I had to start writing about it so people would know how to talk about it. It seemed so inconceivable that you could spend so long working on a film and then you would still have to do something more to explain it to people. Why couldn't you just show it to them? But of course promotion and distribution and other things require these kinds of descriptions. And almost immediately out of my mouth came the term "emotional archaeology." That stands in stark contrast to the dry dates, facts and events that usually make history an anathema for most people. Sure all those shards of information that you were made to remember in class or from that boring film – an expository recitation of what you should know – could be united with a glue that a higher emotional relationship suggests. But I am interested in a higher emotional plane where I think exist the very things that compel most of our personal lives – whether or not we marry someone, what are the elements of love or faith or hate, etc.

**KEN'S FILMS**

*Prohibition* (2011)

*Baseball* (2004-2010)

*The National Parks: American's Best Idea* (2009)

*The War* (2007)

*Unforgivable Blackness: The Rise and Fall of Jack Johnson* (2004)

*Mark Twain* (2001)

*Jazz* (2001)

*Not for Ourselves Alone: The Story of Elizabeth Cady Stanton and Susan B. Anthony* (1999)

*Lewis & Clark: The Journey of the Corps of Discovery* (1997)

*The Civil War* (1990)

*Huey Long* (1995)

*The Statue of Liberty* (1985)

*Brooklyn Bridge* (1991)

*Q – Is "emotional archaeology" how you get at the theme of the project?*

**Ken** – I think that theme is something that can be imposed on something to its potential detriment. I'd rather not impose. I'd rather have the pursuit of a story or in the case of *Baseball* or *The Civil War,* thousands of stories. The management of those stories, the elimination of those that prove not fruitful or the elevation of others that seemed tangential and now have some centrality will as a byproduct, reveal the theme. So rather than this be a didactic imposition, it results in something more organic in its expression.

*Q – I've read that you try to get inside the pictures. What does that mean?*

**Ken** – Stills represent a moment, not just a frozen moment, but suggests a reality before and after the picture was taken. So I could take my old interest as a feature filmmaker and have a master shot into which I could find a long, a medium, a close an extreme close, a tilt, a pan or a reveal that is a zoom out or a push in, and even inserts that would account for details. So when I put up an old photograph in the early days on an easel and a magnet, I may spend half a roll of 16mm film on one photograph. I am sitting in my office right now and looking at a photo of Huey Long giving a speech at a gazebo in some town hall surrounded by onlookers. I spent half a roll on it and used six or seven takes from it in the final film all with the distant sound of loudspeakers and crowd cheers as well as the narrator and the first person voices and the commentary of interview subjects.

*Q – What do you think Elaine and Jerome would say about this technique?*

**Ken** – They are still close friends and I think very proud of my work. I remember a moment when I was working on a film that was sort of my senior thesis and I was pushing back for the first time against suggestions that Jerome was making. The third time I pushed back, he let go and that's when I suddenly realized, *"Yikes!"* He just set me free. I'm on my own now. We engage as craftspeople and artists with lots of techniques. When the application of technique becomes authentic, that is style. By authentic I mean when it is true to that person's needs. When you stand in the middle of a gallery that is filled with Cezanne's, they all look the same. The still lifes and the endless painting of Mt. Sainte-Victoire in southern France. But as you get closer, each one represents its own myriad of millions of problems, in a good way, to be overcome. And if you stand at a distance from my films, it is possible to sort of categorize them or pigeon hole them in an easy way. But if you get close they are uniquely different from the other. What they do share is one person helped by extraordinary compatriots trying to solve the problems of that particular project. It takes awhile to hit your stride when

"It takes a while to hit your stride when it comes to style, but to thine own self be true."

it comes to style, but to thine own self be true. I never wanted to do history. I wanted to be a filmmaker from age 12. And yet it's what I've done for the past 35 years. I use and engage with history as a painter would choose oils and water colors. Or how they would choose to do still lifes or landscapes. It's just the way in.

**Q – You've said in the past you need to have an openness when editing.**

**Ken** – Historical films are generally researched quickly, written and then the writing becomes the form that directs the shooting and the editing. That's not what we are about. We are so open throughout the whole process. It makes the editing longer and more attenuated, but that's where a documentary film is made. We don't want anything to exert some kind of rigid control. We want everything to be pliable. We are willing to learn. So inevitably, the last day of filming may see us adding something that we just learned. Or we just found a new photograph and have to find a way to get it in. Or something that we thought was important and central, now has to be taken out. I think it was how the Emperor of France, Joseph, said so famously in *Amadeus*, *"too many notes."* And when you work in longform like me, twenty-two hours of *Baseball*, seventeen on *Jazz*, eleven and a half on *The Civil War* – too many notes becomes hugely important.

**Q – How do you go about pitching such huge projects?**

**Ken** – First, these films are not invested in – they are philanthropic efforts because I am completely wedded to public television. Not because of experience, but because in belief and commitment to the idea of public broadcasting. However, we are trying to interest essentially three different groups. One I'll loosely call governmental – that would be PBS, the Corporation for Public Broadcasting (CPB) and The National Endowment of the Humanities. And they all have their own requirements that you do for backup, the most being the NEH. But none of them are simply a one pager with a meeting.

The second group is corporate underwriting. I had a marvelous experience with *The Civil War*. I had been trying to get in to see some people at General Motors in the mid-80's. When I finally got in, they asked me what it was about. I very proudly pushed forward the nearly two inch thick proposal that I had successfully given to the NEH. And the guy just sort of thumbed through it like a phone book and said, *"What's this about?"* Anticipating their short attention spans, I pushed forward the subset of that which was a 25 page narrative that had been extracted from that and on the second pass was accepted by CPB. I felt great about that document. But he looked at it and his eyes glazed over and he said, *"What's it about?"* By now I had a lump in my throat and my heart was pounding and I said, *"Before the War, when speaking about our country, Americans said 'the United States are, plural.' After the War, they said, 'the United States is.' I want to make a film about how that was, became and is."* And he said, *"I get it. How much do you need?"*

**Q – Damn! Had you practiced that answer?**

**Ken** – No, that came out of me from sheer panic and terror!

**Q – What's the third group you must please?**

*Ken* – Foundations, which are similar to the first area wherein they need proposals and conversation and fitting into guidelines.

**Q – Do you still shoot Super 16mm?**

*Ken* – Yes. I feel like an NRA member. You know, *"when they pry it from our cold, dead hands."* We have done tape and digital when there are instances where we had to shoot interviews with more rapidity. But all the live cinematography is still Super 16 as are most of the interviews. We finally succumbed to computer editing, but that is a recent thing!

**Q – You've been cutting on Steenbecks all this time?**

*Ken* – Yes. We had eighteen of them and about thirty-five or forty bins. And we had many, many interns trying to find tiny trims or spending their entire semester experience reconstituting footage. But I soon realized that those interns, who in the early 90's sort of thought it was a badge of honor to learn the old way, now saw it like trying to teach someone who wanted to learn how to be a racecar driver to shoe horses. So we went into digital editing. But we still shoot the archives the same we did all those years prior while other filmmakers had switched to tape or digital and did the moves in the editing system. Due to that, all the animation shops that we used to do these minute moves went out of business. So our stills are no longer shot at an archive. They are scanned, digitized and done within the system. I don't think it's as good.

**Q – It does have an artificiality to it.**

*Ken* – There's no eye behind it. In the old days, you would start a move based on your eye and end the move with your eye. So I've had to come down hard and try to impose some intelligence on a system that wants to do it just with ones and zeroes. It's a sort of alchemy. All of what we are doing is trying to give inanimate objects some sort of life.

**Q – How do you feel about The Ken Burns Effect from Apple?**

*Ken* – In some ways it's a technological tail that is wagging the dog. It comes from a good impulse. I have spent my entire career trying to animate old photographs. And I do this with an exploring and energetic camera eye. And it becomes the subject of parody, ridicule and satire – quite legitimately. No one should take themselves too seriously. The folks at Apple took the idea of the emotional power of moving, zooming and panning through photographs and had been trying to develop a program that would do that. So about 2002, 2003, Steve Jobs asked me to come to Apple headquarters and look at what they'd done. I did, it looked great and they said that every Mac computer from then on would have it. They wanted to call it *The Ken Burns Effect*. And while I don't usually do commercial endorsements, we made a deal where they gave me some equipment, which I then gave to some non-profits and educational institutions. It's funny. Some people believe this *Ken Burns Effect* is what we use ourselves, but actually it's a much more sophisticated thing that we do. And yet, people stop me all the time and thank me so profoundly for it because it's made their wedding or graduation or their vacation pictures that much better. But I have to tell them that I didn't do it.

**Q – What advice can you give a new documentary filmmaker?**

**Ken** – The first is Socratic. Be yourself and know who you are. The second is, particularly with documentary film, there is no career path. In fact, the great novelist Robert Ben Warren once told me that careerism is death. The third is that you have to persevere. There is something incredibly attractive about filmmaking on the outside, but it is unusually hard work. I have on my desk several three ring binders, four inches thick of literally hundreds of rejections of my ideas. It's not easy. It's not easy to raise money. But in a way, that's what I love about it.

**Q – What does "documentary" mean to you?**

*Michael* – That's a very important question these days with the rise of reality TV. One of the hazards these days is that, reality is perceived by some people as documentary. If reality goes down the toilet as it surely will, as all things are cyclical, will documentaries go down the toilet with them? So it's nearly impossible to define what a documentary is. But I suppose I'd call it the observation of real life in a non-interventional way. It's important to see the difference with reality, which is at its heart, contrived. Some of it's very successful and illuminating, but it's contrived to put people into situations and see what they do. A documentary has them in a natural setting.

**Q – What advice would you give a documentary filmmaker about choosing their subject matter?**

*Michael* – The great thing about documentaries is that it's totally democratized. At very little cost you can go out and shoot, cut and finish a documentary. Before, it was a whole huge investment deal. That's the good news and the bad news. There are a lot of terrible films made because they don't think it through. *"Let's make a film about my grandmother,"* and off they go and do it. I think the important thing is not the choice of subject - it's your approach to it. Before you approach your documentary, you should figure out a very elementary structure to see what and where you want to go with the idea. The excitement of a documentary is that it's a real thing happening in front of you – you aren't working with a script in a way one does in fiction. But my advice would be to plot out a story so that it does have some purpose to it. Just don't go out there and shoot a ton of stuff on a subject and then hope you or someone else can come in and make sense of it. While it's much easier to make a documentary, it's much harder to get them seen. So if you want that to happen, you have to be doubly thoughtful about what it is.

**Q – What advice would you give to new documentary filmmakers on the topic of interviewing subjects?**

*Michael* – I've found that the best way to interview people is not to be very well prepared.

You know what the subject is and you know what is going on, but to run through a list of questions is usually deadly. The only way to interview someone is to have a conversation with them and listen to what they say. This is best if you want something emotional and intimate. If you want the facts and you need it done crisply and cleanly, then of course, go in as crisp as you can. For all interviews, don't say very much. There's nothing worse than an interviewer who has diarrhea of the mouth. Keep the questions short and don't be afraid of silence. Sometimes silence is your best weapon. People will want to fill a silence and when they do, maybe they will come up with something for you. And don't go through the interview with them beforehand, as you only get it fresh and interesting once. If you blow that by driving in a car or having a cup of coffee with them while planning it out, you're dead. You'll wish that you'd been filming that time in the car or at coffee because you will never be able to capture that moment again.

***Q – Is it difficult to be objective with subjects that you have been following for a long time?***

***Michael*** – You can't be objective. The word objective is bizarre. It means going in and being cold and formal with an interview in a documentary. That's not the way to do it at all. You have to build trust with the person. They have to know they are safe with you. You have to be emotionally involved. You need to be subjective. That's not to say you do whatever they want to do or agree with whatever they say. My point again is that you have to know what you are after. You have to know what your end result is even if it is a circuitous route to getting to it. If objective means distant and cold – forget it. If objective means being even-handed and fair minded, that's another thing and sometimes even that is irrelevant. If you are making a very passionate film about what you think is an injustice then you don't want to be even handed. But you have to be honest at least with the people you deal with. Then the way you approach them depends on what you are doing. If you want anything emotional or revealing then you have to be very much at one with your subject so you will give them

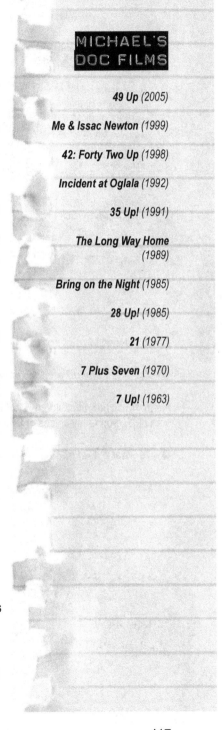

**MICHAEL'S DOC FILMS**

***49 Up*** *(2005)*

***Me & Issac Newton*** *(1999)*

***42: Forty Two Up*** *(1998)*

***Incident at Oglala*** *(1992)*

***35 Up!*** *(1991)*

***The Long Way Home*** *(1989)*

***Bring on the Night*** *(1985)*

***28 Up!*** *(1985)*

***21*** *(1977)*

***7 Plus Seven*** *(1970)*

***7 Up!*** *(1963)*

the confidence to be open with you.

**Q – Are there any differences when you interview children?**

**Michael** – I find with children is not to patronize them. Treat them like adults. Once you start putting on funny voices or talking down to them, kids resent that.

**Q – To what extent should a filmmaker be thinking about their audience?**

**Michael** – Always. We are in the business of entertainment. And too many documentaries show no thought of some end result. You have to make it for people. You are trying to communicate something. You don't patronize the audience. You don't confuse the audience. Pay attention to their needs. Know who your audience is so you can talk the right language to them. You're never making it for yourself.

"For all interviews, don't say very much. There's nothing worse than an interviewer who has diarrhea of the mouth."

**Q – What are the common mistakes that you see new documentary filmmakers make?**

**Michael** – The structure issue. The thought that all you have to do is shoot a lot of material and somehow the story will emerge. It's true with experienced documentarians as well. And it's become more endemic with digital. Have some sense of the structure and the end product in your mind.

**Q – What advice would you give to new documentary filmmakers on ethics?**

*Michael* – It's a private matter. I don't think you can legislate for it. You have to be honorable. You have to tell people what you're going to do and do it. Don't cross any line to them. Don't lie to them. Don't deceive them. You might think I'm going to have to do something because it's very important that I get some statement out here and I may have to misrepresent it. Maybe you do, but it's a question of your personal ethics. I love arguing with people that documentary is a pure form whereas narrative films are contrived. But every edit you make is a judgment. Making a documentary film is full of judgment calls and therefore full of ethical calls as well. And I don't think doing something like paying people compromises things necessarily. I paid people on the *Up* films because it's a business and someone is trying to make money out of it and therefore why shouldn't they. If people are only doing it for money or they're being paid a lot to say something then there may be a strong ethical breach. Then you're buying information. But if you're paying people for their time or the exposure they have to deal with, there's a difference between those two things.

# CHAPTER TWELVE
# CASE STUDIES

## THE DOCUMENTARY
## FILMMAKERS HANDBOOK

**MARWENCOL**

**JEFF MALMBERG**

*Q – What attracts you to a story?*

*Jeff* – I work as an editor and one thing that is a golden rule for me editorially is that you only really have your gut reaction to something. So when I saw my subject Mark Hogancamp's photographs, it lead to a hundred questions to which I needed to find the answers. After a while, I realized that this was a great film subject. The subject matter of your doc has to grab you. If you can put it down, then don't do it.

*Q – When you found your subject Mark, did you do any research about him or post traumatic stress syndrome due to the brain injuries he had incurred?*

*Jeff* – No, because I didn't know I was dealing with that. What I was most interested in understanding were his photographs, his world and what it all meant. Only after I spent time with Mark, did I realize that issues like post-traumatic stress, hate crimes, outsider art and alternative lifestyles were part of his life. Also, I didn't want to make a film about these issues. I purposely didn't want to do the story of a cross dresser who got beat up outside of a bar because I feel that setup cuts you off from the process of getting to know someone. I think there's a lot of value in getting to know someone before you label them. They were surprises to me and I wanted them to be surprises to the audience.

*Q – You don't dwell on his brain injury very much at all...*

*Jeff* – Yes and there were many times when I wondered if that was the right thing to do. But that's where my interest always lay. As I started looking at the footage, I realized all these issues were coming out of this person and I really feel that social issues can be achieved through character and not the other way around. You don't start with a social issue and meet a person, you start with a person and it becomes a social issue.

*Q – And we learn more about his injury and his world that way...*

---

 marwencol@gmail.com     www.marwencol.com

 www.facebook.com/marwencol    http://twitter.com/marwencol

422

*Jeff* – Yes! My girlfriend and producer, Chris Shellen, went to this writer's retreat and there was this novelist there talking about the book he had just written which was based on his article for the *LA Times* about inner city kids. He mentioned that before he wrote the article, he was talking to his wife about how he was going to write it. He was just going to go into the world cold and get quotes from those living there. His wife asked him to name a rappper - just one. He couldn't. So she suggested that he should experience their lives so he could find a deeper meaning of what it was like to be from that part of the world. He did and he ended up with a Pulitzer Prize winning book.

**Q – How did you get Mark to open up to you?**

*Jeff* – I've asked Mark why he let me in so much and he said that one of the first things I asked to do was to go on his walk to the store. No one had ever asked to do that. I really wanted to know this person so I think that assured him early on that I was there for the right reasons. On top of that, I always made sure to show up by myself. I always showed up with low-fi gear. I never set up a light or a reflector. I hardly ever set up a tripod. I balanced the camera on my knee for the longest time. A lot of the time I wouldn't even shoot. I'd just hang out with him for the day and then we'd shoot the next day. Mark is a very intuitive person and he could sense that I wasn't there for money or to steal his art.

**Q – Did being an editor on your day job help you when thinking about how you were going to put the story together?**

*Jeff* – Totally. I remember thinking that I hoped I would bump into a subject that was really deep because I would know how to cut it. Or at least figure it out. Whereas, focusing cameras, interviewing, etc. - I had no experience. But I thought I could cut my way out of it if I had to. Learning how to edit can really save your life because if you look at the budgets of docs, a lot of money is spent on the editor. Someone has to be there twelve hours a day, four to five days a week trying to figure out what it is that everyone just experienced on camera. I feel sorry sometimes for people that don't know how to cut because they have to spend all this time trying to get money together.

**Q – Did you know exactly from the onset, how the doc was going to be?**

**Jeff** – If I'm in the position of not knowing what's going on, which is very much how it was when shooting Mark, your natural instinct is to order things. One of the things that I love about cutting docs is that many of your preconceptions have to melt away in order to see the real thing. Some docs are about writing a script and shooting it, but those in my opinion are the weaker ones. It's nice to get lost. I remember making notes to myself on B-roll. Mark had just told me something about his life and I had no idea what to do with that puzzle piece. And when looking through footage, many times I had left notes to myself telling me not to worry and that I would figure it out. Cameraman me was telling editor me that I would be fine!

**Q – Did you ever feel you were losing your objectivity with Mark?**

**Jeff** – I knew as soon as I met him that all those issues would be tested. Personally, I think they're kind of old school and at their worst they can lead to a lab rat mentality. I purposely just let myself fall for Mark. I knew that as I was cutting it and that I would have to wake up from this dream. Every subject you shoot has its own set of rules, and Mark is no exception. He made a vow in what he calls his second life since the attack, to never tell a lie and it really shows. I know a lot of the things he told me were difficult to talk

about – even on a brain injury level. It actually hurt him to have to remember certain things. But because he was being so honest with me, I wanted to be honest back, so I didn't want that objectivity thing to get in the way.

**Q – With the lying vow, were there times when Mark would speak to you as a director and times when Mark would speaking to you as a friend?**

**Jeff** – Yes, but in my mind those are two separate issues. You have a moral obligation to not put your subject in danger. You realize from watching the footage that there are times where they are talking to you as an interviewee and then there are times when they are talking to you as a friend and the camera happens to be on. Those times you don't use. And even if you look at that footage ten different ways it's going to feel wrong and invasive. Half the reason the film is intimate is because Mark is intimate when you get to know him. It's not because I nuzzled up to him. My form fitted the subject. If you shoot him honestly, he will tell you his inner thoughts. And you can also look at it from the story perspective as opposed to the moral perspective. Putting all those bits in would have taken away from the story.

**Q – How long did you spend with him?**

*Jeff* – Over four years, I think I took sixteen trips. They lasted anywhere between five days to three weeks. That was most of the budget. If you know how to cut and you have a camera, your three main costs are travel, hotels and rental cars.

**Q – Did you do all the shooting?**

*Jeff* – I shot about 95%. And then the three other producers helped at times when we needed more cameras. So maybe six or seven days with three people and the rest was just me. That helped establish a bond with Mark that still lasts today.

**Q – What camera did you shoot on?**

*Jeff* – The Sony PD-150. And I didn't even shoot with that on the first weekend. I don't even know what the first camera was. It was really crummy. All those shots of Mark sitting cross-legged on the couch or him on the green stairs – those are all with the crappy camera. It was all stuff of Mark spilling his guts, so I had to use it. But when I started, I wasn't thinking in those terms. The reason why I had the crappy camera was because the producer I was working with said, *"Oh, you're going to shoot a short? Want my old camera?"* and I said sure. Then when I realized I had this magnificent story, I got a decent camera of my own. Later on in the shoot, I did some Super 8mm.

I hadn't held a camera in a long time and it was awkward. But by the time of the gallery show, wherever my eye went, the camera went. I learned early on to never turn off the camera. Forty minutes – just let it run and pop in a new tape. So for instance, the day of the gallery show I was sitting outside having a smoke with Mark. The camera was pointed down at our feet because I was talking to Mark. He says something and I point up and he says, *"Fucking man shoes."* It became that shot that audiences react to the most. I didn't think anything of it. It was unclear to me at that point as to what this show represented to Mark in terms of how he wanted to present himself in New York City. If someone had asked me that day if it was going in the film I would have said, *"Fuck no!"* A hundred things like that happened every day that didn't make the film. But it is one of the more poignant moments. Who hasn't had the feeling of trying to pull something off and you just can't do it? People can relate to that and it gets a laugh.

**Q – Did you edit along the way or did you let it sit until the end?**

*Jeff* – I so let it sit. I was so afraid of it for a while. I had no idea what it was. I knew it was something big. On a personal level I was afraid of my camera work because I wasn't very proud of it. It turned out it was OK because you can get away with a lot in doc. So when I started to cut, it was a big mountain to climb. I started with a note card system. Any scene I thought of or any idea I had, I would put on a note card. Pretty soon you would realize that two ideas would go together and one would be the sound and one would be the picture. I also set a rule for myself that I was not going to do a paper cut. You can get instant structure that way, but you can never get the real deep meaning. If you are

425

forced to find structure within the footage, you can come out with something better. Each day, my job was to cut one scene – any scene I wanted, whatever I was in the mood to do. One day it would be about him not having had sex in how many years and wanting a girlfriend. Another day it would be a story scene. It kept it fun. If you were tired, you could do a really simple two-person scene. If I were in the mood to struggle, I would cut the art show. I'd show scenes to Chris when she came home from work, always hoping for that home run and getting frustrated when it was not there. But usually they're always right when it's not working. So that was the editorial process and it went on for two years.

### Q – How did you approach the film's music?

**Jeff** – I had worked with this composer before, Ash Black Bufflo in 2007. I had temped out that score with Tangerine Dream, Philip Glass and Radiohead and all this stuff. So he had to do the typical thing where he had to do sound-a-likes and it was really frustrating. So on *Marwencol*, I told him I had a project and I wanted him to start composing music for it now. I never showed him a lick of footage. I just described who Mark was and what some of the scenes were and what his life was about. I showed him some pictures. So by the time I started cutting two years later, I had like 100 tracks that I owned. I didn't have to worry about the spine of the scene being ripped out and replaced by something else. He did an amazing job. It sounded like real film music instead of independent doc music. When you are faced with all that footage, one of the things you can turn to is music. At the very least, you can say the scene that's in my head feels like this.

### Q – What kind of distribution plan did you have?

**Jeff** – When I first started, I never thought it would be distributed. I thought it was some weird little movie project I was doing. I thought it would make an interesting DVD in the back of an art book – like a *Marwencol* art book. When we started getting into festivals, we didn't think it would play in theaters. It was this little insular experience. But somehow when it plays in theaters, it works. There are all these emotional moments built up that people start laughing really hard in places. It becomes this really emotional experience in places. They all come out practically hugging each other. It's amazing. So when we saw it at South By Southwest, we hoped we could get it into theaters.

### Q – What was South by Southwest (SXSW) like?

*Jeff* – It was great. They were picking up everything that we were putting down about Mark. They embraced him and took him into their hearts. They seemed to feel in 83 minutes how we felt about this person and that made me really happy. Festival audiences are usually hyped up and want to like it, but we realized after many screenings that the feelings were real. We then won the Grand Jury Prize and got distribution offers all within a five-day period. We felt like taffy afterwards. Completely emotionally stretched out.

**Q – Was Mark nervous that a lot people would know his story?**

*Jeff* – When we got into SXSW, our first move was to jump on a plane and show Mark the rough cut. And part of this was that the story was about someone wanting to come out as a cross-dresser and they had been beaten up nearly to death for doing that in the first place. I had shown Mark scenes over the years so he wasn't surprised by anything. Once Mark was happy with it, I was done.

**Q – Did you do any special publicity for Marwencol?**

*Jeff* – We put together a book of the stories from the film and sold it as a fundraiser for Mark. It was a nice way to get people excited about the world. At the NuArt Theater show in LA, we turned their alcove area into a gallery and put up Mark's photos. They were surprised because no one had ever thought to do that before. We raffled off the photos and got the entries' emails so we could remarket to them. Haskell Wexler won one!

**Q – Who picked up the film?**

*Jeff* – Cinema Guild for theaters/DVD/Blu-ray and PBS for TV. On PBS it's on *Independent Lens*. Lois Vossen and all the people at PBS were amazing. When I did dare to think about TV distribution, *Independent Lens* was my first thought. I had cut a film that played there in 2007, met Lois and thought they were picking up amazing movies. From a monetary perspective, I don't know what we would all do without PBS' shows. I'm really happy with Cinema Guild, too. They take care of things like VOD and iTunes, about which I have no idea. Especially when you have a day job like most filmmakers. We also sold to Channel 4 in the UK.

**Q – What advice would you give a new documentary filmmaker?**

*Jeff* – You have to love it. You aren't going to get rich doing documentares. I think it was Francis Ford Coppola who said that these days you can't solely be a filmmaker anymore. You have to have some other kind of job to support yourself. Find a day job that you like and do filmmaking when you can. Fortunately, the technology has become so cheap that it has now become like every other art form. You can do it on your own. It may take four years, but you can do it yourself. You should also look for subjects that expand the experience of the film. Mark is still shooting every day so his world is growing beyond the film. Pick a subject that is bigger than your frame.

**PAPER PROMISES**

**SHANE HARVEY**

*Q – Your subject is your father. How did that come about?*

**Shane** – A few years ago, I was dating a woman whose father was a major anchorman for Canadian news. He was very experienced in knowing what made a great story. As we were getting to know one another, I pulled out a piece of paper that my father had given me years earlier. It was a list of the inaugural members of The Country Music Association from their first meeting in Nashville in 1958. It had Johnny Cash, Roy Rogers, Minnie Pearl and a whole lot of other household names on it as well as my Dad, Larry Harvey. So I started telling him the story of my father and he slipped right into journalist mode asking me all these questions. When I was done he said, *"Jesus Christ, Shane. This would make a great documentary!"* The story had been there right under my nose for years, but as is the case many times, it takes someone on the outside to validate it for you. He gave me the names of some people to contact, but they were older, from back in his day, so they weren't really hungry for new stories. Then I got an email through my union about a convention here in Vancouver called FTX West and a documentary course being taught by the authors of this book. So I decided it would be a good idea to take the course and I ended up hiring Andrew to help produce the film.

*Q – Where did you start?*

**Shane** – It started with the list. In the late 1950's, DJs were freaking out because there was a major shift in music going from radio to TV. And when Elvis Presley created such a sensation on TV, places like the Grand Ole Opry decided to start televising their shows at the Ryman Auditorium. The radio DJ's formed the Country Music Association in order to preserve and fight for country music. My Dad was down there at the time fighting it out and joined. They got famous people like Grandpa Jones and Dale Evans to sign up as well as up and comers like my father who had a few hits. So I started to ask myself why does everyone know Johnny Cash and no one knows my father.

---

 info@paper-promises.com       www.paper-promises.com

 www.facebook.com/Paper-Promises-Documenary

*Q – Did you know your Dad's music well?*

**Shane** – It was the soundtrack of my childhood. But as a child I didn't see him in his glory days. I just saw him struggling when things were not going well. There wasn't much talk about his career. So now, I started asking him what happened and I realized there were a few things about what he told me that weren't right. What had happened was that during that time, he had a large fan club based in Newfoundland where he's from. But in the fans' letters, the constant thing that kept coming up was that they couldn't get his music there. Newfoundlanders are very loyal and my Dad got mad at the record company. But King Records in Cincinnati didn't really know about Newfoundland because it was so small. So they focused on places like Toronto or Montreal where they could make money. That didn't sit right with Dad, so he wanted out from his contract. Despite them telling him not to do it, he stood firm and he got out of it. The more I probed about whether he knew how much he was shooting himself in the foot, the more I could see that he had no idea at all. And that intrigued me even more.

*Q – Did he ever play again?*

**Shane** – Not really. He languished away in a parts factory in Toronto. When I asked him about it he said though he didn't realize it then, his commitment was to his family. So alongside the drinking problems, if he wanted to become successful, he would've had to spend more time on the road away from his family and he wasn't prepared to do that. So he gave it up. And when he gave up drinking and became this great lighthearted, loving man, I realized that I wanted to right one of his biggest wrongs. I wanted to get him to play at the Ryman, so that was the focus of the documentary.

*Q – Your father seems like a pretty reserved guy except when he gets on stage. Did that present any character or story problems?*

**Shane** – Well, really it started with a story problem. Once we secured the gig at the Ryman, we weren't sure when to tell my father. There was a time when we went down the path where we'd wait until we got down to Nashville. We would go on a road trip, experience some old times and then when standing in front of the Ryman, I'd tell him that I got him a gig. And I knew his response would be, *"Great. What time?"* He comes

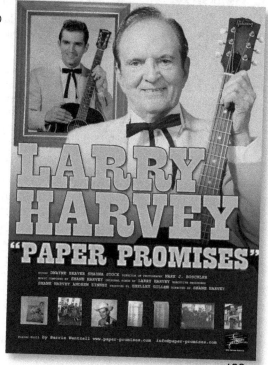

from that old school of not really showing your emotions. Even when we were getting ready to go on stage at the Ryman, I asked him if it ever bugged him that he didn't make it and he said, *"No. I was always famous in my own mind."* So instead, we decided to let him know at his 80th birthday party when I knew we'd have twelve to fifteen active audience members around that I could bounce off in case he flat lined. And though he was quiet, he was welling up.

**Q – How did you come up with the Ryman as a gift?**

**Shane** – My dad told me that he didn't mind not being famous, but he was always a little put out because he thought the Canadian country singer Hank Snow kept him off the Ryman stage. Hank had been putting up songs and making his name before my Dad. So my dad claims that one night Harold Moon of BMI records was going to put him up on the stage of the Ryman because Hank Snow's bus couldn't get there due to a snowstorm. But when Hank heard my dad was going to take his place that night, Hank did everything he could to get back in time and he did. My dad never stepped on the Ryman stage. But when we spoke to a music historian, they told us there's no way that could have ever happened. The Ryman was booked well in advance and there's no way Hank would have been booked so far away that he couldn't make it back. But whatever the truth is, my father never got on the Ryman stage and it seemed to be very important to him.

**Q – How did you get in then?**

**Shane** – I started calling the Ryman, told them the story of my father and hoped it would get us the gig. But the harsh, cold reality of the music business is it's not what you know, it's who you know. They get calls for documentary shooting all the time. So while they said we had a great story, they didn't have the time to accommodate everyone who wants to make a documentary. We were dead. But then a composer friend of mine in Toronto looked at the Ryman website and said that you can rent out the Ryman for weddings and special engagements. So I decided that I would rent it out. But they wouldn't even let me do that! It just added to the tension in the documentary. But I still had to figure out what to do with my Dad. I thought that if all else failed, if we went down and played on the front stairs to the Ryman – my dad and me – that would be a great ending too. I definitely learned that you can't be attached to the outcome in documentaries. You have to be fluid. But I was at the bottom of the barrel. Out of ideas. And thank God for the internet because one night I was up late pushing buttons and on the CMA website there was a list of board of directors. And the international board member was Bruce Allen – Bryan Adams' and Jim Vallance's manager. Over the course of my career, I had developed a relationship with Jim Vallance who wrote songs with Bryan Adams, Ozzy Osbourne, Kiss - all these crazy people. But Jim calling up the Ryman wasn't going to happen. So I called Jim and asked him to call Bruce to get us on the Ryman stage. He said he would do it and he did. He pitched Bruce the story and Bruce made it happen within two weeks!

*Q – How much did you pay for it?*

*Shane* - $14,000. I'm not sure if that's a deal or not, but I didn't care. This was for Dad.

*Q – From a practical standpoint, what kind of challenges came up in production?*

*Shane* – What I discovered is that it's really important to find synergy and a connection with your editor. We had an editor who came with great recommendations. So when she wanted to get paid every week, I said OK when what I really wanted to do was give her a down payment and then give her more when the job was done. Biggest mistake of the project. We get two months in and $3,000 later we had to part ways.

*Q – Did she cut the trailer?*

*Shane* – No. That was another editor. He was more of a button pusher. A good editor when you told him what to do. One thing I learned was that when you ask people to work for nothing or next to nothing and you ask them to change their vision, it's a lot harder than when you're putting cold, hard cash on the table. . But he finished the trailer and did what he said he would do. Then another editor came along and we had similar problems. Maybe the problem was that I wasn't sure what I wanted as the director. But what I did know is that no one could tell the story of my father better than me. And even with Dwayne Beaver who is a fantastic editor, it still wasn't where I wanted to go. Dwayne then said, *"It's your vision so you are the one who's going to have to tell it and I will help you."* So I ended up editing, too.

*Q – Being such an intimate story about your family, what did your parents think when you said you would do the film?*

*Shane* – The first thing I did was tell them that I had to make the film of the truth the way I saw it. Any other version of it wasn't going to happen. So I told them they have to trust me to tell the story honestly. When you do these things you hold the lives of others in your hands. They had to trust me that at the end of the day, audiences would see what amazing people they are. They watch it all the time now. I even watched it with them recently and my Mom said, *"You know, it's a really real documentary."*

*Q – When your Mom has her breakdown on the couch, it definitely was a heavy moment. How did you feel when you were shooting your family like that?*

**Shane** – I wasn't thinking about anybody else. What I was thinking about, especially as a first time filmmaker, was trying to get the right angles. I'm asking them questions. I don't know where it's going. All I know is there's a tremendous amount of emotion going on with my Mom and I'm turning on the camera and getting the shot. And my Mother says, *"And I have all these dreams."* I say, *"What dreams?"* And her answer made the whole scene. One of the best things I learned in this whole documentary project was just to grab a camera and go shoot things like that.

**Q – Some of the footage is SD and some is HD. Did that cause any problems?**

**Shane** – Yes, we had to transcode all the early SD stuff so it would work with the HD footage. We had to format everything with camera frame rates so they would play in sync. Some of the footage was shot at 23. Some was shot at 29.97. So they had to run it through Compressor with ProRes . We used the Sony Z1U with DP Mark Bochsler. The guys we rented out of Nashville were using the Panasonic HPX-500. Then I had a Canon HV-20, which was HDV. And early on I used a Panasonic SD camera with Cinemode on it. We had to put all these effects on it to make it look like old footage so that it worked with the overall look of the film. One interesting problem was that we did this to the first few shots of my film where I introduce my father in the present day. But how can you age footage of something that was supposed to have just been shot? Then I just abandoned the whole concept and figured, *"Who cares?"*

**Q – So the story overtook the technical issues.**

**Shane** – Yes. But that's not to say I didn't get caught up in all of that. I had many sleepless nights where I thought I was going to have to cut all that out because it's not in HD. One of my biggest moments where I surrendered to it being what it is, was when we had to show it to the Toronto Film Festival and I had to do it on SD because that's all the theater could show. And the comment that mattered to me most was when the projectionist said to me, said to me, *"From the first frame that came on, Shane, I didn't care what format it was shot on. I loved the story so much I was brought to tears."*

**Q – You scored the film yourself, correct?**

**Shane** – That's right. Music can be an off camera actor that brings something to the film that is missing. It will help connect all the pieces of the puzzle. With my movie, I realized it was becoming more than it was due to the love of my family. The movie was eighty-two minutes long and there must be seventy-five minutes of music that isn't mine. It's my Dad's. I'm a film composer, so I had to figure out how to accompany that in places where one would naturally place music. One thing I knew was that in no way would I ever eclipse the star of the show – my Dad's music. So I went back to the simplicity of my Dad and a Newfoundler's life. I knew it would be a sparse score. I ended up using spoons because they are well acquainted to East Coast music. And I like to use choral music. I wanted to keep it moving forward because there was a timing issue with the film.

We are going somewhere. So this metronomic clock ticking vibe started to happen for me. Nineteen days before the Ryman. Three days before the Ryman. We were counting down. I wanted my music to convey that as much as possible.

*Q – Since your father owned all his music, getting the rights wasn't an issue right?*

*Shane* – If only! My Dad told me for years that he owned all the publishing rights to the songs. And I believed him. And even if I didn't believe him, I still would have made the documentary. I just would have found more cash! I had had some experience in the music business, but did I know how much those people would take advantage of me? Did I know how ruthless they would be and not caring? No. The wake up call came when I was done cutting the film and we had wall to wall music of my father's and he didn't own the publishing rights. I could have blown a wanker on him. But I knew that was him. He still believes he owns the rights. What he got was the rights to his masters back. So he had the mechanical rights to those specific songs. In the end, I ended up paying $15,000 CAN for those songs. The record company was so unhelpful it was shocking.

*Q – So what's happened to the film?*

*Shane* – It's out and done its run on Super Channel. The response was overwhelming. People were so touched by the story emotionally. One of the things I have been trying to do is get my Dad's unreleased songs out there. One of the biggest tragedies was that all his wonderful songs were never heard back then. Now some of the songs are tied up with the publishing company but I also have an old box of unreleased songs that no one knows anything about.

*Q – Did you have any luck with film festivals?*

*Shane* – We got turned down by every one - even the Nashville Film Festival! Why? I have no idea. I've heard that some things play better on TV than in features. Our other producer Shelley Gillen thought maybe the film wasn't hip enough for the festival circuit.

*Q – Is there anything that you wish you would have done differently?*

*Shane* – That's kind of an unfair question to ask someone who made a documentary that's turned out so successfully because its fluidity. So I would say no because everything that happened lead up to where it ended up.

*Q – What attracts you to a story?*

*Heidi* – The number one priority is that the subject be of deep fascination to us as well as one that we don't know that much about and would like to know more. The film has to be a journey of discovery. It has to be a new experience for us as filmmakers and that way I feel we bring on a more candid and genuine result to the eventual audience. Number two, and it's not a deal breaker, but we would like the subject to have some sort of national relevance. We're not into really quirky, tiny stories – not that there's anything wrong with films that follow a certain job or something – I'll go watch that movie. But I don't want to make it. I want to make stories that an audience member can walk away having made some sort of connection with the subject that means something to them. After that, we do tend to stick with the United States. We both travel a lot and have made several projects in other countries including Saudi Arabia, but the films that we are going to spend years on come from the US because we find it fascinating, enraging, infuriating and wonderful.

*Rachel* – I would add that we look for things that are as complex as possible because we do spend so much time with our subject matter. It needs to sustain two very ADD people for a long period of time. There has to be a lot of nuance to keep us going. Then I'd say not just national importance, but universal truth in it that tackles the big human questions in life.

*Q – When you find a subject, what is your research process especially when it comes to casting?*

*Heidi* – It all depends. *12th & Delaware*, we did a great deal of research before we made any calls. We read everything that had been done on a crisis pregnancy center. We found all the crisis pregnancy centers that were next to abortion clinics. We found out

---

 info@lokifilms.com           www.lokifilms.com

 www.facebook.com/Loki-Films    http://twitter.com/LokiFilms

any legal options or disagreements that had happened surrounding that crisis pregnancy center. That film took a lot of research before picking up the phone because the center's whole MO was to stay under the radar. Their whole existence is based on women not knowing where they are or what's happening. They don't seek national exposure. We spent a lot of time thinking and strategizing, especially because we had made *Jesus Camp* and there were a lot of strikes against us. Most crisis pregnancy centers are evangelical and a lot of evangelicals did not like that film contrary to popular belief.

*Jesus Camp* was different. I was doing a lot of research on child preachers because the child preachers in *The Boys of Baraka* had inspired us. I had heard that there was a school of child preachers in the South and that turned out not to be true. In the course of the research, I ran across Becky Fischer's website *Kids On Fire*. And immediately as the page popped up, I called Rachel and said, *"I found our next film."* It was a gut thing. We decided we had to meet her. We called her and at first she thought it was going to be a film about her and these kids. But very soon we realized that this film was about the Christian right. We had heard about these people who were basically swinging elections to George Bush and here we found ourselves in it. We didn't intend to go there but as we were putting it together we realized that it was a politicized group – even if they deny it. These kids are inside a very strong political culture. And at that moment, we started to see the connection to the Supreme Court.

So that is an example of thinking that it was something smaller and then realizing it was a much, much bigger story that was extremely timely. And that affected our production schedule. We had to go much faster that normal. We used two editors, which we wouldn't do normally because we wanted to get the film out before the mid-term elections. Plus with the Supreme Court nominations, Alito was being vetted and he had a very strong connection to the Christian right. So our schedule and production changed once the material was gathered and that happens on every film.

### Q – Have you ever started shooting and realized you had nothing?

**Rachel** – Happens all the time. You just have to cut your losses. You have to set money aside. Something we've always done with our company is to take a chunk of our profits out of whatever project we are working on and have a research fund. We go out into the field,

435

shoot something, edit it together and see if it will work. When we are between projects we can do a few things like that.

**Q – How did you get the subjects of your films to open up to you, given their well-known distrust of media?**

*Heidi* – We are very transparent. We'd tell them a little about our personal lives, show them our films and our website. You can't hide. No one owes us anything. No one owes me access. Anytime anyone opens their house to me or opens their mouth to tell me something, it's a gift. And I think Rachel and I both have maintained that feeling that this is a favor. They don't have to do this. They can walk away at any time. We take that very, very seriously. So there's an ongoing dialogue with subjects because it's obviously a collaborative process.

I think a lot of documentary filmmakers skirt over the fact that in some way you are in bed with your subjects. It's a strange relationship, but they aren't actors. They can change their mind. They can move. They can disappear. They can get mad and shut the door on you and say don't come back and then you don't have a movie. So we try to be transparent and open. We check in with our subjects when we are not in town. We keep them abreast of what's going on and try to make them feel comfortable. You don't want

someone to feel that you are going to blast in and out of their life. The other thing is that our subjects can tell that we are not highly judgmental people. We don't go in with an agenda and I think that comes across.

*Rachel* – I think the most important thing is to really listen. Sometimes they don't want to talk about what you asked them or what they are really saying. Pay attention to the words they choose and to their body language. And you have to understand their incentive to be in the film. There is a huge range as to why someone would want their privacy deconstructed. You have to be as honest with people as you can possibly be. It puts people at ease and they feel like I'm not looking for them to say anything. I'm not trying to put words in their mouth, in fact, I'm hoping they will say something I can't even imagine. I think it's really important that people know that you respect their decisions to be involved because it is a real gift to have access to someone's inner life. Don't take that for granted at all.

**Q – You once mentioned that your Oscar nomination for Jesus Camp made it more difficult to get interviews.**

*Heidi* – Yes, sometimes it does! People get weirdly intimidated, like, *"Oh, well I'm not that interesting. I don't want you to waste your time."* And sometimes when they see that we were nominated, they think that this is for real. This is going to get seen. This isn't going to be one of these films that goes straight to video. You have to combat that when people start to get nervous that this film is going to be seen by a lot of people. Obviously it is a good problem to have. This film that we are making in Detroit right now, we don't tell them about the Oscar. We walk up to them and say we are making a film, give them our website and then they can do their own research.

**Q – What draws you to certain characters?**

*Heidi* – The number one thing you look for in a character is someone who is exactly the same on camera as off camera. That's hugely important to us because we're looking for a genuine experience. We tend to focus on, I would not call them outliers, but rather passionate, single minded people who are about what they are doing most of the time. Or we will follow people who think there is something great at stake in their mind that is unfolding.

*Rachel* – They have to be true to themselves. It's OK that they contradict themselves because they are complex. A good exercise would be to identify the top twenty characters of all time, fiction and non-fiction and what you enjoyed about them. Doesn't mean you have to like them as a person, but look at what you enjoyed about them as a character.

**Q – Do you and Rachel do the shooting or do you hire DPs?**

*Heidi* – We hire cinematographers usually. There are two or three with whom we work.

**Q – What instructions do you give them when you start a shoot?**

*Heidi* – Stay as small and as invisible as possible. Never yell rolling or not rolling – just keep rolling constantly. Never tell anyone to do something again unless Rachel or I determine that has to happen. Really try to make the person whom we're filming forget that we're filming. We don't want to drag them into the production and make us aware of our process. We like our DPs to stand back as far as possible so we employ a lot of lenses in order to get a distance between the shooter and the subject. Also we don't walk into a situation rolling. If there's a press conference or something we show up an hour before and set up. And then we can shoot the reporters talking to one another or looking through their bags for a pen. If you don't just wait for the "action" to begin you can get the minutiae of a scene. We make sure our DPs understand that it is not necessarily about the obvious action, but it's about what else is happening in the room. The person speaking in the room might not be the story. We don't care so much about sync. Often the most interesting thing is watching the facial expressions of someone in the audience or something going on outside the window.

*Rachel* – Yes, the most interesting parts of an interview are the in between parts, the before parts or the after parts - the parts where the subject doesn't feel like they have to perform or say the right thing. That's what non-fiction film is: bringing genuineness and authenticity to an environment. As audiences get more and more sophisticated, the more they expect things to feel real. So a good vérité DP definitely has a certain skill set. It's opposite of a narrative DP who has a script and knows what to anticipate. Doc is freestyling. It takes years and years for a doc DP to get to the top because they are doing a shit load of work all the time. They have to be really in tune with the director, the subject and the emotional tension in the room.

## Q – What about audio people?

*Rachel* – For audio, we don't have the same stable that we do DPs. So we usually ask them to get the best sound for us and not be so involved with the action. The more people in the room, the more eyeballs going on, the more the wall of observation disappears.

## Q – Do you write a script for your projects?

*Heidi* – We don't use voiceover or narration so that type of script never gets written. We start with nothing. We go out there and see what's out there. Once we get into the shooting process we start writing out a list of scenes. We have a very detailed log and we watch all the material back. And we start writing out scenes that we don't have that would be great to get to help tell the story. We did do a 25 page outline for the film we are shooting now, but we wrote that three months into shooting when we had a real grip on what's going on. We do a lot of that when we're not out in the field. And we look to get out expository information in an interesting way. How's the audience going to know what we know if we haven't filmed that particular scene? Or we missed it? Or it happened before we got there? How are we going to explain that to our viewer in a way that is compelling and cinematic?

## Q – How did you fund your three major films? 12th & Delaware was an HBO film, correct?

*Rachel* – Yes. We came up with the topic together. We told them about crisis pregnancy centers and they encouraged us to go get access to one. HBO funds things outright. For *Jesus Camp*, A & E funded it from the very beginning on a little bit of footage we had. They encouraged us to develop it and we did. They liked it and then financed it. With *The Boys of Baraka*, we self-financed that one for years. We were almost in the edit phase and then we got money from PBS. ITVS specifically. Claire Aguilar. And it ended up on *POV* where we worked with Cara Mertes who was there at the time.

## Q – Any horror stories from any of your productions where you wished if only I hadn't done that?

*Heidi* – I committed a cardinal sin. I was in a hotel room in Saudi Arabia shooting for fourteen hours and it was exhausting. I made the mistake of transferring the material off the cards when I was too tired and I deleted the best two hours of that day. It was the best stuff we had gotten ten days into the project. I was tired and the power went off in the middle of the transfer and I thought it had transferred and it hadn't. I had to tell my DP that I dropped the clutch. I blew it. We tried and tried to get the same thing again and we never got it.

*Rachel* – One of the first things I did when I was working in non-fiction TV was let all the subjects of the film see it before it was finished. That was a big mistake. You have different relationships with your subjects, but that is something I wouldn't encourage. It can cause big problems. People start to get insecure. They think they look bad or fat. It's bad. Have your picture locked and be confident. Don't bring them into the process.

### Q – What is your process like when working with editors?

*Heidi* – Our process is multi-step. First of all, Rachel or myself will have watched the raw material that the editor is cutting. We make fat selections of the material. Our editor Enat Sidi, knows what we like and what's important because we've indicated it as such on a separate Final Cut Pro timeline. And then she's free to cut the scenes. So say there's two hours of material, the first pass on a scene will be at least fifteen minutes, maybe twenty. What I don't want to see is it cut down to four minutes on the first pass. That's not going to fly. Then we discuss the scene and see if there's anything that was thrown out that shouldn't have been. Once something is cut out, it almost never comes back in so it's important to us to keep things long at this point. Then she does another pass and gets it down to like eight minutes. Then we leave the scene and move on. We don't fine cut and polish in the first few months of the edit because there's no need to. You don't know what's going to precede it or come after it. When all the scenes are done that way, we'll do a basic structure and watch a very long output. I wouldn't even call it a rough cut. Our films aren't long, usually around 84 minutes, so this isn't too bad.

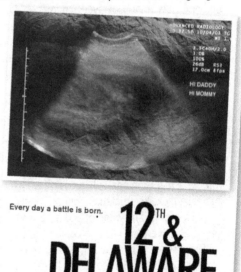

Every day a battle is born.

# 12TH & DELAWARE

### Q – In Jesus Camp, the two opposing sides met via the radio call in show. But in 12th & Delaware, the two opposing sides

*never met. Was there a reason for that?*

*Heidi* – In *Jesus Camp*, at some point we told Becky, the minister, that we were introducing another element into the film – this more liberal Christian DJ. We thought that we should let her know that we were going to be sharing this film with someone else. The film was not working. We needed a counterpoint. So we started filming his show because he addressed a lot of the bigger issues. So we told Becky and she appreciated us telling her and she started listening to his show. Then she said she wanted to go on his show. So we told him about her, but didn't show him any footage for that wouldn't be fair. We told Becky that the next time we would be shooting his show we would let her know and he'll take her call. So we did make that happen. In *12th and Delaware*, it would never happen. It would be totally manufactured. They are mortal enemies. There are lawsuits and restraining orders and fires and hate. That was part of the power of the film, They never have or ever will speak. And yet they are neighbors. We thought that given the stance on abortion in this country, it was a nice metaphor.

*Rachel* – It's a classic storytelling necessity. No matter how big or small, you need conflict. If there's no conflict, then who cares?

**Q – How did the edit for Jesus Camp go?**

*Heidi* – It was a total mess. We were eight months into the edit of the film and it was all one-note. It was the kids over and over again. You get numb to the material. We brought in our friend Sam Pollard to look at it. He was a consulting editor on *Boys of Baraka*. He watched it and said that it was fascinating but it needed another element. Then we told him about the radio guy and he said we should try that because it was definitely not working. Great scenes, my friend, do not make a great movie. New filmmakers need to write that on their hand and on their wall, keep it above their edit machine and the sooner you learn that the better a filmmaker you're going to be. We needed a pressure valve and the radio host was saying what most of the audience was thinking. The audience wants that or they think they are going crazy. How could no one ever not comment on it at all? It was weird. So he commented on the events in general and that worked.

*Rachel* – Yes. Sam basically said that we had no conflict. Even if you have the most interesting, exciting material – and we really had some fantastic scenes in that film with revival meetings and whatnot and access to a world that a lot of people hadn't seen before. But everyone in those communities, everyone was on board. There was no conflict. And with the radio DJ, it was a way for the audience to make sure that we hadn't drunk the Kool-Aid. Someone had to say something. We already had a radio thing going on because Christian radio is hugely prevalent in that world. It was on in every house that we went to. So we were already interweaving it. So Mike Palantonio was perfect because even though he was a progressive, he was a devout Christian.

**Q – How do you handle music? Do you add it before or later?**

*Heidi* – We use temp. We play around with it and about six months into the edit we start talking about composers. You don't want to bring on a composer too early or they are going to waste their chi writing tracks when you're not ready. Their tracks might get cut and it's demoralizing. Composers are very fragile animals and they need to be treated with kid gloves. You have to be ready when you hire a composer. You have to have a vision and know what kind of instruments you want. You have to give them tools, guidance and inspiration so we bring them on very late. Most docs need minimalist music and most composers don't want to write minimalist music. It's always a challenge for us.

*Rachel* – Even coming up with temp tracks is hard for us. It's really tough. It's really where the director has a chance to go overboard or be too subtle in their point of view. So it's difficult to strike the right chord. You want it to be dramatic and you want it to be emotional and you want it to be fun to watch, but you also don't want to overly comment and steer the scene too wildly. You want the audience to feel like it's their journey and not like they are being dragged along.

### Q – Do you have any advice on co-directing?

*Heidi* – Our films take years to make and it's a lonely process making them alone. So it's always best to have someone else there to inspire you or motivate you when you don't feel like it. It's nice to have a sounding board – to get someone else's opinion. We're really great friends and we respect each other, but of course, we have huge arguments in the edit room. You can get mad and irritated and do all those human things, but as long as you respect the other person's opinion and view and skills, you will be fine. Many partnerships break up because they get a little bit of success and everyone wants to take credit for everything.

*Rachel* – That's right. The biggest liability in the partnership would be people's egos. The best thing to do is to ask yourself, *"Why am I feeling this way? Is this going to make the film better or not?"* It's an intimate relationship so you have to do all the things you would have to do in an intimate relationship to keep it healthy and strong. It's not very different from being married to someone.

### Q – What advice would you give a new documentary filmmaker?

*Heidi* – Don't do this job unless you're slightly mentally ill and completely passionate! You have to be like a dog with a bone. If you're not completely interested in a subject, don't make it because it takes a long time to make it. My other advice would be sometimes you have an idea and it would make a better article in *The New Yorker* or make a better short film or a radio piece. Make sure the story you want to tell is right for the cinematic medium.

*Rachel* – Be patient. Making a documentary takes a really long time. Don't hold onto things that aren't good enough. Don't be too self-indulgent. And if you aren't completely passionate about something, cut your losses and don't do it.

**Q – Were you always a filmmaker?**

*Mary Ann* – No. But as a photographer and writer, I have been telling stories in words and images for decades. My early training as a musician and brief stints as an investigative reporter also came in handy. *Quest for Honor* was my first attempt at film. Filmmaking is like picking up a new paintbrush. Or more precisely, it took every skill I had - writing, photography, music, investigative journalism. I had to use them all at one time. Nothing I had learned previously was lost. Filmmaking demanded it all.

**Q – How did Quest for Honor get started?**

*Mary Ann* – In 1991, I had spent six weeks traveling with Hero Talabani, a video journalist and Kurdish resistance fighter. At that time, Saddam had a price on Hero's head. But times changed. In 2005, Hero called me from New York where her husband, Jalal Talabani, the first Kurdish president of Iraq, was speaking at the UN. She invited me to return and told me to bring Sissy Farenthold, our mutual friend. *"You can continue your work on Kurdish women. Maybe do a film this time,"* she said. I spoke with Sissy and with author/filmmaker/professor Elizabeth Warnock "BJ" Fernea, who had made seven films on women in the Middle East. Our original plan was for BJ to be the producer. She suggested London based Iraqi filmmaker Masoon Pachachi as director. Sissy and I would executive produce. Unfortunately, BJ became ill so I picked up the momentum and continued with the project.

**Q – How did you begin to shape the story?**

*Mary Ann* – From the first it was going to be a film to cure the misconceptions of Middle Eastern women which concerned all of us. Since I knew the Kurdish women's world well and could get access to it, we decided to find a story there. So I started working

---

 www.questforhonor.com   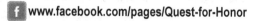 www.facebook.com/pages/Quest-for-Honor

 http://twitter.com/QuestForHonor

442

my network of teachers, journalists, poets, doctors, lawyers, peshmerga and spies looking for the right angle. I knew the Kurdish Good Old Girl Network would work for me. At first, we thought it would be about the organization Hero founded called Zhinan, which means *"women"* in Kurdish. Zhinan encouraged women to develop their talents, especially Kurdish widows created by Saddam's genocide. Through sewing and weaving, it transformed victims into women who could stand on their own two feet, make a living, and raise their children. But when I returned, Zhinan employed a thousand manicured, educated, well-dressed modern young women who were valiant in their own way, but not as interesting as the founders. The story felt old.

New women's voices facing contemporary challenges interested me. And chief among these were women journalists and activists fighting the Kurds' toxic tradition of honor killing. While facing the destruction and pain Saddam inflicted, is difficult, it's not nearly as complicated and intriguing as facing one's own societal demons. So that is where we decided to look for our story. But then I realized that a team of outsiders telling this story wouldn't be as authentic as if I had Kurds on my crew. So I made sure that I had plenty of natives working as co-producers, assistant producers, story consultants, translators and cameramen.

### Q – How did you cast the film?

*Mary Ann* – We cast a large net. Too large of a net, really. We followed too many people at the start. But after much research, one woman whose name kept popping up was Runak Rauf, who, in her sixties, led a march of 150 miles to the Kurdish parliament in Erbil and shamed the men into stopping a brutal civil war. She is the mother of my friend Barham Salih, the then Deputy Prime Minister of Iraq, now Prime Minister of the Kurdistan Regional Government, whom I had known since his days in Washington. She founded The Women's Media Center, which solves honor killings, protects women and educates the public. But even more important, the women there provided an ample diversity in age, social station, and educational background - from a sixty something patrician matriarch to a young woman in her twenties with a sixth grade education. It was obvious that

443

the subjects would be found there.

**Q – What was it about them personally that made you choose them?**

**Mary Ann** – They needed to be articulate. They had to be able to talk about what they were doing and why they were doing it. They couldn't be one-dimensional. They had to have some flaws themselves just like any character in a story. And they had to be engaging.

**Q – Did you have your money in place before you went over there?**

**May Ann** – Yes, because we funded most of it ourselves. We are associated with a foundation and asked people, mostly friends to go through it to donate. It wasn't that easy because I come from a very conservative part of the world – Texas. People aren't used to giving money for filmmaking. But we soldiered on and raised about $60,000 before we went over to Iraq for the first time. But that doesn't last very long with six trips to the Middle East, getting insurance and paying people. We got a lot of in-kind services through the Kurds such as security, cars and lodgings. That mostly came through friends I knew over there. And some times we just stayed in very reasonable lodgings.

**Q – Do you have any tips for filmmakers who want to shoot in a foreign land or even in a different community in their own city?**

**Mary Ann** – I would certainly tell them to know the place and community well before they start shooting - preferably have several years of experience with them. You have to know if there are the facilities to do what you want to do. We went a few places where there wasn't any electricity to recharge camera batteries. Other places had "dirty electricity." In Istanbul, you can go to any concierge and resource something. In Kurdish Iraq there are few to help you if you don't make prior contacts. You have to choose a crew that is up to handling the problems of the place or situation. We lost a few crew members who were not up to the unique challenges of Iraqi Kurdistan.

**Q – How big was your usual crew?**

**Mary Ann** – Two cameras, sound, and myself. Lean and mean, but able to function. In Iraq we picked up our production manager, assistant director, translators, assistant producer, and a third cameraman, who also scouted. Because we were so small, it was important for us to shoot on cameras that could go directly to hard drives so as we were eating we could be downloading footage. That way we could see what we did and didn't have, which reduced unnecessary trips and made being in the field easier.

**Q – Did you have any interesting production problems?**

*Mary Ann* – One of the crew got typhoid when water went bad, and we had to leave the country abruptly once when a shooting at an airliner threatened to close the borders. The Iranians shelled a village we were documenting and the next day all of our subjects fled to parts unknown. Dirty electricity took down some batteries we had to replace, which cost us a few days. But most issues were solved by help from friends who were often ranking officials. When we got in a situation without a restaurant, Kurdish President Massoud Barzani's sister packed picnic lunches for the crew. My "friend and sister" Kurda Khan, Mayor of Koysanjak, opened the small city so that my DP could set up to shoot a cemetery scene at four o'clock one morning. Video and film producer Hirau Ibrahim Ahmad aka Hero Talabani was our guardian angel, making certain we were always safe. Hero is keen on having a film industry in Iraqi Kurdistan.

**Q – How many hours of footage did you shoot?**

*Mary Ann* – All together, a little over 500 hours was collected from six trips from December of 2005 to fall 2008. Much of this is for the foundation's project documenting the rebuilding of Iraqi Kurdistan. All the footage is being archived at the Genocide and Human Rights Documentation Initiative generously supported by The University of Texas Libraries. It was the two trips in 2008 where we really nailed down most of the footage for *Quest for Honor*. Our total footage documenting honor killing practices is about 165 hours.

**Q – When did you start editing?**

*Mary Ann* – We started looking at storylines and sequences in Final Cut Pro in the spring of 2007. Then we edited from September to December – took it as far as we could, then stopped and screened it in various places. After reviewing our input from screenings, we continued editing, then stopped in May, 2008 and went back to Iraq in June, 2008 with a good idea of what we needed to make the story. We finished editing in September, 2008 and were invited to Sundance on our rough cut.

**Q – Based on your photography and art background, did you have a sense of what**

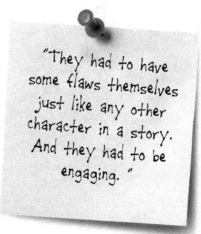

*"They had to have some flaws themselves just like any other character in a story. And they had to be engaging."*

*style you wanted for the film?*

**Mary Ann** – My DP Dane Lawing and I have a similar "eye," and we both know what we want. We both tend to like wide angle and lots of small detail shots - and available light when possible. I love Dane's slow long pans as well. They resemble the wide-angle, low light shots I am known for as a still photographer.

**Q – Did you spend a lot of time in the edit suite?**

**Mary Ann** – At first I didn't because I am a notorious micro-manager. It was tough, but I knew if I went in there I would kill the creative power of the talent I hired. As time went on I spent more and more time in the edit suite. As we begin our second film, I am two or three days a week in the edit suite.

**Q – Did you do anything special in post to enhance the film?**

**Mary Ann** – Everything. To my surprise, I love post. I love the idea of essentially Photoshop-ing a film and telling someone else how to do it! One thing I told the editors to do was to pump up the colors of lush countrysides so it looks more dreamlike. Then in other sections I told them to make things look really natural and we went back and forth between the two looks. It's subtle, not cartoon-ish. On sound, I was influenced by the film *No Country For Old Men*. I love the use of ambient sound in that film, as well as the ambient silence. My music background affected the edit too. I had a real feeling for the tempo - when things should move slower or faster. This sometimes caused arguments in the edit room. Then at the end, my composer Wendy Blackwell would come on the mix sessions to make sure everything was perfect.

**Q – Did you give your composer any special instructions when composing?**

**Mary Ann** – I did. I said I didn't want anything folklore-ish, but it had to sound Kurdish. We found a Kurdish musician in Washington, DC who had about twenty native instruments and he played every one of them for the score.

"You need to have a compelling story...and a great DP doesn't hurt! "

**Q – How did Sundance come about?**

**Mary Ann** – Well, nothing ventured, nothing gained is my motto. Plus, I thought the film was damn good. So I went for it despite some people on my team who thought it wouldn't stand a chance. Actually, them saying that to me is what really made me knuckle down and get the film cut to my specifics and an acceptable Sundance entry.

*Q – Had you ever been to a film festival before?*

*Mary Ann* – No! I loved it! I loved talking to other filmmakers and seeing how they worked. I don't agree with places like *The New York Times* who say you have to know someone to get into Sundance. I was a first time director who knew no one and got invited.

*Q – What advice would you give a new documentary filmmaker?*

*Mary Ann* – You just need to have a compelling story…and a great DP doesn't hurt.

**Q – How did you get the idea for Gasland?**

*Josh* – My father got a proposal in the mail to drill for natural gas on my family home in Pennsylvania. They wanted to use this new technique called hydraulic fracturing or "fracking." Halliburton invented this technique, which involves pumping water and toxic chemicals into the ground at extremely high pressures to fracture rock formations, which hold natural gas. Previously, you would drill down until you hit a pocket of gas and capture it as it rises. With fracking they pulverize the rocks with the pressure of a cluster bomb. I didn't know any of this stuff when I started. When we got the proposal in the mail, we started looking around to all the other leasing that was being done and saw that 80,000 acres had been leased in the Delaware River basin. I started to wonder how it was that we were all of a sudden in a gas drilling area when before we were never in any kind of industrial development area. It was worrisome and disturbing. It's a watershed area. It's beautiful, scenic and amazing. On the other hand, they were offering us $100,000 for the lease and potentially a lot more. Then I discovered that 50% of New York state was being leased. 60%-65% of Pennsylvania was being leased. That meant that land was being turned over at an alarming rate to the gas companies for exploration and if they drilled all those areas, this would be utterly transformative of the entire Northeast. I needed to find out what this process entailed.

**Q – Where did you go first?**

*Josh* - Dimmock, PA. It's about sixty miles away from my father's place. It was a nightmare. Halliburton trucks were swarming everywhere, drilling rigs were all over the place and people's water turned green and brown, smelled bad and fizzed. They could light it on fire! Their children were getting sick. Their animals were getting sick. There was a sense of fear, betrayal and chaos. I looked at that and said, *"There's no way this is happening where I live."* I went back to find out if this was some kind of aberration or was it going on all over the country.

---

 www.gaslandthemovie.com      www.facebook.com/gaslandmovie

 http://twitter.com/gaslandmovie

**Q – Was anyone else talking about this issue?**

**Josh** – Actually, the alarm was sounded first by one of my neighbors. Barbara Arrendale who makes glass sculptures and has a degree in biochemistry from Columbia University lives nearby in the mountains. She started looking into the process and the more she did the more she freaked out. She became scared of the process and all the chemicals they were pumping into the ground. She gave a presentation to a sustainability group showing these moonscapes in these drilling areas in Wyoming. But I didn't know if I could trust these groups. Were they crazy environmentalists? I wanted to find out on my own. What I found out was the actual reality was ten times worse. The people out West that were in the film were all about saying their lives had been destroyed. They said, *"Our water is contaminated. Our homes are valueless. Stop this before it happens to you."*

**Q – Was it easy to gain the trust of your interviewees?**

**Josh** – When people see that you have respect, they appreciate it. I may have been weirded out to go to Texas, but I realized that these people were in crisis. They were dying to talk to anybody - even a guy from New York and Pennsylvania showing up in a beat up 1992 Toyota Camary with no crew. But more importantly, I was in the same boat. They could see that I was sincere. I feel as a director, it's important to be down to earth, never judge anybody and love your subjects. The more you listen and incorporate what they're saying and doing into the story, the more they will help you. As you gaze inside a character, it's your aim to find the most profound thing about them. If you aim for that, your questions are going to be about that, and your responses are going to be like that. I didn't come in there like a network news crew, *"I'm here for 30 seconds. Here's the mic in your face. Give me the sound bite."* I came there to hear what they had to say and spend time with them – even though I was usually only in one place for a day.

**Q – Did you have trepidation about putting yourself in front of the camera?**

**Josh** – I didn't want to be in the film. It made me feel nervous and awkward. But my friends and dramaturge all said that this was my story. I initially developed the voiceover as a placeholder. It was the easiest and best way to give context to a scene. And when we showed segments of

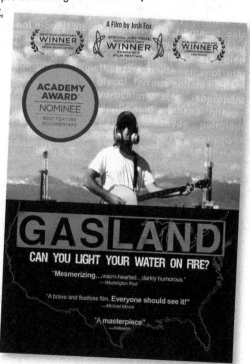

the film, something funny happened. The segments that I was in or narrated, people laughed and enjoyed. The ones I wasn't in, not so much. They would get bored. So we realized that a guide was important to enjoying the film. Look, it's an incredibly dark and depressing subject and you can watch a film about gas drilling and want to blow your head off. We didn't want to do that. We wanted to make sure there was a sense of human hope and positivity. That was the same tone ringing through the interview subjects. They are extraordinary. They are so moving, human, funny and real. If we had not matched that with my story, I think it would have been too grueling. I have a laugh every ten minutes on purpose because it helps keep the audience engaged.

**Q – How much of the shooting did you do? There are several DPs in the credits.**

**Josh** – I did about 75% of the shooting. I'd shot most of my previous feature film, *Memorial Day* and documented about twenty of my plays so I was used to cameras. It's like an extension of my hand.

**Q – What camera did you use?**

**Josh** – I started with the Sony PD-170, which I loved because of its sensitivity to light. When I shot *Memorial Day*, every shot was at night. So I could open up the iris and get these brilliantly washed out colors. When I shot *Gasland*, I'd never shot anything in the

daytime. Now all of a sudden, all of my settings don't work. It looks weird, fuzzy and out of focus. So there are actually several cameras at work in *Gasland*. There's a beautiful pastel, fuzzed out, almost looks like Super 8mm, that's the PD-170. Then you have the Panasonic DVX standard def camera, which I started using midway through the trip because I figured it out one day. And then my editor Matt Sanchez, who is really the co-creator of *Gasland*, had a Panasonic HVX, which is all the HD stuff. When we were in Congress we shot together. On some of the shoots like John Hanger, the Pennsylvania Secretary of the EPA, Matt was there. He's an incredible artist with the camera. The nature shots, the shots of the stream, they are the beautiful moments in the film and they are Matt's camerawork. Molly Gandour, who was one of the research producers was there with me from Grand Junction until Texas. At Divide Creek when I break down, she's the one shooting me. Matt as the editor took all these different visual styles and wrapped them into one cohesive

whole. He chose shots that I never would have because they were artistically beautiful or jarring. I'd be like, *"Why are you going with that completely out of focus shot of a pipe yard?"* Then I'd look at all the other shots and he'd be right. He was very bold to take this very subjective approach to the rhythm of the editing.

**Q – Sometimes when a director shoots his own film, they can worry too much about framing or getting the shot and then lose their connection with the subject.**

**Josh** – No. When I do a sit down interview, I'm behind the camera and the subject is looking at my eyes. So I don't have any problem connecting with people while I am shooting. Of course, I always let them know that they have my 100% attention and focus. I may say, *"I'm also running sound so I may stick the ear piece in and out of my ear to make sure it's working, so don't let it throw you off."* I think there is an unseen connectivity to the person who is in your frame. In my body, I may be looking down to hear the sound or to adjust the focus or exposure, but I'm only doing that as a reaction to what they are doing. The best directing is no directing at all. It's reacting.

**Q – How long was the whole production cycle?**

**Josh** – It was remarkably fast. A year. The road trip across the country took thirty days. The entirety of the editing took about five to six months.

**Q – How did you manage the editing sessions?**

**Josh** – Matt and I worked side by side for months in my house in Pennsylvania and out of my theater company offices in Brooklyn. We had a dual editing system. I'd cut a sequence, and hand it off to Matt. Matt would cut a bunch of stuff. It was really a co-creation process. I'm the director, he's the editor. I'm the writer, he's the refiner. We dealt with structure. We dealt with dramaturgy. I'd write and record voiceover from 4am to 6am and then hand it over to Matt and he would come back with the three lines that were any good. That was the way it was stitched together.

As to how sequences were born, he would take a segment like Wyoming, find the essence of that interview and cut it together beautifully. He created the segment where there are three of me going up the well site on the ladder and there's music there. He didn't understand how to approach Jeff and Rhonda Locker's interview, so I said, *"I think I have to put a little voiceover there."* Then with Louis Meeks, he took a risk in order to get into the interview. He said, *"I am going to take this Esquivel track and the gun fire shots and put it together with Eastern Wyoming. I think this is going to be funny."* I did the first 30 seconds and then he adds in all the stuff with the kids

*"The best directing is no directing at all. It's reacting."*

and the Easter eggs. So after four or five days we have a segment that has this grace and beauty. When you have a creative relationship like that, the results can be incredibly gratifying.

## Q – What were your thoughts on the music and the score?

*Josh* – Music is an instinct and the soul of any work. It's a strictly emotional decision. But it's also a narrative decision. You need to hear that big, jangly Preston Reed as you head into Colorado. We're charging forward. Matt had a take on the music. I had a take on the music. And we had an amazing music clearances person in Sue Jacobs who got everything cleared. We didn't have to change a single track in the film. There were a few nail biting moments where we thought someone might pull out and then we thought this might be a house of cards and the whole thing would fall apart. If we take out this one piece of music, are we going to make it to this next scene without being exhausted and depleted? But from Pete Seeger to Radiohead, people realized that we had a film that was a labor of love made for very little money, so they gave us their music for cheap rates. The music budget came out of the HBO sale. We could not have afforded it without that for we had forty-six tracks and it was going to cost us a pretty penny. And I played a few banjo tracks here and there, too. That probably saved us $10,000!

## Q – Was there an average cost for the licensing?

*Josh* – There was no average. Some pieces cost $10,000. Some cost $500. But once we got through Sundance, the real question was, *"Do you have a $60,000-$70,000 music budget out of money that could be going into your pocket or are you going to make the film that has the integrity it needed?"* There was no question. This is the film that won the Grand Jury Prize at Sundance. This is the film that works. We're not changing a thing. It cost three times what it cost to shoot the whole movie! But there's no *Gasland* without the music in it.

## Q – Did you always plan on submitting to Sundance?

*Josh* – We had no plan B. Sundance was plan A. Matt and I had both premiered our first feature films at CineVegas, so we had a relationship with Trevor Groth, who was a programmer there. We did a lot of late night, Vegas, Gray Goose fun together. So when we were submitting, I think he was very surprised that either Matt or I were submitting a doc. We knew people in our community loved what we had shown them of the film. But we had no idea if it was going to translate to audiences who weren't under attack. Are people going to care who aren't in the drilling zone? That was one really big nerve wracking question. When we showed up at Sundance, we were totally star struck. We had been shot out of the cannon. We were so excited and we had spent the last six weeks not sleeping at all. The film was literally finished the day before the festival. When we got there, the elevation gave me the worst stomach pains, back pains and headaches. And then our assignment was to go to these Hollywood-y parties and try to explain hydraulic fracturing to people. They would say, *"Oh that's interesting. I'm going to go over here and talk to the girl from Twilight."*

By the end of Sundance, we overheard people on the shuttle bus explaining hydraulic fracturing to each other. That's when I knew it was going to work. We got standing ovation after standing ovation at Sundance. We were the best-reviewed film. It was such a relief to know they didn't hate me or think I was a jerk. I don't think I'll fully understand what happened at Sundance until five years from now. It was such a weird event.

**Q – When you show the water being lit on fire for the first time, I think everyone is hooked.**

*Josh –* That's interesting because when we were testing out which sequences to keep in the film, we thought we were going to go chronologically. I actually went to Arkansas before I went to Colorado where that happens. In Arkansas, we had some of the most horrible incidences of water contamination. You can see that footage on the DVD. But I told Matt we had to have that water on fire within the first twenty minutes because the minute we have that, we've got our audience. It was a hard decision, but it was a rhythm based decision. People can fill in the gaps. They can figure out that I drove from Pennsylvania to Colorado without stopping in Arkansas. We had an interview with a Congresswoman and we ended up cutting that. We had to beeline to that scene. The sense of humor of the whole film comes out of that moment. It's gallows humor and Mike Markham, Amy Ellsworth and Renee McClure are genuine beautiful human beings in a

very tough spot. They're not being paid attention to by the government. In fact, we got kicked out of the Colorado Oil and Gas Conservation Commission's office even though we had a scheduled appointment!

**Q – How did you structure the film?**

*Josh –* We were making a road movie and the structure of any road movie boils down to *The Wizard of Oz*. In each place, you have to meet the Tin Man and the Lion. In Dimmock, PA, we showed the initial shock and confusion by the people there. In Colorado, the families are documenting what's going on with the TV crews coming in. In Wyoming, there's the chemical contamination in the water. Then we get to Western Colorado and the health crisis. Down in Texas, it was about the air. Louisiana, it was about the discovery of the dumping of the wastewater. And at the end of Act two, when I break down by the side of the stream it's like the poppy fields in *The Wizard of Oz*. In New

York City, we show the crisis that twelve million people's drinking water could be affected. Then to DC to watch the industry just lying to Congress.

**Q – What are you doing next?**

**Josh** – *Gasland 2*. There was an assumption when we made *Gasland* that we called attention to the problems on a big enough scale, that is to say if we were a big enough success, which we have been, that there would be action taken and the problem would be solved. That was a naïve assumption because what we've encountered since is a year and a half worth of attacks, smears, obfuscation, misinformation and a multi-million dollar PR campaign to try and discredit the film on behalf of the National Gas Industry. Their MO is to lie to the government.

So *Gasland 2* is an inquiry into the very way our government processes information. In addition, gas drilling is not just an American problem. It's spread out all over the world. We do a fair bit of international reporting in the next one as well. The big alarming fact, though, that compels us to make the next movie is that it has been scientifically shown by a study out of Cornell, that fracking contributes more greenhouse gas into the atmosphere than burning coal, which is the worst of our fossil fuels. The climate change issue with natural gas and how it speaks to switching to renewable energies is going to be part of a trilogy of films about our energy choices. The third part will be about renewable energy, which we are also filming right now.

**Q – When you were on The Daily Show with Jon Stewart, he really challenged you on the facts of the film.**

**Josh** – That's because the oil and gas industry blasted his office with phone calls and misinformation trying to discredit the film. It was the most terrifying thing of my life. Everyone watches Jon Stewart. My mom watches Jon Stewart. He's unpredictable. You don't know what he's going to say. I thought he took it seriously. Though at times, it was almost like a Mutt and Jeff routine. He would lob them up and I would knock them down, then I would lob them up and he would knock them down. He would say, *"Well, if it's just your water, why would I care about you?"* Then I would say, *"Well, interestingly where I live supplies you with water."* Then he made that Jon Stewart face like, *"Dammit!"* Then I try to get serious and talk about the Halliburton Loophole and he says, *"That sounds like the worst sexual position of all time."* And that's unbelievably hilarious! But three days after our Oscar nomination, he lets T. Boone Pickens on and softballs questions to him and let's T. Boone off the hook when he says he's had no problems with fracking. My fans went ballistic. We had a little payback when Tom Ridge went on Stephen Colbert and Colbert had a field day with him. Ridge was the Governor of Pennsylvania, the first director of Homeland Security and now lobbies for the gas and coal industry. He started lying about how the gas is naturally occurring and not harmful. So Colbert said, *"Which of these toxic chemicals should I have my toddler drink?"* Then he showed a big clip of *Gasland*. It would have been nice to have seen Jon do that to T. Boone, but at the same time by having me on he broke the doors down for everyone learning about fracking.

Between that and PBS and CNN, it was part of a media week that has not ceased. MSNBC played *Gasland* for three days in a row. So I will always be thankful to Jon Stewart for having me on.

**Q – It's a weird thing with the media because you are the media in this film.**

*Josh* – Right. That's awesome because I can go on CNN in front of 300,000 people, but when *Gasland 2* comes out we are going to have a viewer-ship of millions. We're reporting honestly and humanly which means we will get that kind of audience and we hold it sacred. What bothers me is that independent investigative journalism is seriously on the rocks right now in American. We rank last in industrialized countries in supporting public media as a nation. That's why you see documentaries doing so much of this long form journalism because newspapers and other media outlets are not doing it. I can always tell if I'm on a show with someone who's studied the topic. Jon Stewart hadn't gone out to the field. And yet, his staff told me they had received one hundred phone calls and faxes from the gas industry. So in a way the interview was colored with the fact that the oil and gas industry came breathing hard. Now Carol Hoye from CNN went into the field and interviewed people from across Pennsylvania. When I did my interview with her, she was 100% on the side of the reporting that we did and had to conceal her bias.

**Q – What was the Oscar experience like?**

*Josh* – It was an incredible thing to happen because it allowed us to get right back in the media at a very crucial moment. At Sundance, I met Mark Ruffalo who lives in my area. He's been an anti-gas activist for over a year. We were both nominated for Oscars and have become friends so we hit the campaign trail. We went to DC and lobbied. We went on CNN. It was huge. We did very little Oscar campaigning to win and we didn't, but I think we got so much more out of the experience. As for the event itself, there's no real way of being at the Oscars. When you watch it on TV, you're not there. And when you're there, you feel it's not as real as when you watch it on TV. And when you're in documentary, you know you're not the main event. Everyone wants to talk to Nicole Kidman and Natalie Portman and that's fine. I kind of wanted to, too! I did spend time with the most incredible documentarians. It was an incredibly surreal experience. And nerve wracking. I had to use internet and Youtube instructions on how to tie a bowtie. It's the most incredible honor of your life to be honored by your peers. To be welcomed like that. To have people say you have made one of the best documentaries of the year – there's nothing like it. The last thing about the Oscars is that it meant an enormous amount to the people in the film. It validated everything that they have been going through.

**Q – What advice would you give a new documentary filmmaker?**

*Josh* – Get the hell out there and don't wait for money. Grab your cell phone, grab whatever video camera you can and start working. That's how you learn. On the other hand, *Gasland* is the culmination of 20 years of experience telling stories. You have to realize that you're on a timeline of craftsmanship that's going to take you your whole life.

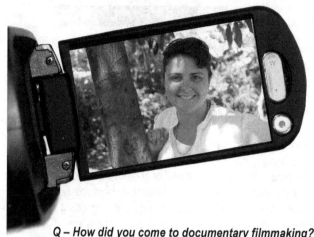

A SMALL ACT
JENNIFER ARNOLD

**Q – How did you come to documentary filmmaking?**

*Jennifer* – Totally by accident. I went to UCLA film school and made a short film that got into Sundance called *Maid of Honor* that was bought by HBO. I took development meetings all over LA, but it took me a long time to write my next script and when I was done, there was a writer's strike. I had this idea to do a documentary on mullets at a time when they were back in the mainstream. In a meeting, I cavalierly pitched an idea for a mullet documentary; it took off and a deal came together very quickly. After all this time having difficulty getting a fiction film off the ground, I got the doc sold in ten minutes. So off we went and I was making my first documentary. It sold to Palm Pictures, Lionsgate put it on DVD and it did an art house run. It became a little underground hit and soon after everyone was asking me about my next documentary subject.

**Q – You had spent time in Kenya during undergrad. Is that where the idea for A Small Act came from?**

*Jennifer* – Yes. I was getting a history degree with a bent toward African Studies so I did a year abroad at the University of Nairobi. I met the woman who is Chris' cousin in the film, Jane. She lived in the dorm room next to me. We became close friends and stayed in touch. Years later, I decided that I wanted to sponsor a child and I called Jane to get advice on how to do it and find out if there was a good organization with which I could get involved. She told me about Hilde Back, who once sponsored Chris' education and how she and Chris were founding a new education fund as a thank you for the generosity they once received. That was the genesis of the idea.

**Q – What did you see in Chris and Jane's story that made you think this was filmic material?**

*Jennifer* – That's a two-part answer. First, I started the film in 2007, it was pre-Obama,

---

 harambeemedia@asmallact.com     www.asmallact.com

 www.facebook.com/asmallact     http://twitter.com/asmallact

456

it was the Bush regime and the Iraq War was in full force. I was feeling that as an individual, your voice wouldn't be heard. It didn't matter if you voted. It didn't matter if you protested. As a regular, everyday person you didn't have much power to create change. I'm by nature a cynic. I love black comedy and irony. But I couldn't even joke about the world anymore. It was going in a direction I was so against. When I heard Chris' story about how one person did a small act and it helped so many people – it had saved lives - I realized it doesn't matter how bad the world is, you still have to be involved.

The other thing I liked was that I could see the narrative arc. Chris wants an education, he gets it and then he wants to thank the woman who sponsored him. So instantly there was a journey. The only problem was that when I heard the story, Chris and Hilde had already met. I thought I had missed the key moment to the film until I heard that it all had been videotaped. I asked them to send me the tape and it was a three-hour extended play VHS recording, but it had what I needed. Then I started to ask Chris what was happening with his fund. He told me that they were taking new applicants; that to qualify for a scholarship, the students had to take an aptitude test and get a specific score and that the scholarship board would announce beneficiaries in a big meeting. As soon as I heard all those points, I realized those were dramatic story beats. The film could be touching and dramatically solid.

**Q – Were you fighting your cynical nature the whole way?**

*Jennifer* – I feared it would be schmaltzy and sentimental, so I tried to keep it as real as possible and since I spent time in Kenya I felt I knew the culture decently enough that I thought I could keep the tone honest. The funny thing is that people would see it and say, *"Your film is so sappy."* And then other people are like, *"Wow, you could have made it a little more sentimental. It's dry."* Personally, I'm proud of the tone, not too cynical and not too schmaltzy either.

**Q – So once you had the concept, what was your next step?**

*Jennifer* – I had the idea about three months before Chris was going to meet Hilde for the second time and we knew that filming the second meeting would be crucial. I realized that I didn't have much time to do

A single gesture. Limitless possibilities.

**a small act**

a film by Jennifer Arnold

research. I either do it or I don't. I had no money. I'd never made a film longer than fifty-two minutes. It was across three countries and all these different languages. But I said whatever, let's do it. So I looked around to see what I had. What I had were a lot of friends who worked on other films with me. So I wrote up a three for four-page proposal with a small business plan and looked through my address book to see whom I could take it to. The first meeting I had, they gave me money in the room! Not enough money to make a film of this scale, more like enough to make a short. But I took it and now I thought I have to do it. I did get a few other investors but we still only had a quarter of the budget. I then went to Patti Lee who shot most of my other films and said, *"Hey, want to go shoot a film in Kenya for free?"* She said, *"Make me a producer and I'll shoot it for free."* I gladly said yes. So we decided to scale the production back to the money that we had. We figured out which airlines let you take two bags for free and which airlines still let you have luggage that weighed seventy pounds. We brought four suitcases - our clothes in one suitcase and all of the gear in the other three. We bought our camera, the Panasonic HVX-200, and had a Diva light and a tripod - which counted as two of the four suitcases. We couldn't afford production insurance so we didn't have it. We put it all on our credit cards hoping that might provide some insurance.

### Q – Did you do any tests before you went?

*Jennifer* – Yes. I knew the theme of the film was that we are all connected in the world and that a single action can ripple out to impact a lot of people. We tried to come up

with three visual effects that would illustrate that idea. We came up with the cloud idea. Kenya has the most amazing clouds. So I thought we could go into the sky and come out of the sky and show that we are all in one world and under one sky. Then we had the idea of rippling water. We also wanted to shoot crowds to show that any stranger in a crowd could affect your life in some way. We went to downtown Los Angeles and tested our crowd shots and our cloud shots. The only thing we had trouble with was the spinning of the camera. I wanted to start in the sky and then pan down to the dark of the ground. Then you will come out of the dark and back into the sky and you will be on the other side of the world. Patti didn't think it was going to work. We tried cutting together the gray of a freeway with a lush green neighborhood doubling for Kenya and it didn't work at all. Patti decided to spin the camera horizontally. She came up with the idea of loosening the tripod all the way, pushing the handle and then ducking. We played with the shutter speed as well and it worked. It looked like we were spinning from one place to another. So we made sure to do a camera spin wherever we went.

**Q – Who ran the sound when you were over there?**

*Jennifer* – I did. We couldn't afford a sound person. I'd done a little sound, but not a lot. We borrowed a sound rig from some kind friends with the promise that if we lost it or broke it, we'd buy them a replacement. It was really hard at first, but we figured it out. We went to Sweden first for Hilde's birthday party and then we went to Geneva. Then we went to Kenya where we had no electricity in the village so we had to figure out ways around that. To keep the lights up, we got a bag of rocks and hung them on a lighting stand. We would take tree branches and tape a reflector to it for lighting help. We built elaborate lighting set ups with rocks and sticks. It was like *The Flintstones*! But we both knew the principals of lighting, so we made it look good.

**Q – Did it all work out in post?**

*Jennifer* – Actually, it did. The lighting was fine and for the sound we were using wireless lavs that went into a three-channel mixer. Then I had a boom on the camera and a boom on a pole. It all fed down to two inputs in the camera. So because we had two separate tracks, there was always reliable audio. Everything on the shoot worked out…although we did have several car crashes. We were fine, but it was a crazy shoot. Luckily, there were no robberies or wild animal stories. We did get tear-gassed. We shot some of the political violence and got too close to a political party demonstration that got gassed. The police were pushing us back. It was the first time I had gotten tear-gassed, but we didn't feel like we were in real danger because there were a lot of reporters around us. And we could easily run back to the hotel. When we told our Kenyan friends it was like we had gone through a rite of passage. They thought it was cute!

**Q – How did you manage to charge the camera batteries and transfer the files if there was no electricity?**

*Jennifer* – We rented an apartment in Nairobi, which was about an hour away from the village. It had electricity. There was some electricity in the village, but definitely not in the kids' houses. We had about four to six batteries for the camera and a knock off version of a light panel, which had a battery and that was it. We had a power inverter for the car so we could use the cigarette lighter, too. We both had laptops so we would shoot, fill up a P2 card, download it through the laptop through a bus powered hard drive. Three quarters of the way through the day, the laptop battery would die, but there was a second laptop or we would use the power inverter.

**Q – Was it difficult to manage all your media in such a remote area?**

*Jennifer* – We flew from LA with hard drives. But we started running out of hard drive space. You could get hard drives in Kenya but they were really small and expensive. Most were USB and not Firewire. But we had this amazing organizational method. We took two drives out into the field with us everyday and we loaded the P2 footage onto them, once to drive A and once to drive B. That way there were always two copies before we wiped a P2 card. Then the field drives would come back to Nairobi and we would copy drive A to negative drive A and we would copy drive B to a negative drive B. So we always had drives that were like "film negative." We would make sure it all transfered before we wiped the field drives. Everything was very organized and it worked really well until we started running out of space. Then we had to shove files wherever we could.

### Q – Was it difficult to get the kids or their parents to trust you?

*Jennifer* – What really helped was that Chris and Jane who were from that village introduced me. We explained what we were doing so very few people said no to us. The real problem was that once we started filming two things happened. One, they thought that because we were filming them they were automatically going to get a scholarship. For several weeks, we had to explain that the filming was separate from the scholarship selection. The other thing is that because we were foreigners we would automatically become guests. So we would show up and they would stop whatever they were doing, put on their best clothes and make us lunch. It took a few weeks, but with one family when they saw that we were going to come every day, they realized they didn't need to make us tea. With another family, we told them that we were going to stop coming because they were spending all their money on making us meals and that wasn't good for them or us. After a few weeks, they understood what we wanted to do and we understood what they expected.

### Q – How did you find working with the children? You had some very intimate moments of them crying.

*Jennifer* – We were there for three months so the kids got really used to us and we formed relationships with them. It was hard. As a human being, we were in situations where we totally wanted to get involved, but as a documentary filmmaker, you can't. It was hard to watch them cry and get their hearts broken. And it was great to watch them when they were happy. There's no special trick to that. It's just a natural thing.

### Q – How did you direct the kids?

*Jennifer* – They all had limited English so what I'd do is ask them questions in English and then have them respond in English. Once I got the gist of what the answer would be I would say, *"Great. Now tell me everything that you just told me in Kikuyu and go into greater detail."* I had no idea what they said so I turned to the driver/translator and he would tell me. But that was a problem because the translator wanted to be helpful and he would fill in details that the kids didn't say. So I would ask the kids if they were sad because they didn't get the test scores they wanted. And he or she would give a very short answer in Kikuyu. Then the translator would say, *"Yes, I am very sad. I know I had to get a 380."* And then I would get the translation back and the student had indeed just said, *"Yes, I am."* Mostly though, as my relationship with the kids grew, they would just tell me how they were feeling in English.

**Q – Did you have any other problems shooting in Kenya?**

*Jennifer* – We got permits so we didn't have any problems with the government. The hardest thing was the language barrier. I speak a little Swahili and thought that would be useful, but although most Kenyans speak Swahili, they all speech a local dialect at home. The students I filmed all spoke Kikuyu. They could understand me, but I couldn't understand any of the verite conversations in their homes. So we shot hours and hours of footage having no clue what people were saying. We had a driver/assistant who did everything for us. He was a friend of a friend of mine in Kenya. I told him to tap me on the shoulder if they ever start talking about school fees or Caroline's mother's illness – basically any kind of story point. So he would tap me on the shoulder and we would film. Then I would get it translated and get it back three weeks later. All the footage would be banal stuff like, *"Did you feed the cow? No, did you feed the cow? No."* I went back to our driver and said, "I thought this was all about school fees." And he replied, *"Yeah, they were talking about school fees and then I tapped you on the shoulder."* I had to tell him to tap me earlier because I need to record that part. Eventually we got a system down. On the plus side, since most of the documentary subjects knew we couldn't understand them, they would usually speak very freely. I think we got a lot of great footage because people knew we couldn't understand what they were saying while we filmed.

**Q – Did the political violence cause problems?**

*Jennifer* – We didn't expect that at all. No one did. Not even the Kenyans. The violence was sparked by elections and we hadn't shot a lot about the run up to the elections so we were scrambling to figure out how to add that storyline. We shot two shots of campaign cars, which are cars with big speakers on their roofs, purely because the noise was constantly getting into our interviews and we needed a way to show where the noise was coming from. We used every frame of those shots in the final edit, that's pretty much all we had to show that an election was coming.

**Q – Did Chris have any concerns?**

*Jennifer* – I don't think he was concerned about how we would tell the stories. But he had a lot of ideas of what documentaries are and that was good and bad for us. We would interview him and he would give us very long answers that would sometimes meander. I would go back and ask him to speak about just one specific point or clarify something with a succinct sentence. And he would stop me and say, *"Can't you just have the narrator set that up? They can clarify*

it." I told him that we weren't planning on having a narrator. He said, *"That's impossible! All documentaries have narrators."* And that was because he loves golf and all the documentaries he's seen have been on Arnold Palmer or some other sporting event. I guess most golf films have narrators, so he was really surprised when he saw the final film as his interview actually serves as narration.

### Q – What about transportation? You said you had a driver.

*Jennifer* – Yes. We rented a car, but we couldn't afford an SUV. We had a Toyota Corolla and it had a cracked radiator. So every ten miles we had to put water in it. One day, I opened the trunk and there next to all our gear were two full jugs of water with no lids. It was just plastic wrap held in place by rubber bands. I told the driver to please not put open water containers next to every piece of gear we had. So it was things like that which happened everyday and we just had to get used to them.

### Q – How was the transcription process handled?

*Jennifer* – In our minds, we were going to have the footage transcribed in Kenya while we were there. But we didn't have money to hire a real transcription service, so I hired university students. While I was out shooting during the day in the village, we'd leave a laptop behind in our apartment and have a student do it. It would take forever. Two days of shooting would take two weeks. After we got to Los Angeles we ended up burning video CDs because our transcribers didn't have DVD players in Kenya. So we made these reels and burned time code into them and gave them to the Kenya transcribers on video CD. We had to FedEX them back and forth which costs about $200 between Los Angeles and Kenya. So we would wait until we had like fifty reels to send. It took six months to get all our translations back. The other issue with transcribers was that they were very literal. So they might write, *"Don't you out the mouth loudly!"* And we had to figure out that was, *"Don't yell at me!"* Eventually, when we got to a rough cut, we found a Kikuyu speaker in Los Angeles who would check our dialog edits and subtitles for us.

### Q – How long did the whole edit process take?

*Jennifer* – About two years. We got it to a long rough cut in a year. We worked seven days a week around the clock in my garage. We were always about to run out of money. But once we got that long rough cut, we made the presale to HBO. Then we had the money to finish.

### Q – Did you or Patti edit the film?

*Jennifer* – No. We first hired a friend of mine from film school. He loved the film, but he didn't have a lot of documentary experience. So he got it to a certain point and then we got another investor who allowed us to hire Tyler Hubby who cut *The Devil and Daniel Johnson*. He came in at the rough cut stage and helped us finish.

*Q – What were your thoughts on music?*

*Jennifer* – I always knew I didn't want African music. This wasn't a story about Africa. This was a story about how small acts can have a big impact. It's about interconnectivity. Our lives are interwoven even if we don't realize it. So I didn't want Kenya specific music. I liked the way someone like Sofia Coppola would take a period piece and put modern music in it. I originally wanted to get a Los Angeles band to do the score, but we ended up getting into Sundance and we had to finish before I could really figure that out. HBO had suggestions for a composer, one of them being Joel Goodman. I listened to his stuff and really loved it. He did the music very quickly and I absolutely love the score.

*Q – It seems like you pushed the colors a bit in Kenya. Is that true?*

*Jennifer* – I wanted to make sure each country had it's own unique look, so yes we did and we did a lot of it in camera, which was sort of a risk. We debated about shooting it clean and pushing the colors in post, but we didn't know how much money we would have for that. So we boosted the colors of Kenya and de-saturated the greys of Sweden.

*Q – Did Hilde have any concerns?*

*Jennifer* – She was the most hesitant one. She agreed to do it, but she doesn't like to talk on the phone and she doesn't have email or a computer. So we did our initial correspondence through written letters. She didn't want us to go to her house before the filming. She didn't want to be bothered because she was putting together her 80th birthday party. So we asked her if we could just come by once and see the house before filming because we were concerned about the lighting. Would it have windows? Would it be dark? It was hard to convince her of that. And when Patti and I got there, we saw that Hilde, being Swedish and socially conscious, had something like two light bulbs that were sixteen watt fluorescents. We freaked out and went to Ikea to buy a bunch of lamps so we could get exposure. Also, Hilde has tons of energy, but she's very structured. She was very much like, *"You can stand here, but you can't stand there."* After a few days though, she decided that it was fun and everything was fine.

The other thing with Hilde is that she hadn't talked a lot about her Holocaust history. She doesn't talk a lot about her parents and we weren't sure she would be willing to go there. She did talk about it, but she would say, *"I don't think it affected me very much."* I had to make a decision about whether to push her or not and at one point I said, *"Hilde, your parents died in concentration camps. How could it not affect you?"* Eventually she started talking about it. When we went back for pick ups a year later she stated that she had been speaking about it a lot more over the year.

*Q – Did you plan for the second trip or did you realize you had to go back after seeing the footage?*

*Jennifer* – We always thought we would have to go back. We only spent a week each in Sweden and Geneva. We put some money aside to go back and kind of hoped we wouldn't have to so we could use the money for something else, but that wasn't the case.

**Q – When did the themes of genocide and using education to get out of bad situations become evident?**

*Jennifer* – What I knew in the beginning was that Hilde survived the Holocaust and Chris worked in an organization for human rights. He'd done a lot of work in genocidal situations in Africa. I also knew that education plays a role in political manipulation. Ignorance is a political weapon. But it wasn't until the violence happened in Kenya that it all came full circle in the film. Before filming, I wrote a script of how I thought the story might play out, even though I knew I couldn't really anticipate what would happen. But I had certain story points in mind and I think that comes from my narrative filmmaking background. The way my brain works is I have to have an idea of what the end of Act 1 is going to be. What the end of Act 2 will be and so on. So when the violence happened, I started to realize that the end of Act 1 was Chris talking about the link between poverty, political manipulation and his education fund. Then the end of Act 2 would be the violence itself. We thought originally that the kids getting their scores would be the end of Act 2 and there might be a happy kid and a sad kid. But ultimately the violence became the true Act 2 end point.

**Q – Did you shoot any other kids that fell by the wayside, or did you always intend on featuring the three you ended up with?**

*Jennifer* – We sort of knew they would be the ones. Because we started the film so late, we went to a bunch of schools and looked for the smartest kids. We found one kid who was so smart and very sweet, but he didn't have a ton of screen presence. Then we met Kimani. We went to his school as a last ditch effort and he had so much charisma. The students in Kenya take a test called the mock, which is like our PSATs and Kimani had scored really well on it. Well enough that if he repeated that performance on his real exam he would qualify for a scholarship. We needed more kids, but for practical reasons, they all had to come from Kimani's school. We thought it would be too time consuming and too confusing to film at various schools. Kimani's main rival is Ruth. She got the same test score as Kimani on the mocks. We were going to film Kimani's best friend, but Ruth was very shy and she kept bringing her friend, Caroline, to her interviews. Ruth didn't want to be filmed alone so we shot Caroline with Ruth.

Then, it turned out that Caroline had an amazing story as well. So suddenly we had our three kids. Intermittently, we filmed other kids with high test scores just in case. But we didn't have time to devote to them fully. So we gambled.

*Q – How did HBO find out about your film?*

*Jennifer* – We got into IFC's Spotlight on Docs on our second try. We had a rough cut of maybe two and half hours and we also had a fifteen-minute sample reel. Through IFC we got a meeting with HBO and gave them the sample reel. We gave it to them on a Thursday and Monday they called us. We had a great time with HBO. We grooved with them well. All the notes they had were things we wanted to do to the film as well.

*Q – What was the Sundance experience like?*

*Jennifer* – We got into the competition section, which has sixteen films, and I swear almost everyone else had an Academy Award nomination or some major credits to their name. So I was a little intimidated. We already had the HBO deal in place. I already had a foreign sales agent attached at that point, so it wasn't like I had to get ten people with feet on the ground to help me make a sale. The great thing that happened at Sundance, and this was totally unsolicited; the audience started donating money to the Hilde Back Foundation. They gave cash and checks right to Hilde, Chris and Jane. In the ten days of Sundance, $90,000 was donated. So the audience was literally changing peoples lives. Since the film has come out, the Hilde Back Fund has raised over $750,000 and now has gone from a village-wide fund to a nationwide fund.

*Q – Wow! That wasn't your intention going in though, right?*

*Jennifer* – No! I just wanted to make an engaging film with a good story. There are a lot of informative docs that promote social change, but I think people are much more likely to join a movement or take action if they go on an emotional journey and feel something.

*Q – Looking back now, is there anything that you would have done differently?*

*Jennifer* – I wish we'd started our social outreach campaign earlier. The film has done a lot, but we could have done even more if we started earlier. I think it's tough to ask filmmakers to make a great film, which is next to impossible, and then ask them to save the world via outreach and audience engagement, too.

*Q – What advice would you give a new documentary filmmaker?*

*Jennifer* – Always have a strategy in mind. Try to figure out who the audience will be for your film ahead of time. Think through the look of the film, and how can you achieve that look on any budget. Think about what partners you can engage early on. Think through as much as you can because thinking doesn't cost you anything.

*Q – What kind of story are you attracted to?*

*Bill* – I don't know if it's stories that we're after initially. I think that it has been more about the location and the idea of those locations, such as the imagery of the places that have stuck with us during our travels of the past. When we get there, then we start looking for storylines that pull us through.

*Turner* – We're definitely based on a more experiential viewpoint. All our lives we've been documenting things, going on travels, picking people's brains. The most natural extension of that was to combine the technology of making films with what was more in tune with what we like to do with our own personal lives. So what we are doing now is going to places or people and seeing what happens as we acclimate. Then we try to establish a sense of place and feel and create an artifact based on that.

*Q – So do you go to these places cold? Or do you do some research on the places to get a better understanding of them?*

*Turner* – So far nothing has been cold, but that's a remnant of having traveled through most of the States. Our next film is on New Orleans and it's a place that we spent a lot of time when growing up. It's a very intriguing place culturally. It's a very vivid place in the world. We didn't go to capture a certain thing, but we went there to seek out the sense memories that we had from our childhood.

*Bill* – At the end of the day, our films are a way to have an adventure. To meet new people and gather great stories to tell when we are old men. It just so happens there's a film in the end!

*Turner* – The best stories though are not the ones we capture on camera. The real

---

 www.45365movie.com           www.rossbros.net

 www.facebook.com/rossbros     http://twitter.com/rossbros

stories of these things are being in a time and a place.

*Q – 45365 seems like it was a time and place in your hometown.*

**Turner** – That's what we set out to do, capture something very dear to us that I guess at the end of the day we didn't completely know as well as we thought we would. We were kids growing up there and we went back as adults and found a place that was on one hand very much what we remembered and yet somehow different. We went in there with some preconceived notions, but then blew them all away and discovered other things. You think that would be really hard to do in your hometown, but it really wasn't. What comes out in the film seems like a single season, but we spent almost a year back home trying to dig in to what that place was all about by capturing moments with people.

*Q – The film feels like it starts in August. So you're saying you were shooting prior to that?*

**Bill** – The film is not chronological. We tried to make it feel like you existed in this place for nine months. But stuff we shot the first day shows up at the eighty-five minute mark. So it's a construction to build this feeling we were after.

**Turner** - We aren't after these things for some social issues and telling some sort of scientific, anthropological truth. In it's construction it may feel like the glow of autumn, but it tells a greater truth or conveys a more honest feeling than if we were to go back there and do some chronological, linear survey.

*Q – When you were going through all the footage, what made you decide on certain characters to follow?*

**Turner** – Going into each film we always have a very generic layout of the people we think we want to spend time with. So on a very basic level in *45365* we knew we wanted to spend time with a teenager, we knew we wanted to spend time with a police officer... And then we are always open to everything as it comes. Then we go out and find those people to fill in that cast that we are after. And usually finding those people leads to other people who are more interesting than what we had conceived going into it.

*Bill* – Once it starts it really starts to cast itself because you find these really engaging leads and inevitably in their periphery are other people that branch out into other environments. I guess by judgment you filter it out and you end up with this vast array of people and places and intimate environments and we sort of go for it.

*Turner* – It also comes down to following your instincts. If it feels good, follow it. In a way, we love everyone we shoot with no matter how confused or awful that person seems to others. We have to love them somehow.

### Q – Was it difficult to get the ride-along with the cop?

*Bill* – No. I thought it would be. We weren't the most well behaved kids growing up there!

*Turner* – Unless those people are involved in really specific governmental shit where they are not allowed to perform in front of the camera, they usually seem to be all about it. *"This is me doing my job and I look good doing it."*

### Q – Did they remember you?

*Bill* – They did. I remember my first night shooting was during a night shift with that guy.

It was a slow night, nothing was happening. It was 3am and I had been driving with him since 11pm. He starts to make small talk and says, *"Well, Bill, have you had any involvement with the Sidney Police Department?"* And I said, *"Yes, I have, but if you don't mind I'd like to leave it at that."* And he thought that was fair enough. He knew.

### Q – What are some of the things you practice to get your subjects to let you into their world and inner feelings?

*Turner* – It's going to be different in every situation. Walking into the Ritz Carlton is different than walking into The Silver Spur Saloon. You have to acclimate to a different environment when going about things. We always bear in mind that we're being given an opportunity and we try to be as honest and as gracious as possible. From our end, we try to tell people what we are doing and then do it. Just go in shooting or working and try to establish what it is and gain their confidence. But in environments where we might be different, it's important for us to let people know they are

allowed to be exactly who they are and that's all we want them to be. So even if it's off color and not something we agree with, it's their life and world. So we have to be welcoming of them at the same time.

*Bill* – We only film for about a third of the time anywhere. It's a lot of hanging out, conversations and going to BBQ's and church. Whatever it is they do. We build friendships. We stay in touch with everyone that we film. It's a positive experience.

## Q – Do you both do the shooting?

*Bill* – It depends on the circumstances. If it's a bigger event, we both shoot. If it's a more intimate event like sitting at home watching TV, only one of us will go.

## Q – Do you find it easy or difficult to direct and shoot at the same time?

*Bill* – We don't have a problem with it because all we do is exist in a space.

## Q – So you don't ask questions when the camera is on? You're just capturing life?

*Bill* – Pretty much. Sometimes it gets to a point where nothing is going on then maybe we'll ask a question that will start a conversation between the people that we're filming.

*Turner* – It's up to us to be in the right environment at the right time to capture the right moment. Once you have done the forward thinking to put yourself in the right place then it's really just a matter of directing the image. It's not posed.

## Q – How do you do your audio?

*Bill* – Whomever we are following we always mic them up with a wireless and then we have an onboard mic.

## Q – What camera did you use to shoot 45365?

*Bill* – We used two Panasonic DVX-100Bs.

## Q – How did you come up with the idea for the train passing by as a transition?

*Bill* – I think there was definitely a discussion during the shooting where we were going to use things like that. The train is a thematic device. It's glue that holds things together.

## Q – Did you edit all the way through production or wait until you finished?

*Bill* – We waited until the end and that was always the plan. We always reviewed the footage, but no cutting. We saw it as gathering ingredients and in the end I'd assess what we had and then make soup out of it.

**Q – Were you discussing what might make good scenes or were you really keeping your heads out of it?**

*Bill* – No. Being brothers we try to out do each other. So at the end of a day, I would say, *"I definitely got a scene in the film. How about you?"* When something is cooking, you can just tell. For example, the shot at the end of *45365* when the football players run out onto the field, when I digitized that I knew that was definitely going to be a scene.

**Q – How many hours of footage did you have?**

*Bill* – Approximately five hundred hours.

**Q – How was your process for handling that much data?**

*Bill* – I'd digitize all the footage at the end of each night. Then when we were done, I took my hard drives out to Los Angeles and just sat in a room for a year. In the beginning, I watched every second of it and took notes on my initial impressions – what could work, what storylines we had in there. So I had this big book of notes for each tape. Then I went back through them again and made selects of things I thought could work for each character and each location. So I had in my Final Cut Pro project, bins with people's names or trains or musical numbers. And in those bins would have the selects. That broke it down to make it more manageable. So for the first six months, it was just myself cutting rough selects and scenes together to see how they would play off of each other.

*Turner* – For the first four months, we didn't talk at all. Bill needed to be left alone for two reasons. One, we had spent all this time doing this shit and we needed time apart. Two, there was this daunting amount of footage to sift through before we could even get to a place to have a conversation. Periodically, Bill would send cuts, ideas and notes and we'd get together and have conversations. It wasn't until we were seven or eight months in that we had a major breakthrough of what this really needed to look, feel and be like. At that point, Bill went straight back into it and really made it work.

**Q – What was the tipping point for the breakthrough?**

*Turner* – Bill gets lost in this world of editing. He's back in this place where we were filming, but I get some distance from it. So when he sends me these things, I get to see them with fresh eyes. About six months in, he sent me a double disk. On one was a four hour rough cut of what he thought the film needed to be like. The other was a DVD called 'Things I Like'. It was images and tiny moments. Really outstanding selects. The rough cut was more dealing with character and moving through the town and place. The 'Things I Like' disk was far and away the best of it all. It was honest. There would be a beautiful shot of a wheat field and then you'd be in a room having a conversation with people, then a little kid on a bike and then a sign in a yard. It was magical to see it and drift through that space. Then Bill came to visit and we had a long conversation and it became more of what we were striving for. The film was going to be more ambient. It was going to breathe and let things speak for themselves.

*Q – Sometimes when one team member lives with the footage for a while, they can become frustrated as the other plays catch up when the project is shared. Does that happen to you?*

*Bill* – I get very frustrated at that. I've arrived at a decision in the edit after I've tried it a million different ways. I have determined that this is the only way it will work. Then Turner sees it and says, *"Well, why didn't you do it this way?"* So we have to backpedal all the way to the original idea to come all the way back to the final decision. Then he will either understand or it will create a discussion and makes me see it in a different light. So while it's very frustrating, it's also very beneficial.

*Q – How long did it take you to edit the film? And did you do anything to the color or the sounds?*

*Bill* – A full year. And no we didn't do anything special. We had a sound guy who helped us clean up the sound, but that's it.

*Q – What were your thoughts about music?*

*Turner* – It's kind of an organic process. In terms of music used, it was informed by the fact that we shot at a radio station and that we were in cars with people with radios. Those would be jumping off points. When we were in that space we would listen to that music being played and get emotional about it, then we would write down what we and other people were listening to.

*Bill* – We kept a running log of what people were listening to whether it was on a jukebox or a car radio. Then when I was editing I could go back to those notes and if a song made sense I'd place it in the scene. We always want the music to be organic.

*Q – So all music comes from the environment? There's no score in your films?*

*Bill* – There's a little. In *45365*, I was shooting these guys playing guitar on a back porch. We didn't use the scene, but we used the music and put it under something else.

**Q – Did you give them any instruction?**

*Bill* – We told them we wanted to evoke a certain kind of feeling. I don't really know how to speak musically, so I'd send them samples of stuff. Then we'd send them the footage, leave them alone and let them toy around with it. Then they would send us all this stuff back and we would match it to picture and see what worked.

**Q – How did you get around all the rights issues? Did you evoke Fair Use?**

*Turner* – We didn't get around it. That's why it's not on DVD. We are stuck in a rut. We need $30,000 if you know anybody! We were able to get it on PBS because they have a special scenario because they are public television and they have some deal that allows them to air things without rights clearances. Most of our screenings have been specialty screenings such as art houses, museums, film festivals that have their own deals. We didn't have a wide release and we don't have VOD and DVD because we don't have the money. The amount of non-Fair Use music in the film is not immense, but we need to have those legal statements written and then we need to clear that music. The amount is about the same as we paid to make the film.

**Q – What kind of distribution deal did you get?**

*Turner* – We didn't know what we were getting into so we ended up with some folks that don't operate the same way we do. Now we're in a quagmire trying to get the film off the black market. We just don't have the money. We've contacted entertainment lawyers and Fair Use people. We've got deals in place, even a DVD one but no support and no funding. It's amazing how bureaucratic something so simple can become.

**Q – What were your initial thoughts on distribution?**

*Bill* – We were just happy it was done and wanted to move on to other projects. We didn't think about submitting it to various film festivals or going a certain distribution route. We just finished and started cold submitting the film to festivals through Withoutabox. But in the end, we both went back to our jobs on Monday.

*Turner* – We didn't intend for it to be a commodity and it was beyond our grasp that it would do very well. We only received one bite from a small regional film festival and we thought that was great. Then a couple days later we got a call from South By Southwest who wanted to know if we'd like to be in competition there. We weren't ready for that. We weren't trying to be salesmen, so we hid in a bar for the weekend. At the end of it, we went to the awards ceremony and they said our film was great. When something like that happens the thing has a life of its own. It's been a wonderful experience because it allowed us to keep doing it. As soon as that happened, we started getting distribution offers – most of which petered out once people saw the film. But we looked at each other and said that this was something we could do. So we started in on the next one.

*Q – What was South by Southwest like?*

*Turner* – It's a great festival and Austin is a nice town. The festival is a big spectacle and a lot of fun. It's very laid back and we had a hugely positive experience.

*Q – Did you guys do any publicity or marketing for the film?*

*Turner* – Zero. We put it out there cold. The reviews were cold. We didn't butter anyone up. We didn't do anything except go to the venues where they wanted to screen it. I don't know why it's worked so well, but we are excited that it has. It earned us a couple of grants and a lot of good press. And we've made a lot of good friends along the way.

*Q – What were the grants?*

*Turner* – The first one we won was the Truer Than Fiction prize at the Independent Spirit Awards. That came with a prize sponsored by Chaz and Roger Ebert. That was awesome. That gave us some credence and that got us a grant for our New Orleans project from Cinereach. They are a small organization that sponsors independent films.

*Q – Some of our readers, especially the newer ones, worry about making mistakes. What do you say about that?*

*Turner* – We screw up daily. We've developed a mantra that is you're going to screw up and when it happens, you just have to move forward. If it gets stuck in your head, then you're going to be incapable of doing anything. So you keep shooting and keep going.

*Bill* – You can't get everything. You are going to miss things. Even if you miss what you think was going to be the greatest moment in your film, you can't hold onto that. You have to let it go or it will eat you up.

*Q – What advice would you give a new documentary filmmaker?*

*Bill* – Make mistakes. I think too often people get caught up in *"my stuff's not good enough."* Before this film, all I was doing was making mistakes. But I just kept making stuff and I knew if I kept at it I might just arrive at something I could go public with. My other favorite piece of advice is, *"Don't talk about it, be about it."* Everyone sits around and talks about that great novel they are going to write, but it never comes.

*Turner* – And if a rancher in South Texas says, *"Do you want to stab the hog?"* then stab the hog! We hunted a three hundred pound wild boar with a knife.

*Bill* - I had to prove myself to these guys or they weren't going to take me seriously. As soon as that thing was dead, they looked at us very differently. So back to how do you earn trust, you always say *"yes."*

TWO SPIRITS

LYDIA NIBLEY

## Q – What attracted you to the story of Two Spirits?

*Lydia* – I've been intrigued for a long time by the idea of how important the balance is between the masculine and feminine and I'm concerned about how imbalances impact so many issues globally. When I learned the details of Fred Martinez's life and murder; that he expressed a mix of male and female; and that this range of expression had been respected in many Native American tribes for thousands of years, I thought this film would help people see things from a fresh perspective.

## Q – How did you get access to this very personal family story?

*Lydia* – A friend who lived in Cortez and who was a local LGBT (Lesbian, Gay, Bisexual, Transgender) activist was also a close friend of the Martinez family. He told us about what was going on behind the scenes with the murder investigation and how it was influencing the community. Russell Martin, my producer, and I, started researching aspects of the story to see what could be done with it. Was it a book? Was it a film? I knew I could make a film when my friend showed me a photograph of Fred dancing with his arms outstretched and his face turned up to the sun. This was taken just a few weeks before Fred was murdered and a few feet from where his body was found. The image communicates his essence - his courage, his expressiveness, and the hope of what his life could have been. It became one of the creative keys to the film.

## Q – What kind of research did you do so you could feel confident connecting with communities of which you were not a part?

*Lydia* – I'm a natural hunter-gatherer when it comes to stories. I read a number of books and scholarly articles to ground myself in the subjects of the film and then I talked to respected experts so I could understand things from the inside out - as much as a

 lydianibley@ridingthetigerpro.com     www.twospirits.org

 http://twitter.com/TwoSpiritsFilm

474

straight, white woman could. By the time I wrote the shooting treatment I had a solid understanding of the subject matter. My commitment was to make the best film possible and to find the right people to tell their own stories so that the film would represent their experiences and concerns. I'm very happy that this approach worked and that Native Two Spirit people have embraced the film.

**Q – How did you gain their trust, especially Fred's mother?**

**Lydia** – If you know someone who is close to a story, you have credibility and access. But even though the introduction to Fred's mother came through a mutual friend, it still took time to build a personal connection. There are times when you'd want to maintain distance from your subjects as a filmmaker, but for *Two Spirits* it was very important to work up close and with a sense of emotional intimacy with the people in the film. I had to be connected to Fred's mother in order to provide the safe environment where she could deliver the "performance" at the heart of the film. She had to expose her raw emotions and let the audience into her pain and that was supported by the trust we built over time.

**Q – You chose to hold off letting the viewer know about the murder until very late in the film. Was there a reason you did that?**

**Lydia** – Films tell you how they want to be told and this story did not want to be a true crime story about the murderer, the victim, and the details of the crime. There's no suspense in this case because the police knew immediately who had killed Fred. The murderer was covered with blood and bragged about having *"bug-smashed a fag."* It was a hate crime, but I didn't want to make a film about hatred, I wanted to make a film with a hate crime in it but one that was really about love. I focused on the unconditional love of a mother for her son, the love of many tribes for their LGBT and Two-Spirit people, and the ways a variety of gender expression contributes to society. I wanted the audience to feel connected to Fred as a living person and to know him well before he is killed toward the end of the film. Then there would be a sense of mourning

TWOSPIRITS

Fred Martinez was a Navajo boy who was also a girl. In an earlier era, he would have been revered. Instead he was murdered.

THE AWARD-WINNING DOCUMENTARY

"Riveting." *LA Weekly*

when he was lost. Not only of his short life, but of what we all lose when kids commit suicide or when acts of violence are committed against LGBT people. That's why the mother's story is so important. Her love anchors the film and in the end her grief is also so deep that we can go there with her as well.

**Q – What were some of the signs that said the story wanted to go this way?**

*Lydia* – This film could have been executed in a way that would have made it a very niche film - perhaps made specifically for Two Spirit or LGBT audiences. But I wanted *Two Spirits* to connect with millions of people in general audiences in the US and throughout the world because I thought the film could do the most good that way. I wanted to serve the Two-Spirit audience by telling their story for one of the first times on film, and to add to the body of work that supports the move to full equality for LGBT people, but the film had to appeal to general audiences in order to be really successful. There's a line in the film where activist Richard LaFortune says, *"We've had gay marriage on this continent for thousands of years - long before it was a glimmer in the eye of Stonewall."* Those kinds of breakthrough ideas needed wide exposure. I personally connected with the storylines of the film in a profound way as a straight woman who is a mother and I knew that I could make a film that would move general audiences as well.

**Q – Where did you get your seed money?**

*Lydia* – The first funding came from one of the co-producing partners of the film, Just Media. The early money is the bravest and most visionary money - when a funder goes on instinct and trusts that you'll be able to deliver the film you're pitching without much to show yet. *Independent Lens* acquired the film after it was completed and when it was making the rounds at film festivals.

**Q – On what format did you shoot the film?**

*Lydia* – We shot as much of it as we could on HD, but one of the challenges of making *Two Spirits* was having so many eclectic sources of material. That's something many documentarians face. You get so many formats going at the same time it can blow your mind. But in the end we came up with a production design that made the most of the eclectic mix of footage and still photographs and used it as a creative strength.

**Q – How many shoots did you have and in how many locations?**

*Lydia* – There were several shoots around the country. And there were times when we had to pick up a one day shoot and I couldn't go because we didn't have the budget to both shoot and have me travel. So in those cases I directed over the phone! This was a few years ago, before video on smartphones so I'd ask my DP to describe the framing of the shot to me and then have him put the phone down on the table so I could hear what the interview subject was saying. I sent detailed instructions to cinematographers about how I wanted a scene to look and feel - it was wild!

**Q – What were some of those notes like?**

**Lydia** – I'd ask for things like, *"Shoot right on top of the subject and get them to look into the camera Errol Morris style, or get a Gus Van Sant long shot of the high school and just hold it."* We had a shared language and it worked. We had to make our days and get exactly what the film needed, so there wasn't any wiggle room.

**Q – Was there a method to the shots you chose?**

**Lydia** – I wanted to make sure the characters seemed at home in their environments and that they felt connected to each other as a linked cast of characters. I didn't want experts dropping out of the sky to make a comment and then disappearing from the film. I showed the relationships between people and how they were connected. But we didn't have the budget and shooting days to follow people around or have the luxury to see what might happen. I had to make sure the right things did happen so I started with a tightly written treatment and then moved to a detailed shooting script with specified B-roll. Some documentaries are made by shooting lots of footage and then "finding" the story of the film within that footage in post-production. *Two Spirits* was constructed in the opposite way by imagining the finished film, writing a script based on what I knew I could get from pre-interviews, and shooting specifically to get there.

**Q – How long did the project take to complete?**

**Lydia** – Five years from start to finish, but that wasn't continuous work. There was some starting and stopping and making a living doing other projects along the way. It was over a year of research and relationship building before we started any shooting in Cortez.

**Q – What was the tipping point that moved you from pre-production to production?**

**Lydia** – The big leap came when the cinematographer David Armstrong jumped in and had the time available to shoot in the Four Corners and that momentum was joined by Henry Ansbacher at Just Media stepping up with enough funding that we could shoot for a full week. Once you have a rough cut of some sample footage and you can show the tangible impact of your film, the project becomes less of a gamble for funders. At that point less imagination is required to understand a film and people can see what it's about, how it works, and how it will look and feel.

*"once you have a rough cut of some sample footage and you can show the tangible impact of your film, it becomes less of a gamble to investors."*

**Q – Other than directing over the phone, were there any other unusual problems you encountered?**

*Lydia* – We didn't have the budget to cast the actors for the re-enactment of the murder. Those kinds of sequences are always a challenge because they have to be done right. I wanted the sequence to be impressionistic and also to convey the terrible brutality of the murder. But because we didn't have trained actors I was worried that we'd have to find a local Navajo boy to be killed on camera by a local white kid who might have the same sort of attitudes of the murderer and I didn't want to replay those awful dynamics, even in an acted situation. Fortunately, the documentary gods were kind and we found a young man who happened to be straight and Navajo and who was committed to social causes to play the part of Fred Martinez. He wanted to do anything to help the film and he did a wonderful job. The person who played the murderer happened to be gay and was someone who had suffered hate-crime violence himself. He had been beaten so badly he was hospitalized and his attacker had been successfully prosecuted and he also wanted to be a part of the project.

It was cathartic for both of these nonprofessional actors to reenact the experience and we all felt great about the impact of the resulting footage. Also, it was a little dangerous and probably not the wisest thing but we reenacted the murder in the actual location.

Another problem we just couldn't solve was that some of our digital files were corrupted and lost. I couldn't obsess about what was lost in those fourteen files, I just had to work with the remaining files and know that it's always a challenge to be creative with the elements you have or can acquire. All filmmaking has limitations of some kind or another.

**Q – Did you change the script in any way once you started production?**

*Lydia* – Yes. We couldn't get any of the local cops to go on camera and I thought those could have been great interviews. But there's a kind of magic that happens with a project when it's developed enough and strong enough that it starts to tell you how to make it. It's hard to explain but there's a time when a project has a life of its own. And there's always a better solution that can evolve when you listen carefully to what a story wants and let go of what you wanted to impose.

**Q – Did you edit the film yourself or did you bring on an editor?**

*Lydia* – Darrin Navarro was a great fit to edit the film. I had shot to create a tight three act structure but within that we had the flexibility to move sequences around to get the right feeling for things. Darren has a strong aesthetic eye and he also understands what an audience needs to experience in order for the story to unfold properly. He was technically very solid - fast and smart and he could often solve problems in the moment. We worked closely together for months and it was a great collaboration.

### Q – Were there specific instructions you gave him about the edit?

**Lydia** – *Two Spirits* has two storylines that intersect throughout the three acts and so it's a complex narrative structure. I didn't want one storyline to dominate the other. So we had to make sure that the historic and contemporary information about Two-Spirit people didn't overwhelm the story of Fred's life. He was only sixteen years old when he was killed and so we had to make the most of the few family photos and our reenactment footage to build his character throughout the three acts and to create the right balance between the storylines.

### Q – Did you always intend for it to be an hour long piece?

**Lydia** – The first cut of the film that screened in festivals was a longer version and then when *Two Spirits* was picked up by *Independent Lens,* we had to get it down to their broadcast hour, actually to the frame at 51:20. There were a couple of scenes that ended up as DVD bonus material, but that's why God invented the DVD bonus category, so sequences you love and are attached to, can be cut from the film and still have a home!

### Q – The music is fantastic. What inspired you to make the choices that you did?

**Lydia** – Music is very important to me and I knew *Two Spirits* needed a rich range of music. We ended up with thirty-two cuts of music in a one hour film. We worked closely with Canyon Records to include a diverse range of Native American music from ethnographic recordings to punk rock and Pow Wow, and some of their artists even created music specifically for the film. It was a great partnership. I also got a grant from First Nations Composer's Initiative funded by the Ford Foundation so that Juantio Bicente, who is a Navajo composer and a character in the film, could compose music for key sequences. And the great Patti Smith gave us *Gone Again,* a song that ends the film with just the right quality of fierce mother love. I'm very grateful to Patti for that.

*"There's always a better solution that can evolve when you listen to what a story wants and let go of what you wanted to impose"*

### Q – How did that happen?

**Lydia** – The doc gods were kind yet again. That song was a key creative inspiration. I wanted the ending to be uplifting, to get beyond the wound to the healing of the wound, to give people a sense of hope that change is possible. I didn't know Patti, but our editor knew a music supervisor who put us in touch with her lawyer. We showed her a rough cut of the film so she could see how her music could finish *Two Spirits* so beautifully. My intuition from the beginning was that we'd get that piece somehow, so I didn't even look for an alternative - I knew that it would be just right.

**Q – What was your strategy for distribution once you were done?**

*Lydia* – We worked closely with Peter Broderick. He's the king of rights splitting and helps filmmakers craft distribution that fits their particular film. It feels appropriate for artists to maintain as much control over their work as possible. It no longer makes sense to release all the rights at once and to one entity, but to find the right constellation of distribution partners. Peter thought that PBS was the right home for the film and he was absolutely right. They also have the iTunes distribution. The educational distributor is The Cinema Guild. And I always maintained the right to distribute the consumer DVD. The CBC is broadcasting the film in Canada. And I am looking for the right partners to distribute the film internationally literally country by country, because with a film like *Two Spirits* there are places where it won't connect with people as much and other countries where it will work very well.

**Q – What was your interface like with Independent Lens?**

*Lydia* – They did a great job with the film and promoted it well as their final film of the season. Our team worked social media as hard as we could and their web team was wonderful to work with as well, so together we created the most online activity they had ever had for a film, not just in that season but in the entire history of the program. Millions of people hit *Two Spirits* web content on the PBS site around the 1,495 broadcasts of the film over 140 stations throughout June of 2011. Lois Vossen and her team were marvelous to work with and we all had a very positive experience.

**Q – A film like this seems a natural for social media outreach.**

*Lydia* – Yes and all the way through the process I worked to create relationships with non-profit organizations that could use the film to make change at the grassroots level. I felt the responsibility to both make the best film possible and to make sure as many people would see it as possible. This film needed to serve as a tool to make change over a long period of time. Over sixty non-profit organizations signed up as outreach partners and the film is being used on an ongoing basis in many programs and on campuses as part of the curriculum. All of this work helps the broadcast reach of the film as well. If you don't do anything to support your film one million people will see it, but if you work really hard you can have six million people tune in. Which would you choose?

**Q – Did you use social media as a key part of your outreach strategy?**

*Lydia* – Yes. I wish we could have raised grant money so that we could have done more, but time ran out and grant writing was a slow slog that wasn't working. So our band of volunteers just had to do our very best to spread the word about the film and connect new audiences to it. In the end we were successful in generating a great deal of interest.

### Q – What advice would you give a new documentary filmmaker?

*Lydia* – Pick your subjects carefully. Make sure you feel compelled to tell a story and that you are fully committed to what it will take to get through the process. It's a long journey and there will be many times when it will be easier to give up than to keep going. But if you know the film must be made, you'll get through the dark times that are inevitable in any project. It's very satisfying to see the impact a film has - how hearts and minds are forever influenced by the time an audience spends with your film.

**MY PERESTROIKA**

**ROBIN HESSMAN**

### Q – How did you find the topic for My Perestroika?

*Robin* – I lived in Russia from 1991 to 1999. When I came back to the States, I was often asked for a sentence or two to explain "what was Russia like" or "how Russians felt about the transition from communism to capitalism." I found it incredibly difficult to sum up this incredibly complicated experience, which I also lived through. For every story I could tell, from which you could form one conclusion, I had a million at my fingertips that would lead to the opposite. I started to think about making a film that would tell the story of my generation of Russians, who were the last generation of Soviet kids to grow up behind the Iron Curtain. They grew up in a Soviet Union that was assumed to be eternal. Then, as teenagers when they were coming of age, Gorbachev comes to power and all of a sudden everything begins to be questioned, and the foundations of their society begins to shake. Finally, the year that the subjects of my film graduated from college, the Soviet Union collapsed. They had to reinvent themselves, no longer assigned jobs as they used to be. They had to invent themselves as adults in a brand-new society.

From the beginning, I thought it would be a helpful framework to focus on several people who had been childhood classmates. For the most part, people in the USSR (and in Russia today) are with the same twenty to twenty five classmates from kindergarten to the end of high school. Even if they don't stay in close touch, they share an enormously important common history. I even know people in their 70's who still have class reunions every year. As a director, you try to create situations that allow for possible opportunities. Perhaps the classmates would have contradictory memories of the same events, or maybe one would remember something that another had forgotten. One of the additional benefits in filming classmates that I hadn't counted on were the home movies. All along I had planned to saturate the film with images of childhood from the 1970s and 1980s - the intimate view of life behind the Iron Curtain that people in the West never saw during the Cold War. I knew that 8mm cameras were rare at that time so assumed I would only

---

 info@myperestroika.com

 www.myperestroika.com

 www.facebook.com/myperesroika

 http://twitter.com/myperestroika

find films of people the same AGE as my subjects, who would stand in as childhood of that generation. But, to my amazement, one of the subject's fathers actually had a 8mm camera, and filmed his son incessantly. To my utter joy, he also went into the class and filmed all of his son's classmates – so I didn't fill the film with images of strangers who happened to be the same generation as my subjects – I actually had images of each of them, personally, when they were kids.

### Q – How did you set out finding your subjects?

**Robin** – I started working on the film in September 2004 and I knew I had to get back to Russia. So I started looking for grants and became a filmmaker in residence at WGBH in Boston. It has a small stipend and it was a great base for me from where to write my early grants. I got my first grant in the spring of 2005 and immediately headed back to Moscow. When there, I started speaking to lots of thirty-somethings from all walks of life. Friends of friends, talking to people I knew, meeting new people all the time, describing the film I was planning to make. All of that time I was also looking for home movies and was already going into archives and screening the official archival footage I wanted to juxtapose with them. I borrowed a camera and started pre-interviewing these people for two to three hours at a time. There were many interesting people, and I loved hearing their stories, but no one gave me that "a-ha" moment. My approach was that once I had met the first person whom I felt just HAD to be in the film, then I would seek out his or her classmates.

With a character-driven documentary, the choice of the characters is the most important thing. It's also the moment of no return. I came back to the States and tried to raise more money. One of the hardest parts about writing those early proposals was that as the film was character-driven, and I still didn't have any concrete characters, I still had to convey effectively what the film was going to be like. So I created four sample characters, three of which were composites of friends of mine from the decade I lived in Russia. And I found myself describing a fourth character that was a history teacher in elementary school. At a certain point, I realized the extent to which I was curious to speak with someone of this generation who was teaching history in Russia today. That would mean that they had been taught history under

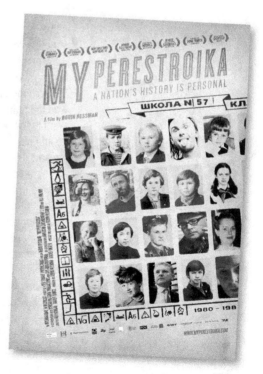

the Soviet regime and were just coming of age when archives were first opening up. So all of sudden, the truth of what they were taught as children was being turned upside down. And now, today, they would be teaching kids who were all born after the collapse of the USSR, and for whom the country that their own parents grew up in, is like Ancient Rome.

Also, there is a very famous expression, *"Russia has a very unpredictable past."* Certainly, most countries re-evaluate their take on the past as time goes on such as how American textbooks talk about Native Americans or the Civil Rights Movement. But Russia has a great tradition of erasing people from history and creating totally new narratives. Stalin commissioned portraits where he would be next to Lenin as if he were his heir apparent. People were erased from photographs after they had been sent off to the gulag. So between the first and second trip, I found myself constantly wondering about the perspective of history teachers. I didn't know at that point they would become part of the film – but I knew I was drawn to learn more. As an aside, Borya and Lyuba, the married couple who wound up being in the film, were studying to become history teachers the very year when all history exams for the Soviet Union were canceled – in 1988 – since nobody knew what the right answers on the exams would be anymore. It's also been fascinating to hear how they, as teachers, have been watching children of many generations go through the changes since the fall of the Soviet Union.

### Q – How did you find teachers to speak with?

**Robin** – Word of mouth mostly. I asked friends, and friends of friends. I went to some non-profits that worked with educational and civil rights organizations like Memorial. I had notebooks I filled with people's names and phone numbers. Along the way, someone had told me there was a teacher at School 57 who was the right age and was a history teacher. His name went in the notebook as well, but I didn't know how to find him. Luckily, I had an intern at the time and he saw my open notebook and said, *"Oh, 57 was my school. I will take you there tomorrow."* So we went and he introduced me to Borya. I was thrilled to hear that his wife was also a history teacher at the very same school. For about twenty minutes I told him about the film and he was intrigued enough to invite me home for dinner the following day. So then I met his wife, Lyuba, and Mark, their funny and precocious nine year old son. Borya and Lyuba are very passionate historians and have fantastic ways of tying in their broader cultural and historical understanding with very specific anecdotes and understanding of how things affected them. Then I asked them, as I was asking everyone I met, if they ever knew anyone who had an 8mm camera in the 70's and 80's. Borya answered that his father filmed him constantly as a child. He opened a closet that had a huge stack of film reels and then set up the projector and screen. Mark had never seen any of the films before. We sat around for the next few hours watching the films together and talking and it all finally clicked. In fact, I knew it was them before Borya showed me the films. They would have become the heart of the film, even if they hadn't had any films – but that was the icing on the cake. I then asked about their childhood classmates and from there I met Ruslan, Olga and Andrei. I originally didn't want five people in the film because I thought it was too many for the audience to really get to know each person as deeply as I hoped. But each of them has their own story and voice, so after meeting all five of them, I couldn't imagine the film without any of them.

*Q – Did you get any grants that made it possible to go back that second time?*

*Robin* – Before the first trip, I got an Irex grant, which is for scholars to do research for books in other countries, but nowhere in the guidelines does it say film is ineligible. It was a small grant of $3,500, but it was enough to get me to Moscow. I also got a LEF Pre-production grant, which is for New England and California filmmakers. I spent a lot of time trying to raise money from individuals, as I'm a member of Filmmaker's Collaborative, a non-profit in Boston. So when people donate money to the movie, they get a tax deduction. That's a very important avenue for raising money for film. Before my second trip, I got a Sundance Development Grant and an NEH grant that they don't have anymore that was called the Consultation Grant for $10,000. That got me to Russia the second time. Then the NEH said they wouldn't allow me to be on their grant path anymore because I had too much contemporary vérité footage in it. It had to be purely historical for their needs. Now they have a program called Bridging Cultures through Film, which is friendlier to films more like *My Perestroika*.

*Q – How did you get the other subjects in the film to trust you?*

*Robin* – I lived there for eight years so I'm fluent in Russian, which helped a lot. I think each of them in their own way found a way to connect with me. I also wasn't some foreigner coming in with a camera crew and putting a microphone in their face. For the most part, it was just me and them. That was the advantage of shooting most of the film myself. Then of course, there was my specific relationship with each of them. Olga and I talked a lot about personal things – we shared our pasts. With Andrei, I talked more about politics. It's funny for me to remember, but I was a bit apprehensive about meeting Ruslan the first time as this big punk rock star. In the end, I spent the most time with the Meyersons. They became good friends along the way. I think they all liked my intentions to not have an agenda or specific message of a conclusion about Russia that I was trying to hammer home and how I wanted to let multiple voices be heard and show different and genuine experiences. And it wasn't 1991. It was 2006, 2007 and some time had passed since those events, but not too much time. And in the busy pace of life, there isn't much time to stop and reflect on what's happened to you. I think that appealed to them. But none of them had been burning to tell their stories to the world. They just all generously agreed to take part.

**Q – Did they have any pre-conceptions of what a documentary is and if so, did it help or hinder the process?**

*Robin* – Not really. When I was there, I curated the documentary program of The American Film Festival in Moscow. That meant I brought retrospective docs as well as four to six contemporary ones to be screened to the Moscow public. I made sure to bring over different kinds of formats and subgenres of documentaries - personal films, long-form observational films, essay films, historical films, such as *51 Birch Street, Trouble the Water, Helvetica, Kurt Cobain, About a Son, Roman Polanski, Wanted and Desired* and *Street Fight*. And most of the filmmakers came out for the festival as well. Most people in Russia had never seen these kinds of independent non-fiction films. And in Russia, the word "non-fiction" is often interchanged with the word "non-artistic" as a means of saying a film is a documentary. It drove me nuts when I was in film school in Moscow in the early 90's – even though I was in a fiction class. I would say, on the whole, in Russia, documentary films are considered to be at first glance nature films or true crime shows on TV. But I can say definitely, that none of the people in this film had any idea about independent documentary films and would joke about how they couldn't even imagine what the film would be like in the end. Andrei didn't get why I wasn't making it for someone specific, and that no one had hired me to make this film – that I was doing it because I wanted to, and I was going to do whatever it took, to make sure the film got made. I think they all thought this was pretty bizarre behavior. Especially as it took so many years to make. I think they were all a little amazed at the persistence needed to make this kind of film.

**Q – Have you spoken to the subjects since, about what they thought of the process?**

*Robin* – Borya and Lyuba have told audiences at Q&As that they stopped noticing when I was shooting or when I was just spending time with them without the camera. I guess they all got used to me.

**Q – How many trips did you do in total?**

*Robin* – Five shooting trips that lasted between two and seven months.

**Q – Did you have a crew or did you one man band it?**

*Robin* – I one man banded it for the most part, with a few exceptions. I really wanted to have a cameraman for the whole film so I could focus on the subjects and not worry about white balance and focusing. But during my trip in April of 2006, I realized it was impossible to have a cameraperson. I found that I could either find a news cameraman, who didn't care what the shots looked like or about composition. News guys are used to just getting the information in the shot. Or you have people who shoot huge fiction films on 35mm and are used to three hours to set up lights with huge crews. There aren't a lot of people there who do vérité. I did manage to find someone who had worked with the BBC on some vérité films, but soon I realized I wasn't going to be able to afford him because I never knew in advance when I would be able to shoot, as it all depended on the subjects. It would have meant keeping him on retainer for months at a time – which of course was absurd and impossible. But another reason I couldn't use him was that the moment he walked into the room, the whole atmosphere changed. The Meyersons would get shy. Mark, the son, didn't like him. The kitchen was so small that I had to do the interviews from under the kitchen table. It just didn't work and I realized, with trepidation at first, that I was going to have to shoot the film.

*Q – Had you shot on video before?*

*Robin* – No. I went to VGIK – the All-Russian State Institute of Cinematography - in Moscow and we shot on 35mm. Video was new to me. So I just grabbed the camera, went over to the Meyersons' and went for it. It was very exciting and empowering to not need anyone else. It changed the trajectory of the film due to the freedom that I had to film at a moment's notice.

*Q – What camera did you use?*

*Robin* – I used the Panasonic DVX-100B. It's an SD camera and I shot in 24p mode.

I loved that camera. It was a great size for me. I shot mostly on a monopod that I put in my pocket. It made it easier to move from room to room in an apartment than if I had the camera on a tripod. Hand held was tough for me because I'm really not strong enough to film for hours and it not be shaky. I never got tired with the monopod.

*Q – The camera handled light well, especially the mixed lighting. Did you use any special lighting?*

*Robin* – No. All natural lighting. The only exception to that was the scene where they are watching home movies because I needed enough light to be able to see their faces as they were watching the films, which was tricky. I worked with a professional cinematographer to light that scene, as I couldn't have done it on my own.

*Q – Did you play with the colors in post at all?*

*Robin* – We just made them look better. The color person I worked with at Final Frame in NYC, Will Cox, is amazing and he does great stuff. We didn't distort anything, just tried to have the real colors come through more – and make the blacks black, and the whites white. After the color correct it looked like a grimy film had been taken off the image.

*Q – Was there anything that came up in production that caused unusual problems?*

*Robin* –The rock concert was a challenge for me to shoot because there was no way I could've walked through that mosh pit by myself. I hired a 6' 3" camera guy for some of that shoot. That was a crazy day of shooting. It started at 6am with us shooting on two cameras in front of the school, on the first day of school, which is the last shot of the film. Then we went with Lyuba's class outside of Moscow to celebrate their first day of being seniors. Then, we had to return the camera I had rented, and go off immediately, only with my camera, to the reunion concert where Ruslan was playing. On top of it, I was leaving the next day to go to the States for seventy-two hours, and on the train platform going back to Moscow, my wallet was stolen including all the cash I had to pay the camera guy. And then we reached the concert and it was an utter madhouse. But we got through it and the day ended at 2am. There were so many things that happened on this shoot, it was incredibly intense. But it's common for all documentary films that things go wrong along the way.

All in all, it was an intense four years of shooting. And now, with distribution, it will soon be 7 years of my life – full time. I never thought the movie would take as long as it did. Part of that was raising money, though the film probably turned out better for having more time with the subjects and being able to follow the trajectory of their lives and the country. I remember the day that I was going to Moscow for the first research trip, I had a meeting with Cara Mertes when she was still at *POV*. She told me that films like this usually take three to five years to make. I was so confident that it would take two to three years max!

*Q – Did you have any other misconceptions?*

*Robin* – Yes. I expected to get all my funding from Europe because I thought nobody in the US would be interested in Russia anymore. I thought maybe I would get one US acquisition down the road. And the opposite happened. There was tremendous support from US foundations, individuals, and of course, POV. Europe has been a slower and harder process to get on board. The nice things we have in the US are foundations who give money for docs – both big and small, and individuals who donate money.

*Q – What was the final budget of the film?*

*Robin* – Approximately $750,000, but that didn't include distribution.

*Q – Were you editing the film as you were going along or did you wait until the end of production? And when did you start structuring the film?*

*Robin* – I always had a basic structure in my head. There were going to be three chapters in the film: Soviet childhood, Perestroika youth and contemporary life today. And I knew I wanted to interweave the five stories with the story of the country, and 8mm home movies with the "official" images from the state archives. I'm not an editor and because I was working by myself on the film for so many years, I didn't want to edit it by myself. I digitized most of the footage before the last shooting trip, so I could identify any holes that needed to be filled. The last trip for shooting was in the spring of 2008 and editing began in May of 2008. Then there was one trip to Russia in the fall of 2008 together with the editor where she was editing and I was going out and doing pick up shoots, which was a very useful setup. In the end, the film was edited by two really talented, wonderful editors. It was also helpful that the first editor, Alla Kovgan, was Russian and had a very deep, intimate knowledge of this world, as did I from having lived there. But together, it was hard for us to have an outsider, American perspective on the film. We were both too inside the story. The second editor, Garret Savage, was American and didn't have any Russian connection, so he came to it with fresh eyes.

*Q – Do you usually work with the editor or do you let them go off and bring you a cut?*

*Robin* – I usually sit in the same room as the editor but I'm not involved with what they're doing the whole time. I might be on my computer doing something else for the production, but I'm always at arms length in case they want to talk things through or to look at scenes. I know some editors like the directors to go away, but as we had only one small office there was nowhere else for me to go, anyway! When Garret was cutting the film, my desk faced away from him, my back was to him when I was working, so it's not like I was just staring over his shoulder the whole time.

*Q – How did you speak to Garret about the film since he was so fresh?*

*Robin* – I gave him a book or two about Russia to read. I talked about my hopes for the film – in terms of the intimacy with the characters I was striving for. When he came on board, we already had many utterly beautiful scenes edited by Alla, but the whole flow of the film hadn't gotten there yet. We also struggled a lot in getting the introduction of the characters right. But we were lucky enough to get to go to the Sundance Edit Lab together and that was incredibly helpful. At that point, the film wasn't terrible. It was interesting, with really great moments, but it was still losing people. It was long and shaggy, and at times confusing, and we were trying to figure out how to fix it.

*Q – So what was the tipping point that made the film work?*

*Robin* – When we got to the Sundance Edit Lab, I was obsessed with solving the beginning of the film. At that point it was taking much too long before we met all the characters – I think about 11 or 12 minutes. At the Lab, we showed the cut to everyone else and to my total shock, they all said, *"The opening is working fine."* But then I remember editor Mary Lampson said something about needing to focus more on the characters. It was so ironic because the whole reason I made the film was to get into these characters, and they were getting a bit lost in some of the archival footage and explanations. Garret and I had made color coded cards for each character and for the archive and plotted them out on a corkboard. But what we hadn't done was isolate each character's arc through the whole film and work on them by themselves. Once we did that, went back to the roots of what was important in this film, it became sharper. As a funny aside, two months later after we worked on the characters, we had another rough cut screening with a bunch of friends, some of whom had been at the Labs too. The main criticism from that screening was about the opening, *"It takes too long to get to the characters."* It was very funny. On the one hand, I felt vindicated. And I was also amused that no one had agreed with me a few months earlier. But Garret was probably right when he said that at the later point, when we had fixed all the other problems, the thing that was still a problem was now glaringly obvious. So we worked more on the opening, had to throw out some amazing archival footage, which is always sad and we sharpened it down. Karen Schmeer, who was a brilliant editor, was a close friend of both mine and Garret's and she came into the editing room and gave some great feedback too. We now have a Fellowship in her name, after her tragic death in January 2010. For all editors out there, please look into the Karen Schmeer Film Editing Fellowship, which we are granting once a year.

**Q – How long was the whole editing process?**

**Robin** – May of 2008 to January of 2010. So eighteen months or so.

**Q – How did POV come into the picture?**

**Robin** – I let them know about the film in 2005 when I met with Cara Mertes, and she said I should send in something so they could open a file on the film and track it. I kept forgetting to send anything in, since it was so early in the process. But finally, in 2006, I sent in my Sundance development grant proposal and a 10-minute demo reel thinking it would go into a file in a drawer until I was further along. But instead, Yance Ford called me when I was shooting in Russia in October 2006 and told me it had all been put in front of their committee already and they all loved the project and were officially "interested." That was a great surprise – since I only had a 10 minute demo reel at that point. In March of 2007, when I was still in early-mid production, I got a call from Simon Kilmurry at *POV* who said they had decided to get officially on board. I was very lucky they agreed to take a chance on me like that and commit so early on in the process. Just at about the same time, ITVS also came on board, so that was very helpful.

**Q – Did you make any other sales worldwide?**

**Robin** – I made a pre-sale to YLE in Finland based on the ten minute demo reel back in 2006. Since, there have been a handful of other sales internationally. I am working with Annie Roney at Ro*co Films. I've spent a lot of time personally working on various aspects of US distribution.

490

**Q – Were there any issues in distribution that caught you off guard?**

**Robin** – I wasn't prepared for all the costs of distribution. You're so busy working to raise the money just to finish the film that you aren't thinking about publicists, post cards, posters and building a website. I've found very few grants for distribution. Perhaps if my film had more of a politically active message it was advocating for, there might have been interested institutional organizations who would want to partner up and help support distribution costs. But in my case, doing so much of the distribution on my own, I find myself relying on individual contributions to cover those costs, and to my surprise, it's been a lot harder raising those funds with a finished film that was well-received by critics and has won awards, than when it was just a work-in-progress and not clear what would become of it. Odd, but true.

Now that filmmakers are splitting their rights more and more, you aren't as likely to have an all-rights distributor who comes in and pays these costs up front. My educational distributor is New Day – which is a filmmaker-owned co-op and I'm very happy I made that choice, but each filmmaker in the co-op is responsible for paying the expenses for the manufacture of the educational DVD and for all promotion. I think it works out better in the end, as you have a lot more control, but there are up front costs you have to find ways to cover. Even when you're just launching a film – there are the costs of applying to the festival, FedExing things places overseas and then, once you get in, shipping posters, and tapes, not to mention sometimes actually going to the festival itself. I'd recommend that any filmmaker find an executive producer early on who can help raise funding for distribution. Often there are costs you'll need to make decisions about like Oscar qualification. I was having fundraising screenings as we were onlining the film in order to pay for some of the Sundance costs for *My Perestroika*. So let people early on know there will be a phase where you will need help whether it's a grant, tax-deductible donation or an in-kind donation.

**Q – What advice would you give a new documentary filmmaker?**

**Robin** – Giving up and not making this film was never an option. I was going to slog through it no matter what it took. The only question was that I didn't know how long it would take me, but at a certain point, I made peace with that. If you adopt that way of thinking, that not finishing isn't even possible, then you will finish your film. Similarly, if I had looked every day at the entire project from a bird's eye view at everything that has to happen to finish, it is an incredibly overwhelming, daunting concept. And you have to do that occasionally just to think ahead. But if you're focused on your immediate To Do list, which will get you to the next stage, then it's all manageable. And also, be part of the documentary community. Go to screenings, join D-word, talk to people, ask questions. We are so lucky to be in this field filled with passionate, smart, people who are curious about the world, and generally open and generous. None of us are in this to get rich, and there is a wonderful spirit of community in this profession that I think keeps us all going, when times get rough.

**Q – What does documentary filmmaking mean to you?**

*Sam –* It's a way to engage with the world and a way to make some meaning out of my own experiences. It's a great pleasurable part of my life.

**Q – With your films, you seem to like looking at how principled people become that way, and then watching those principles battle reality...**

*Sam –* Someone once said that you always make the same film over and over again. And to a certain extent that's true. I can certainly see a thread running through all of mine. People who are earnest or noble or idealistic in order to change the world for the better, appeal to me. And many times it doesn't work out as people hoped it would. So I think a lot of my work is a collision between idealism and the constraints of "human nature." Usually as a filmmaker when you are drawn to certain topics, it comes from a personal and emotional response to something. It's not abstract. Even my previous film *The Rainbow Man* really resonated with me and I felt a strong connection to that subject. And a lot of the times, my films help me try to make sense of those themes. I didn't make *The Weather Underground* so Baby Boomers could have a walk down memory lane. I did it to try and make sense of a situation as to how it ties to the present.

**Q – How do you select your subjects?**

*Sam –* I see a photograph or hear a conversation or story that resonates with me and gets under my skin in an emotional way. That usually inspires me to look into something. Sometimes there's nothing there. And sometimes it takes a long time to find it but then a film develops out of it. In all of my films, I am trying to express a feeling. Films are great for getting facts across but books are way better. What film is so profound at doing is

---

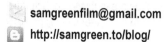 samgreenfilm@gmail.com     www.samgreen.to

http://samgreen.to/blog/

expressing feeling through music, images and sounds.

*Q – How did The Weather Underground come about?*

*Sam* – I was at the Library of Congress in Washington DC doing research on another project. I was killing time waiting for some books to come up and I was at the computer card catalogue, and I started typing in some random phrases. I had been interested in The Weather Underground since I was a teenager. I liked the subversive aspect of it, blowing up buildings and the like. So I typed it in and this two hundred page Senate report came up that I'd never known about. I got it and in the middle of it are these series of pages of the photos of the people. They mesmerized me. Younger people think of the 1960's and they often imagine it as peace and love – smiling hippies with flowers in their hair. These Weather Underground kids had short hair and looked mean and hard! At the same time, I could also see these they were middle class white kids like me trying to look hard, and that was intriguing. Who were these people? As I starting looking through their names, I realized that I knew one of them – a friend of a friend. When I got back to San Francisco, I called him and asked him if he was in The Weather Underground. And he said, *"Oh, so you found out about my secret life?"* So I asked him if I could come over to his house and ask some questions. He said yes and I went over and found that he was really articulate and smart. And the more he spoke, the more I started to see that it sort of made sense what they did. I could also see how crazy it was too. The moral ambiguity interested me and the project evolved out of that.

*Q – Some of our readers wonder about how you take that first step to getting a project going. It seems this one was a bit serendipitous.*

*Sam* – Yes, but even it I hadn't known the person, it would have been possible to get in touch with people from the group. Most of them were more or less accessible. It really helped though because at that point I was doing it out of curiosity. I might not have taken that step otherwise. But taking that first step is hard. It helps if you're curious.

*Q – How long was it before you could start filming members of The Weather Underground?*

*Sam* – That was one of the big challenges of the film. I did that film with my friend Bill Siegel. We knew

that we couldn't make the film without a number of the former members of the group. When we contacted them they all thought it was a terrible idea. It took a long time to get people's trust and get them on board. At some point someone told me something that was really helpful – I think this is a rule for sales-people – and that is: never give people the opportunity to say no to you. It's simple, but it was extremely helpful to us. So you start out just asking someone if they will have coffee with you so you can tell them about the project; almost everyone will say ok to that. When we were getting in touch with the former members of the group, most of them hadn't even thought about those experiences in a long time or talked to their kids about it. There was tension around it. So we did this very slow process of getting people to introduce us to other people in the group. We kept meeting with people over a long period of time, and slowly built up trust with them. It took two years before we started asking people to be in the film. But it was invaluable because that's how you learn the story. Documentaries are only as good as the relationship between the filmmaker and the subjects.

**Q – Did you struggle with objectivity? How did you keep asking tough questions when you knew them well?**

**Sam –** I think most people don't believe in objectivity in that classic sense. Most people realize that a film, or a newspaper article or a non-fiction book, is a construct. For me,

what I work toward is fairness and accuracy. You can't do 100% of either. It's a struggle though, especially when you have developed relationships with a subject. Being accurate means you may have to say things they don't want to hear and that came up a lot with *The Weather Underground*. When I was in the editing room, there were things that I wasn't sure I should put in due to my allegiance to the people we interviewed. But at some point someone said to me, *"In the editing room you only have one allegiance and that's to the viewer."* That made a huge difference to me. And even though there's some criticism of the group in the movie that the former members may not share, I think that ultimately they respected us for including that stuff and also knew that that made the film better.

**Q – From your two year research process, did you have a basic idea of what the structure of the plot would be before you started shooting?**

**Sam –** Early on I had this fantasy about making it a very experimental film where you never saw anyone's face and it was just voiceover with

494

images from the time. I wanted to do that because I was making a film for 20 year olds who had no connection to the time. So we wanted to make something that was as far from a talking head movie as possible. And we didn't want 60 year olds on the screen. We wanted 20 year olds on the screen so that a younger viewer would connect with them. We learned quickly that that idea wouldn't work. This was my first feature length doc so I was learning too. It wasn't like we did pre-production, wrote an outline, shot the footage and then edited. It was very messy as the various sections overlapped. But what we realized early on is that it made sense to structure the film chronologically. It's no secret why a lot of films do that. The trick was figuring out how much context to put in it.

**Q – Was there anything that you really loved that never made it into the film?**

**Sam** – Sure, lots of things. There was the story of The Weather Underground and then there were all these stories that shot off from that, which needed context. What we realized was that the story of The Weather Underground could only support so much. There was a story where the members of the group almost got caught. They went to get some money that was wired to them and when they got to the Western Union office they noticed some undercover looking guys. So they took off and there was this car chase all over town and we had all this great footage. But it was too much detail. It's hard because you work so hard to shoot something like that and then you cut it. Then you thank God you did.

**Q – How has getting archival footage changed from making The Weather Underground to your more recent film, Utopia in Four Movements?**

**Sam** – It's changed a lot. If you look back at some older archival films like *Twist* by Ron Mann in the 1990's they are loaded with archival footage. They were real accomplishments. Back then, images were not as accessible as they are now. You had to go to archives. You had to get people to mail you a VHS tape with stuff on it. It was a lot of work. Now you can locate just about anything quickly – it's just that the quality of the stuff on Youtube isn't all that great. So finding the footage is great, but getting a good copy of the footage is still tricky. You still have to deal with archival houses like Getty Images who charge a lot and drive me crazy. Networks are still expensive. But then on the other end you have a friend of a friend who shot all this archival footage and it's in his attic and he'll give it to you for free. Also now you have different rights you have to negotiate for, like Video On Demand.

**Q – What do you look for in an editor?**

**Sam** – Well, I've edited all my own films so it's a little hard to say. With a documentary most of the time you don't have a script or even a rough

> "Documentaries are only as good as the relationship between the filmmaker and the subjects."

idea of where you are going, so the editor almost becomes the director. It's hard to imagine someone else doing that part. Plus I can edit for cheap and I never have enough money to hire someone else. I just did a short recently and I worked with an editor and we collaborated. That was interesting. She did a lot of great things that I wouldn't have thought of or couldn't have done. So I have to say that now I have opened myself up to working with people. Still the film becomes an expression of them and I want it to be an expression of me. It's tricky.

**Q – Sam Pollard, Spike Lee's editor, said that editors have to be curious. Do you think your curiosity helps you when editing?**

**Sam** – I think curiosity is the impulse for all documentaries. What I've noticed is that great editors can inhabit the material in an almost superhuman way. This editor I worked with would always laugh at certain funny bits. I was numb to it after seeing it so many times, but she never did. I think great editors create this profound relationship with the footage and internalize it some way.

**Q – What are your approaches to voiceovers and music in your films?**

**Sam** – I, like most filmmakers of my generation, were very much down on voiceover. It

was always like this Voice of God or something. It gave the impression of stuffy old boring documentaries. But after struggling a lot with the editing of *The Weather Underground* I realized there were things I couldn't communicate with the material alone. So eventually, I accepted the fact that there had to be a little voiceover. With *Utopia in Four Movements*, when I first showed it to people, they had no idea what the film was trying to say. It was an experimental film about four stories about Utopia. I was going for something like *Fast, Cheap and Out of Control*. I didn't want to link the stories together in any explicit way – I wanted the audience to make those connections. So I had to add voiceover to tie all these different sections of the film together. In a strange way, films usually end up telling you what they want to be. So it evolved into an essay film. It's live and there's a lot of talking. Through the experience of making that film, I developed huge appreciation for voiceover and I think it's so rarely done because it's hard to do. It's much easier to make a film where you show both sides. But I'm finding myself bored with that. I want people to actually say something. So now I'm a huge voiceover fan.

Adam Curtis, the British filmmaker who made *The Power of Nightmares*, is really good. His writing is brilliant. In terms of music, I always start the edit with music and build a scene around it. All my films come out of an emotional interaction and music helps me achieve that. My footage then has the feel of that music. I can't edit without music and I can't get into a film until I figure out the music.

**Q – With Utopia, what are the different segments?**

**Sam** – One section is about the world's largest shopping mall, which is in China and turns out to be a total failure as a business. There are almost no stores open at this point and very few customers. It's an absolutely bizarre place. Another section is on the language Esperanto, which is an artificial language that a Polish guy invented in the late 1800s with the hope that if everyone in the world spoke it, we could overcome war and racism. It obviously didn't come to pass, but surprisingly there's still a worldwide movement of people who speak it. Another is about Cuba and an American revolutionary who is living there. It looks at revolution. The fourth is a meditation on a time capsule that was buried at the 1939 World's Fair that was supposed to be dug up in 5000 years. It's really hopeful. It's an experimental movie that puts all these things together in a way that they become more than the sum of their parts.

**Q – Did you structure them in a certain way that follows a story arc?**

**Sam** – It's roughly chronological. It also progresses from very funny and light to serious at the end. It's more of an emotional structure throughout.

**Q – I believe you have a live band play when the film screens?**

**Sam** – It was a weird way to work. Dave Cerf, who I made the film with, and I live in San Francisco. The band, *The Quavers*, who played at our Sundance screening, live in New York. I had known Todd Griffin, one of the people in the band for a long time and asked him how to work with live music and film. Todd has done lots of that kind of thing. When we got into Sundance, we asked Todd if they would do live music for the film and he said *'sure.'* So we sent them QuickTimes of sections and they made music. We went back and

FROM THE OSCAR-NOMINATED DIRECTOR OF THE WEATHER UNDERGROUND

# utopia in four movements

A LIVE DOCUMENTARY BY SAM GREEN AND DAVE CERF

forth. We met in Sundance a week before and holed up in a condo rehearsing working all day and night to put the piece together. It was nerve wracking, but it worked! The great thing about doing live events is that you can always rework the music for each show coming up. So it's grown and gotten better over time.

**Q – What did you actually present to Sundance for them to say yes?**

*Sam* – We did a performance for some of the programmers. If you videotape yourself doing this kind of live performance film, it usually turns out really bad. It's like a dance performance on videotape. You get a sense of what it is, but it's not the actual performance. There's no sense of experience. So we had to do it live for them in person.

**Q – An Inconvenient Truth was sort of like that. Did you get any inspiration from there?**

*Sam* – I have seen it, but I hadn't thought of the similarities until much later. *Utopia* is a live presentation and *An Inconvenient Truth* is a documentation of that live presenation.

**Q – Have you noticed any differences in the distribution between your two films?**

*Sam* – Things have changed a lot. *The Weather Underground* was a successful movie for a small documentary. It did about $800,000 at the box office and sold a lot of DVDs. I don't think that would happen these days. It's a lot harder to get a movie out there now unless there's an easy to promote angle. That's one of the reasons I did *Utopia* as a live event. I knew I had to do something different because it was so experimental. Now with technology you can reach a niche audience way easier. In the past, my Esperanto documentary would have been very difficult to market. You'd have to write letters to people to see if they would be interested. But now with the internet and social media you can get it out there in a profound way.

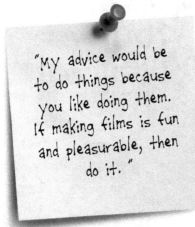

"My advice would be to do things because you like doing them. If making films is fun and pleasurable, then do it."

**Q – What advice would you give a new documentary filmmaker?**

*Sam* – When I was in my 20's, I had this big weight on my shoulders about what I was going "to be." But when I was around 27, I said I wasn't going to answer that question. I decided just to do what I liked. I started to work on *The Rainbow Man* movie and got some jobs working as an editor. I liked doing it. And when I put out *The Rainbow Man*, people came and liked it. So I guess my advice would be to do things because you like doing them. If making films is fun and pleasurable, then do it. And under the right circumstances, you'll be able to do it for a long time. If you do it because you want to get famous, make a lot of money or get laid a lot, you aren't going to be able to sustain that.

# INDEX

## THE DOCUMENTARY FILMMAKERS HANDBOOK

# INDEX

## SYMBOLS

## A